I wanted a fantastic, glorious, wonderful relationship.

But for this to happen, I knew I needed to do a better job of meeting Mr. Right. I felt I'd tried everything in London. Maybe it was time for a more radical and far-reaching solution?

Rather than traveling to recover from Mr. Wrong, what if I went traveling for Mr. Right? I mean, I was sure Fate had him out there waiting for me, so why was I wasting time in London moaning when I could be out in the world searching? I'd put my heart and soul into my job; maybe it was time I put the same amount of effort into my love life.

So, after some soul-searching, I quit my job. I had a new job now: finding my Soul Mate.

Around the World in 80 Dates

A True Story by

Jennifer Cox

Around the World in 80 Dates

Jennifer Cox

doWn
tOwn
press

New York   London   Toronto   Sydney

DOWNTOWN PRESS, published by Pocket Books
1230 Avenue of the Americas
New York, NY 10020

Copyright © 2005 by Jennifer Cox

Originally published in Great Britain in 2005 by William Heinemann

Library of Congress Cataloging-in-Publication data is available.

ISBN: 1-4165-1315-9

First Downtown Press trade paperback edition April 2005

1   3   5   7   9   10   8   6   4   2

DOWNTOWN PRESS and colophon are
trademarks of Simon & Schuster, Inc.

Photo Credits: Chapter 1, Charlotte Hindle; Chapter 4, Kompani Bastard;
Chapter 7, Rosalind Cox; Chapter 8, www.deanz.com;
Chapter 9, Frank Roberto; Chapter 12, Charlotte Hindle; Afterword, Frank Roberto

Manufactured in the United States of America

Designed by Jaime Putorti

For information regarding special discounts for bulk purchases,
please contact Simon & Schuster Special Sales at
1-800-456-6798 or business@simonandschuster.com.

To my parents, Brenda and John Cox,
with love and thanks for putting up
with years of my nonsense

And to G., who has all that to come

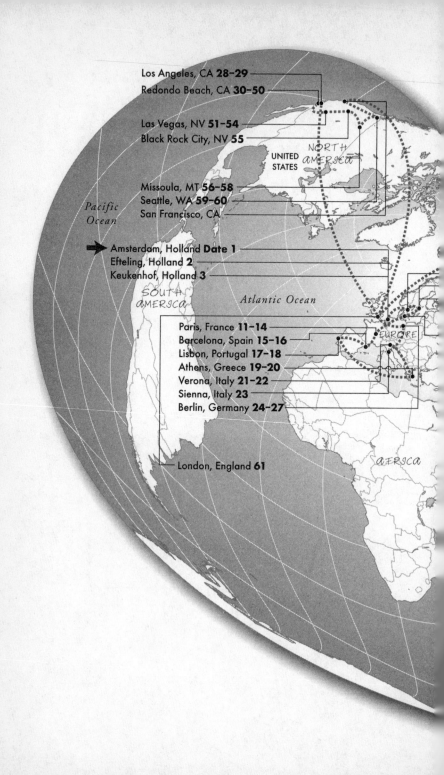

Los Angeles, CA **28–29**
Redondo Beach, CA **30–50**

Las Vegas, NV **51–54**
Black Rock City, NV **55**

Pacific Ocean

Missoula, MT **56–58**
Seattle, WA **59–60**
San Francisco, CA

NORTH AMERICA

UNITED STATES

Amsterdam, Holland **Date 1**
Efteling, Holland **2**
Keukenhof, Holland **3**

SOUTH AMERICA

Atlantic Ocean

EUROPE

Paris, France **11–14**
Barcelona, Spain **15–16**
Lisbon, Portugal **17–18**
Athens, Greece **19–20**
Verona, Italy **21–22**
Sienna, Italy **23**
Berlin, Germany **24–27**

AFRICA

London, England **61**

Around the World in 80 Dates

Tokyo, Japan **62–63**
Beijing, China **64–66**
Bangkok, Thailand **67–68**
Kuala Lumpur, Malaysia **69**

Gothenburg, Sweden **4–5**
Stockholm, Sweden **6, 8**
Birka, Sweden **7**

Copenhagen, Denmark **9–10**

Perth, Australia **70–71**
Melbourne, Australia **72**
Sydney, Australia **73–74**

Pacific Ocean

ASIA

AUSTRALIA

Indian Ocean

Auckland, New Zealand **75, 80**
Blenheim, New Zealand **76**
Queenstown, New Zealand **78–79**

Middlemarch, New Zealand **77**

ANTARCTICA

So that's me, packed and ready to go: passport, little black dress, and the names of eighty men I'm going to date in seventeen countries over the next six months. I'm off to find my Soul Mate, and I'm not coming back to Yonkers till I do.

chapter one

This Time Last Year

Time to leave London and start dating.

Settling into a steady rhythm of drinking, crying, drinking, crying, I became aware of the music for the first time: *"Stand by your man, give him two arms to cling to . . ."* I glared at the radio: I've always hated that song. My feeling was that if the only way a man could remain standing upright was by leaning heavily on you, surely it was best just to let him fall right on over. But since today was the day I'd discovered Kelly had been cheating on me for pretty much the five years we'd been together, I let out a long, ragged sigh, too exhausted to cry anymore. It was also the day I had to accept that maybe there's a little bit of Tammy in us all. I really loved Kelly. Which was surprising because he actually wasn't that lovable. He was very sexy—one of those dark, brooding types, with piercing green eyes and a tangle of curly black hair. He was tall and strong, with a gentle mouth and a chest broad enough to do a week's ironing on. But he was also self-centered, secretive, and moody. The kind of guy who sits in the corner of a bar, smoldering over a beer and a shot. For some reason I was drawn to "the difficult ones," and Kelly was as difficult as they came. A man who would sooner eat broken glass than tell you where he'd been, what his plans were, or if he loved you. I have no idea why I kept trying, when he'd wanted to go to parties on his own, stayed out late, kept a phone number with just an initial next to it. . . . In fact, for some reason it made me try harder. Over our five years together, as Kelly morphed into Clint Eastwood, I increasingly turned into Coco the Clown, pulling out all the stops to entertain him, make him feel involved, get his attention. I did the emotional equivalent of driving a small red pedal car around the ring of our relationship, frantically tooting on my little horn as bunches of flowers popped out of my shirt and small men in orange wigs emptied buckets of custard down my trousers and twanged my big red nose. It was not dignified. And, ultimately, it was pointless. I knew in my heart we would only ever share a "now." Never a future. Then I rang the number with the initial next to it, and our "now" was over.

As soon as I split up with Kelly, I went straight to the airport and got on a plane to New York City. The experience of being in New York is like stroking a man-eating tiger: As much as it scares the bejesus out of you, for those moments it allows you to touch it, you know you are blessed and immortal.

And on this occasion, like every other I'd been there, New York uplifted me. I lost myself in the markets, boutiques, and coffee shops around Greenwich Village and Harlem, whacked softballs in the batting cages over at Coney Island until my arms sang. Being in the city didn't cure my heartache, but it distracted me and stopped it getting worse, and for that I was grateful.

I actually had to be in New York for work, so in a way it was good timing (if such a thing exists when you're talking about splitting up with your boyfriend). But then again, I worked in the travel industry, so it wasn't that unusual for me to be heading off somewhere. I loved traveling and had been determined to get a job in the industry from the moment I discovered its unerring ability to make me feel really good.

This was especially true after an ugly breakup. Some say that time is a great healer, but I discovered years ago that it's actually travel that quite literally moves you on. Staying on the crime scene of an awful breakup is the worst thing you can do: too many painful memories and reminders. I subscribe to the "pack up your troubles" school of relationship recovery, and let me tell you, it works. It had been almost by accident that I'd learned travel mends a broken heart. I was eighteen and William was the first big love of my life. We were at school together and shared the kind of pure and trusting love only possible when you have yet to experience that first deep cut. When William dumped me out of the blue for Melanie (a girl who shopped at Miss Selfridge, who had never even been to Glastonbury), I was completely unprepared for the shock. I spent that whole summer after my exams moping around, crying on my best friend Belinda's shoulder, making her come for long walks so I could tell her (again) how awful it was and how I was never going to get over it. But when, at the end of the summer, I left home for Leeds University, I was really surprised to discover that out of sight really was out of mind. Here I was in a whole new place, with no painful memories. There was no danger of bumping into Will and Mel in Leeds; I didn't have to go to *our* places on my own or have people drop into conversation that they'd all been out together the night before. So, free from constant reminders of my old Will and his new girlfriend, I got over him and on with my life.

All thanks to the M1 motorway and National Express buses. But my lesson in the healing power of travel didn't end there. It was my next boyfriend who taught me that travel makes things easier for the dumper (as opposed to the dumpee), too. Peter was the guitarist in a band I sang with in Leeds, and we lived together for most of my time at university. He was gentle, kind, and very cute. But sadly, as time went on, it became increasingly clear that "gentle and kind" wasn't enough. I really didn't want to hurt him—Peter didn't deserve that, plus I remembered how bad it felt—but as much as I loved him, I felt restless and the need to move on. But I couldn't end it. I really tried: I'd psych myself up, telling myself I was going through with it this time, but at the last minute I'd think about how upset Peter would be and I'd lose my nerve. Actually, a couple of times I did end it, but Peter persuaded me to give us another chance. I was hopeless: I just couldn't face his heartache and make a clean break. Until I went to Australia.

It was one of those whimsical decisions that only makes sense after you've done it. I'd just graduated from university and had no idea what I wanted to do next. Going to Australia on my own for three months suddenly seemed the perfect solution: It would be both an adventurous challenge and the chance to think everything through.

So I flew into Perth, Western Australia. And virtually the first thing I did when I arrived was to call Peter and split up with him. As crazy as it sounds, I needed to go to the other side of the world to do it: I wasn't there to watch him fall apart, knowing it was my fault and still caring about him. And because I didn't feel wracked with the guilt I would have felt at home, I got over it far more quickly (as did he). I was free to fall madly in love with Australia, and I stayed, traveling all over Australasia for the next six years.

· · ·

I think I have to be honest at this point and confess it wasn't only Australia I fell madly in love with. I might have been Peter's girl-friend when I flew into Australia, but six months after arriving I was Philip's wife.

I'd been in Australia for two weeks when I met Philip. He worked at a theater company where I'd landed a job, and it was love at first sight. I immediately recognized Philip, a spellbind-ing, charismatic, risk-all outback Romeo, as one of my Soul Mates. (Well, cats have nine lives, who's to say we are limited to a single, solitary Soul Mate?) He wasn't afraid of anything, and when I was with him, life was exciting and full of possibilities. We fell deeply and passionately in love. Although we got married very quickly, we *clicked* so powerfully together it felt the natural and right thing to do. Neither of us had really done much travel-ing, so we set off to explore, experience, and discover together. We spent six months driving through the hot, red outback in an old Holden panel van, living on wild fruit, swimming with dol-phins, wrestling with spiders. We trekked through craggy out-posts of India and Nepal, spent weekends snorkeling in the coral-studded waters around Vanuatu and the Solomons, took crazy surf-trips to Bali, and sailed boats down the muddy Mekong in Vietnam. It was amazing. And in the end, maybe that was the problem: Man cannot live on thrill alone. After six years of wonder and discovery, I was all amazed out. I'd had one brief visit home in all that time. I missed my family and friends; I missed normal old England. I missed Marks & Spencer's potato chips; I longed to sit in a pub on a damp autumn day (Australia doesn't do seasons) and pretend I cared about soccer; I was des-perate for a colorful argument about politics and the chance to browse through some decent weekend papers (MAN LEAVES CHANGE ON CONVENIENCE STORE COUNTER was about the level of reporting in Australia). It was time to come home, and as much as I loved Philip, he was a creature of the outback. Beautiful, passionate, and wild, he had—and wanted—no place in Britain, with its crowds, traffic, litter, and drizzle. I went to Australia alone. Six years later, I returned home the same way.

It had been a year now since Kelly and I split up, and thankfully I was past the I'll Never Fall in Love Again stage. I spent a lot of time thinking about why we stayed together for as long as we did, also trying to work out how I could avoid making the same mistakes again. And during that year going over past choices and future options, I learned two things. Firstly, anyone who wants to know anything about Cher or Def Leppard should tune into VH1 at 3 a.m. Secondly, trying to find even a halfway decent boyfriend in London is a total nightmare. If you know the latter, chances are you've already discovered the former. Londoners have the longest working hours in Europe, and the highest number of stress-related diseases to prove it. It's hardly the setting for a romantic Barry White–type encounter— *"You're my first, you're my last, you're my intray?"*—yet precisely because we spend the majority of our time in the office, inevitably this is where we're hoping to meet Mr. Right. And failing to find him. Manners may maketh the man, but work unmaketh him pretty damn quick. It used to be exciting meeting someone in the office, but nowadays it means sifting through a pack of lifeless men so stressed and depressed that the only relationships they have the energy or confidence for are with their laptops and their lads' mags. And we SIWWIDs (Single-Income Women, Working Instead of Dating) have bought into the whole "mustn't try harder" myth: that being successful at work and having fun with our friends makes us independent and therefore unattractive to men. This really isn't the case: It's simply that the office—all floppy disks and soft launches—is not the place to find a satisfying relationship. Ten years ago when I moved from Australia back to England, I had to accept the sad truth that my marriage wasn't moving back with me. But I knew my love affair with travel was a relationship that would flourish wherever I went, so I lost no time getting a job in the travel industry. I became spokesperson and head of PR for the guidebook company Lonely Planet Publications, as well as a travel writer and correspondent for the BBC.

And as I traveled to and from my office in London, and to and from my work overseas, I was struck by how much more interested in women foreign men are, compared with British men. At times it feels as if you can't find a decent date in London to save your life, the bar being so low now that I mean any man who knows how to use a fork and possesses a matching pair of shoes, but you virtually have to fight them off with a stick in every other capital city around the world. I don't want to sound like an international hussy here, and I'm not even vaguely God's gift—I don't have Britney's butt or Melanie Griffiths's lips . . . though, to be fair, neither does she. But it is so much easier to meet men when you're abroad. Walk down the street in any other country and there'll always be men checking you out, coming over, chatting you up. In London, the only guys who make eye contact with you are the inmates on the subway. I'm not saying British men are totally to blame: We women have to take some of the responsibility, too. There are only so many hours in the day, and chances are that if you have a successful career, it's your job that takes up most of them. As the economy flourishes, are we in the grip of an emotional recession? Have we made our jobs the primary relationships in our lives, settling for so-so boyfriends because that's all we have the time to either find or maintain?

I say *we*, but of course I mean *I*. Had I loved my job more than I loved my boyfriend? By putting in and getting back so much from my career, how much did I have left to give Kelly?

And how much did I really need from him in return? If I had needed Kelly more, would I have been forced to accept sooner that the relationship sucked and saved myself from going through "Jen and Kel—The Crap Years"? I know this sounds terrible, but is it really possible to have a great relationship and a great job? And if not, which would you choose?

And to get back to talking about me again (oh, go on), if I was right and all the *great relationships* were wandering down streets in every country other than the one in which I lived, what was I going to do about it?

Before we go any further, I think we need to take a moment to discuss terms. It's important to clarify exactly what I mean by *great relationships*. What I'm not talking about is a shag. One-night stands are the emotional kebabs of the relationship world: easy to get after the pubs close, leaving you feeling like rubbish for the next three days. No, I'm talking about meeting someone I actually like and want to get to know. Someone who makes me laugh, reads me bits out of the newspaper, will run out for tampons, lets me cut his hair (badly, once), has a bath while I sit on the loo seat cutting my/his toenails. Someone I'm willing to introduce to my friends. I'm talking about a Soul Mate. And I'm completely serious when I say I don't believe he exists here in London.

If you think I'm being harsh and haven't given the locals enough of a chance, or perhaps you're new to London and are considering the perilous climb up Mount True Love yourself, I'll outline the options. There are a number of well and wearily trodden paths to a new man. Your friends unconsciously reveal what they really think of you by the kind of *someone I thought you'd like to meet* man brought to dinner parties. Rather than catching up on your paperwork, you could squeeze in some *best of a bad lot* power-flirting on the commute to work (and be devastated when, even though you didn't fancy him to begin with, he brushes you off). Maybe you're considering signing up for online dating or going to places where you should, but absolutely never will, meet someone suitable? Since over the last year I've tried them all, I'll share what I've learned with you. I've sat chatting to Belgian lawyers in Starbucks (willing them to be even a little more interesting); I've dabbled with online dating (where all the guys have done the *Nick Hornby's Guide to Women* course and are single parents with angelic but troubled kids, or run small, quirky, yet failing businesses). I don't even want to think about going to another cultural event (to meet graduates of the *Tony Parsons' Guide to Women* course: bitterness over ex-wife, partially concealed by exterior of witty self-loathing, which in turn is momentarily obscured by an encyclopedic knowledge of early punk bands). Maybe you can tell me about evening classes. I can't work out whether eligible guys need to do Woodwork 101 or if the classes will just be full of women like me. Likewise, I haven't signed up for a fourteen-week religious or spiritual workshop and I won't go near any therapy that involves garden hoses, buckets, or splash mats. I'm not looking to discover the meaning of life. Get karmic social services on to me, because I'm really not interested in my inner child. I just want a decent boyfriend. And by all means share your experiences with your girlfriends, but I am completely serious when I say that the actual task of searching for your Soul Mate, like getting your bikini line waxed, is strictly a one-woman job. It's a selfish, solo occupation that can't involve all your other single female friends. When too many of us in relationship recovery get together, new boyfriends are the last things on our minds. Instead we perpetuate and mythologize our misery, building a shrine to our exes out of empty wine bottles and Kettle Chip packets. I don't want to talk about old relationships. I don't want to spend months trying to understand what went wrong. If your car plunged through the median of the highway, you wouldn't spend a year showing your friends photos of the happy days when it was safely parked outside your house. You'd just go out and buy another one. Get right back into the fast lane. Move on.

But we're so busy working, we don't have the time to find the person we want to *move on* with. So we turn to the *labor-saving devices* on the market, designed to lead us to Mr. Right in the small amount of time we have allocated to the task. A perfect example of this is online dating. Online dating seems convenient because you can do it surreptitiously from your desk, during meetings at work, or with flirtatious, drunken abandon when you get home in the early hours of Saturday morning. That's pretty much where the convenience ends, though, because no matter how good the profile and nice the picture, you need to know more about him before deciding if he's worth meeting. So, you chat back and forth via email, maybe send a text message or two, then you're ready to talk on the phone. The first physical contact (i.e., ear-to-ear) is crunch-time since you can generally tell from his voice and conversation if you want to meet him or not. Unfortunately, it's generally "not" but by this point you're involved with him and finding a reason to end that involvement—even though you don't know him—is cringingly hard (tip: keep a fictitious "unresolved ex" up your sleeve for these occasions). Hope turns to guilt as you become locked into a continuous and exhausting process of assessing candidates, like interviewing people for a job you know they'll never get. And in the meantime, that's another two hours a day spent in front of your computer. Something has to change. Enough of these *relationship patches,* which, like nicotine patches, stave off the need without satisfying any of the desire. I wanted a fantastic, glorious, wonderful relationship. Otherwise, what's the point?

But for this to happen, I knew I needed to make a better job of meeting Mr. Right. I felt I'd tried everything in London. Maybe it was time for a more radical and far-reaching solution?

Rather than traveling to recover from Mr. Wrong, what if I went traveling to find Mr. Right? I mean, I was sure Fate had him out there waiting for me, so why was I wasting time in London moaning when I could be out in the world searching? I'd put my heart and soul into my job; maybe it was time I put the same amount of effort into my love life.

So, after some soul-searching, I quit my job at Lonely Planet. I had a new job now: finding my Soul Mate.

The business and management skills I'd developed over the years would most likely come in handy. Making programs for the BBC had honed my research and interviewing skills. Setting up and running Lonely Planet's European publicity and promotional operations meant devising campaigns while jumping on and off planes to oversee launches and train staff, plus doing a ton of interviews and public speaking stints. Like anybody with a big, fat job, to do this well I'd had to be able to network, research, talk people into doing things they weren't that keen on, time-manage, meet deadlines, budget, and plan.

So, traveling would be the answer to London's dearth of suitable men, and my professional skills would hopefully lead me to possible candidates, eliminating the unsuitable, undesirable, and unstable from among them. But where should I start looking? I couldn't just get off a plane in another country shouting, *"Soul Mate, I'm here. Come and get me."* I was confident Fate had a number of them out there for me to meet (as I've already said, I believe we have more than one), but where, and who could they be?

I decided that the first step to answering this question was to work out who they *had* been. If finding my Soul Mate was now my job, as with any other job I'd need to put together an up-to-date résumé. A Relationship Résumé: a document that set out my romance history, giving me an insight into the kind of person I'd gone for in the past. In short, whom I dated and when; the role I undertook in the relationship and the reasons for leaving it. Based on that, I then needed to write a Soul Mate Job Description, outlining the position I was looking to fill. The task was too big for me alone, but I was hoping that my global network of friends would help. If I emailed them the Soul Mate Job Description, they could act as Date Wranglers, sending it out to *their* global network of friends and corralling suitable dates for me around the world.

The more I thought about it, the more I wondered why I hadn't done this sooner.

Okay, the Relationship Résumé:

DATE: 1984–85
TITLE: First Love
COMPANY: William
MAJOR RESPONSIBILITIES: Going to festivals; riding around on the back of a motorbike; protesting at Greenham Common; finding politics; losing virginity.
REASONS FOR LEAVING: Laid off; replaced by someone who drank Bacardi Breezers.

DATE: 1985–89
TITLE: First Live-in Relationship
COMPANY: Peter
MAJOR RESPONSIBILITIES: Learning to cook; having lots of dinner parties; buying things for the flat; having Sunday lunch with his family; getting engaged.
REASONS FOR LEAVING: Applied for a position overseas.

DATE: 1989–95
TITLE: Wife
COMPANY: Philip
MAJOR RESPONSIBILITIES: Being spontaneous and not worrying too much about tomorrow; sharing adventures; being supportive of each other's dreams; saying "No, Philip, that's too crazy."
REASONS FOR LEAVING: Was relocated back to the U.K.

DATE: January 1996
TITLE: Transition Relationship
COMPANY: Dan
MAJOR RESPONSIBILITIES: Drinking Jack Daniel's and staying up very late; watching a lot of Tarantino films; listening to heavy-metal music; bursting into tears.
REASONS FOR LEAVING: Short-term contract.

DATE: February–June 1996
TITLE: Career Advisor
COMPANY: Edmund
MAJOR RESPONSIBILITIES: Going over to his house or sitting on the phone every night and listening to what he had written that day on his book. Criticism was not welcome, only attention and praise.
REASONS FOR LEAVING: Communication breakdown.

DATE: August 1996
TITLE: Fellow Adventurer
COMPANY: Jason
MAJOR RESPONSIBILITIES: Swapping travel stories and talking about all the crazy places we had been/both wanted to go.

REASONS FOR LEAVING: I met Jason a week before he was due to set off to pedal the planet for four years. NB: Carried out some freelance work for this company over Xmas.

DATE: 1997–98
TITLE: Company Trustee
COMPANY: Grant
MAJOR RESPONSIBILITIES: Listening to Grant complain about his ex-wife and how glad he was they had split up.
REASONS FOR LEAVING: They hadn't split up.

DATE: 1999–2004
TITLE: Coco the Clown
COMPANY: Kelly
MAJOR RESPONSIBILITIES: Feeling everything was my fault and that I was too demanding/needy/neurotic/successful; believing things would get better if I could only understand what the problem was.
REASONS FOR LEAVING: I was unwilling to job-share.

Hmmm. Writing the Relationship Résumé had been an illuminating but not terribly uplifting experience: It looked like I hadn't been in a good relationship for ages. For a moment I wondered if I was better off forgetting about romantic relationships and sticking to having fun with my millions of other single female friends.

But that was silly. My single friends wanted to be in a relationship as much as I did; even if *I* wimped out and stayed single, there was no guarantee *they'd* stay that way (and I hoped for all their sakes they wouldn't—I wanted them to meet their Mr. Rights, too).

No, I wanted to be in a good relationship. I missed having

that close connection with one person, feeling that I was at the center of something rather than bobbing around the edges. But I wanted one of the early happy-style relationships, not one of the hard, rubbish ones I seemed to have specialized in in recent years. Clearly the Soul Mate Job Description needed serious consideration if I was to avoid disappointment and disaster.

First I needed to decide on the kind of person I wanted to meet. Well, since I was five feet eleven, height was very important: I needed the chemistry when someone's tall enough to put his arm around my shoulders—I absolutely could not date someone shorter than me. I wanted someone who was affectionate without being overbearing—such a hard one to get right. Someone who was smart, funny, and adventurous and had his own friends. Since divorced men have a marriage-shaped hole in their lives that they are looking to quickly fill, and single women have a disaster-shaped hole in their lives they want to keep empty for as long as possible, I didn't want someone who was going to take me over completely.

What else? An interest in music was good, too much interest in TV was bad. I am a vegetarian, and although I don't mind meat-eaters, anyone with a love of offal should probably not apply. I don't like smokers (good-bye, Jean Pierre) but distrust anyone who doesn't drink. They don't have to have their own library card, but a few books on the shelf would be good (science fiction and self-help don't count). I don't mind guys who are slightly overweight, but "man breasts" are a complete no-no. Skinny guys are out: If their waists are smaller than my thighs, it's not going to work. I quite like laid-back guys, but absolutely no slackers, potheads, or wannabe poets (if I want to see the beauty in anything, I'll go to the Mac cosmetics counter, thank you very much). Sporty is good, but don't expect me to come watch if it's raining.

Having said all of that, I *was* open-minded and probably needed to challenge what I thought my type of man really was—with the exception of man breasts and offal; they were non-negotiable.

The next step was to assemble my network of Date Wranglers (DWs), including Belinda, Charlotte, Simon, Cath, Ian, Eleanor, Sara-Jane, Hector, Jeannette, Jo, Posh PR Emma, Paula, Sophie, Madhav, Jill, Matt, Lizzy, Grainne . . . All old friends, either in the travel industry or journalists who have worked overseas for years. These First-Generation Date Wranglers all had an extensive network of contacts and friends around the world, who would be either Dates or second- or third-generation Date Wranglers in their own right. I'd already talked to everyone about my plans, but it was now time to send out a briefing email and get the team to work.

Dear Date Wranglers

A few of you have asked what kind of person I'm looking to meet and what I want to do on the date (thank you, Sophie—José the Chilean sheep farmer sounds lovely. And Jo, yes, Jason the Buddhist lawyer in Nova Scotia might be perfect). I've pasted a Soul Mate Job Description below. Please read it carefully. If it sounds like a single someone you know anywhere in the world, and they'd be willing to date me, please let me know. I'll then sit down with a list of potential Dates and pick the ones that look most promising and fall relatively easily into a route around the world. Dinner at my house on the 12th for questions/brainstorming/reality check.

Lots of love, J xx

Soul Mate Job Description

I am a 38-year-old writer living in London. I've
done a bit of traveling over the years and am planning another big trip soon. When not schlepping my
backpack on and off Indian trains, maxing my card
at Macy's, or eating gelati in Italy, I love London
Life. Sunday papers and coffee with my friends,
plus shows, gigs, and movies. I'm a bit sporty, especially running (though not very far or fast) and
cycling (see "running"). I'm bad at spelling but
good at cooking. I sing along to music and always
seem to forget Xmas cards till the last minute. I'm
fairly laid-back about most things, though get pathetically competitive playing poker.

And what am I looking for in a man?

I'm pretty tall at five foot eleven but old-
fashioned enough to want to feel "ladylike," so
looking for someone over six foot. What else?
Well, I'd like to meet someone who makes me smile,
lets me read them bits out of the newspaper, has
beliefs they're willing to arm-wrestle for, and
tells me interesting things I didn't know. Like me,
you'll believe that life is short and you should
make the most of it; unlike me, you'll probably
realize that TV isn't real and remain calm when
Lassie doesn't come home. An interest in music
and books is good, a sense of fun and adventure
essential.

The response was instant, overwhelming, and very reassuring:
everyone was fired up with suggestions and ideas. Maybe all my

competitive friends just wanted to prove they each had the best
contacts, but I actually think everyone genuinely wanted to help
and believed that they had just the person for me.

Queries started flooding in. Sophie bluntly asked:

```
Do you want to sleep with them all or just
dinner/chat about life etc. . . ? Lemme know,
it'll influence who I put you onto. Love S
```

I have to be honest, this panicked me a bit. My journey had already been dubbed "Around the World in Eighty Lays" by most
of my friends. I automatically replied with an *It's not about sex, it's
about romance* mantra but was secretly worrying whether every
date was going to end in a wrestling match.

Posh PR Emma rang and asked in cut-glass tones if I wanted
to date a count. Her impeccable accent made the *o* completely
silent. Realizing how it sounded, she kept repeating the question,
which drew attention to the mispronunciation, making it worse.
I felt like replying: "Ems, I've already dated so many."

As my DWs went to work and word of what I was doing
began buzzing around, potential dates started pouring in. Every
morning I would log on to find up to a hundred emails from people looking to get involved.

First-generation DWs introducing me to second-generation
DWs:

```
Jennifer, meet Abigail, she is the most high-flying
woman in New York—head honcho, inspired party gal,
groovy traveling companion of many years and dear,
dear friend . . . AND I think she has the perfect
date for you . . . she will tell you more . . . I can't
wait to hear the outcome . . . SJ xxxxxx
```

Third-generation DWs signing up and asking for basic clarification:

Does he need to speak English? Would you be willing
to go on a ménage à trois with a translator?
Hannah, emailing from Budapest

Giving me a *wake up and smell the fertility* reality check:

P.S. You say you don't want to date men younger
than thirty. I have two words for you: sperm motil-
ity. If you're still in the race to have a child
before, say, forty-five, you'll need energetic
critters rather than those about to retire. Leslie,
emailing from Moscow

And forcing me to face the facts:

These are the details of the English lady I was
telling you about: I hope she sounds interesting to
you. She's a very nice lady, aged thirty-eight (but
this is quite normal in the U.K. to be old and
still single)....

And so read the email trail between Alex and his friend Beaver in
Lithuania.

At the same time that I was being contacted by DWs and their
Dates, I was also out looking for myself, spending hours on the
Internet researching places or events that might yield my Soul
Mate. Anything to do with Love or a love of mine should have
potential, I reasoned. I scoured the search engines like an intrepid
love detective sleuthing for clues that would help me identify and

locate my missing man. In some instances, this threw up dreadful red herrings. I am a huge devotee of the yeast spread Marmite, for example, and thought this might make me compatible with the man who ran a Marmite appreciation website in America:

```
I started the Marmite site because I take Marmite
into work with me on a Friday (the company I work
for supplies breakfast, mainly bagels though we do
have toast as well and sometimes yogurt, though I
don't have Marmite with the yogurt. Just the
bagels. And the toast, if they've run out of
bagels). Other than eating Marmite, I write infor-
mation management and delivery software for the
Internet. . . .
```

Thankfully, other leads proved to be more fruitful, such as the Costco Soul Mate Trading Outlet, one of the theme camps at the annual Burning Man Festival, held in the Nevada desert. I didn't totally understand what they were about, but I did manage to establish that Costco was a kind of anarchic dating agency at the festival. The CEO, Rico Thunder, agreed that I could be part of their camp and work on their "front desk" in exchange for some light flirting duties. I felt I'd have some useful expertise to contribute by the time I'd made it through Europe and the West Coast of America to Nevada, plus I fully intended to skim off any suitable Soul Mates for myself. Rico also put me in touch with a Seattle-based audio engineer in TV sports who was one of the Costco crew. He matched my Soul Mate Job Description perfectly and emailed:

```
The things you write in your description could have
been written by me! What is up with that?
```

Love: Cooking, building/restoring cars (just
finished an Alfa), music, road trips
Hate: Working out (still do it), rigid
people, being cold for long periods of time,
speed bumps

The only way I could cope with the huge volume of correspondence was to ruthlessly compartmentalize. In the process of establishing a tentative rapport with the desirables and gently filtering out the inadvisables, Europe was given priority over America, which in turn took precedence over Australasia.

Big picture, that was how I saw my route working: Europe, U.S., Australasia. It wasn't logical from a geographical point of view, but it made it possible to attend specific events at certain times, plus—as importantly—ensured that I'd always be traveling with the sun. This meant I could stay warm, pack light, and see people at their/my most foxy. There are valid reasons that all the feel-good songs—"Summer Breeze," "Summer Lovin'"— "Summer of '69"—are written about the summer rather than the miserable winter months. Who looks good with chapped lips and a scarf?

Communication all had to be via email: It was the only way I could keep track of what I'd said to whom, and reply to people in my own time rather than real time. Most people were fine with this but occasionally someone insisted that we had to speak on the phone:

I don't want to rush you but I much prefer speaking
as opposed to typing. Feel free to call me on 877-
722-****. Toll-free USA. In Canada or elsewhere
561-178-****. Christopher, Florida

This always put me in a spin. I didn't really have the time for more than a single conversation with any one person and there was no way they'd just want to talk once; inevitably they'd want to know all about me as well as when I was coming over, how long I was staying, and all the other details of my trip. But I didn't have answers to these questions yet, and the stress of organizing this mammoth undertaking was taking its toll as I comfort-ate, putting the "ate" in "date" just at the time I really needed to look my best.

I was tentatively working toward a route that would start in the Netherlands, head up through Scandinavia, then down through Mediterranean Europe and central Europe and on to the States. This was just guesswork, though, because—for example—until Henk in Amsterdam got back from his skiing trip, I had no way of knowing if he was free on the 27th? If he was, that would mean I'd be able to make it down to see Frank on the Belgian border, thereby arriving in Barcelona in time to meet Carlos before he set off for his conference in Russia:

. . . though I am in with my good friends in St.
Petersburg and maybe it would be that you like
to join us there if you are in a visit to this
place?

I just needed everyone to stay still long enough to give me an answer that would allow me to include them in or eliminate them from my itinerary. Then—knowing they were locked in—I could work out who, logically, I should see next. And that was just the dating side of it. My friend Karin, who worked at the Netherlands tourist board, was hugely helpful in trying to work out how I would get between three dates spread over two hundred fifty miles:

I've been looking for public transport facilities
from Schiphol to the Efteling and from the Efteling
to the Keukenhof and I must say it's not good
news. . . . It will take you two and a half hours to
get from Schiphol to the Efteling and three hours
to get from the Efteling to the Keukenhof. I knew
it would be bad as you have to use both trains and
buses, but I didn't know it would be this lousy. A
taxi is not really an alternative, that will be really expensive, but I was thinking you could maybe
rent a car for two or three days. Do you have your
driver's license and would it be a good idea? I've
attached an information sheet with car rental com-
panies at Schiphol and in Amsterdam. If you like
the idea, you could phone them and ask for prices.
If you do prefer to use public transport I can tell
you exactly which trains and buses you have to
take, so just let me know.

I felt guilty, as she clearly wanted me to make a decision and all
I could do was be vague and noncommittal. The problem was
that she was asking about the minutiae of one aspect of three
dates while I was in a totally different place, struggling to get
the big picture straight on *all* aspects of *all* eighty dates. It felt
akin to being dragged from a burning building by the emergency
services, only to have them demand back an overdue library
book.

   With so many options and nothing actually nailed down, I
started feeling the enormity of what I was attempting. I was getting a tad tense trying to stay focused while having to remain upbeat and chatty corresponding with the avalanche of potential
dates. I knew I wouldn't get much in the way of sympathy (*"Help,*

I am being hounded by an endless supply of eligible, international bachelors, all wanting to date me. . . ."), but even if I'd been foolish enough to ask, I wouldn't have got anyone's attention at this point. Brimming with enthusiasm and support, the DWs had gone off on a mission of their own.

I had clearly said I wanted to date my Soul Mate and explained in detail who that person was. But suddenly, girlfriends were less interested in helping me find *my* ideal man and more interested in helping themselves live out a cherished fantasy. They had found a way to date The One Who Could Have Been.

Could Haves are those intense, poignant relationships that, for some reason, never get acted upon. But despite this, or maybe because of it, these people become imbued with an aura of exquisite perfection that only increases as the years go by. A pocket of my (mostly married) DWs had just realized that I could go on the date they had always longed for. No guilt on their part, plus I would be able to tell them afterward if the date was as blissful as they had always imagined.

Jen, I have always, always had a huge crush on Paul but we were never single at the same time. You lucky girl, he's free now—I want to know EVERYTHING. Lucinda xxx

P.S. Get him to take you to the Dove—we always used to go there together for drinks after work; it's really romantic. Sit at the table by the window. The chardonnay's great. Order the fish.

Or they'd become distracted by their own idea of what the optimum Soul Mate was like, rather than working to mine: "Oh, you should date a circus performer," Dea said with great conviction, no explanation, and a faraway look in her eye. "Ohmigod, you could date a tramp," Jo exploded, then gazed off in a similarly mute manner, lost in her own thoughts.

Clearly, I needed to get them to refocus, and I knew the only way this would happen would be if I made them competitive about coming up with the best Dates. I sent another email to the group:

I am so grateful to you all for coming up with such great contacts, and the current joint favorites for the (Little Black) Booker Prize are Paul Mansfield and Belinda Rhodes. Eleanor Garland pulled away from the pack toward the end of last week, though, and is now gaining fast.

I am now fully dated up for N. America and Australia. Holland is looking good, too. Can anyone help with France, Germany, Spain, and Italy? How about Asia—HK, Thailand, and Singapore?

Thankfully, this led to a fresh deluge of dates, but also to a new phenomenon: Date Wrangler Anxiety. Hector, a journalist friend at *China Daily,* emailed from Beijing, frustrated that he didn't seem to be able to come up with any good dates. He felt he was letting me down and not being a good friend. "Write an article about it," I suggested. "Interview me about why I'm doing it and include my Soul Mate Job Description, and then anyone who thinks they're 'it' can email me at a special email address I'll create." Overwhelmed by the greater task in hand and consigning it to the *I'll worry about it when I'm on to Australasia* pile, I promptly forgot all about the conversation. Until two weeks later, when Hector sheepishly sent me a link for that day's paper. On the cover was a huge picture of me, smiling vacantly. Underneath, the caption read: IS THERE A MAN IN CHINA TO SATISFY THIS WOMAN?

Most of the time that I was working on setting up this International Tour of Shame, as I'd affectionately come to think of it, I was too engrossed and in the zone to think about anything else. But occasionally there were stone-cold moments of sober clarity, when it really hit me how it must have looked to other people.

The *China Daily* cover was one of them. I sat in front of my computer, shocked and rather ashamed, wondering why I had started this crazy adventure in the first place. But then, as the responses to the article started pouring in, I was once again too frantic keeping up with the task at hand to have any more perspective or qualms.

Replies ranged from Tom in Hong Kong:

I am currently seeing someone but we don't really
get on that well and on the off-chance I've split
up with her by the time you get here, can we please
stay in touch?

And Larry, the pilot:

I've seen your picture. You're not that good-
looking and you make no effort with your hair; I
like that kind of confidence in a woman and I'll
definitely date you. But don't expect to go to expensive restaurants or be a nosy parker and talk
about me to my friends.

To Tan, the businessman:

I look forward to meeting a western woman, so different from Asian women: you with your "fuller"

body and more voluptuous breasts. In a country of billions, you will certainly stand out.

Well, my comfort eating *was* getting out of hand now, and I was putting on so much weight I'd started wondering if I should just cut out the middleman and staple the cookies directly onto my thighs. Despite the weight gain, however, I felt sure I lacked the prized voluptuousness that would make me a worthy ambassador for Breast Western. And the idea that a billion people were going to be disappointed with my cleavage was frankly too much pressure to be dealing with right now.

Fortunately, I was saved from dwelling on this thought because a combination of brute force and plaintive begging had finally pulled my European schedule loosely together. There was still a huge amount to be done: I knew who I was meeting and where, but still had no idea where I was staying when I arrived, or, indeed, in most cases how I would arrive at all. I accepted that I would have to work this out along the way.

It was time to start dating.

chapter two

The Netherlands

Date #2—The real Prince
Charming in Eftelling, Holland

He ordered for both of them: "Two toast with butter and . . . d'you want a coffee, Debs?" She nodded without looking up from her handbag-rummaging. "And two coffees: a latte coffee and an ordinary one."

The North Terminal of Gatwick Airport didn't exactly smack of romance, but it positively reverberated with relationships and everyday intimacies. It was awash with people who had shared many breakfasts and went on holiday together without giving it a second thought. Booked on the 7:30 a.m. to Amsterdam, I was sitting on my own, ordering my own breakfast and feeling a touch out of sorts. I hadn't started out on my Dating Odyssey yet, but I couldn't quite suppress the small voice in my head that whispered: *It's not too late—you don't have to go through with this.*

Like getting a tattoo, I sensed, once I began this journey there would be no turning back. I would be changed forever. The problem was that I had no idea whether the change was going to be good or bad, and that uncertainty was unnerving.

Debs and "ordinary coffee" husband were on my left. On my right, a guy my age was sitting on his own, reading *Q*, my favorite music magazine. I glanced at the remains on his plate: It looked like he was a vegetarian too. Did I really need to travel around the world to meet somebody? Wasn't it just possible that this man right next to me could turn out to be my Soul Mate? I sighed impatiently, disgusted with myself as I pulled on my jacket and signaled the waitress for the bill. I loathed people who relied on palmists or tea-leaf readers to "learn" what was wedged up the sleeve of Fate for them. Yet there I was, divining my future among the smears of ketchup and greasy remains of a vegetarian sausage. Exactly how desperate had I become?

Desperate enough to go around the world in eighty dates, I told myself matter-of-factly as I pushed a tip under the plate, picked up my bags, and started the long walk to flight BA8111 and Date #1.

Date #1: Henk—Amsterdam, Holland

I was staying at Amsterdam House, a comfortably quirky hotel on a quiet part of the Amstel River, in the old diamond district. You could sit in the lounge flicking through piles of magazines, drink great coffee, and watch the world go by. Well, *you* could, *I* couldn't: I was up in my tiny attic room, waiting to get the call from reception that would announce the arrival of Henk, my first date.

I met Henk through Sandrine, a third-generation DW whom I'd initially acquired through Belinda. Henk and I had emailed

back and forth a couple of times, but all I really knew about him
was that he was balding, sporty, and confident.

I started up my laptop to look at the photo he'd emailed,
saved into a regional file along with those of all the others I was
dating in that location. He looked quite cute. I wondered why he
was single. And if he worried about it; he didn't look the neurotic
type. I also wondered—and I know this sounds terrible—if I
could go out with a bald man.

Wondered was about my level of interest and anxiety over
what I was shortly to do. I didn't feel at all nervous, more detached with a sense of curiosity, an eagerness to get on with it,
and a wish that I'd had time to go round the shops I'd passed on
the way to the hotel.

In short, I was in denial.

Although the knowledge that I had a date with Prince
Charming tomorrow, with Willem the next day, and so on, took
a lot of pressure off: If the date didn't go well, there'd be another
along soon enough. What I was doing was a form of speed-
dating, but more far-reaching: *"Today's Monday and Rome, you
must be Date Number 12."*

I had no idea what we were going to do on this date and, security aside—one of the reasons I set up dates through friends
and carried a cell phone with me at all times—that was fine by
me. I'd served my time planning thoughtful, lovely treats for
boyfriends; I was really happy to have someone else in charge—
and to learn to be okay with the results.

Thirty minutes had passed and Henk was late. I still wasn't
nervous but I did wish he'd hurry up and get here. It was now
11:50 a.m. and I had perfected my *"Henk . . . it is so great to finally meet you"* smile; I was done with all the clothing crises my
limited wardrobe allowed. I'd hidden my new duty-free Mac lip

gloss in the bottom of my bag; I'd been applying it for over an hour to pass the time. If he tried to kiss me now, his face would skid off mine so fast, he'd get whiplash.

Peering out the window, I saw no sign of anyone who looked like Henk. Time to go to the loo one more time? I was hungry but didn't know whether to eat or not. This was a drawback of not knowing what we were doing: If I didn't eat, guaranteed we'd go for a ten-mile hike; if I did, he'd immediately take me for a meal. Mulling it over, I unwrapped yet another gorgeous little spice cookie and found myself hoping we'd go for a beer.

Ummmm, yes, a beer. Suddenly I really wanted a drink. God, if I was like this watching out for all the Dates, I'd be a three-hundred-pound alcoholic by the end of the trip: from Date Watcher to Weight Watchers in eighty easy lessons.

The phone rang. Reception. Henk was here.

I was determined not to get tongue-tied and nervous, so before I had the chance I grabbed my bag and a jacket and, slamming my room door shut, ran down three flights of stairs to the lobby.

Henk was waiting for me, looking a little nervous himself. "Don't think about it, don't think about it," I was chanting in my head as, ignoring the amused look on the receptionist's face, I walked over to shake Henk's outstretched hand and thereby officially commit to my dating fate.

Henk was about six foot three, with an athletic build, blond hair, blue eyes, and a nice smile. My very first thought was: not as bald as I imagined, nice-looking, tall and rangy, a bit preppy, sensitive. "I have a boat with me," he said, smiling shyly. Beaming appreciatively in response, I was groaning inwardly: Even looking at a boat makes me want to throw up. As Henk helped me onto the thirty-five-foot barge, he added: "I thought I'd take you on a bit of a spin around the canals and we'd have something to eat along the way."

Out of the hamper by his feet, he pulled sashimi, strawberries, and champagne. The date had begun.

I was touched. He had obviously put a lot of effort into making the date as romantic as possible. Unfortunately—and I didn't say this to him—it was more someone else's idea of romantic. I've always wanted to be one of those women sophisticated enough to function on a diet of protein and alcohol, but as a lactose-intolerant, lapsed Catholic vegetarian, I'm sadly more of a potato-and-bread girl, with a limited capacity for raw fish. But that was the old me. So, sailing up Prinsengraacht, I settled back in the sunshine and smiled at Henk as he passed me a glass of champagne as chilled as the music on the boat's MP3 player. We toasted each other's health and I silently toasted the elegant new me: Watery Hepburn.

Floating past the flower market full of roses and sunflowers, the queues outside Anne Frank's house, the red-light district packed with drunk British men (T-shirts declaring they were on "Steve's Stag Weekend"), I asked Henk about his relationship history. People on bridges smiled down indulgently, thinking us the perfect couple, while Henk described how he had been happy with his first long relationship at university but wasn't ready to settle down. His next relationship was a bit of a disaster: The girl had been intense and spiritual and it hadn't worked out, but he'd stayed in touch with her. His next girlfriend had treated him badly but he was crazy about her. ("She was very passionate," he said helplessly, then added rather alarmingly, "You remind me of her a lot.")

As Henk expertly navigated the waterways, I thought of the last time I'd been to Amsterdam. It had been with Kelly: We'd argued fiercely about who knows what and I'd stormed off in the pouring rain. Why had Kelly never done anything like this? And, having to ask that, why then did I still miss him?

Meanwhile Henk sailed on, turning us into endless canals, reliving endless romances. It was cold and dark now; we'd been on the water for about seven hours. Although I hadn't felt quite as sick as I'd first anticipated, an unhappy blend of sashimi and champagne swirled ominously in the pit of my stomach as I listened with a growing sense of impatience while Henk talked. It dawned on me that other people's love lives are like other people's dreams: only interesting if you're in them, and then only if they're good. I started feeling a bit disheartened: *Another seventy-nine of these conversations to go . . .*

I didn't want to be mean. I had actually really enjoyed being on the water with Henk. But I didn't fancy him, it was getting cold, and I had to be up early to drive to Date #2 tomorrow morning. Fortunately, at this point Henk told me he'd booked a sofa at the Supper Club, which gave me the excuse to say, "I've had a great time, but I have to say good night." I could tell he was disappointed, but he was a good guy and turned the boat around obediently to start sailing back to the hotel.

We got back just before 9 p.m. and Henk helped me (as I shook uncontrollably from the cold) onto the towpath. Thanking him—with an effusion born of guilt—for a wonderful day, I suddenly realized we had entered the Long Good-bye, that awkward time at the end of a date when he wants to kiss you, but you don't want to kiss him. I have always been completely hopeless at getting this right and, as someone about to date eighty men, I needed to fast-track this skill. I'd always opted for the Quick Peck and Hug (QPH) maneuver, the one where you say, "Okay, thanks for a lovely evening," give him a quick kiss on the cheek, then dodge into a hug before he can lock his mouth onto yours. This was an utterly rubbish technique that could go on for days, as the man let you hug him but then kept talking to you, so you had to endlessly start over.

Henk deftly neutralized my QPH. I admitted defeat and agreed to another date with him two days later, knowing I'd be on a plane when the time came. I felt bad but was too cold to come up with a better plan.

Date #2: Frank—Efteling, Holland

Horribly early the next morning, I picked up a rental car from Schiphol airport and drove south toward the Belgian border for Date #2.

I'd heard about a place called Efteling: an amusement theme park and hotel designed around classic national and international fairy tales. I'd arranged to spend the night in the Sleeping Beauty Suite, and my patient friend Karin had set me up to date the guy who played Prince Charming at the park.

I felt a little uneasy about Henk (I should have just said no, rather than copping out and making him think we'd have another date—note to self: Be firmer), but it was a gorgeous spring morning and soon I was enjoying the uncomplicated feeling of being on the road again.

That feeling lasted about ten minutes.

My pastoral appreciation of fields, churches, and cows was soon completely overshadowed by the discovery that the Dutch, mostly a calm, liberal, egalitarian people, evidently treated motorways as the place to exercise their ids and drove like complete maniacs. Cars shot across lanes into tiny spaces between the speeding vehicles without any warning or regard for safety. Convoys of huge trucks randomly (or so it seemed to me) honked their horns, making me increasingly paranoid that either the trunk was open and my luggage was spilling out or I was breaking some vital Dutch driving law. Or were they just being friendly? I had no idea and it was very disconcerting. I arrived at Efteling late, harassed, and somewhat distracted.

As ever, I overcompensated by being very businesslike. I swept into the lobby of the Golden Tulip Hotel and up to the front desk. "My name is Jennifer Cox," I told the neat-looking receptionist briskly, "I'm here to date Prince Charming."

I knew how ridiculous it sounded, but it had been a trying morning, and I gave her a look that stated very clearly: *"Say 'Ooooh, aren't we all' and I will disembowel you where you stand."*

But she didn't. Instead she smiled sympathetically and said: "Ah yes, we've been expecting you, Ms. Cox. I'm sorry, but I have some bad news: Prince Charming has unexpectedly been taken ill. But please don't worry, he has arranged for his friend Frank, who runs the local bike shop, to date you instead. He's waiting for you over there."

As she pointed somewhere over my shoulder, I sagged against the counter and squinted at her in uncomprehending astonishment. This was not good. Really not good at all. I'm not a hippie, but I do believe in karma: When Prince Charming can't be bothered to show up and is replaced last minute by the local bike mechanic, romance is not writ large in the stars.

"Be calm," I told myself evenly and unconvincingly. "Fate is just testing you to make sure you're serious." I took a deep breath and turned to Frank, who was sitting patiently waiting to introduce himself. I forced a weak, wobbly smile onto my face as I walked over to meet him. My first impression was that he was nervous (who could blame him?) and a bit thin. He looked good when he stood up, though: about six feet two, with slightly curly, reddish hair and very blue eyes. He looked shy but

not wimpy (I hate wimpy) and surprised me by taking my hand and saying firmly: "Come with me, Jennifer, I'm going to date you."

And that's exactly what he did.

Efteling theme park dated back to 1952 and was full of your regular fairies and Red Riding Hoods, but also, weird, freakish gargoyles called Laafs, who were a sort of cherished national goblin. The park had the air and appearance of a 1970s Disney Does Brueghel fantasy—rather dated and a bit disturbing—but in a nice way, with lots of bright flowers and excited schoolkids running around.

Frank walked me round the gargoyles and daffodils with a sense of purpose. He had planned where we should go and was quietly in charge (which I liked). But I'd been up for five hours, had eaten nothing all day (the whole pre-date "To eat or not to eat" question again), and was really starting to feel the effects. Noticing I was getting a little vague, Frank took me to a cafeteria by a huge aviary.

Food is always a nightmare for me in Europe: There's either too much dairy (France), too much meat (Germany), or too much lard (pretty much anywhere east of Zurich). There was nothing I really wanted but I'd left it too late to be fussy, so bought us both smoked-salmon open sandwiches. Feeling a little faint, I went to take my first bite and the sandwich slipped out of my hand. Lightning reflexes honed by seven years on the school softball team kicked in as I caught the sandwich in its upward trajectory, snatching it out of the air. The salmon, however, continued to fly pancake-esque upward. It flipped over lazily before plummeting back down and slapping wetly onto the back of my hand, covering it completely like some vile-smelling glove. I stared at it helplessly. You don't eat food that's been on the floor, but what's the protocol for food that's been worn? Frank, who had stood quietly watching my freakish display, reached over, unpeeled the fish from my hand, and folded it back onto the top of the sandwich.

"Shall we walk as we eat?" he asked politely. I nodded meekly and we set off to explore.

Once I'd eaten, I started to relax and enjoy myself. The park was great: Dream Ride was a fairy kingdom full of scary porn fairies with open mouths; Panda Dream was a highly inventive 3D film, in which Martin Luther King was reincarnated as a panda concerned about the environment. My favorite ride was the "Arabic" boat trip along an indoor river that sailed past scenes from *Tales of 1,001 Nights.*

We cruised around blind corners scented with apple incense, into market scenes where cheesy shop-window dummies with rolling eyes jerked stiffly on magic carpets. We sailed out of one dark, smoky tunnel between the legs of a huge genie, whose vast jowls hung down over us, disconcerting, like giant testicles.

The ride reduced us to helpless, conspiratorial giggles. Suddenly, I didn't resent that I'd been stood up by Prince Charming, as Frank was turning out to be the male equivalent of Cinderella: a slow burner full of fun. Earlier in the day he'd touched my shoulder a few times to make a point, and at the time the intimacy had made me feel uncomfortable. Now when he did it, I felt relaxed and fond of him.

Despite the fact that I was having a good time, by 6 p.m. the spring air had grown cold and we were flagging, so Frank suggested we return to the hotel bar for a drink. Finding a table by the window and ordering wine, we were chatting and laughing easily by now. As we sat with our heads close together, Frank said something I didn't catch. I turned and leaned closer to hear him better. Without warning he took my face in his hands and kissed me full on the mouth. I genuinely wasn't expecting this at all and I gasped out loud in shock (though not unpleasantly surprised).

"You can't kiss me in the bar," I spluttered, pulling away and laughing.

"Where would you like me to kiss you?" Frank replied with a challenging smile.

I know this is going to sound completely naïve, but I hadn't even thought about what I'd do if someone kissed me. It wasn't that I didn't like Frank—I did—but I had another date in twelve hours. I had already started to detach emotionally and was really looking forward to the peace and quiet of my room. I needed some time out to curl up in bed with a beer, chips, and a movie, not talking to anyone at all.

Although I knew I was staying in the Sleeping Beauty Suite (cute and silly, with a spinning wheel in one corner and a life-size snoring knight in another), there hadn't been time to check in yet. While Frank and I were in Kiss Negotiations, the hotel manager chose this moment to walk over with my stowed luggage and introduce himself.

"Good evening, Ms. Cox," he said cheerfully. "We hope you are enjoying yourself?" I blushed guiltily as he continued, "I just wanted to let you know, we have moved you from the Sleeping Beauty Suite to the Bridal Suite. We are sure you will enjoy the room." And, with a smile, he walked away.

The Bridal Suite was the one with the huge rotating bed and the Jacuzzi in the middle of the room. I didn't even have a chance to react—Frank was on his feet. "Let's go," he urged.

Suddenly it felt as if the date had accelerated past me and I was having trouble keeping up. "Frank, you are NOT coming to my room," I told him firmly, though feeling extremely flustered.

Frank acted as if he hadn't heard me. "Come on," he said. "I want to kiss you."

That he was so confident and focused disoriented me completely. "Frank," I squeaked, struggling to stay calm and sound like I meant what I said. "There is no way I'm going to sleep with you."

And I meant it: Frank was cute and he was fun, but he wasn't The One. But even as I said it, I was aware that Frank was compellingly sexy. God, I really hadn't thought through the whole attraction thing.

"Why not?" he asked, sensing my confusion and smiling lazily, like a cat not so much with the cream but with the entire cow. At gunpoint.

I breathed hard, gripping the edge of the table to steady myself. "Because I dated a guy yesterday, I'm dating another guy tomorrow, and I'm dating another seventy-seven after that. I can't sleep with all the Dates; what would that make me?" I beseeched indignantly.

But Frank had no pity. "I'm not asking you to sleep with all the Dates," he replied reasonably, stroking my hand almost sympathetically, "just this one."

God, he was good. This was like being back at a school disco with the cute bad boy trying to charm you out of your knickers with the selfish logic of, *"Well you'll be taking them off later anyway . . ."*

I had to act fast. I jumped to my feet, grabbed my suitcase, and ran to the lift. Frank got there first. We were both laughing and flushed now. There was dangerous electricity that crackled between us, growing by the second.

"Frank, you are not getting in the lift with me," I said firmly as the lift doors opened. Frank and I got in. The doors closed.

Frank didn't say a word; he just turned, pushed his weight against me, and started kissing me with a slow, hard certainty that made my head spin.

As the lift ascended, Frank and I staggered from wall to wall, locked in a deep, wet passion that lasted eight floors.

I fell out the doors as they opened on my floor, face red from Frank's stubble and eyes wild from the excitement. I was having trouble focusing. I had a teaspoon of self-control left, though, and I knew I had to exert it. "Frank, stay in the lift," I commanded hoarsely, swallowing hard. He looked at me steadily, his hair messed, his mouth wet, and his foot jammed in the lift door.

Then, coolly maintaining eye contact, Frank stepped out of the lift. The doors closed behind him and he started walking toward me. I was lost; there was no way I was going to be able to keep resisting him. And, if I'm honest, I was starting to wonder why I was even trying.

I was transfixed and helpless as he moved toward me.

But suddenly, the mood was broken by the noisy chatter of a Dutch family rounding the corner, a nice-looking young couple with two kids under ten. They stopped their animated conversation abruptly and looked at us uncertainly. They must have sensed the tension in the air, and hesitated in front of the lift next to us. They asked Frank something in Dutch which could well have been: "Did you just kiss the face clean off that woman?" but was probably just "Are you getting in or out of the lift?"

The lift doors opened, and Frank stepped away from them, taking my arm as the family got in. I knew we were at the point of no return: With my last shred of willpower, I shoved Frank hard, making him stumble back into the lift. As the doors slid shut, Frank and the family all stood staring at me in astonishment. I grabbed my bags, ran to my room, and locked the door behind me.

I sat on the bed panting, then, catching sight of myself in the mirror, burst out laughing: I looked like I was on the school playground, resting in the middle of a game of kiss-chase. And kissing was good. But on a first date, anything more than kissing seemed a bit much. It wasn't that *anything more* was completely out of the question, it was more that I imagined it would be tender and romantic and with The One. I was two dates in and both had ended in a tussle, with the Dates wanting to go further and me just wanting to go. Maybe my friends were right to call my journey "Around the World in Eighty Lays." But it was no big deal: I'd just forgotten what it was like to date; in future I'd be more prepared. Actually, in many ways it was quite reassuring—the world might have changed a lot since I was a teenager, but dating didn't seem to have changed at all.

The next day, before I left, I checked my emails. There was a lovely one from Frank telling me in broken English how much he had enjoyed our date and how he hoped:

> . . . to meat you again.

I believed him.

Date #3: Willem—Keukenhof, Holland

Another early start heading northwest to Keukenhof, the famous tulip fields that have graced a thousand postcards. There had been a silly misunderstanding with my Dutch friend Birgit. I'd told her briefly over the phone what I was doing, and she thought I'd said I was looking for my Soil Mate. She knows I love my teeny backyard and just assumed it was a gardening thing and had set me up to date Willem, a gardener at Keukenhof.

Once I got past my eye-rolling about the date and started thinking about what Willem might be like, I was actually pretty excited. I imagined a sun-beaten, Lawrencian antihero: dirt under his nails; shirt pulled back roughly over his strong forearms; and the little eye contact that was made would be both mocking and smoldering.

Still dizzy from nearly being Franked, I happily daydreamed as I drove, cramming sweet almond-studded rolls filled with cinnamon cream into my mouth. I was not going to start this date digestively vulnerable. I was going to be prepared and ready.

It was another beautiful day and—like a plague of locusts off buzzing another field—the crazy drivers and hooting truckers had vanished. Sunny fields of cows and windmills, gorgeous churches with proudly domed roofs, and canals bobbing with pretty barges, all hinted at a life lived less hectically.

I was in a great mood but a bit tired, mainly from the effort of emoting and drawing the Dates out of themselves. And the dates had been long, too, both lasting most of the day and well into the evening. That's not a date, that's a DAY.

I had to find a different way to run the dates, I thought: One, limit the amount of time we had together, and, two, not let them talk about their old girlfriends too much. It would end up being exhausting otherwise and not much fun for either of us. Being able to talk through their Relationship Résumés was probably quite therapeutic for the Dates, though. Being a dumpee is the very definition of self-absorption, and here I was, some stranger parachuted in for a day, encouraging them to open up about things their friends were probably sick to death of hearing about.

But it would be a big disappointment if that's all I did over the eighty dates: got dressed and Mac'd up just to listen to other people's problems. You know, it's funny, I'd focused on how much effort it had been setting up the dates, but it was only just dawning on me how much work going around the world in eighty dates could actually turn out to be. I really hoped it was going to be more fun than having eighty *trapped in the kitchen at a party* conversations. I almost wanted to speed-date all eighty for ten minutes, then just have a proper date with the top ten. But I'd be cheating Fate and shortchanging myself that way: I'd only meet my Soul Mate if I entered fully into the spirit of my Dating Odyssey, no holds barred.

Meanwhile, all this pondering had distracted me from reading the map properly and, as a result, I got lost on the ring road around Rotterdam and arrived in Keukenhof an hour late for meeting Willem.

I screeched to a halt in the parking lot and raced through the front gate, barely taking the time to check my hair and makeup. A sweet old man, unsteady on his walking stick, chatted about the seven million bulbs that had been planted at Keukenhof that spring, as he led me to the walled garden where Willem was waiting for me.

Willem was not what I expected.

Less Lawrence, more landed gentry, Willem had reddish hair, green eyes, and pale skin. He was wearing a tweed jacket over a crisp, white shirt and pressed trousers. He also wore an expression that said he would rather be absolutely anywhere but here.

He rose formally from the wooden bench as I approached, and stiffly held out his right hand to shake mine. In his left he held a beautiful tulip. Long-stemmed and luxurious, its feathery yellow head pouted engorged lips like clams. I smiled, thinking how beautiful it was, and he caught me admiring it. "This is what we Dutch men traditionally give on blind dates," he said self-consciously in a voice that was deep and educated. I had no idea if he was serious or not, but noting his discomfort and sympathizing (let's face it, it was a bizarre situation), I smiled encouragingly and waited for him to give me the flower.

But he didn't give me the flower. Instead, he sat back down on the bench, smoothing out the creases in his impeccable trousers and straightening his cuffs. Feeling more than a little disconcerted, I followed his lead and sat down next to him. Together we surveyed the rippling rows of nodding tulips stretching up to meet the weak spring sunshine. Row upon row of frilled heads: lilac, black, yellow, white shot with scarlet, some feathery, some furled, puckered tight, some blown and fading, all color and life spent. It was magnificent, and, in a way, an intimate and emotional sight to share.

The atmosphere between Willem and me, however, was anything but intimate. It was completely silent and increasingly awkward. I was waiting for him to take the lead, but not only did he show no indication he would, he showed no indication that he even knew I was there.

"Do you know why I'm here?" I asked brightly, trying to hide the hurt I felt at his distant attitude and determined to break the mood.

"Not really," he replied stiffly with the dignified resignation of a highly decorated military man who, due to circumstances beyond his control or understanding, now finds himself selling sex toys in a shop in Soho.

"Well," I said brightly, taking a deep breath and launching into an explanation that was meant to be both reassuring and intriguing. "It's just we all work so hard," I trilled. "We have no time for love, so I'm traveling the world dating people to see if I can find my Soul Mate."

I finished with a flourish and turned, expecting to see Willem smiling, relaxed, and ready to talk. Clearly I had fallen short of the tone I was striving for: Willem was still surveying the flowerbed, staring ahead stonily but now with a grim expression that unflatteringly hovered somewhere between disgust and disbelief. It was as if I'd suggested we both take off our underpants and look at each other's bottoms. A moment passed. Then another. Not a word was said. I sat rigid with rising panic, feeling a wave of hot shame wash over me, completely and horribly mortified. And this was only Date #3.

Willem, maybe sensing my distress, maybe just wanting to end his own, got to his feet.

"Shall we have some lunch?" he asked politely. I nodded gratefully, misery robbing me of the ability to speak. As we walked past the raspberry posies that peppered the rhododendron and the soft papery apricot of the azaleas, I watched Willem take the tulip he had picked for but not actually given to me. As he walked, he neatly and methodically folded the flower over and over and over on itself until its broken stem and crushed head were no more than a ruined, sap-bleeding ball. I pretended not to notice when he silently dropped it into a trash bin at the side of the path and continued marching without breaking his stride.

Willem relaxed a little over lunch and actually turned out to be quite amiable, with a dry sense of humor. But after a gentle walk around the beautiful gardens and a look at the gorgeous displays of scented lilies, I was grateful to be back in my car and heading for Schiphol airport, alone with my thoughts about the journey ahead. What if my Dating Odyssey failed to find me a boyfriend and just succeeded in making me feel freaky and bad about myself?

As I took endless wrong turns and dodged through rush-hour traffic, trying to make it in time for my connection, the phone started ringing on the seat next to me. An Amsterdam number. It would be Henk ringing to collect on the promised second date. I frowned and gripped the steering wheel harder, ignoring the phone; I just didn't have the emotional energy to deal with Henk now. Also, I don't mean this horribly, but I didn't want to go back over old Dates; I wanted to look forward and get on to the new ones. I was flying to Sweden in the hope that my next Date would give me some much-needed insight and perspective on the journey I had undertaken. Professor Lars-Görsta Dahlöf at Gothenburg University was one of the world's leading authorities on psychology and sexology—the science of love and attraction.

This was one Date I'd happily devote a day to.

chapter three

Gothenburg, Sweden

Date #5—The mysterious Anders in Gothenburg, Sweden

Gothenburg does itself no favors having a Volvo museum. Drawing attention to the fact that it's the birthplace of arguably the dullest, least-adventurous car in the world is not a PR coup for a city that's easily as hip as Stockholm and just as much the party town as Malmo.

But Sweden generally seems to suffer from a bit of a personality crisis, and I don't think I'm going to win any awards for insight by suggesting it's probably due to the weather. Nearly a sixth of Sweden is north of the Arctic Circle and winter nights last anything up to eighteen *stay indoors, stare at the walls for four months* hours. From May to August, however, the height of the sun and the tilt of the earth's axis go to the other extreme, creating the midnight sun and up to twenty-three hours of sunshine a day.

And when the midnight sun shines, so do the Swedes. Everyone seems to spin and show, like overwound ballerinas in a music box, making the most of every bright second before the lid slams shut for another winter of introspective darkness.

But maybe the city does its thinking in the dark, because over the last forty years, Gothenburg has been at the forefront of pioneering research into sexology, the science of human sexuality and how it affects us chemically, socially, and physically. And I had an appointment at the university to meet one of the world's leading sexologists; I had come to date the Love Professor.

Date #4: Professor Lars-Görsta Dahlöf—Gothenburg, Sweden

I'd come across Professor Lars-Görsta Dahlöf in an online article, reporting on a conference he'd held called "The Science of Love and Passion." At the time it was casual curiosity: I thought it would be fascinating to learn more about his theories and ideas. But now that I was here, I realized my questions were less theoretical and more personal. I was slightly unsettled by how my journey was turning out and hoped he'd have some theories that would help me establish whether I stood any chance of success, or could, at the very least, emerge with a shred of dignity. The memory of Willem's blatant disapproval still stung.

The plan was that we'd meet at the reception area of my downtown hotel and then drive out to the Japanese Gardens past the university for a walk and a chat. Now it was 11:30 a.m. and I had literally just checked into my room when reception rang to say the Love Professor was downstairs waiting for me. Damn, he was forty minutes early. I'd hoped to have a quick shower and a moment to gather my thoughts before I met him.

I flipped my bag onto the bed. I'd packed my waterproof

jacket and sweater on top—even without his early arrival, I'd known it would be a tight turnaround. As I pulled the jacket out I noticed a puddle of sticky white fluid on the sleeve. I stopped dead and looked at it, mystified. Gingerly I checked my bag; nothing was broken. I really didn't want to smell it, but—and I had no good feelings about this—what the hell was it?

I was tired and feared I was going crazy, but . . . was it possible a baggage handler had opened my bag and . . . ?

NO, it was too much to even think about. Why would they do that? Holding my breath and grimacing, I plucked the coat carefully out of my bag and took it into the bathroom to sponge the fluid off, all the while painfully aware that the Love Professor was downstairs waiting to meet me. At arm's length, I dropped the sleeve into the sink and, stepping back, turned the tap on full. As soon as the water hit the sticky mess, it started frothing and foaming. Foam? I hadn't expected foam. I looked at the sleeve in confusion, turned the water off, put the wet coat down on the edge of the sink, and walked back into the bedroom. Minus my coat, there was now more room in my case to investigate. I gingerly lifted out the rolled clothes and peered cautiously underneath them.

A bottle of shampoo I had missed earlier was lodged in the corner of the case, its lid unscrewed and white soap oozing out of the unsecured top.

I closed my eyes and groaned in exasperation. Apparently, it wasn't just the lid that was coming unscrewed. Was the fact that I was meeting the Love Professor making me see sex everywhere, or was I doing this to myself by undertaking this journey? Just think what kind of interpretation he would put on this: "Ahh, so, Jennifer, you imagine your traveling persona to be the focus of unsolicited sexual attention, and yet it is a journey you have chosen to make. Is it not possible that you are filled with a desire to have your 'baggage handled' by strangers and you are seeking to make this fantasy a reality?"

The Love Professor was looking out of the window into the Nordstan shopping center outside when I finally made it down to reception. He was a kind-looking man, about 50, with a Woody Allen Does Academic appearance, a lived-in tweed jacket, and sparse brown hair framing a thin, contemplative face. My entrance felt a bit scattered, in utter contrast to his quiet, serene pose at the window, and on seeing him I became gripped with the urge to fling myself down onto the reception sofa and blurt out everything that had happened to me so far. With steely resolve, I resisted the impulse. Instead, waiting for the Love Professor to transfer a huge armful of papers from right to left, I smiled warmly, shook his outstretched hand, and answered: "Yes, I had a lovely journey here, thank you, no problems at all. Quite uneventful. I'm sorry if I kept you waiting, shall we go?"

He drove me out to the Japanese Gardens, a tranquil refuge at the top of a steep trail in the public gardens beyond the university where he worked. As we settled in a wooden arbor, off the path overlooking a bamboo garden, I explained my theory and mission to the Love Professor. If I did meet my Soul Mate, I asked, how would I know he was The One? Were there any signs or signals I should be looking for?

"Well, we have a physical response which we define as sexual . . . ," he began cautiously, as if realizing for the first time that I had a vested interest in his answers. "Also understanding that although we all fall in love, few of us know anything more about it than how we feel." Like technology: I can send you an email without either of us having the faintest clue how it got from my computer to yours. The Love Professor was about to explain the

Love Equivalent of firewalls, IPs, wireless applications, and the laser printer.

". . . but it starts in the earliest relationship: the one between the mother and the child. It is an intense experience of trust and well-being: feeling everything is as good as it could be. To fall in love and to be close to another human being at any age in your life . . ." Uh-oh, not the whole oedipal thing.

"So when you fall in love," I interrupted impatiently, "you're looking to relive those bonds of comfort and security?"

"Yes, you are seeking to relive something you don't consciously remember but your body does," he replied.

I knew this must be relevant somewhere, but time was short and I wasn't looking to date either of my parents on this trip, so I moved it along.

"So apart from my historical needs, what about the physical side? How will I know if I'm attracted to somebody?" An obvious question, with an even more obvious answer, but the Love Professor didn't seem to think me odd for wanting to know. Apparently you fall in love in three stages: lust, attraction, and attachment. Each stage has distinct characteristics, accompanied by set behavioral patterns and a variety of hormones. Evidently it was more complex than just thinking someone looked good in a leather jacket.

The Love Professor gave me an example: "There are a number of factors working beneath your consciousness, and one of them is smell. Not only does smell influence you, your smell also carries information about your genetic makeup."

This was intriguing. "So am I wasting my time kissing when I should be sniffing?" I demanded.

The Love Professor looked momentarily confused and then replied, "No, because kissing is a good opportunity to take a good sniff."

We both laughed. "I'm intrigued and a little concerned for your kissing technique," I teased. Funnily enough, I found the fact that we were compelled to do romantic things for practical reasons really reassuring; almost as if it wasn't totally my fault if I made a mess of it, nature had to take a share of the blame, too. "Okay, that's a fantastic piece of information." I beamed; we were getting somewhere now. "Are there any other things that will help me work out if my Dates are compatible or not with me when I first meet them? I only have one date with each of these people, so I have to take in a lot of information and make a lot of decisions very quickly."

The Love Professor warmed to the subject. "When two people are attracted, we send messages that we are interested and want to become better acquainted, often by mimicking each other's actions. If a woman strokes her hair, the man will make the same movement a second later. After a while, if everything works and there is a mutual interest, there will be a perfect synchronicity. We tend to like a partner who is a reflection of ourselves: A person who mirrors you in such a positive way is very easy to fall in love with."

Presumably the same was true from a negative perspective, too: If you felt like rubbish, were you more likely to pick a partner who made you feel you were rubbish?

Again, the Love Professor concurred. "If you have a secure and positive image of yourself—being nice, liking yourself—you will be more likely to pick someone who sees and affirms that in you. However, if your self-esteem is absent or very low, you find it harder to believe there is someone else out there like you or who will like you."

I could see how that would be true. "So you're saying: Work at making yourself feel good before you get involved with anyone else, because they'll only be good for you if you're good to yourself." But what did this mean for me? I was a pretty positive person—generally cheerful and comfortable with myself—yet I had chosen relationships that had not been in my best interest. Wasn't it possible there were other important factors that played a role in who you chose as your partner? I had my own theory on the subject and wanted to ask the Love Professor what he thought of it.

"So, to go back to the idea of selection. I have a theory—which I'm hoping is wrong—about work and relationships. Basically, work is where we meet our partners, but work is more demanding than ever, and men are coping less well with the pressure than women. As a result, working women find their jobs the most emotionally satisfying relationships in their lives, so they either settle for so-so romances or end up chronically single. Could there be any truth in this?"

The Love Professor thought for a moment. "Traditionally, the most important reason for being in a relationship was to reproduce: Couples married and had children. The man supported the family; the woman stayed at home and looked after it. Most women these days are not looking for partners in order to have babies, or at least not right away. A change has taken place in a very short period of time; men and women have become more equal. Although we have acknowledged the change, we have yet to address how the needs and expectations of relationships have changed as a result."

I genuinely found this sad and disturbing: Was the implication that men were only attracted to women who wanted to have children? I tried to get it straight in my head:

"You talk about how we telegraph information in nonverbal ways, through smell, etcetera. . . . If women want careers, could we be unconsciously transmitting a desire not to have children and be less desirable or attractive to potential partners as a result?"

The Love Professor considered what I was asking. "I don't know about that, but body odors are certainly affected by high levels of stress. Working too much, too many problems, no time for leisure, etcetera, can—on a subconscious level—be recognized in the way you smell."

So maybe the issue wasn't about wanting or not wanting kids; it was that career women literally smelled like hard work. I felt the need to bring the conversation back around to me. "But I've quit my job, I'm not stressed, and I've nurtured a positive self-image. I should be smelling relaxed, right?"

The Love Professor nodded noncommittally, not sure where this was going but willing to let me carry on until I got there. I got there: "Do you think I'm going to meet Mr. Right?"

Faced with such an emotionally charged question, the Love Professor retreated to the safety of science. "Our research has shown that when you are waiting or starving for a relationship, you will be very open to all types of stimuli that will tell you this is the right person. That means you will probably be quite uncritical. . . ."

The scientific way of saying "desperate" . . .

"Looking at it from a scientific view," the Love Professor said evenly, "when two people meet and get involved, they each bring their own history with them. How you bring these histories together provides the condition for the future of your relationship. A person who gives you too much of his 'history' shows an inability to choose or prioritize his relationships."

This reminded me of a guy I dated, Grant—"I'm separated, I just forgot to tell my wife." He seemed incapable of going anywhere without at least two of his friends, and his cell phone never stopped ringing when we were out. It baffled him that I thought this was a problem.

"And also, from the opposite perspective, it can be quite disappointing when the one you want to share your life with will not share very much of his or her own life with you. The person who will not share their past is unlikely to see you in their future."

This was Kelly: Captain Compartmentalize, never wanting me to meet his family or friends.

Interesting stuff, but, looking at my watch, I realized I was running out of time. I was meeting my friend Ann-Charlotte for a drink at 6 p.m. to hear about tomorrow's date with her foxy-sounding friend Anders.

I asked if, after all his measuring and dissecting, the Love Professor believed in the existence of Love.

He answered immediately, with total conviction and heartfelt certainty: "Yes, yes, I think it exists. And there is so much data supporting this. Being touched and caressed by your partner will stimulate the brain to release the chemicals oxytocin and vaso-pressin—both have been linked to our ability to forge strong and lasting emotional bonds. When you meet someone you're attracted to, within two seconds your heart rate will increase dramatically, your blood pressure goes up, muscle tension increases, and your intestines shut off, giving you that 'butterflies in stomach' sensation.

"Your brain should interpret this as enjoyable," he added helpfully.

"But I always get really anxious and start babbling," I confessed. "I talk far too much and make far too many hand gestures. And in my head I'm going, *Shut up, shut up, you're being weird*, but I find it really hard to stop." I said all this in a small, pained voice, before asking equally pathetically: "I mean, do guys find that attractive?"

The Love Professor looked at me sympathetically, clearly thinking, *This woman will have died of anxiety-induced exhaus-*

tion by the end of eight dates, let alone eighty. He took a deep breath, paused a moment to find the right words, then said: "I think this is a way of handling a fear of losing control. One way—which is perhaps not the best way—to try and regain control is to talk, talk, talk."

He said this very gently as I hid my face and squirmed on the park bench. Bemused parents out walking with their kids—memories of the horrors of dating long erased—looked over quizzically. I caught sight of my watch; it really was time to go. I had a lot of information, but did the Love Professor have just one tip for my date tomorrow? Was there one thing above all others that I should do?

He looked at me with the kindly expression of someone who knows no amount of advice will help. "I think you should not plan too much," he said simply. "Just let it happen. Use all your senses and take in whatever comes. You should not watch too much what kind of message you are sending. Afterward you can analyze, but not at the time. What is attractive to the person you are dating is that you are present in all aspects: mind, body, and soul. That is a very good start."

We sat and looked at each other for a moment, both a bit drained from the intense conversation, and me from the recognition that I felt far more exposed and unsure about my journey than I had ever realized. I gave him a big hug and thanked him sincerely.

As we walked back through the park to his car, we chatted about "normal" things: family, work, places we had visited. We strolled under the comfortable shade of linden and oak trees; it was a beautiful place and I hoped to come back one day when I was less preoccupied. The Love Professor had given me plenty to think about—not all of it easy to hear—but I'd have the chance to talk about it all tonight with Ann-Charlotte, over a large drink.

I knew Ann-Charlotte from when she'd worked for the Swedish tourist board in London. I'd been sad to see her move back to her home city of Gothenburg the year before, but was reaping the benefits now. Not only had she promised to take me to the "only locals know" funky parts of town, she'd also done a great job as local Date Wrangler-in-Chief.

Back at my hotel, getting ready to meet her, I felt happy and relaxed, looking forward to the uncomplicated evening I knew we'd spend together. I'd just started to realize how important it was to intersperse my 80 Dates with some normal socializing, preferably with female friends. Dating was really demanding: There was all the stress of preparation and anticipation. Then there was the date itself, fraught with revealing body-language and full of silent *I can't believe he just said that* moments.

We were obliged under the International Girlfriend Charter to reenact dating highlights for each other's entertainment, but, just as importantly right now, I needed relaxed, no-agenda fun with girlfriends to help offset the pressure of dating and stop me obsessing about the *I can't believe I just said that* moments of my own.

Avoiding the Avenue (the main tourist drag), Ann-Charlotte took me to a place in Linnégatan, a cosmopolitan area awash with trendy bars and chichi restaurants. It was next to Slottsko-gen, another of Gothenburg's big parks, and close to Haga, the old town where tall Brothers Grimm wooden houses lined the twisting cobbled streets.

After we caught up with old news, Ann-Charlotte sat rapt with fascination as I explained the Love Professor's scientific theories on love and compatibility. Wine flowed like wine, as we compared notes on how scarily accurate it all was: exes who had refused to be intimate; girlfriends with ready excuses about why their awful relationships really weren't that awful.

She asked if I was going to test what I had learned from the Love Professor on Anders, the friend of hers I was dating tomorrow. But since Anders had insisted everything about him and the date remain a mystery until the date itself (I was starting to see this as one of the ways Dates felt they could retain a degree of control; maybe it made them feel special and not just "one of eighty"), it was impossible to know how I was going to be with him. But, in theory, "of course," I told her. I would sniff him, mimic his movements, give him enough but not too much of my history, try not to talk too much, and—most importantly—let it happen. BUT, I stressed to Ann-Charlotte, only if he was cute. The last thing I needed was more flirting flotsam, to attract another guy I wasn't seriously interested in, when I needed to concentrate my efforts on finding Mr. Right.

As we stumbled back to our beds at 4:30 a.m., the streets were full of people; the people were full of alcohol. Ann-Charlotte and I were no exception. It was as bright as the afternoon and there was a friendly party atmosphere, the warm air heavy with possibilities. As the night porter of my hotel opened the taxi door for Ann-Charlotte to climb in, she gave me a big hug and wished me luck for the days ahead.

"I think maybe it is a crazy thing that you are doing, Jennifer," she said intensely. "But you are brave enough to do what the rest of us can only dream of. Go date the world for every woman," she declared flamboyantly, collapsing into the back of the taxi and giving me a wobbly salute. I watched the taxi drive off. Just as it rounded the corner, I heard her shriek: "And don't forget—for your date with Anders, you must take a bikini."

Date #5: Anders—Gothenburg, Sweden

When I woke at 11 a.m. that morning, I was immediately confronted by two facts: Firstly, I had the kind of hangover that made my eyes look like a hamster's cheeks stuffed with peanuts, and secondly, in six hours I had to wear a bikini.

I'd brought one with me. Before I'd left London, Ann-Charlotte had repeatedly impressed upon me that it would be needed, but I'd managed to block it out until she'd reminded me last night that I was actually going to have to wear it.

All she'd told me about tonight was that her friend Anders would pick me up from my hotel at 5 p.m.; I should pack a bikini and be ready for a boat trip.

As I have already explained, I will never be ready for a boat trip.

My crushing hangover made it impossible to focus on anything, but—as much as I was capable—I was worried. People who don't suffer from seasickness refuse to accept that the condition is genuine. Instead, they see it as a kind of laziness that can be cured with a little effort and a better attitude. I was forever being told by sailing friends: *"Oh, if you sit up on deck/eat a cookie/keep your eye on the horizon . . . you'll be fine."* Did they not think I had tried all these things? I mean, it wasn't like I was some kind of aquatic bulimic and wanted to be sick.

Mariah and Whitney don't do stairs; I'd told everyone who had anything to do with my journey, I don't do boats. My Dates seemed to think they knew better, though, stubbornly championing the inherent romance of *man woos woman on the open seas.* Well, fair enough, maybe they'd see the inherent romance in *man watches woman throw up on the open seas.*

However, my concerns about being sick were nothing compared to my feelings about wearing a bikini in front of a complete stranger. I had great thighs, and I don't mean that in a good way.

When I first heard about the whole bikini nightmare, I went straight to the gym and asked my Swedish trainer, Emma, for a high-impact, fast-result program. As I sweated and shook through a series of lunges and lifts, I explained the reason for the emergency. Emma immediately wrinkled her perfect nose, pursed her pink, cupid-bow lips, and declared, "Oh, but Swedish men are so boring."

"Really?" I gasped, turning to look at her, my lunge wobbling off to the side. "I thought they were all tall and utterly gorgeous."

"Exactly," she replied with the judgment of Solomon. "They have never needed to develop a personality. You should try Australians," she added helpfully.

Could this be true? Had the Swedish gene pool developed a race so beautiful, evolution had deemed personalities as superfluous as the male nipple? Or did we all just have a "familiarity breeds contempt" attitude toward our homeboys?

Pushing all futile thoughts to one side, I booted up my laptop: I had work to do. I needed at least three hours a day, every day, to keep on top of the practicalities and logistics of my trip, as well as taking care of the minutiae of "normal life." Although I had started my traveling and dating, there was still so much to be done.

Logging on, I found the usual deluge of dating detail emails. Italy was demanding decisions. I was meeting Umberto, a guy who ran a "traffic dating" website. (Stuck in a traffic jam and fancy the driver two lanes over? Note down their license plate, search for it on Umberto's website, and send them an email suggesting a date.) Umberto wanted to know, were we meeting in Siena or Rome?

I was going to Verona to do the balcony scene with Romeo. The people who looked after Juliet's house wanted to know my medieval dress size.

Meanwhile, over in Paris, I was going on a Skate Date and the guy I was to skate with wanted to know my foot size.

There was also a two-day-old email from Anders:

```
I have heard the weather shell be sunny on friday
so you dont need any warm clothes, i will recemend
jeans, maby a windbreaker, and of course bikini
(leasure).
```

Hmmmmm.

I worked my way through the emails. I also surfed the Net trying to work out if it was feasible to get from Paris to Berlin by train, and if not and I needed to fly, could I go direct or did I need to backtrack via London? I'd forgotten to pay my credit-card bill and had left my online password in my Palm Pilot at home (in a misguided attempt to travel light), so I needed to call the bank and sort that out. I also checked my answering machine in London. My sister Toz had called: What day was I arriving at her house for the bank holiday weekend? Gareth had rung from Wales to make sure I was still on for the hike over the bank holiday weekend. On my cell, Cath had texted to see if we were still on for Norfolk over the bank holiday weekend. Obviously, while I meticulously cross-checked my dating schedule, I'd forgotten to pay the same attention to my home life and had now triple-booked myself. I couldn't face hearing all those irritated voices now, so made a mental note to call them later.

I looked at my watch: 4 p.m. No time to catch a nap, I had to get ready. An hour later, hoping I didn't look as hungover and sleep-deprived as I felt, I grabbed my bag (including the dreaded bikini) and made my way down to reception.

I had no idea what Anders looked like, but felt sure I'd know when I saw him. As I looked discreetly around the lobby, the door crashed open and a large woman in a tailored black jacket stormed in. She pointed at me. "You are Jennifer?" she boomed, as if daring me to disagree.

I nodded, hesitating in my confusion. Where was Anders?

"Then you come with me," she commanded, turning on her heel and striding back outside without a backward glance.

It wasn't quite what I had expected. Unsure of exactly what was happening, I walked slowly out the open front door after her. Scanning the street, I spotted her waiting in the driver's seat of a taxi, engine running. She motioned impatiently for me to get in. I knew Ann-Charlotte was in on this, plus I had done crazier things making travel programs (on one national radio show, listeners were invited to show me, unaccompanied, around their home cities. As I climbed into a strange man's car in Istanbul, I remember wondering if we had really thought through the personal security implications of the program and if I'd ever be seen alive again).

We drove south out of town through the busy port area. The shipyard was hard at work, huge cruise liners moored alongside fleets of fishing boats, proving that Gothenburg was wise or fortunate enough to have more than one industry paying the bills. The industrial warehouses looked successful enough, for now, to resist the yuppie developments claiming more vulnerable waterfronts around the world, from Auckland and Sydney to Vancouver and London.

My taxi driver chatted as she drove but I wasn't really listening. I was thinking about how I was being played. Anders was keeping me guessing: He obviously liked to be in charge, calling all the shots. "Let him," I said to myself, smiling. I had no problem with that. This was going to be fun.

After fifteen minutes of driving along the coast road, we came to a stop at a picturesque wharf. Although small sailing vessels tugged gently against their moorings, the air was still and, even this late in the day, the sun was hot on my skin.

The driver parked the car and together we walked the short distance to a wooden pier on which a cheery man in his sixties seemed to be waiting for us. He looked like an ad for *Crewing Monthly* with his turtleneck sweater and pipe, periwinkle eyes flashing mischievously in his tanned face. I had thought Anders would be younger, more edgy. Although he looked fun, I was a little disappointed. I shrugged it off, though; it was fine, at least the waiting was over, and I was sure there'd be more game players further down the line.

The driver introduced us: It wasn't Anders, it was one of the local captains. Another twist—Anders and I had yet to meet.

The driver made her excuses and disappeared for a moment, leaving the captain and me to chat. Was I going out on a boat? he asked. Memory of the date with Willem made me hesitate: Was there a good way of explaining that, not only did I have no idea what I was doing here, but I was doing this eighty times over with strange men around the world? It was a tricky thing to say nonchalantly to someone not in on my plan (and, as Willem had demonstrated, sometimes tricky to say to someone who was).

I was saved from having to explain my presence by the return of my driver. She was accompanied by a man in his mid-twenties, with classic Swedish looks: fine, clean features, white-blond hair, incredibly clear skin, and blue, blue eyes. Was this Anders? Again, I felt a twinge of disappointment. Fresh-faced and sweet-looking, he was young and had the air of an earnest, uncomplicated boy, quite at odds with the foxy game-playing vibe Anders had been putting out.

He walked over, holding out his hand to shake mine. "Hello," he said. "I'm Martin."

Ahhhh, I thought with a grin, *the game is still on.*

"If you will please come with me, I must take you on my boat. Anders is waiting for you."

I laughed and picked up my bag, following Martin onto a small, incredibly sleek speedboat. I sat on the jockey seat next to him, strapped on the life jacket he handed over, and braced myself as we gently accelerated away from the wharf and into the open water.

The water in question was part of the Scandinavian southern archipelago, where the North Sea forms Kattegat, a wide channel between Sweden and Denmark. Even while I was concentrating on my soothing mantra of *"don't be sick, don't be sick,"* I could appreciate it was intensely beautiful. We knifed through the clear water; the sharp-edged waves from our boat had turned to gentle ripples by the time they reached the shores of the tiny islands we passed. I could hear the local children chatter and laugh as they milled around in rock pools and dived off rafts into the cool water. Behind them, pine trees crowded down to the boulder-studded shoreline, like kids around an ice cream van. The occasional tiny red stave house peeped shyly from between branches, pristine white roof bright against the deep green of the needles. We flew across the clear blue water; the air felt clean and fresh. I was both nervous and excited: I felt sure this was the final leg of the journey before Anders and I would meet.

Some of the tension must have shown on my face. Martin, sweetly misunderstanding, took one hand from deftly skimming the boat from tip to tip of the bouncing waves. "Don't worry," he shouted over the noise of the engine and crash of the water, touching my arm reassuringly and frowning with concern. "We have all been told you get very, very sick on boats and I am to watch and see if you will vomit."

I smiled weakly and wiped some of the salty spray from my

face to hide my embarrassment, as we plowed ever onward into the surf.

Half an hour later, I was watching a cluster of tacking boats filled with orange-life-jacketed children learning to sail. I reflected on how wonderful it would be to grow up having sailed dinghies, ridden horses, or hiked and biked mountains virtually from the age you could walk. In England, it seems everyone has watched TV or idled in traffic from the age we could sit. I snapped out of my ruminating: The roar of the engine had become a gentle purr. Martin had slowed the boat and was standing at the wheel, scanning the horizon.

"Are we lost?" I asked, suddenly really nervous about meeting mysterious Anders. Maybe going back to the hotel, having a big bath, and catching up on sleep wouldn't be such a bad thing.

"No," Martin replied politely, but preoccupied as he eased the boat through a rocky channel, all the time scanning the horizon. "They are here somewhere."

Where the hell am I being taken? I suddenly thought crossly. Why didn't Martin know where they (THEY?) were? What was next? To get into a submarine? Who was the goddamn date with—Captain Nemo?

I was starting to get impatient. Enough was enough. *Let's get on with the date or take me back to the hotel so I can watch cable and be as one with the minibar.*

But at that very moment, Martin pushed the throttle down on the boat and we sped forward: He had spotted them.

I was about to meet Anders.

We were sailing toward a floating pontoon moored to a rocky outcrop in the middle of the sea. It was a big pontoon, about eighteen feet by thirty, a large cabin in the middle with a deck front and back. I could make out two men standing on the front deck, one pale, fiddling with ropes, one tall and dark, looking straight at me. He waved.

Oh, my God, it was Anders. Finally.

Except, all of a sudden, "finally" felt like it had arrived far too soon. I didn't feel ready. Clutching my bag protectively to my chest, I felt completely overwhelmed with nerves and I suddenly wished my date had been with lovely, sweet Martin after all.

I waved back to Anders with a confidence I didn't feel.

The sun was bright on my face. My hair had been whipped insensible and my eyes were stinging and weeping after an hour being buffeted by the salty wind and surf. As Martin sailed closer to the pontoon, Anders steadily came into focus. I groaned to myself wretchedly: He was absolutely gorgeous. Completely and ridiculously handsome. I was utterly out of my depth.

As Martin navigated the boat alongside the pontoon, Anders, who had been leaning against the railing watching our approach, stepped forward to help me aboard. My legs wobbling, my nose running, I pleaded with myself not to fall in or do or say anything stupid, as he reached down, took my hand in his, and pulled me up toward him.

Now both on deck, we stood six inches apart and gave each other a long, appraising look.

Anders was about six feet three and in his early forties. His skin was tanned golden, his thick brown hair wavy and swept back from his face, which was lined in a manner that suggested he knew his own mind and was used to getting his own way. He was deeply handsome, his green eyes offset by a strong jaw and full mouth. He was obviously very fit, dressed casually in a white T-shirt with a khaki shirt loosely buttoned over it, strands of hair curling up from his chest.

He looked a lot like Mel Gibson.

What the hell was Ann-Charlotte doing with a friend like this? How was this possible? She was like me: We didn't know people like this. We knew normal people, people who played table football and smacked into the full-length mirrors in the Met Bar, thinking it was another room. We knew people who looked like the boy next door, because in all probability they lived next door. This man was in another league altogether.

"So, I shall go now, Jennifer. It was a pleasure meeting you." I stopped staring at Anders and spun around. Martin was climbing back into the speedboat with pale, rope-fiddling guy, and they were getting ready to head back to the shore.

I would have paid any amount of money to go with Martin rather than stay here with Anders, but I knew that wasn't going to happen. Plus, I told myself sternly, attempting a degree of control and to stop my thoughts free-falling, *This is what my journey is all about: to challenge my "type comfort zone" and be open to the possibility that a "new type," although unfamiliar territory, might actually make me happier.*

And with a friendly wave, Martin motored off. This was it: Short of faking a burst appendix, I was committed to dating Anders.

Maybe sensing my apprehension, Anders did the best possible thing. Dipping into the cabin and emerging with a bottle of chilled Moët and two glasses, he gestured that I should sit on one of the chairs by a long, wooden bench.

"Jennifer," he said in a deep voice, his Scandinavian accent drawing out the syllables, "it is a pleasure to finally meet you. I think your story is a brave and fascinating one, and I am very much looking forward to hearing more of it. But first, I hope you are a little hungry as I have prepared some light food for us. I must return to the kitchen for a few moments, so why don't you just sit and relax and enjoy the view."

I remained standing: I was still keyed up and didn't feel comfortable being waited on.

"Oh, Anders, please let me help," I protested, but Anders just smiled warmly, handed me a glass glistening with bubbles, and pulled out the chair for me to sit on. Realizing Anders was being gracious—and knowing it would be undignified to argue—I settled into the seat. His hand lightly brushed my shoulder, then I heard him turn and walk into the cabin—which I now knew to be a kitchen—behind me.

Moments later, the sound of strings, gliding like a shoal of fish around Frank Sinatra crooning "Young at Heart," came from speakers mounted on the side of the cabin.

When I was a kid my parents used to play us *Songs for Swingin' Lovers*; I've always loved Frank. I immediately relaxed and smiled appreciatively. I was allowed to do this. I could let someone treat me really nicely without over-thinking or fighting it. I remembered the Love Professor and realized this was one of my tasks: to learn to surrender a little control and trust that my feelings would still be considered. Also that I wasn't the only person who could make events run smoothly.

It was about 7:30 p.m. by now and the sun was still hot and bright. The water seemed to have a soft haze over it, a gentle mist that floated above the protruding rocks, making them appear like the heads and shoulders of a small crowd dressed in cashmere sweaters.

I was enjoying both Frank and the Moët but I was also very curious about Anders. I didn't want to interfere with his preparations, but maybe he could cope with me chatting while he cooked (one of those comfortable relationship intimacies that I really missed).

I walked with my glass over to the cabin door. "Room for a passenger with a lot of questions?" I asked.

Anders looked up from a chopping board full of smoked fish and lemons, a ramekin of what looked like dill mustard dressing in his hand. He smiled welcomingly. "I would like that very much," he replied. "Please make yourself comfortable. Maybe you would like to look around, too?"

The kitchen was surprisingly well equipped: a full-size stove and fridge, plus, from what I could see, cupboards full of crystal glasses and fine china. The windows were fringed with blue and white gingham curtains; a stack of pressed white linen tablecloths and napkins sat on a counter. Agreeing that I would set the table outside, I busied myself with cutlery.

Stepping between the lovely kitchen and the picturesque deck looking out onto the water, I found it a little hard to get my head around how perfect this all was.

"Anders, you really do have the most incredible boat," I told him. "I'm so happy that you invited me out here, thank you." Anders, who was ferrying trays of cheese, crudités, and fish out to the table, laughed.

"I wish it was my boat," he said sincerely, "but I have just borrowed it for tonight. Besides," he continued, returning to the kitchen and pausing to inspect the open fridge before selecting a bottle of wine, "haven't you noticed, it's not a boat, it's a floating sauna."

I laughed out loud, not particularly because I thought he was joking but more because it seemed too far-fetched to be true.

He smiled back at me. "No, I'm serious. Go and have a look." He gently took my arm and turned me toward the back of the galley kitchen. Still laughing, I walked over, pulled aside the curtain, and stepped through into a narrow corridor. To the left, another curtain screened off a little toilet and sink; at the end of the corridor was a glass door, the view beyond it obscured by the steam streaming in rivulets down the length of it. Gingerly turning the handle on the door, I was immediately hit by a blast of heat that made my eyes sting. Anders had been serious, it was a full-size sauna: two long, wooden benches, white towels and gowns folded on the end, a grate filled with glowing coals in the middle. At the end of the room, another glass door looked out onto the rocks to which we were moored. It was incredible. I'd never seen anything like it.

Anders, who was still busy with the food, and, I suspect, keeping a respectful distance in the kitchen, looked up when I walked back in. "Well?" he asked playfully. "Did you find the sauna?" I rolled my eyes at what seemed to me the insane opulence of it.

"Anders, that's just crazy," I stated with incredulity.

"Why crazy?" he asked with a grin.

For a moment, I was worried I would appear a bit of a country bumpkin. "It just seems so extravagant," I replied slowly, trying to put my culture shock into words. "In England, to go to a sauna is a real treat, to go sailing is a bit of an event. To go sailing on a sauna seems the equivalent of bobbing for Godiva chocolates in a barrel of Moët."

He laughed at this, appearing as it must have to him like a scene out of *Pygmalion*. He reassured me by putting it into context: "Don't forget, in Sweden we think to take a sauna is very normal. And as for the floating part, this is a coastal city: Water is a big part of our lives."

He seemed gently charmed by my reaction and I in turn felt more relaxed that we had subtly acknowledged our differences but not found them too much of an obstacle. When I had arrived, Anders had scared me. He was too *everything:* handsome, rich, powerful . . . He was still all those things, but I was less fazed by them now that I was starting to get a sense of his personality.

I did still feel apprehensive about one thing, though. "So, that was why I needed to bring the bikini, then?" I asked, trying to keep the I-would-sooner-throw-myself-over-the-side-than-let-you-see-me-in-a-bikini note from my voice.

Suddenly Anders looked awkward, too. "Yes," he replied. "I thought it might be romantic, but . . ." My heart leaped at the "but." " . . . maybe it is too much too soon? Perhaps it is good just to relax and enjoy each other's company?"

I could have kissed him.

And Anders, maybe sharing my performance anxiety, looked relieved, too. Picking up the final tray of food and flipping a cloth over his arm, he bowed mockingly. "If madam is ready, dinner is served," he announced with a flourish.

Sitting across from me at the table on deck, Anders unveiled exquisite dish after dish: strawberries dusted with sugar and threaded onto skewers; hot, tender fish sandwiches dressed in a piquant sauce, each a single mouthful dripping warm olive oil down my forearm; baked cheese coated in crunchy herbs served with a tangy mustard dip. Crisp chunks of bread and brimming bowls of glossy salad acted to counterpoint the rich flavors and textures.

We ate with our fingers, after a while forgetting to wipe them clean on our napkins so that, unnoticed, our wineglasses became imprinted with buttery impressions of our lips and fingertips.

And all the while we talked. We talked about my journey, our friends, our lives, and what we thought might be our futures.

Anders was a local events organizer and had just finished his two big shows for the year: a huge arts and music festival and the Gothenburg Grand Prix. He admitted he was exhausted and was looking forward to catching up with friends, but mostly to spending time on his own in his very basic log cabin in a nearby forest.

"Really?" I asked in surprise. I must have said it with a little too much surprise, as Anders raised his eyebrows quizzically. "Sorry," I said quickly. "I didn't mean that rudely, I just meant . . ." I groped for a tactful way to say he looked too urban and sophisticated to rough it. "You look like someone with a taste for city life. I can't quite picture you drawing water from a well and combing your hair with twigs."

He smiled, looking vaguely flattered. "I need time in my cabin," he explained. "It is my retreat, the place I go to recharge my batteries and switch off from everything that pulls and makes demands of me."

I could understand that. "I get like that, too," I agreed, "but I always feel guilty: I spend so much time traveling and away from my friends, I feel I have to put the time in with them when I get back or they get really irritable and difficult." And, to be fair, I wanted to put the time in, too: Traveling for work might be wonderful, but it was also pretty lonely.

Anders looked a little sad. "Yes, it is hard with friends as they do not understand that, yes, my work is fun, but it is also very demanding and with long hours. As I have become older, I am less troubled by the demands of others and enjoy my own company more and more." He explained that it had caused his most recent relationship to break up, as they were both traveling extensively for work and spending long periods of time apart. Although he looked hurt by this, I also sensed that Anders was someone happy to be on his own, reconciled to and actually enjoying his own company in a way I suspected I never could. He had a grown-up son from a marriage long over. When you're a guy and you've had children, maybe that particular need is sated and it's your own company you value for its peace and continuity.

We talked for hours. We talked through dinner; we talked through juicy spikes of chopped tropical fruit; we talked through rich, bitter chocolates; we talked through coffee; we talked through cognac. We talked through Frank Sinatra, U2, Bruce Springsteen, Matt Monro. And as we talked about Gothenburg and London, and relationships we'd loved and relationships that had broken our hearts, jobs we'd adored . . . I knew he was not my Soul Mate. I enjoyed being with Anders and found him very attractive, but ultimately we were looking for different relationships. He was an educated, passionate man with a true appreciation of fine things. But he was a loner. Being on my own scared me to death: I wanted to meet someone who was open to the possibility of falling in love, running the risk of getting hurt along the way, but still believing there was someone wonderful out there for him. I didn't want to experience life solo, I wanted a Soul Mate to share it with, and was willing to travel the world to find him.

By now it was 3 a.m. There was still light in the sky, but it had a silvery luminosity about it, like it was the moon shining rather than the sun. We both had early starts the next day, Anders to help a friend move house, me to catch a train to Stockholm. He rang another of the ubiquitous captains to come and tow us back to land.

Back on dry land, a taxi was waiting. We sat very close on the backseat as we drove back to Gothenburg. I felt we had really shared something—I'm certain he did, too—but I was unsure exactly what.

When we arrived at my hotel, Anders got out and walked me to the door. We stood looking at each other without speaking, just as we had done all those hours ago on the deck of the boat. But so much seemed to have happened since then. He held my hands in his and studied me, smiling enigmatically. He then took me in his arms and pulled me tightly against him.

"You are a very special woman, Jennifer, it has been an extraordinary evening," he said in a low voice, tense with emotion. I felt the same way and got quite teary. "Will you be okay to catch your train?" he asked softly. "It's early, isn't it?"

I made a face. "Eight thirty," I told him. Loosening his hold on me a fraction, he looked at his watch. It was 4 a.m. "It's fine, though, there are a ton of trains to Stockholm," I said. "I can easily get a later one if I'm too tired." I sensed he knew that nothing was going to happen tonight and he wasn't going to make a move. I'd started thinking that breakfast together would be nice but didn't want to suggest it myself.

"Maybe you'd like breakfast, then?" he suggested.

I beamed. "That would be lovely," I replied. "But I know you have to help your friend move."

A cloud flitted across his face and he frowned for a moment. "Ah yes, my friends. I will have to call them and see what can be done. In the meantime, though," and again he held me close, this time brushing his lips across my ear, "I want to thank you for this evening. It has touched me greatly."

And then, taking my face in his hands and tilting it up toward his, he looked into my eyes and kissed me very lightly on the lips, touching my mouth gently with his fingers. Complicated emotions played across his face: sadness, indecision, desire? I was unsure, but he held my gaze intensely. Mesmerized, I held my breath. Tracing his fingers up my face and stroking my hair, he kissed me lightly once more, then turned and got back into the taxi. The door closed and it pulled away.

I have to admit, I was so tired by now that I was almost relieved to see him go. I desperately needed some sleep. But watching him gaze at me through the window of the taxi, I felt thrilled and tantalized. The whole exchange had been romantic, electric, complicated, and unresolved. Would I hear from him tomorrow?

Did I want to? Too tired to search for answers, I went up to my room, lay down fully clothed on the bed, and fell into a deep sleep until the alarm went off three hours later.

By 9:30 the next morning, the train had already carried me an hour east of Gothenburg.

When the alarm had gone off, I'd taken a quick shower and packed, listening for the phone the whole time. It hadn't rung. Neither had it when I'd queued to buy the ticket to Stockholm. I'd boarded the train in a dream: It would make a mess of my schedule if he did call and I had to take a later train. But if I couldn't deal with a change in my plans, there was no point in me being on this journey in the first place.

But seriously, were we even compatible? He looked like someone used to women with drawers full of sheer lingerie, who wouldn't need to sit at weird angles to attain the illusion of a perfect fit. My underwear drawers were full of "favorite" (i.e., unattractive but comfortable) bras, mismatched socks, and bars of soap I kept meaning to use but constantly forgot I owned. Was I too old to change? Was I an old dog that could be taught new tricks? It was hard to know. I suspected that in order to meet my Soul Mate, I needed to embrace new ideas, but if those ideas were too much of a stretch (or squeeze), I'd never really be happy.

Had Anders known all this? Or had I been putting out *not interested* vibes? Or was it all part of him being a loner, that he didn't feel the need to follow up? Or maybe he had a whole basket of issues I knew nothing about?

It felt unresolved, but, curiously, I was fine with that. Although I wanted the satisfaction and closure of him calling, I wasn't troubled by the fact that he hadn't. My self-confidence wasn't free-falling and I didn't feel rejected.

Then my phone rang and I nearly fell off the seat. Was Anders opening it all back up, just as I was going through the rationalizing ritual of closing it all down? No, it was Ann-Charlotte, incandescent with curiosity about how the evening had gone. She oohed and ahhhed and ohmigoded through my account before exploding: "And so, has he rung?"

"Of course not, you nit, or I wouldn't be on the train," I retorted in exasperation.

"Well, for goodness' sake, Jennifer, call him. You must call him, what are you waiting for?"

But I wasn't going to call. I'd spent one magical evening with Anders and had enjoyed every moment of it. But I knew that that was it and—unlike in the past—I was going to trust my instincts. We'd had fun, but we weren't right for each other; more time together wouldn't change that.

Then it suddenly hit me with a jolt: Hey, *I don't get seasick on floating saunas.* Pleased with my newfound expensive tastes and certain it was only a matter of time before I'd be bobbing for Godivas, I curled up on my seat and fell into a deep sleep that lasted until the train pulled into Stockholm five hours later.

chapter four

Stockholm, Sweden, & Copenhagen, Denmark

Date #7—The Viking Date in Birka, Sweden

You've got to admire the nerve of the Swedes. At a time when the rest of the world was denying it had ever even owned a tank top, let alone worn a pair of beige slacks that fitted snugly around the (pre-thong) bottom, Sweden—in particular, Stockholm—was embracing and refining its entire 1970s back catalogue.

Man-made textiles were cherished, not vilified, and everything from couture to cutlery came in a variety of bold designs, resplendent in the entire rich spectrum of the color brown.

And then, as the rest of the world came back around to the idea that the seventies' look wasn't gauche after all but actually knowing and cutting edge, Stockholm was crowned the most knowing of them all. If cities were people, Stockholm, absorbed in its own fashionable introspectiveness, was Andy Warhol.

I've always wondered if the whole thing was just a double bluff. Was Stockholm really that hip, or was it more a case of not knowing any better than to have a soft spot for flares and flammable fabrics? Isn't it possible Stockholm just got lucky that the rest of the world was too insecure to call them out and folded first?

The reason I'd been contemplating design issues was also the reason I'd been reluctant to get a later train: I had a Designer Date in Stockholm.

Date #6: Thomas Sandell, Designer— Stockholm, Sweden

Thomas Sandell was an über-award-winning Swedish designer whose interiors and furniture designs had earned him commissions ranging from the Swedish government to Eriksson technologies. He was even represented in the stores of what was arguably Sweden's most effective cultural ambassador: IKEA.

I say the date was with Thomas, but it was actually with one of his designs. Stay with me on this: I'll explain.

I was booked into the Hotel Birger Jarl, a hip, modern hotel in which all the rooms had been created by Sweden's top designers. I was staying in one of the two rooms created by Thomas.

I wanted to test my theory that if your job is your most important relationship, it will eventually start to resemble you. I mean, dogs famously take on the appearance of their owners, so is the same true of a job? How much of who you are can be seen in what you do?

Specifically, would I get a true sense of Thomas by staying in a room he'd designed? I'd check into his room, then meet up with him in a couple of days, tell him the impression I had of him from his work, and see if I was right.

Feeling groggy from my weird new sleep patterns, and arms aching from dragging my case over cobbled streets (*"God, it can't be much farther"* being the misguided mantra of travelers everywhere), I arrived at the minimalist lobby of the Birger Jarl. As I checked in, the desk clerk, chic and understated in his black suit and Bond-baddie wire glasses, handed me a number of messages.

I immediately wondered if one was from Anders. I didn't think he knew where I was staying, so I doubted it, but that didn't stop a flame of hope flaring up. So much for my *trusting my instincts/ he's not the one for me* moral high ground.

Scooping up the messages and the key to room 705, I went up in the tiny lift, en route to the first stage of my Designer Date.

A plaque outside my door told me my room was called "Mr. Glad."

Oh, at last, an upbeat boyfriend, I thought as I slid my keycard into the lock and let myself in.

The first thing I did when I walked into the space was laugh. The room was long, bright, and silly. The windows that ran down the far wall were fringed with white window-boxes of bright green Astroturf. It didn't even look vaguely natural or pastoral; instead it seemed like someone was growing green plastic broom-heads.

In the middle of the room, a white gauze curtain acted as a gossamer screen between the room and a larger-than-life bed, like something out of *Goldilocks and the Three Bears.* The white wall behind the pillow-laden headboard was covered with black-painted dashes, reminiscent of a cow-print design. The chairs in front of the bed were equally *who's been sitting in my chair*–esque.

Putting my bags down on the floor, I clambered up onto the bed. The whole room felt friendly and funny, generous and openly welcoming. *Thank God,* I thought as I bedded down in a nest of pillows and fished the messages out of my coat pocket; I could so easily have ended up in the scary room with the black bed and claustrophobic black-and-white-checked walls.

Hotel rooms are like relationships: intimate and powerful. The good ones nurture, making you feel relaxed and happy. The bad ones get under your skin and fill you with impotent rage.

Well, I was Ms. Glad; so far my Design Date was going very well indeed.

I opened the messages. The first one was from Lorna confirming my 10:30 at the Nobel Museum in a couple of days. Second message was from my sister Mandy, just calling to check I was doing okay. Third message was from Maria, my Designer Date Wrangler. "Uh-oh." I sat up on the bed, sensing bad news.

"Hello, Jennifer, I hope you have arrived safely and are enjoying the hotel. I wanted to let you know that unfortunately Thomas will be on business in Moscow for the next few days and may not be back in Sweden in time to meet you. He has left his number if you want to call him."

Not wanting to think about how much it would cost on my cell phone to bounce my voice via satellite from Sweden to England to Russia to England and back to Sweden, I decided to call tomorrow. It was a lovely evening; I was going to take a walk, find some food, then have an early night. I was dating a Viking tomorrow and needed to catch up with myself.

The hotel was a short walk from the funky Odengatan and grungy Kungsgatan areas, and I soon discovered that my trip to Stockholm coincided with a big Metallica concert and that the fans owned the city that night.

Heavy metal was king in Scandinavia, and Metallica was probably its oldest ruling dynasty. The streets were crammed with roving gangs of teenage boys looking strangely like baby hedgehogs, the backs of their denim jackets spiky with tiny metal studs. The bars spilled over with long-haired bikers—fueled by excitement and Jack Daniel's, they roared across the street at each other like Norse warriors going into battle.

I have a bit of a heavy-metal soft spot and ordinarily would have enjoyed the display, even seen it as a warm-up act for the Viking tomorrow. But the atmosphere seemed tense and volatile rather than fun. I stopped at a supermarket for some chips and cookies (just because I was traveling was no reason to let my diet go) and settled in the hotel bar with a book and the internationally ubiquitous chill-out music of designer hotels.

Date #7: Ny Björn Gosterssen, Viking and Archaeologist—Birka, Sweden

At 10 a.m. the next morning, I boarded a ferry from the quay outside City Hall and set sail for Birka.

Birka was an island, situated one and a half hours west of Stockholm, along the inland archipelago of Lake Mälaren. Although there wasn't much to see now, this UNESCO site was an important part of the Viking heritage. Founded in the eighth century, Birka had been Sweden's first city and a busy trade center between Northern Europe and the Baltic Sea. It also contained the largest Viking-age cemetery—more than 3,000 graves scattered throughout the island—and excavating archaeologists were still uncovering important finds.

It was actually one of the archaeologists I was on my way to date. Each summer a number of them, specializing in Viking-age studies, stayed on the island as part of a living history display but also to learn more about the Vikings by emulating what is known of their living conditions and habits.

This was all good news for me, as I wanted to date a Viking.

I know this is going to sound terrible and wildly politically incorrect, but I've always thought the Viking image deeply sexy.

Ruthless warriors conquering all in their path, Vikings always seemed to be depicted as having big hair, bad attitudes, and hard, hot bodies. I realized as a peaceful vegetarian I should have found this image appalling rather than appealing, but there you go, that's hormones for you. Vikings were the stuff of daydreams, as far as I was concerned, and this was my chance to find out if my fantasies survived scrutiny.

Stockholm had been really warm when I'd left, but as I walked from the ferry down the metal gangplank into the steady drizzle that enveloped Birka, I didn't need to be told I had got my outfit completely wrong. Although I'd thought to wear a waterproof coat, underneath I was freezing and being bitten to death in my open-toed sandals and capri pants. Rain and mosquitoes? I was failing Viking 101 from the outset.

I followed a gravel path toward a thin copse. The sound of wood being chopped rang energetically through the trees and echoed off the rocks, scaring dark clouds of guttural crows into the darker rain clouds that hung low above Birka. I knew that Ny Björn, archaeologist and part-time Viking, was re-creating a Viking-age kitchen with his fellow archaeologists. Unless IKEA dated back much further than I realized, I guessed that sound was them cutting up trees and building the kitchen from scratch.

As I came through a clearing, I saw a group of people surrounded by tree trunks stripped of their bark and piles of fresh shavings. The stakes were loosely laid out on the forest floor in the shape of a small one-room house. A cold-looking woman in a long woolen dress was crouched at the edge of the clearing, stirring a cauldron over an open fire. The rest of the group were men and stood in the center of the clearing, blunt saws and axes at their feet. Two wore long, woolen, monklike robes, cinched at the waist by long twists of thin rope. The rest wore sturdy leather trousers and boots, topped with rough woolen shirts and tweed jerkins. They all stared at the arrangement of wood, hands on hips and nonplussed expressions on their faces. Maybe it was early IKEA after all?

Catching sight of me, they immediately busied themselves, moving around bits of wood and generally trying to give the impression that they were very busy and knew exactly what they were doing. I was touched that they were bothered about impressing a woman who was dressed as if going for coffee in the south of France, when actually on a rain-sodden island that clearly hadn't seen the sun in months. But I suppose none of us would have been on the island if we didn't have some issues to work through.

One of the group, in leather trousers and a crazy flat cap, smiled and strode toward me. "Auch, hellooo, Jennifer, welcome to Birka," he called out in a broad Scottish accent. I was confused: I thought my Viking was Swedish—Ny Bjórn was surely never a Scottish name?

He got close enough to shake my hand, by now so cold it was shaking anyway.

"Hello," I said. "Are you Scottish?"

"Ooh, noo," he replied with a grin. "But I've done a fair bit of excavating in the Scottish Highlands, so I've got a bit of a burr." He actually had so much of a burr that just saying the word took him about fifteen minutes.

"But you are a Viking?" I asked, looking to establish some facts. "Or at least you're dressed like one."

"Yes," Ny Bjórn replied, "or as we assume they dressed, from the remains we have found in Denmark, York, and Northern Germany."

Rather than the ruthless warrior I had imagined, Ny Bjórn actually looked more like a wandering minstrel. My first impression was of a tall, thin, and engaging man, clearly having the time of his life on this cold, wet island. His long reddish-blond hair tied back into a ponytail, Ny Björn had a mischievous-looking face, punctuated by an energetic goatee that wagged up and down like a happy dog's tail when he laughed. I knew straight away that he wasn't my type: He looked like the smart kid you enjoyed chatting with because you sat next to him in chemistry but never fancied. I didn't mind, though; I was still fascinated to learn more about him and what he was doing here.

Ny Björn and I retreated to a large, cold rock to talk. He explained that until they finished building the cookhouse in two weeks' time, they would be sleeping rough on rainy Birka.

I had my first inkling that maybe Vikings were tough not because it was cute and sexy but because they had to be. And I—with my pathological hatred of the cold, not to mention mosquitoes—might not find myself a natural fit into Viking society. I asked Ny Björn to explain who the Vikings actually were.

"The word 'Viking' is used for all people in the North cultural sphere, but Vikings were really just a tiny part of the community, mostly those who went raiding and taking things with force," he replied.

"So they were like unionized burglars?" I asked.

"Exactly, that's the Viking part. They were seen as heroes by the local community who watched them come back loaded up with bounty, but by the end of the Viking age, to call someone 'a Viking' was really seen as quite rude."

"Umm, so as a Viking you could be fairly prosperous, by the sound of it." I found this reassuring from a comfort point of view, but what about from a dating point of view? The key question (which I was too ashamed to ask outright) was, exactly how hot were the Vikings?

I paraphrased: "We have an image of Vikings as being rough,

roguish types and you're sitting here in leather trousers, which have gone on to become the uniform of rock stars. Were Vikings seen as the sexy rock-star gods of their age?"

That was me—a Pulitzer just waiting to happen.

Happily, Ny Björn didn't seem to think the question too idiotic. "The famous ones, absolutely. You just need to look at the Icelandic sagas to see that: Gretty the Strong—"

"Ohhh, I like the sound of Gretty the Strong," I cooed, all pretense of dignity completely abandoned. "It sounds like the lead singer in a heavy metal band."

"Oh, yes," Ny Björn replied with equal enthusiasm, clearly warming to the subject. "He lived in the early eleventh century, and although he was finally killed, he was outlawed for eighteen years and seen as the superstar of his days."

"Really?" I swooned, knowing absolutely nothing about him, but instantly having a huge crush on him anyway. "What did he do that was so great?"

"Well," said Ny Björn excitedly, suggesting that if he wasn't a man and a Viking and a thousand years too late, maybe he would have had a bit of a crush on Gretty too, "he did a lot of things: He was a great warrior, he was really strong, and he was a good wrestler."

The idea of wrestling cooled my ardor for a moment, conjuring up images of bouffanted fools basted in baby oil working the WWF circuit, but then I had a mental picture of huge leather jerkins being ripped off broad, sweaty chests, as muddy warriors grunted and rolled around on the ground for real. I could barely contain myself. This was great: Vikings were every bit as sexy as I had imagined.

"He even killed a ghost once. . . ." Ny Björn boasted, like a kid getting carried away in front of a playground audience and saying his dad could beat up all of theirs.

"Huh?" Dragged from my daydreaming, I picked up on Ny Björn saying something about ghosts. Ghosts? I wasn't interested in "ghosts." Ghosts weren't sexy.

"Oh, yes, he was the idol for people back then," Ny Björn continued unabashed. He was on a roll, delighted to have an audience for a subject that he clearly lived and breathed. "People who were 'good at the trade' of being a Viking were pretty much the role model of what men should be back then. There was deep resentment about the Vikings who came to settle around York, or Yorvik, for example, because they took away all the women from the Englishmen there. And the reason was that the Vikings washed every Saturday and combed their hair, etcetera. They were really well-groomed by the standards of the times."

Back on safer ground and feeling that we shared an appreciation, albeit for different reasons, I summed up: "So can I just clarify, the Vikings wore leather and washed?"

"Yes, yes," Ny Björn replied.

I gave a big happy sigh. "This just gets better and better."

We both laughed.

I knew why I was into Vikings, but what about Ny Björn? What was the appeal for him? The leather? The machismo? The beards?

"No, no . . ." he spluttered. "It's . . ."

"Oh, come on," I persisted, determined not to let him off the hook.

"Well, okay, yes," he admitted sheepishly. "But the real attraction is I'm totally into artifacts. I really like 'things' and gizmos and how they were made. This is a great way for me to increase my understanding of things made by the Vikings."

All my instincts went on "geek alert" when Ny Björn said this, but I suppose you don't live on a cold, wet island for the summer unless you are seriously passionate about the place, and who was I to judge? I was passionate about Vikings; Ny Bjórn was passionate about Vikings' "things," that's all.

"I mean, cooking fish over an open fire in an enamel pot," he continued, now lost in a romantic reverie of his own, "it worked back then. If we can make it work here, we can learn from it, that's one of the main reasons I do this."

I was proving myself to be superficial and shallow: I wanted to go back to hearing about strong men wrestling, not how to cook fish over a fire. I guess that was the thing, though—the guys who were satisfied with leather and machismo were the ones who'd been gathering for the Metallica concert in Stockholm the night before. Here on the island, the fascination was with the life behind the myth. I'd arrived a thousand years too late.

Frozen to the core, I stood up and gently massaged some blood back into my hands and feet. The ferry back to the mainland had just docked and it was time for me to go. I had loved meeting Ny Bjórn, even if he hadn't turned out to be the Viking of my dreams. I was interested to see how immersed he was in his work—even if my Designer Date didn't end up proving my *you look like your job* theory, Ny Bjórn certainly did.

I wished him luck building the cookhouse and for the summer ahead, then walked woodenly back to the warmth of the boat and the challenge of the next seventy-three dates.

Sailing back, it was so cold and wet I had to sit below deck. There was one spare seat at a coffee table, where two women leaned toward one another, deep in conversation. They invited me to join them and I did, but although busying myself with my book, I found it impossible to ignore their conversation.

Sarah was in her thirties, from London but working for the

EU in Brussels. Katia was in her fifties, living and working in Stockholm. She was a part-time therapist who also made money selling diets over the Internet. They were several hours into a conversation about their love lives.

Sarah was torn between a relationship with a cute commitment-phobe in Brussels and a safe-bet/dull-as-ditchwater back home in London. The thing she was really struggling with, though, was, as she put it: "We are all born alone and die alone."

I could see how that would put a damper on the evening.

Katia only had the one relationship to contend with, but it was more than enough by the sound of it. She was in love with an ex–Soviet general and was unresolved as to if and how she could accept or change his fierce anti-Semitic views.

The places, faces, and details changed, but I had had these conversations a million times on the road over the years. Wherever you travel, there will be women struggling to come to terms with the big, emotional issues in their lives. I liked to think I was less desperate and better dressed about it, but I had been that woman over the years, too. Who knew, maybe I was that woman now. As I watched Katia pick up her copy of *The Answer Within: Learning to Love Yourself* and disembark with Sarah, I knew I would never discover how their dilemmas worked out. But maybe that wasn't the point. Having the chance to think and talk about your issues was what was important. Perhaps that was where the idea for my Dating Odyssey had come from, except I didn't want to talk about my past, I wanted to be talked into my future.

When I got back to the hotel, I called Thomas in Russia. We agreed I would email him my impression of him and he would

email me back his response, so, in a way, our date would have
taken place in spite of his absence. I got to work immediately:

Okay, so to my impression of you from your design:
    CARING—You wanted me to be happy.
    CALM—The room, although bright, was very tran-
quil.
    THOUGHTFUL—The room had "breathing space," like
you were encouraging me to take the time to think
about things.
    SMART—You knew how to control the mediums and
get the effect you wanted.
    FUN/SENSE OF HUMOR—I loved the larger-than-life
bed—it made me think of Goldilocks and the Three
Bears!
    SENSITIVE—Feeling for textures and subtle
form.
    In short, the sense of you that I got from your
room is that you are a kind man and selfless friend.
Someone who listens, returns calls no matter how
late, and puts others before himself. You are reliable and thoughtful.
    There is a darker side that most don't see,
though (the bathroom has an utterly different mood
to the bedroom): You feel the need to keep that out
of view and compartmentalized "for yourself."
    You are also a passionate perfectionist, with a
strong, restless vision. You cannot rest until a
project has been completed to your high standards.
    Thomas, I do hope I haven't said anything insen-
sitive or too personal here. You came across as

being utterly lovely from your room and I hope that
is clear in what I have just written. I'm curious
as to how right and wrong I am.
   Take care, Jennifer

Date #8: William—Nobel Museum, Stockholm, Sweden

The next morning I walked to Rådmansgatan Station and caught
the Tunnelbana metro to Gamla Stan, Stockholm's medieval center. It was built on an island and was good for lazy sightseers, as
the charismatic castle, cathedral, parliament buildings, and mu-
seums were all within spitting distance of each other.

It also meant that it had the highest concentration of tourists,
expensive ice creams, and customer-only toilets of anywhere in
Sweden. I bypassed all of these and headed straight for the Nobel
Museum and my 10:30 with William.

William was a student here. He was also the brother of my
friend Lorna from Australia. I had more than enough Swedish
dates already, but Lorna had begged me to meet up with him:

Think of this as a favor to me, Jen: He doesn't
know a lot of people there as he's pretty shy so a
bit slow making friends. I know he'd love to have
the chance to talk to someone. I'll owe you big-
time.

To be told someone will "owe you big-time" means you're pretty
much being told to expect the worst but for noble reasons. It
wasn't the Nobel Date I wanted, but "it's just coffee," I told myself firmly as I hiked up the steps outside the Nobel Museum.
"It's one morning out of my life." Get in, date him, and boom—
I could be heading out of the country and on to the next date in
under four hours.

It had just gone 10 a.m. as I walked into the entrance hall. I wanted the chance to have a look around before I met William. The Nobel Museum honored the 743 laureates who had tirelessly devoted themselves to the fields of physics, chemistry, medicine, literature, economics, and, of course, peace.

The museum was wonderful: As you entered, a huge Orwellian tract ran around the ceiling of the entire building, laminated portraits of the laureates rattling along it on hangers. At various points the track dipped down so you could read the profiles.

The museum was divided into sections by solid screens of what looked like chicken wire covered in Plexiglas, white fiberoptic lights glowing inside. I bumped into the publicist, Anna, who pointed me in the direction of the electronic museum, where I wanted to surf the online database of the laureates' acceptance speeches.

Martin Luther King Jr., Marie Curie, Samuel Beckett, Kofi Annan, Mother Teresa . . . Reading them, I was struck by how much passion these people had poured into the ideals they championed. Out of curiosity, I entered the word "love" and searched for references to it among the speeches.

The screen filled and I scrolled down. The laureates' love of ideas; their love of humanity, freedom, God, science and discovery, home; even their love of cars. It struck me very powerfully that this kind of love was a dedication: a devotional love, abstract, not interpersonal. There was no mention of romantic love; no real celebration of people other than as concepts or ideals.

Clearly the laureates were accomplished, unique people. But was being accomplished and unique at the expense of something more everyday and vital to our happiness? In short, to be a great idealist, did you need to be pretty self-centered and emotionally unavailable? Were they just a smarter, more noble version of me, choosing a job over a partner? But since they were making the world a better place rather than writing about where to go on holiday, did that make it okay?

Another thing that really struck me was how few of the laureates were women: only 31 out of a total of 743. What did that say about gender roles and the pursuit of ideals? Were women more interested in people, and men in ideas, or was the judging system just crap?

But it was time to meet William. As I walked back out to the lobby, I bumped into Anna again. I asked her if she thought it was true the laureates didn't value romantic or personal love.

Anna smiled wryly. "You know, when I started working at the Nobel Museum, I was told: 'Here you are not loved for being witty or beautiful, you are loved for your ideas.' Most of the people associated with the Nobel Prizes—winners and staff—give up their families and well-paid jobs so that they might explore and prove their ideas. It takes a certain type of selfishness to be so dedicated."

So it was as true for Nobel Prize winners as it was for guidebook publicists: Too much work wrecks your love life.

William and I had arranged to meet at the Kafé Satir. Modeled on Café Museum, the Viennese intellectuals' hang-out in the early 1900s, it was where the Nobel Museum encouraged you to debate and reflect. I figured if William didn't have much to say for himself, at least there'd be enough going on around to distract us. The café was small; I should have no problem spotting William: brown collar-length hair, bookish, and "normal-looking," according to Lorna.

There was only one person in the café when I arrived. Sunk low in his chair, huge booted feet propped up on the table, a young man with long, greasy hair slouched with his eyes shut and his mouth open. The serving staff stood tensely behind the counter, watching him with open hostility, outraged at the bad manners, worse attitude, and unforgivable hair.

This could not be William.

I don't know why I even bothered thinking that, because I instantly knew that it was. This heavy-metal dating disaster was "shy," "normal" William. And from the look and smell of his T-shirt, he hadn't been home since the Metallica concert the night before.

Rather than feeling worried or intimidated, I felt like someone's mum arriving home unexpectedly to find her son blowing off school and reading Dad's hidden stash of porn.

Walking over to where William sat oblivious to my stern judgment, I gave the staff an *I'll deal with this* look. Putting my bag and coat on the table next to William's feet, I sharply rapped on the sole of one of his boots. His eyelids flickered, his brow creased, but he continued to sleep, the studs on his jacket rising and falling gently with each deep breath.

"William," I said crisply. This time his eyes snapped open and he looked around in alarm, completely disoriented, clearly not recognizing where he was. "William," I repeated, this time a little more gently but still with a *wait till I get you home, young man* tone to my voice. He blinked twice and blankly focused his gaze in my direction. Like being behind a student driver waiting and waiting to pull out on a busy roundabout, sometimes you have to give them a nudge or you'll be there forever. "William!" I shouted, knocking him hard on the shoulder.

Pausing as if manually connecting brain with body, William shambled into life. Crashing his legs off the table onto the floor, he stumbled to his feet. As the chair toppled over noisily behind him, the counter staff flinched collectively. The smell of cigarettes and alcohol was overwhelming. William looked at me uncertainly: He knew he was expected to speak but was obviously having difficulty knowing exactly where he was and what he was meant to say.

I revved my engine and shunted him into the oncoming traffic.

"William, I am Jennifer," I said briskly, Mary Poppins suddenly my default personality.

"Yes?" he asked dully. Something about this sounded familiar; he just needed more time to work out what.

"I am a friend of your sister Lorna's. She arranged for us to meet."

William was suddenly completely in the moment, totally lucid, and very much awake. "Hey," he said slowly, looking at me attentively as if seeing me for the first time. "You're that chick going round the world banging all those guys," he reported matter-of-factly. I sensed all movement behind the counter come to an abrupt halt; the kitchen staff stopped watching William and—like spectators at Wimbledon—collectively turned their attention to me, their faces alight with frank incredulity and wonder.

Although the café was designed to foster the lively exchange of ideas, I doubted very much that this was what they had in mind.

"William," I said witheringly, summoning all the dignity I could manage, "I am not—as you say—'banging guys around the world.' I am on a quest, traveling the world in search of my Soul Mate." I snorted at the ridiculousness of his statement, as much to convince the staff in the kitchen as William.

"But you bang some of the guys, right?" he asked hopefully.

I rolled my eyes. I didn't have the time or energy to explain the niceties of my Odyssey to some teenage boy optimistically and inappropriately awash with hormones. With a dignified sniff, I picked up my bag and coat. Casting a disdainful eye in the direction of the counter staff, who by now had given up all pretense of rearranging the chocolate cookies and were openly following our conversation, I thanked William for meeting me.

"I'll tell Lorna you looked, ummm . . ." I struggled for a suitable description. " . . . well."

William just stared at me, his unwashed face puckering into folds of exasperation as he realized I was going, and he was not coming with me. "Maaan," he groaned in frustration, "I only came here because I thought I was going to get laid. I'm telling you, there is no way I am ever doing my sister a favor again."

Doing my sister a favor?

Whatever did he mean? I was the one on the mission of mercy here. Had Lorna given him the impression *I* was the one who needed help? Her desperate friend destined to end up Internationally Single, but if he could help make up the numbers, at least there'd be a shag in it for him? Could she really have said that?

I never got the chance to ask, because William, like a child who's been told "No more *Robot Wars* until your room's tidy," had already stomped out of the café and up the street, without so much as a backward glance.

I raised my eyebrows and let out a long, steadying breath. That, I said to myself, was what happened when you dated a Viking. Giving the kitchen staff an *at least wait until I am out of earshot* look, I left the museum for my hotel, where I packed and left for Denmark.

The man sitting in front of me on the plane to Copenhagen was easily the most nervous flyer I've ever seen in my life. He puffed and panted through gritted teeth like he was flying Air Lamaze.

At one point I was woken by him shrieking, "Oh, my God!" involuntarily, before returning to his steady panting.

No one watched the film; we all watched him.

I shouldn't have taken this as a bad omen, but I did. I was in an ugly mood. I still felt irritated, less by how William had been and more by what Lorna might have said. Although I only had two dates in Copenhagen, I'm afraid to say I didn't feel in the mood for either of them.

Date #9: Lars—The Free State of Christiania, Copenhagen, Denmark

My mood was not improved by getting soaked on the way to Christiania. It was dead in the water by the time I'd finished dating Lars.

Christiania was on the site of an abandoned military barracks on the edge of Copenhagen city center. Taken over by squatters in 1971 and declared a "free state," it was now home to around eight hundred people, with another seven hundred–odd who worked within the community.

Christiania was a self-governing, car-free society that functioned as a collective. It ran its own school, recycling programs, and small businesses that catered to both residents and the tourists who flocked here (mainly to buy the pot openly sold on "Pusher Street").

Its very existence was a challenging expression of civil liberties. I had loved the sense of community I got from living in a housing co-op in Leeds when I was a student. Could my Soul Mate be found in this community?

My date Lars had just split up with his girlfriend. His friend Vessie, who was a friend of my friend Kirk, thought it would cheer Lars up to meet me. I have no idea if it cheered Lars up, but it depressed the hell out of me. "I'm only here so I don't have to be on my own at home," he told me bluntly the second we met.

Our date consisted of three hours walking along Christiania's muddy paths in the pouring rain, as Lars poured his heart out. His girlfriend had left him for someone else; he was a good guy who couldn't catch a break; she'd never appreciated him, he was too good for her; what was so great about macho guys anyway . . . ?

Regardless of the fact that Lars had just been dumped, to me he seemed one of those people who had a horrible, negative attitude anyway. When we parted company, I felt like asking for his ex-girlfriend's phone number just so we could go out for a drink together and bad mouth him.

Date #10: Paul—Tivoli Gardens, Copenhagen, Denmark

I slept badly after my date with Lars. His negativity weighed on me and made me feel despondent about my own chances of success—not because he had been unlucky in love but because I feared I might be unlucky enough to have another seventy-one dates just like him.

But my next date was with Paul, a chef who worked in one of the "It" restaurants in Copenhagen. We'd both been too busy to talk or email, but my friend Georgia had arranged for us to meet on the Kissing Bench at Tivoli Gardens, the Victorian amusement park full of old-fashioned rides, street orchestras, and beautiful flower gardens. It was one of my favorite places and I knew it would cheer me up.

But four hours later, as I sat solo on the Kissing Bench in the pouring rain, I realized that rather than being cheered up, I was being stood up. Paul was a no-show. I shouldn't have been as

upset about it as I was, but I took it really badly and very personally: Not only did he not want to see me, he couldn't even be
bothered to let me know he wasn't coming. Too embarrassed to
get in contact with Georgia and too wretched to do anything
else, I went back to the hotel, ran a hot bath, and cried.

chapter five

France

Date #12—The Gallic Date
in Paris, France

I love Scandinavia: Like the Netherlands, its people seem liberal and smart without making a big deal about it. In complete contrast, the French national identity has an air of disdainful elegance, like old money at Ascot. But the back-to-back dating disaster in Copenhagen, preceded by William in Stockholm, made me sincerely glad I was heading for the complicated cosmopolitanism of Paris. I needed a complete change of scene and atmosphere.

The last time I had come to Paris was Kelly's and my four-year anniversary. After extensive nagging, he'd agreed to go to the Buddha Bar. Apparently, the beer was too expensive, the staff too fashionable; it hadn't been a great success.

If I hadn't been traveling for the purpose of dating, I think I might have resented that so many cities around the world seemed to contain little Kelly booby traps—painful or irritating memories that exploded out of nowhere. But I was determined not to be one of those people who stayed involved with the bitterness longer than they'd been with the person who'd actually caused it.

And if I step off my martyr's pedestal for a moment to be honest, Kelly wasn't the only man I thought of when I came to Paris. Wild, sexy, and dead . . . I also had a thing going on with Doors singer Jim Morrison. Over the last five years I must have visited his grave, just inside the eastern edge of the Périphérique, half a dozen times, either to make programs or with friends.

I've always been fascinated that Jim Morrison—a parallel—Elvis: sexy, iconoclast gone to seed—ended his days in Paris. Erotic and playful as he, Paris was also cultured and subtle. As the Lizard King became the Lard King and tired of himself, maybe that was what drew him here.

I suspect that as a boyfriend, Jim Morrison would have been an absolute nightmare: unfaithful, self-indulgent, and often cruel. But he was also a lithe sex god who created the sound-track to my teen years, and the affinity I felt with him ran deep. I decided to spend the day with him at his grave in the stately Père Lachaise cemetery, to try to pinpoint the attraction.

Date #11: Jim Morrison, The Doors—Cimetière du Père Lachaise, Paris, France

Père Lachaise was the most visited cemetery in the world and had been a fashionable address for the afterlife since its inception in 1804. It was Napoleon who converted what was originally a slum neighborhood into a vast cemetery, arranging to have Molière reburied here at the "launch party." Its reputation as the in place for the over crowd thus established, its million residents now included Gertrude Stein, Edith Piaf, Oscar Wilde, Pisarro, and

Proust. But as you made your way up from the metro, the pro-
liferation of signs, maps, and memorabilia overwhelmingly
pointed to Jim Morrison being the grave célèbre here.

Finding Jim Morrison's grave was quite tricky: Père Lachaise
still had all the winding avenues and tree-lined boulevards from
the days when people lived (rather than died) here, and it was
easy to get lost. Getting lost wasn't such a hardship, though, as
the cemetery was a moving and beautiful site: Tombs varied from
Art Deco Egyptian pharaohs and larger-than-life muscular
bronze angels to austere black granite obelisks, painstakingly
scrubbed mirror-clean by stooped middle-aged women every
single day.

Like Cemetery Number 1 in New Orleans, this was a place
where the living had an ongoing relationship with their dead.
And nowhere was this more true than at Jim Morrison's grave.

I was grateful for the short shadows cast by the broad trees as
I walked through the cemetery looking for Jim Morrison. It was
only 10 a.m. but the sun already probed like a dentist's drill, bur-
rowing ruthlessly into the top of my head. The air was hot and
still; a raven perched on the marble head of a weeping Madonna
watched me balefully as I marched by full of purpose. My backpack was heavy with bottled water, the Doors biography my sister Mandy bought me when I was fifteen, sunblock, and other
bits to get me through the day. The bag bunched my cotton skirt
up at the back, but sweat glued it to my legs, preserving my mod-
esty in this place of rest.

Around the corner of a wide boulevard, in a spot hidden
among the headstones and next to a large tree trunk, I found Jim.
Or, rather, the crowd around Jim.

Three nineteen-year-old boys were camped on one of the
tombs, the ubiquitous backpackers' banquet of plain French
bread and Orangina spread before them, plus an assortment of

boxed CDs and Walkmans. Two were baseball-capped, fresh-faced Americans, the other a baggy-sweatered, straggly-haired Frenchman. They had one set of headphones between them and were taking turns, passing it around like a joint.

" 'L.A. Woman' . . . that's my favorite song. Maaan, this song is amazing," said the first young American, transported by the music in his headset. Suddenly a furious Frenchman burst from between the trees and marched over: *"Ce que faites-vous ici?"* he bellowed. "What is wrong with you that you are sitting on the burial place of the dead eating your lunch? Have you no respect?"

The boys quailed and looked uncomfortable. The French-man, too agitated to remain still, angrily paced on the path a few feet away. The two Americans turned frowning to the French boy. "Man, was he talking to us? What did he say?"

The French boy shrugged sullenly.

Back on the path, the Frenchman became incandescent. "Ah," he snorted in disgusted English. "Tourists! What do you know?" and he stormed off, leaving clouds of dust hanging over the gravel path in his wake. The teenage boys left maybe half an hour later.

In the five hours I stayed by or near the grave, around a hundred people visited. The Frenchman was right to say that the tourists were insensitive, but he was wrong to say they lacked respect. It was the very reason they were here: out of love and respect.

Jim Morrison's grave was unimposing. A plain, squat head-stone stated without fuss that James Douglas Morrison lived from 1943 to 1971. The grave itself was a shallow granite frame around a sandy pit, maybe three by six feet.

Every mourner stepped up to the grave with a sense of the theatrical, individual players each featuring in his or her own one-act drama. A group of Latino boys in gang insignia silently regarded the grave, their heads bowed in fresh grief as if Jim Morrison had died yesterday, not thirty years ago. The tallest of the group took a bottle of bourbon from his bag. Passing it between them, they each took a swallow. Taking an extra swallow, the leader then poured a measure directly onto the grave before placing the bottle gently on the headstone. Standing straight, he touched two fingers to his heart, his lips, then the headstone. One by one each of the gang repeated the sequence. Ritual completed, without a word they turned and walked away.

A midwestern couple in their forties pointed to the grave and poignantly told their three teenage children: "When we were your age, he meant everything to us. We wanted you to meet him."

Finding a lull in mourners, I put down my bag and walked over to the grave myself. It wasn't just bourbon bottles, half-smoked joints, and cigarettes; the grave was full of poems and dedications. As I read the dedications, I wondered why I—and all these other people—nurtured such enduring love for Jim Morrison. The Love Professor had described successful, healthy relationships as ones in which our positive traits are reflected back by our chosen partner. By choosing Jim Morrison, were we claiming some part of his creative, sexual vitality as our own? By liking Jim, were we saying we were like Jim?

Or could it simply be that we didn't want to forget how good it felt to be young, passionate, misunderstood, and alive? Music is a powerful memory and mood trigger, and Jim Morrison was a Door that took us back to that time and state.

There was also the fantasy element. The Love Professor said we all had to know and nurture *the real me* to be truly happy. But I loved fantasizing about the *imaginary me,* the person I could but never would be. Apart from traveling, the best time for this is at the start of a relationship: Unhindered by routine or too much information about the other person, you imagine both of you doing all the things you've always dreamed of. You see yourself going horse riding every weekend (you've never been on a horse in your life) or taking a Spanish evening class together (you miss enrollment). Fine, what does it hurt to savor the thought you'll get a chance to do all these things, whether you actually do them or not?

And if I was shacked up with someone as crazy and unstructured as Jim Morrison, surely the conversation would be elevated above whose turn it was to put the kettle on, or how bad Saturday night TV was these days. His energy would inspire and stretch me.

Yes, yes, I'm a feminist, too: I know I shouldn't need to be in a relationship to do these things, but it makes it easier.

So, how much of my love was about Jim Morrison and how much was about me? Did I imagine a relationship with Jim's juju would allow my as-yet untapped potential to be the coolest, smartest, sexiest person on earth to be realized? Was I interested in him as a person or just for what he could do for me?

But I was pulled from my introspection by two Australian women walking over to where I was sitting. "Aww, I'm really sorry to disturb you," one asked awkwardly, "but would you mind taking our photo? We want to see what we look like post-Jim."

I smiled as I took the camera: Whatever ego issues I was suffering from, I was clearly not suffering alone. The girls stood on either side of the grave and smiled into the camera as I took their picture.

Amanda and Luciana were both in their late twenties and spending the summer visiting France and the U.K. When I told them I was here to date Jim and why, they both squealed their approval. "Oh, I know why you would want to do that," Amanda burst out, squeezing my arm in emphasis, "he was really gorgeous, really wild, too. Sexy and crazy."

Luciana sounded far more downbeat. "Men aren't like that anymore," she observed ruefully.

They asked me some questions about my journey. Was I going to Sydney? I confirmed I had several dates lined up there. "Oh, good luck," Luciana said bitterly. "And trust me, you'll need it finding a man there."

This shocked me a little, as Luciana was gorgeous: a voluptuous, curvaceous "Italian" figure topped with a glossy cloud of curly brown hair and fantastically trashy earrings. She saw me noticing her figure and looking surprised. "I dressed up for Jim," she said with a sly smile. Amanda laughed, picking up on my *you get more attention away from home* theory: "You know, you're so right," she agreed. "It is just incredible how much more the guys notice you here. And in a good, fun way, not sleazy."

Luciana chipped in. "Like those guys last night," she said excitedly, nudging Amanda. "We were walking past some steps and these guys were just hanging out. Anyway . . ." Luciana and Amanda were both in fits of giggles by now. ". . . when they saw us, they called out, 'You are beautiful, come and kiss us.' It was so nice, so cheeky and flattering. It'd never be that way at home."

We all sighed together, thinking about how much fun cheeky guys could be.

And that made me realize: As much as I enjoyed the fantasy of Jim and the life I'd have with him (if, you know, he wasn't dead), I actually liked the life I already had. I had fun being me; I didn't want to morph or be molded into someone else. What I needed was to find someone else like me: a Soul Mate I could relate to.

And I wanted fun with cheeky guys. I wanted to laugh and feel sexy. It was time to bury my dead and make a date with the living.

Date #12: Olivier—Paris, France

I was booked into a hotel in the Marais, my favorite Parisian neighborhood. Touristy in parts, the area was mostly elegant and couture but, thankfully, its relentless chicness was softened by pockets of pretty squares fringed with pungent *fromageries* and cafés stocked with casually fantastic pastries.

I rushed back and changed in a hurry: I had an hour before my next date.

Showered and dressed in my new baby-blue linen top (I had spotted a gorgeous boutique on the corner of my street and raced in on the way back from the metro), I took the short walk from my hotel to the Place des Vosges. This elegant square of houses dated back to 1612, and among its former residents were Richelieu and Victor Hugo. The park at its center was once used for dueling; tonight it would be used for dating. This was where I was to meet Olivier, Date #12.

I was very curious about Olivier. He seemed extremely French: flawlessly educated and virulently contemptuous. He worked in the French film industry and would leave long gaps between emails since he (and he described it with pulling-teeth loathing) had to be at meetings everywhere from Brussels to Cannes. His emailed photos were taken from about five hundred yards away, the only discernible features a crazy mop of dark hair and severe horn-rimmed glasses.

I was curious about him, but didn't feel I knew or had developed much of a rapport with him. He admitted in one email he could "*stay mute and prostrated for hours, not even noticing someone is sitting by my side . . . depends on my mood.*"

This might have made me nervous but for the fact that the date had been set up by my friend Muriel, a smart, exuberant

Frenchwoman living in London. I knew any friend of hers was going to be worth meeting.

It was a warm early summer's evening and the pavement cafés were already full of loquacious Parisians enjoying the sunshine and unhurriedly sipping glasses of red wine (the French were restrained enough to order wine by the glass—to the binge-drinking Brits, this felt about as logical as buying a house by the room).

I spotted Olivier as soon as I walked into the park, but skirted around a statue so I could check him out before he saw me. First impression: tall, slim without being skinny, but glasses and hair—as in the photos—the dominant features. Was an evening with Olivier going to be hard work? I took a deep breath and stepped out from behind the statue to introduce myself.

As he turned to greet me, I was shocked by something I had not prepared myself for.

He was cute.

Under that mop of dark-brown curly hair and the severe glasses, Olivier had gorgeous green eyes, clear, freckled skin, and a fine nose. I smiled instinctively. I'd been prepared for an interesting, possibly argumentative date; I was quick to revise my opinion and put my "flirt face" on.

"Hi, I'm Jennifer," I said unnecessarily (we'd both seen each other's photos), holding my hand out to shake his. Olivier's hand was warm and firm in mine.

A middle-aged man a few feet away waited patiently for his dog to finish adding yet more crap to the park. He whiled away the time watching us with a neutral expression. We were clearly on a blind date; maybe he was glad he was beyond all that. Maybe he was sad that on such a beautiful evening his only companion was a crapping dog.

I tended not to get too nervous about the dates (apart from Anders, of course), as I knew it was actually harder on the Dates than it was on me. Up until they met me, the Dates treated the occasion as a sort of community challenge, as they, their Date Wranglers, and gradually most of their friends became involved in designing the Perfect Date. My date-a-thon was like a street carnival where each Date and his group wanted to make and show off the best float.

My date-a-thon also revealed the competitiveness of men: They were so concerned with imagining what the other seventy-nine might have arranged and whether they could do better, they quite forgot that when the time came they'd be on their own dating a real live woman (me). As a result, during the first thirty minutes of the date, the guys tended to suffer from DRI (Dating Reality Impact) and all my energies were focused on getting them safely through the transition period until they felt normal enough to *be* normal.

However, because I hadn't expected Olivier to be good-looking—plus he was French, so he didn't care what I thought anyway—I was caught off guard and went straight into full-blown DRI myself. I launched into a manic account of how my mother and sister used to live in Paris and wasn't the weather great and wasn't Paris better than London because it was so much smaller and oh, I love the Marais, there are so many cute shops . . . I listened with horror as the anecdotes and opinions poured uncontrollably out of me at top speed. Olivier studied me with an amused expression, which was all he could do as my jabbering made it impossible for him to get a word in.

But suddenly, just as I'd launched into an excruciatingly su-perfluous story about bees, the wise words of the Love Professor floated—Obi-Wan Kenobi–esque—into my head: *Jennifer . . .*

*Jennifer . . . just let it happen. Use all your senses . . . take in what-
ever comes. . . ."*

And I stopped talking.

Olivier waited to see if I would start again. I didn't. So he
smiled and asked, "Would you like a drink?"

I nodded gratefully, and we left the park and began our date.

It was a wonderful evening. Olivier and I wandered along the
banks of the Seine, stopping for glasses of wine, dinner in a little
bistro, coffee in a café by now lit by moonlight, whiskey in a
crowded after-hours bar. . . . We walked and talked through the
romantic streets of the Marais; crossed the Seine to the touristy
twists and turns of the Latin Quarter and back again through the
crowded club-land of rue de Lappe and Bastille.

Olivier was every bit as challenging as I'd imagined and ten
times as interesting. He had lived and studied all over Europe and
was passionate about art and films. His personality was like a medieval city of switchback streets opening up into beautiful court-
yards: impenetrable and magical by turns. And as he opened up,
he became more tactile, touching my hand to make a point or
standing close behind me and reaching over my shoulder to show
me something fascinating and obscure about a building.

I had decided after Denmark that I was only going to stay out
late or agree to see the Date again if I felt he was a genuine
prospect. It was now after 3 a.m. and I still felt intrigued and utterly entertained by Olivier. I was also attracted to him and felt
comfortable enough with the pace at which things were progress-
ing to anticipate with pleasure the French Kiss that I was confident would come at the end of the date.

By 3:30 a.m., we were both completely talked out and I was
glad when Olivier offered to walk me back to my hotel. I'd had a

wonderful evening and felt really good about seeing him the next day if he asked. It was the perfect time to end the date.

Thirty minutes later, we stood together outside my hotel, our faces gently lit by the fading streetlights and the approaching dawn that now warmed the sky.

Olivier admitted, "I really did not know what to expect from this evening, Jennifer, but it has been extremely enjoyable. It is unlike me to talk of myself so much; you are charming and very good company." Studying me through his glasses, his eyes were dark and intent. He was about four inches taller than me, so when I told him how much I had enjoyed the evening, too, I had to tilt my face up toward his to answer, smiling warmly into his eyes.

I watched his mouth as he talked; I was going to get kissed and I was feeling really good about it.

"If you have time, I would very much like to see you again to-morrow," Olivier said.

"I would like that too," I replied simply.

Olivier smiled. "It is agreed then."

I relaxed. He smiled at me, I smiled at him. I waited happily; I was in no rush.

"Umm, okay, then I shall see you tomorrow," Olivier suddenly blurted, and with an awkward half-shrug he turned and walked off down the street.

Huh?

I watched in astonishment as my cheeky-guy fun vanished around the corner. What had just happened? Why hadn't he kissed me? I shook my head vigorously, as if trying to shake some sense into it. I didn't understand: Why hadn't he kissed me? We'd liked each other. He'd asked me out again. Why didn't he want to kiss me? Why?

I suddenly felt furious with him: How could he do this? I'd

stayed out most of the night with him and would now undoubt-edly spend the rest of the night wide awake, agonizing over why he hadn't wanted to kiss me. I mean, I knew he didn't have to, but I was really sure he'd wanted to. What terrible thing had I said or done that had made him change his mind? Could I isolate the thing which had made me an Unkissable?

One thing was certain: I had no intention of ever seeing him again. I know that sounds harsh, but I have absolutely served my time dating men who are hard work and take tons of understand-ing. I was here on my Soul Mate Mission, and that did not in-clude second dates with men who disturbed my self-confidence and peace of mind by treating me as an Unkissable.

I said all this over breakfast the next morning to my friends Jilly and Stevie, who were over from London for the weekend.

"Oh, Jen, that's not fair," Jilly remonstrated as we divided up the last buttery flakes of croissant, trying to catch the eye of the waitress so we could order some more. "He sounds lovely, you must see him again."

"Bugger that, why must I?" I protested indignantly. "The whole point of what I'm doing is to find someone who'll make me happy and not invest time in guys who *don't* anymore."

"Maybe he's a slow starter?" Stevie observed reasonably, while attempting unsuccessfully to flag down the waitress.

They were being sweet and lovely. I knew they wanted the best for me, to see me happy and with a boyfriend again. But if I was going to ignore my instincts and make excuses for someone from the first date, I might as well have saved myself all this effort and settled for the first ("you've got") male who came along. I knew from personal experience that to give him another chance was just courting trouble and disappointment.

"Stevie," I said firmly, licking the delicious pear confiture from my fingers and pouring out more coffee, "I really appreciate you saying that and maybe you're right, but it's not like I'm upset because he didn't propose to me. It's a kiss we're talking about here. It was a date, we liked each other. It shouldn't have been that difficult."

But none of us had had much sleep the night before and the task of getting the waitress to serve us turned into a major production. Soon the topic of whether I should see Olivier again or not was forgotten by everyone.

Except me. When my phone rang, I pushed it deeper into my handbag and nudged my bag under the table with my foot until the ringing stopped.

Date #13: Max—Paris, France

I would have dearly loved to have gone shopping that afternoon, or even to have popped back to the hotel for a quick nap, but I had a date in a few hours with Max, an old friend of Clare, one of my neighbors from home.

Max was a lecturer in art history at one of our neighborhood schools and Clare had been trying to orchestrate a meeting for months. He was spending the school break taking a school group around Paris, and when Clare heard I would be there the same week she nearly broke her fingers trying to dial his number and lock us into a date before I could come up with a reason why it wasn't possible.

It wasn't that I hated the thought of meeting Max; he just didn't particularly sound my type, a little too earnest and proper. But Clare was determined we should meet and I had run out of energy to keep persuading her otherwise.

Max had an afternoon off from the kids, so we had arranged to meet outside Varenne metro station at 2:30 p.m. He was easy to spot: around six feet five ("You can't say he's too short for you,"

Clare boasted triumphantly) and extremely thin with a long, pale, but boyishly eager face, crowned with an explosion of curly red hair. There was a Cambridge University scarf wrapped tightly around Max's neck (even though the temperature must have been about seventy degrees) and he was sniffing vigorously.

He beamed as soon as he saw me and stalked straight over. "Ah, Jennifer, what a pleasure, what an absolute pleasure to meet you." He smiled and sniffed, nervous and excited in equal measures. Towering over me like a huge praying mantis, he bent his upper body down to kiss me "hello." I wasn't prepared, he misjudged my height, and at the last minute I overcompensated and stretched up to meet his kiss.

It was an awkward mess: I got a mouthful of shirt as I ended up kissing his collar; he missed my head altogether, his mouth sucking the air two inches right of my cheek. He sniffed and laughed in embarrassment, but as he pulled his head self-consciously away, he caught one of my big silver hoop earrings in his hair and ripped it clean out.

I let out a high-pitched yelp of pain and surprise. Max frowned in alarm; he had no idea why I was shrieking, and he also had no idea that one of my earrings was dangling incongruously from his tight red curls.

Following my astonished stare, he gingerly reached into his hair and found my earring. He beamed in confusion, now sniffing furiously, like a beagle at customs angling for a promotion. "Ah, well, yes," he stammered, "I, ermm, well, but . . . this must be yours. . . ." Max pulled the earring from his hair and plummeted from his great height back down toward me. I realized with horror he intended to try to put it back in.

"No," I shrieked automatically, taking a sharp step backward, my hand clamped protectively over my throbbing ear. "I mean . . . please don't worry," I managed to say, slightly less dramatically. "I'll take it, it's fine." And I took the earring from between his long, outstretched fingers and dropped it out of sight into my handbag.

Words didn't exist to describe how much I was hating today. I mean really, really, really hating it. It wasn't really poor Max's fault, and it was important that I didn't make him feel it was. You can't blame someone for not being your type; it was myself I blamed for giving in to Clare—she had the married person's compulsion to match up singles, the way some tuck in a stranger's sticking-out shirt label on buses: The desire for neatness is greater than their sense of tact.

But this wasn't working. In fact, at that moment, it seemed the whole premise my Odyssey was based on wasn't working. Clearly, there were far more "wrongs" than Mr. Rights out there. And I was wrong about the ones I thought were "rights," as they all turned out to have something wrong with them in the end. Was I wasting my time? Should I be back in London, either trying harder or accepting my single life? Did this mission have any chance of success at all?

At school when I was about five, I picked up someone else's sweater by accident. One of the teachers noticed and asked me to give it back. Perversely, I insisted it was mine, and before anyone could take it away I tried to put it on. It belonged to a girl half my size, though, and the sweater got stuck over my head. Embarrassed at being caught out, enraged at not having pulled off the bluff, and very, very agitated at having my head trapped in someone else's sweater, I had the kind of whirling-dervish, feet-stamping, screaming-my-head-off meltdown that on a slower day would have made it into every single textbook ever written on behavioral difficulties.

The same kind of impotent rage was rising up dangerously in me now. I was trying on and getting stuck in ill-fitting Soul

Mates; I'd nearly lost an ear in this one. It was really starting to get on my nerves.

As I furiously debated these points in my head, outside in the real world I was still standing with one hand clamped to my ear, staring murderously at Max. His sniffing long stopped, he stood mute with anxiety and embarrassment. God, I was being a total bitch to poor Max.

"Max, I am being rude, I am so sorry," I apologized gently. "I'm just feeling a bit all over the place at the moment." My heart went out to him as he gave a wobbly smile, like a little kid whose ice cream just fell in the sand and was trying to be brave about it. He gave an exploratory sniff, as if testing the waters, then another. "Ah, please don't . . . that's to say . . . umm, well, then I really do hope you like sculpture, Jennifer," he said, gradually regaining confidence and enthusiasm. "Because I am going to take you to see one of my absolute favorites. It's at the Musée Rodin. I'm sure you'll know it." His face lit up happily. "It's called *The Kiss*."

I could have killed him.

Actually, it turned out to be a fascinating visit. Rodin's impressive eighteenth-century house now houses his work, and I enjoyed hearing Max talk about the artist as we walked around the museum and gorgeous landscaped grounds (where we bought equally gorgeous *glaces*).

Rodin sounded difficult as hell, and his muse and lover Camille Claudel spent the last thirty years of her life in an asylum as a result. There were too many tourists around *The Kiss* to get a good look at it, so instead Max and I inspected the clay working-model prototype next to it. Although the lovers were passionately entwined, their mouths were actually a good inch apart. The most famous kissers in the world did not actually kiss at all.

Maybe Olivier wasn't the only faux French Kisser. And no wonder poor Camille ended up bonkers.

Date #14: Nick, Skate Date—Paris, France

It was raining when I said good-bye to Max back at the metro, which was a shame as I needed good weather for my next encounter: the Skate Date.

Every Friday night in Paris, up to 28,000 people took part in the Pari Roller: three hours spent whizzing twenty-five kilometers round the closed-off streets on in-line skates. I'd made a program about it a couple of years earlier and thought the atmosphere was so incredible—retirees blowing whistles, kids zipping in and out between their parents' legs—I wanted to take part myself. I also thought this would make a perfect date.

I'd spent six weeks wobbling round Fountains Leisure Centre in west London, being shown not so much the ropes as the wheels by Citiskate, the people who organize something similar to the Paris event in London.

My class was just the nicest bunch of people, and—all as hopeless as each other—we quickly bonded as we encouraged each other to make it through the embarrassing, painful learning curve. A group of about twelve of us had vowed we'd all get good enough to do the Pari Roller together. And one of the group, Nick, had shyly asked if he could be my Skate Date, even though our conversations had rarely consisted of more than "Oohh, that had to hurt" or "Waaaatch ooooout" as one of us smacked into a wall or body-checked an oncoming skater.

Well, tonight was the night. I ran through a curtain of rain back to my hotel. I needed to quickly check my emails, then change and pick up my skating gear (kindly delivered and being taken back by Jilly and Stevie). As I dumped my bags on the bed, I noticed the voice mail light flashing. It was from Nick: "*Hey,*

Jennifer, hope you're doing okay. How f**d is this rain? I just spoke to Marianne and she said it's probably off tonight. We're meeting at Bastille anyway, see you there—and, hey, get your skates on or you'll be late!"

He never tired of that joke.

If tonight was canceled, it would be disappointing though no great surprise. Actually, it was probably a good thing: My skating skills were a triumph of enthusiasm over ability. Speed-skating the wet, cobbled, hilly streets would invariably result in me completing the rest of my dating tour on crutches.

I got stuck on the computer trying to finalize a soccer date in Barcelona and writing another pleading email to the Date Wranglers to help me out on the U.S. leg, which was proving to be a nightmare. When I rushed out of the metro at Bastille, wearing an old pair of jeans and clutching a bag with my skates, helmet, and padding, there were only a few skaters around. Clearly the efficient website had spread the word that the skate was off.

I couldn't see Nick but spotted Marianne from our class, with Anne, Russell, Lisa, and about five others. They were huddled under a café awning looking very wet. Marianne waved happily as she saw me sprinting over. "Jennifer, can you believe this bloody weather?" she shouted over the din of the rain. "All that work and now we won't get to skate." I smiled sympathetically: She was the best skater in the group and had been itching to do this since we started.

"So what's happening?" I asked, hugging her and the rest of the group. "Is Nick here yet?"

"Oh you just missed him." She shrugged. "He wasn't sure if you were coming so he went off with some of the others to some Irish pub." We both rolled our eyes: Irish pubs—the McDonald's of the new millennium.

I shrugged too. It was fine: no skate, no date. There was almost a logic to it. But just then, Nick and the rest of our group careened around the corner, running from canopy to canopy, yelling madly as they got increasingly drenched. Nick saw me with Marianne and came straight over, giving me a big hug. "Hey, Skater Dater, I thought you weren't coming."

I laughed as he flicked his wet coat at me. "Sorry, I got held up. Hey, I thought you guys had gone Oirish?"

"That we did," he replied. "But we thought we'd better come back for the rest of you Roller Rookies."

We all laughed at this, then trooped into the café and found tables at the back big enough to fit the whole group around and dump our gear under. Nick sat next to me, and for about twenty minutes we chatted about my date-a-thon and life in general. But soon the rest of the group joined in, and our gossiping, teasing, and storytelling was still going strong when closing time came hours later.

And not only was that fine—it was wonderful. I realized that, in a way, my date was with the whole group. Together we'd worked really hard to get to the point where we could attempt the Pari Roller. And okay, after all that work, here we were, unable to skate because of the weather, but we'd all made it this far, hadn't we? That was surely something worth celebrating.

Kicked out onto the street, we hugged and shouted our goodbyes. I felt comforted and rejuvenated by the camaraderie of the evening. Our joint failure had turned into something lovely and reassuring, which instinctively gave me courage and hope for my own journey. I realized I had to make the time to celebrate the little triumphs, taking pride in how far I had come, rather than getting bogged down in one or two bad days and dates, believing they set the tone for the rest of my life.

chapter six

The Rest of Europe

Date #22—"Oh Romeo, Romeo . . ." Verona, Italy

Dates #15–27: Barcelona, Lisbon, Athens, Verona, Siena, Berlin

When I say the next thirteen dates were whirlwind romances, I'm talking about the traveling rather than the quality of the dates. I hurtled in and out of capitals so fast, I barely had time to open my bags before I was off again.

Back when Phileas Fogg embraced the challenge of traveling around the world in eighty days, Heathrow meant *man bowling*. But now traveling is so cheap and easy (we ask when rather than how), I went online and booked the short flights between Paris, Barcelona, Lisbon, Athens, Verona, and Berlin without giving it a second thought.

Maybe *thinking* was something I was trying to avoid?

Paris had taught me an important lesson: I needed to be less melodramatic. Date & Go, Date & Go; stick to the schedule, stay focused. If I was to survive all eighty of these dates without my self-esteem crashing and burning altogether, I had to establish some boundaries. I needed to find a cutoff point for the amount of time and energy I invested in each of the dates, so I wasn't continually churned up about something someone had/hadn't done/said. I couldn't take it all so personally.

I've never been the best at keeping things in perspective, but it was imperative I learned to do it now. I don't mean being cold and unfeeling (I really did want to find my Soul Mate on this journey, not just meet my quota of dates); I just needed to be more sensible. These were dates, social engagements; I had to stop being oversensitive and stick to logistics.

It was only when I paid some long overdue attention to logistics, however, that I discovered logistics were having a few problems of their own.

I was so busy dating, traveling, and—in any spare moments—arranging the next lot of dating and traveling, I'd forgotten to build in any downtime. I was becoming tired and disoriented. I'd wake up in the middle of the night needing to pee, but could only start looking for the bathroom once I'd remembered which date I'd just had/was about to have, therefore which country, city, and then hotel I was in.

I was also having to buy knickers and T-shirts since all my clothes were dirty and there was no time to do laundry. I knew I should make the time, but I also had to apply for my Chinese visa, check the trains between Verona and Florence, plus see if that cheap hotel in L.A. had any rooms available.

And every single day was a new day for potential future dates, making initial chitchat contact to test the dating waters. I wanted to email back, *"For chrissakes, you're one of eighty: Date me or don't, I don't have the time to talk you into it,"* but I knew I couldn't.

It felt like there wasn't a minute to lose; taking time off to do laundry just seemed impossible.

And then there was the issue of personal grooming.

My decision to travel with the sun made for a waxing dilemma. The hair on my legs was long enough to be noticeable but not really long enough to be waxed. Should I boil to death in trousers or stick to dinner dates so I could hide my legs under the table?

The same applied to my bikini line. Could I bear to leave it, as I normally did, until I got Koala Ears—when it appears there's a koala down the front of your knickers with the ears sticking out the sides—but then risk literally being caught *out* on an unannounced bikini date?

These might sound like small considerations, but they were what preoccupied my thoughts as I crashed into furniture looking for the bathroom in the wee small hours.

I raced from date to date, country to country.

Steve (Date #15) in Barcelona was a friend of Hillary's from university. We had a date to watch soccer in a bar: England versus one of the Spanish teams. I love watching the big championships and thought I knew enough about soccer to hold my own. Steve soon put me straight. "Are England in the white strip?" I asked just after kickoff. Mortified, he spun around to see if anyone had heard, before hissing, "Keep your voice down."

I was just another girl who thought that because she could name three players from Man U, she knew soccer. England lost; the date didn't go into extra time.

Ray (Date #16) I vaguely knew through my friend Theresa. For years he'd been a financial broker in the city before burning out and giving it all up to move to Barcelona. Like me, he'd invested all his energy in his job and taken radical steps to find a more healthy balance. I wondered if it had worked for him and if he felt he'd made the right decision.

Theresa had omitted to mention Ray now worked as a street mime on La Rambla. When he arrived at the tapas bar, he was still dressed for work: silver catsuit and body paint. Apparently he was in the middle of a turf war with his rival, the Clockwork Bronze Man, and couldn't stay long.

I don't think I'm exaggerating when I say we were the subject of a fair amount of attention. I was mortified. Ray was silent—an admirable quality in a mime, less so in a Date.

I caught the first flight to Lisbon the following morning.

Paolo (Date #17) and **José (Date #18)** were friends of Jane, a South African woman I'd met traveling through Europe years ago. I knew Paolo played flamenco guitar and was taking me to the famous Pastéis de Belém café for *pastéis de nata*.

We drank intense, bitter espressos to balance the rich pastéis, crisp buttery cups of flaky pastry filled with creamy custard, dusted with powdered sugar, made to a closely guarded secret recipe. Paolo was chatty and funny, but there was no spark.

It made me feel good to dance off some calories, clubbing with José in the trendy Bairro Alto district. He was extremely charming and his friends were lovely, but my "dancing till dawn every weekend" days were behind me. José was fun but not The One.

I went straight from the club to the hotel, to pick up my bags, then on to the airport for Athens.

Drakoulis (Date #19) was the cousin of Effie, a Greek friend of mine from the gym. Maybe I could have coped with his heavy smoking—it was Europe, after all. But when we went to dinner, *everyone* in the restaurant smoked constantly and I struggled.

I'm not being fussy but it was disgusting. The air in the restaurant was heavy with thick, painfully acrid smoke. It was like having dinner in a burning furniture warehouse. Drakoulis took me on to a fantastic Rembetika club (a type of traditional Greek gangsta folk music), but my head throbbed and my eyes stung. I felt guilty leaving during the players' first break, but I had set and reached my limit.

Effie had also set me up with an AE (Amicable Ex). **Joseph (Date #20)** was a tour guide, and since his first group arrived at 10 a.m., we'd arranged to meet at the fish market for an 8 a.m. breakfast date. If it worked out and he didn't mind, I thought I might go on the tour with him afterward.

But I'd had five hours' sleep in two days and woke with a start at 8:30 a.m. I repeatedly called his cell as I scrambled to dress and get to the market on the off-chance he was still there. But his phone rang unanswered and there was no sign of him at the market.

Forget it: He'd probably drive you as crazy as he drove me, Effie replied breezily to my apologetic email. *Though it would have been interesting to hear why he split up with Claudia.*

Damn her: Joseph obviously wasn't an AE at all. He was a UE (Unresolved Ex) and Effie was using me to get an update. As I left for Italy, I silently congratulated myself on avoiding what sounded like unfinished business.

Verona was the home of Romeo and Juliet, arguably the world's most famous lovers. Some might argue that a couple whose poor communication skills resulted in joint suicide were perhaps not the best relationship role models. But up to 5,000 people a year saw it differently, writing to Juliet's house and tomb, asking for her advice about their own love lives.

Local poets and writers had been responding to the letters since the 1930s, but in 1975 Verona intellectual Giulio Tamassia founded the Juliet Club and arranged for ten unpaid, multilingual "secretaries" to answer the letters. In addition, he established the Dear Juliet Award, which is presented to the most romantic letter writer each year.

I'd been emailing Eleanor, the secretary responsible for Italian, Spanish, and English correspondence. With the explosion of the Internet and online dating, I wondered, were people increasingly emailing Shakespeare's heroine?

Now, we do receive some emails, but mainly letters; writing by hand is more intimate, especially if you talk about love, feelings, and emotions. . . . We answer all the letters, by hand.

Eleanor had been a huge help, arranging not only for me to meet this year's Dear Juliet winner but also for me to stand on Juliet's balcony and date "Romeo."

Whatever the outcome, I reasoned, it would be interesting to see what dating two of Italy's most romantic men was like. As terrible as it sounds, I suspected I would find dating an intensely romantic man a bit claustrophobic and annoying; all that fetching and carrying and fussing around would get on my nerves. Either that or I'd assume they'd done something really bad and were overcompensating.

I know, why I'm still single is a mystery to me, too.

$\cdot$ $\cdot$ $\cdot$

This year's Dear Juliet winner was Davide, a Verona man in his thirties. As we waited for him at the Juliet Club offices, we watched a group of women chatting amiably around a huge table, sorting hundreds of letters into different piles. Eleanor told me it was easy to spot which country a letter was from: "French people are very passionate, very romantic. Italians and Spanish like flowery phrases; like South Americans, they are verbose, using a lot of words to say just one thing."

I wondered if it was mainly the Latin countries that asked for advice about their love lives. Was there some truth in that stereotypical hot-blooded image?

"No, no." Eleanor shook her head vigorously. "We get letters from China, Japan, Russia . . . all over. Latin people tend to be extremely forthcoming about their feelings. Americans are the other extreme: They'll write just a five-line letter saying, 'She's blond, I like her, what should I do?' It's very frustrating. I want to tell them, 'Say a little more: Do you know her, does she like someone else?' It's difficult to give advice when you know so little."

British people are resigned to scoring badly in any kind of international personality contest, but I went ahead and asked Eleanor what the British were like. She thought for a moment before answering carefully: "Reserved at first, but then—since they are writing—they become very deep and introspective. It takes them a while to open up, but when they do it is heartfelt."

Apparently, some think that Juliet is a saint or goddess of love: "People often don't go into that much detail because they think Juliet already knows their problem. And if their problem is resolved, people come and thank Juliet for her help. An Italian lady left a message at Juliet's tomb last month saying she had come three years ago single and here she was now, with her new husband. She saw this as a miracle and wanted to thank Juliet for helping her find love."

Italy is reputedly one of the most romantic countries in the world, yet even here finding a decent boyfriend is considered a miracle. That didn't sound good.

Then **Davide (Date #21)** arrived. Just under six feet tall with short dark hair, he had large, soft brown eyes, like huge chocolate cookies ready to be dunked. Davide didn't speak English, so Eleanor was going to translate for us.

I hadn't had a chance to read Davide's letter; I wondered what had made it more romantic than any other that year.

(All translated by Eleanor.)

Davide: "It is not easy to tell people my story, so it took effort to write to Juliet. I had to be sure I was writing to someone who would understand. It started eleven years ago at a moment in my life when I was very alone and sad.

"I was walking through a cemetery and noticed a tomb full of dust that no one had taken care of for many years. I started cleaning it, and as I cleaned I uncovered a picture of a young woman on the grave. I saw by the inscription that she had died in 1927 when she was twenty-three, my age at the time I found the tomb.

"I have always believed in another life, but, as I cleaned, I had a strange and powerful feeling that Elena—the young woman in the grave—was calling me to take care of her.

"So I did.

"And, little by little, in addition to the sense of compassion that compelled me to look after her grave, over the years another feeling for her developed: one of true love."

Davide stopped talking and looked at me shyly. I realized that the entire time he had been telling his story, I had been holding my breath. I inhaled sharply and blinked hard. I couldn't believe what he was telling me, but I knew I had to say something or he'd close up.

"So you fell in love with Elena after you stumbled across her grave?" I clarified in a neutral tone. "Why were you in the grave-yard in the first place?"

Davide explained he was there because he was in love with a real girl who sold flowers outside the cemetery. The feeling wasn't reciprocated, he admitted with a gentle shrug.

As Davide and Eleanor talked, I quickly read a translation of Davide's letter for the first time. When they finished talking, I showed Davide the translation. "In your letter—which is really beautiful—you say: 'Her angelic face was covered in years of dust. I was moved and saddened by her image so I cleaned up her grave and bought some flowers.' "

Had he ever bought flowers for Elena's grave from the flower seller as an excuse to talk to her? He said at first yes, but as he fell in love with Elena he'd forgotten all about the flower seller and stopped buying from her.

I asked how much he knew about Elena's background. Davide explained he'd visited the records office in City Hall and read up on her family, initially with the intention of contacting them to let them know how neglected the grave was. He found she'd been born on the same street as Juliet in the center of Verona. Her father was a trader; she had two brothers and one sister. All were dead now.

As Davide explained, I watched him closely. For the last eleven years he'd been in love with a girl who'd been dead for nearly eighty. Did that make him mad? He looked normal and sweet, but was this the sign of a lonely man or something more sinister?

But as easy as it would have been to dismiss his feelings out of hand and ridicule his situation, I didn't want to do that. It felt very important that I kept an open mind about what he was telling me. What if he really did love her? And what if loving her didn't make him mad or deluded but actually incredibly brave to recognize and honor his feelings?

Rather than making assumptions and judging him, I wanted to hear what he had to say. I asked what his friends and family thought of the situation. Also, "when you go to parties and people are there with their partners, don't you wish you had someone with you?"

Davide shook his head. "Although my family knows, I don't tell my friends as most wouldn't understand. I just say, 'I'm alone, maybe I will find someone one day.' And anyway, when I go to parties, I don't mind that nobody 'real' is there. I am quite happy."

I asked what it was about Elena that made him happy. Davide considered the question for a moment, then said: "I feel a deep sense of joy and peace. Even though she can't speak, she communicates with me. I feel her presence; otherwise this wouldn't have gone on for so many years."

He paused, then said simply, "I believe we all have a Soul Mate—just one—either in this life or the next. Sooner or later you meet: This is how I feel about Elena."

I was moved by Davide's devotion, though I didn't agree with his Soul Mate theory. As I see it, when you are young, you go through a lot of fast-changing stages. As you get older, the stages change more slowly and you are in each for a progressively longer time. I believe there is a Soul Mate for each stage. If you are lucky, you find them. If you are luckier still, their stages coincide with yours and you stay and grow together. I suppose that's why I can be positive and believe there is a Soul Mate out there for me.

With luck, I will find him.

But what if you believed there was only ever going to be one Soul Mate for you, and you found them after they'd died? How incredibly strong or lonely would you have to be to be true to them anyway? Would you live like Davide and be true to your Soul Mate—no matter how hard—or would you just give up and settle for the easier option of a living mate?

I asked Davide how he knew she was The One.

Davide told me that, although he felt connected from the moment he first saw the grave, it was only little by little over the years that he realized how deeply involved he was with her. "She leads me," he said simply. "She gives me signs."

"What kinds of signs?" I asked.

"Like encouraging me to write to Juliet," he said. "I am convinced she wanted me to tell the world about us. I wrote to Juliet about our relationship and the letter was awarded the prize. After the letter was published, a lot of my friends and colleagues saw it and congratulated me. I had done the right thing."

I asked if he found loving Elena easy.

"No," Davide replied gravely. "You must feel ready, otherwise it is impossible to live this life. But, if you have been lonely and suffered with that loneliness, you find love where you thought you never would."

I didn't want to judge Davide or patronize him with my pity, but it sounded a hard life and I did feel sorry for him. I thought back to the Love Professor observing that when you've been single for a long time, after a while anything will do. I asked Davide if—having experienced such a deep love with Elena—he thought the experience would make him more receptive to loving someone living.

He shrugged; possibly, but that person would have to accept his huge love for Elena, otherwise it would not work. Part of his heart would always be devoted to Elena.

One of the things I loved about being in a relationship was

coming home and relaxing together, chatting about our days, having someone to share moments and thoughts with. How did Davide and Elena's relationship work on a daily basis?

Davide explained that he led a normal life; he took fresh flowers to the grave often but not every day. Either way, he always felt connected and close to her. "I've always been very reserved, I don't have many friends. Every time I feel sad or down, I turn to her and she gives me comfort and love."

I suddenly noticed a ring on Davide's left hand. "Oh, is that a wedding ring?" The question just popped out.

Davide smiled proudly and touched it gently with the fingers on his right hand. "Yes, with her name inside."

I wasn't prepared for this and was deeply shocked. An involuntary groan escaped before I could stop it. I tried to turn it into a more appreciative noise: "Ooooh, did you have one made for her, too?"

Davide nodded and explained that in Italy, after a certain period of time has elapsed, it's legal for people to dig up family coffins and rebury the remains inside a smaller casket. Davide had dug up and reburied Elena last year. Inside the new casket, alongside her remains, he had placed his wedding ring to her, his name engraved inside.

"Right . . ." It took me a moment to collect my thoughts. "So, when you put the ring in with Elena's remains, was that your wedding as well as her reburial?"

"Yes," he confirmed. "By then our relationship had been going for ten years. I was sure of how I felt and wanted to give her a sign of my love, a symbol."

"Davide, did you invite anybody else along to the wedding or was it just the pair of you?" I asked evenly.

"My mother came. She knows all about Elena and is fond of her."

Davide went on to explain that his mother was at first extremely uncomfortable about the situation with Elena, but "when she saw how happy Elena made me, she accepted and grew to care for her, too." Initially after the reburial, they felt bad "for disturbing her sleep," but now they were happy: She was no longer neglected and was being taken proper care of.

As Eleanor translated, Davide reached into his pocket, took out his wallet, and tenderly removed a small black and white photograph. It was Elena. He looked at the picture fondly, before holding it out proudly for me to inspect. It was a copy of the original photograph on her gravestone. A young girl stared shyly out. She looked polite and neat, her hair bobbed short, her face heart-shaped and pretty.

I felt incredibly moved that Davide was showing me the picture, but also unbelievably awkward. I knew I needed to say something complimentary about it, but, honestly, it felt more like I was being shown an old family photograph of someone's grandmother than the "wallet shot" of someone's wife.

"She looks very fun-loving and open," I said after the briefest pause. Were people "fun-loving" back in 1927? I didn't want to say the wrong thing and offend Davide, but he seemed fine, obviously happy to be able to include her in the conversation: "Her sweet eyes look beyond time and life; I fell in love with her look."

"She looks lovely, thank you," I said, handing back the photo. I caught sight of my watch: It was time to go.

"What are your plans for the future?" I asked, as we all got to our feet. Davide said he just hoped for a good life, to find a good job.

"But if you are asking about my heart, I am happy now, fulfilled. And even though people don't understand and even if I meet someone else, Elena will always be a great part of my life. I feel happy with that."

So I wished Davide and Elena luck and we all said good-bye. Eleanor drove me back to my hotel. Lost in our own thoughts, neither of us spoke much.

In the alleys off Via Cappello, in the shadow of Juliet Capulet's house, pairs of Italian teenagers fall in love. Heads close, they talk and laugh quietly, locked in a private world of mutual desire, delighting in each other's company. Randomly, conversation gives way to urgent kissing, moped helmet dangling from one hand, cell phone from the other.

Out on the main street, cumbersome knots of American and Japanese tourists mill by, oblivious to the teenagers. They are making their way to the structure symbolizing the only kind of Italian teen-love that interests and moves them: Juliet's balcony.

In Verona everyone seemed wrapped up in their own desire. In a city famous for lovers who would rather die than compromise their feelings, maybe this was appropriate. Davide's story had saddened and perplexed me, though: Even if he was happy, I felt troubled for him.

Unable to distract myself by shopping (all the clothes were either too small, too expensive, or too white), I felt preoccupied and restless. I didn't want time on my hands with three gelaterias right outside my hotel (BRITISH TOURIST DEAD FROM FREAK ICE-CREAM OVERDOSE), so I rang Eleanor and we went out and got really drunk instead. It was great.

There was a courtyard around Juliet's beautiful fourteenth-century house. Over the years, the courtyard walls had accumulated such a collection of graffiti that people now wrote their love poems on wads of chewing gum that coated every inch of wall, like rubbery, multicolored tiles.

Under the balcony was a bronze statue of Juliet. Folklore had declared it lucky (though possibly not for her) to touch Juliet's right breast. The statue of the fourteen-year-old girl—breast corroded a pale orange by the acid sweat of a million would-be Romeos—looked on stoically, as a hundred stamping and baying tourists took turns being photographed groping her. Like the audience of *Blind Date* transported back in time, with each squeeze the crowd roared its approval.

I watched with a huge hangover, knowing that in about ten minutes, I was going to have to put on a velvet gown and dress up as Juliet.

Despite my misgivings, Eleanor took me into the house and persuaded me to go into the utility closet and change into the dress. It was a heavy red velvet floor-length outfit, laced up the front, cinched round the waist with a jeweled belt, and topped off with a red spongy headdress.

As I emerged, the crowd spotted me immediately. They poured in from the courtyard, pushing inside to get a better look, roaring replaced by quiet, rapt expectation. *The first person who tries to rub my breast will quickly discover they are anything but lucky,* I thought grimly.

Actually, as the dress trailed across the floor, I felt my spirits (and hangover) lift. I immediately understood the attraction of dressing like this, so voluminous and red that I could have spent my whole life living off croissants, gelati, and pizza, and nobody would have been any the wiser.

Then "Romeo" **(Date #22)** arrived. Sporting a deep-red velvet tunic, green tights, and a codpiece that made me instinctively avert my eyes, he was a hyperactive mid-thirties Italian called Solimano. He looked vaguely consumptive and a foot too short but had a mischievous smile. Solimano marched across the courtyard into the hallway and through the parting crowd, like Moses on a mission. Stopping directly in front of me, Solimano sank down onto one knee, snatched my hand, and kissed it passionately.

To my astonishment and the delight of the crowd, he declared: "I am here, your Romeo. Now we will be together forever." He finished with a flourish, then, jumping to his feet, vaulted out the window, onto the balcony. "Come now, my Juliet," he commanded. "Come to the balcony, so I may speak of my love for you."

"Oh, sweet Jesus," I sighed. My head was starting to throb again; the spongy headdress was itching uncomfortably. Back out in the courtyard, however, the remaining crowd had no such misgivings. Hands paused mid-gumming and groping, they let out a collective sigh. This was the romance they had come for. The floor show had begun.

Fortunately, Eleanor took one look at my face and pushed through the crowd to where Solimano was now waiting expectantly beneath the balcony. "Come along, Romeo," she said briskly. "Jennifer knows that bit of the story already. Let's find somewhere more private for your date."

Solimano looked dejected but trailed obediently after her. The crowd followed with their eyes, mutinously disappointed, like children told they could not throw their pet from the window to see if it could fly.

Eleanor found us a couple of thrones on the first floor and the date began.

Solimano was fun, sensitive without taking himself too seriously. We chatted about life on the road. He traveled all over Italy performing, but always played Romeo when he was home.

"Don't you ever get bored of it?" I asked. Unexpectedly, a look of guilt and frustration stole across his face. Solimano quickly looked away to compose himself, then turned back. "I love

Romeo," he protested, "but the problem is that he is young and his emotions are not . . ." He waved his hand around, searching for the word. ". . . developed." He leaned forward and lowered his voice in a conspiratorial manner. "I am not telling anyone this yet, but I am thinking maybe now I am more interested in Mercutio."

He looked deep into my eyes, watching my reaction to his confession for signs of . . . I have no idea what. Outrage? Ridicule? He was clearly going through a bit of a character crisis and my question had unwittingly opened the floodgates.

Actually, most of my Romeos seemed to be at a crossroads, going through something (hey, who wasn't?), but it never occurred to me that even *the* Romeo would be.

Fresh from my intense meeting with Davide, I knew how to keep a poker face. I also knew a reaction was expected. "So, why Mercutio?" I asked conversationally.

Solimano looked troubled; then, leaning in close again, pausing to assemble the words before speaking, he answered: "Mercutio is—how you say?—the central pillar of the play."

All around us, cameras flashed incessantly as groups of tourists stood inches away posing for photos with us. I slapped away hands that tentatively snaked over my shoulder (this was the first date where I was actually more concerned about being groped by the passersby than by the Date). Of course, the crowd had no way of knowing that they were not witnessing perfect love in action. Juliet was halfway through a rejection—Romeo didn't want to be with her; in fact, he didn't even want to be with himself.

But Solimano was unaware of or immune to the crowd, and he continued to unburden himself: "You see, at first it is a play about life. But then Mercutio dies and it becomes a dark, brooding play about death." Solimano sat up straight, his speech gathering momentum and intensity. "Mercutio is the play's turning point; he is so strong, he can change the play from day to night, light to dark. . . ." Solimano spoke with a feverish passion; he clenched his hands and arched his body in the chair. ". . . He is the most powerful person in *Romeo and Juliet* and I want to be him. I am sick of love, I want power. I have had enough of being Romeo. I want to be Mercutio."

Reaching the climax of his speech, Solimano cried out this final pronouncement. He paused, suspended in the intensity of his realized feelings. Then a huge smile lit up his face and he collapsed back in his chair, sighing deeply, all tension gone from his body.

But I was busy having a revelation of my own: I'd come all this way only to be proven superfluous. Romeo was cutting Juliet out of the deal altogether and going straight to the afterlife on his own, as Mercutio. Love was passé; Death was in.

No wonder Davide had won the bloody Juliet prize, I thought bitterly. When it came to the most intense relationship, it seemed nobody beat Death.

"Thank you, Jennifer," Solimano breathed. "I have never told a soul this and now I have told you. You were sent to me: I know now what I must do. No more Romeo, I am to be Mercutio."

The cameras continued to flash and Solimano leaned back, spent and content with his revelation. I sat with my mouth slightly open, trying to work out what the hell had just happened.

I said good-bye to Eleanor (without whom I very much doubt I would have got out of Juliet's house alive) and embarked on a long cross-country train journey via Bologna to Florence. After two hours by bus through the soft green hills and vineyards of Tuscany, I arrived in Siena.

I had a date with **Umberto (Date #23).** He ran the traffic dating website www.motoristmail.com. I knew from our emails that the idea had come out of Umberto's frustration at being cut off in traffic:

```
One night while I was driving inside a tunnel a
fast car cut me off, and I couldn't contact it (to
tell him "how smart you are"), so I thought what a
beautiful idea if I could write to its license
plate numbers by an Internet site.
```

But Umberto was a businessman and he soon realized his website could be put to better use as one of the *labor-saving devices* for busy single people. It was now a dating website custom-built for Italians who spent most of their lives stuck in their cars in traffic. Rather than registering the license plates of bad drivers on the website, it now allowed you to register your own license plate if you were single and looking to meet someone. So if you saw someone you fancied in a traffic jam but couldn't get to talk to them from your car, you just went to Umberto's website and, if their details were registered, emailed and asked them out on a date.

The idea had caught on, and Umberto's site now got six thousand posts a day.

This and all Umberto's other businesses kept him so incredibly busy, however, that he could only spare the time to date me over lunch. So we met at a teeny pizzeria and chatted at a table outside in the bright Tuscan sunshine. I was fascinated to hear about the site and really liked Umberto, who was shy but charming. But he seemed a total workaholic. I was sad for him but not surprised to hear he didn't have a girlfriend. "I'll get one when I have more time and lots of money," he said matter-of-factly before having to rush back to work.

. . .

After our pizza date, I caught the train to Pisa and flew to Berlin. As the plane taxied for takeoff, I took one last look out the window at Italy. Another country done. It had been fascinating and I had met some lovely people, but I was now more than twenty dates into my journey—a quarter of my potential The Ones met—and I was still no closer to finding my Soul Mate. Was I doing something wrong, or was it simply that I hadn't yet achieved the critical mass that statistically contained my new man? What were my Soul Mate odds: one in how many?

How many more before I met him? Was I close? What more could I do to speed up the process, or be confident I was even on the right path? If I held my breath until we took off, if the man next to me finished his chapter before the captain said we could undo our seat belts, would I meet my Soul Mate in Germany? Was our meeting a matter of such superstition or random luck?

Did I have to work harder at finding my Soul Mate, or did I have to work harder at trusting Fate? I wasn't exactly losing hope, but it was a surprise that so many people had yielded—and I don't mean this in an unkind way—so little. And in the meantime, I seemed to be loading up my romantic mystery tour bus with a huge number of people who all quite understandably expected my energy and attention. Was I in danger of becoming so busy picking up passengers that, when the time came, there wouldn't be room for the one person I wanted on board?

This was a very real possibility.

Although Berlin had regained its status as capital of Germany, most airlines had yet to build this into their schedules and fly direct. As a result, although travelers might just make the tight connections, their bags generally weren't so lucky, and lost luggage had become the norm.

Sure enough, I got to Berlin but my bags didn't. And I'd made the mistake of agreeing to meet **Ede (Date #24)** in Arrivals. Even on a normal day, I like to arrive at my own pace. Today, with makeup and dating clothes in my lost bags, I felt particularly unprepared.

Ede was waiting with a single yellow rose (which, unlike Willem in Holland, he gave me straight away) and didn't seem at all troubled by the fact that we couldn't leave until I had reported my bags missing. There was a huge line at the lost luggage office, so we went for a coffee.

It was to be my first—and, I hoped, last—airport date.

I sneaked a look at him as we queued: mid-thirties, tall and slim, with long legs and a slightly mysterious air. He was nice and easy to talk to, but I struggled to concentrate on the conversation; all I could think about was my bags and if I'd ever see them again.

Four hours later, we finally made it to the front of the line. The clerk assured me that my bags would be delivered to my hotel by 5 p.m., although "there may be a delay as all streets are being closed for the Love Parade."

I knew all about the Love Parade. It was the reason I was here.

Since 1989, Berlin's Love Parade has been the world's biggest techno street party. It might take two to tango, but it took up to two million to techno, as big-name DJs on flamboyant carnival floats pumped up the volume in Tiergarten Park, surrounded by huge crowds of ravers. I wanted to see if I would be lucky in Love in Berlin.

Ede was lovely but he didn't have my attention. It was no one's fault. I liked him and in a different situation we might have clicked, but not this time. I felt bad when he dropped me at my hotel: I halfheartedly said maybe I could see him later but secretly hoped he wouldn't be too disappointed when I didn't get back in touch.

I was staying in Prenzlauer Berg. Part of old East Berlin—one of the few areas to resist Hitler's rise to power—this was where the radicals, intellectuals, and students lived. It felt like a place only you know about, and it was fascinating to stumble across quirky galleries, stark buildings with beautiful features, plus loads of funky bars and cafés.

I was staying here, but apparently my bags weren't; there was still no sign of them.

I went out to see an art installation in the cavernous and scary basement of a water tower up the road. When I came back, there was still no sign of my bags. I went for a long walk round the Berg, poked round shops, found a great bar, and settled down with my book until 11 p.m. The bags were still not at the hotel when I returned. "Maybe midnight, maybe tomorrow?" the receptionist answered without looking up from his paper.

I knew there was no point in getting angry: It would just give me a headache and the Tylenol was in my lost bags.

I came down to reception the next morning. "Any sign of my bags?" I asked in a monotone.

"No, we have no idea where they are," the receptionist replied cheerfully.

Sometimes I think there is nowhere more foreign than Europe.

I went back to my room, drank some coffee, turned my knickers inside out, then set off in two-day-old clothes and no makeup to join some of the most beautiful people in the world dancing for joy.

It was a shame I wasn't at my best, as I had quite a tricky dating day ahead of me. I was to go to the parade with **Paul (Date #25),** a raver I'd met via one of the Love Parade websites, then date **DJ Frank from Holland (Date #26)** on his float, then **Franz-Philipp (Date #27)** on his float. I knew from my BBC Radio 1 days how incredibly resistant club people are to being nailed down; any arrangement was going to be fluid.

At school, I was always very sporty. Love Parade gave me an insight into how it must feel when no one wants you on their team.

I made myself up in a department store using the testers on the cosmetics counter. I then met Paul, who was very young and completely hyper on E. Ten minutes into the date, he scaled a lamppost and that was the last I saw of him (I was wearing a skirt and two-day-old knickers; I wouldn't have joined him even if I'd been able to). DJ Frank's float had been detained at the Dutch border, and the bouncers on Franz-Philipp's float took one look at my appearance and refused to even pass on a message saying I'd arrived.

And the whole time, a psychiatrist called Wolfgang followed me around asking me out for a drink. I was worried that since I'd had a couple of no-show dates, Fate might think I wasn't living up to my side of the deal to date eighty men. So to appease the Numbers God, I went for a coffee with Wolfgang. Apparently he had just moved from Brussels and didn't know anyone. He'd come to the Love Parade because "I'm at a crossroads and I thought I might meet someone here."

I felt a bit sorry for him but also worried that, in his own way, maybe he felt just as sorry for me. Did I also appear an unconnected outsider, randomly jumping into the slipstream of other people's fun, hoping to be swept up and carried along with them?

I'd given it my best shot, but every fiber in my body told me that as hard as I tried, I was not going to find my Soul Mate hanging with the ravers at the Love Parade. I'd tried it, it hadn't worked. It was time to go home and regroup my energies and those of my Date Wranglers for the next stage of my journey: America.

Oiled and toned in leather bikinis, plastic dresses, and pink fur boots, ravers blew their whistles and savored the narcissistic tang of dancing and being watched dancing. I let the crowd push past me as I forced a path through the oncoming tide of revelers, back to the station and my hotel. "Oh, Ms. Cox, good news: Your bags have arrived," the receptionist announced, beaming at me as I walked into the lobby.

"That's lovely," I responded with an empty smile. "I'd like to check out, please."

I flew back to London. As I walked through passport control at Heathrow, one of the officers asked where the flight had just come in from.

"Denmark," I replied blankly.

The man behind me laughed.

"You're a bit lost, love—it wasn't Denmark, it was Germany. Sounds like you don't know where you're going."

Everyone laughed, except me. I was just too tired. Too tired to laugh, too tired to talk, too tired to explain why I had no idea where I was. He was right, though: I had no idea where I was going, I was just plowing ahead blindly. And when I thought of how much more traveling was still ahead of me, I wondered if it was really worth carrying on.

chapter seven

London

Catching up with my sis's kids, Isaac and Tabitha

But I felt better as soon as I got home; it was the perfect tonic at just the right time. To be able to shut the front door and feel the stillness and silence slowly soak into my bones, like milk gently coloring black coffee caramel, drop by drop.

Until I had to leave for the U.S. two weeks from now, my time was my own: no dates, no traveling. It felt like an impossible luxury. And in the meantime, I could see my friends, sleep in my beloved bed, pick any outfit from my entire wardrobe, and do all the things I'd missed so much about my daily life in London. I was off-duty and I was going to relax.

Except I couldn't.

My brutal Date & Go, Date & Go schedule had become ingrained and there was still so much to be organized before

I'd be ready to leave again. I was completely incapable of switching off.

Plus there was the backlog of London dating traffic that had been accumulating in the time I'd been traveling through Europe. I haven't really mentioned this before, but despite deciding to travel in search of my Soul Mate because London seemed such a dating desert, for some reason I couldn't bring myself to give up on my home city altogether. I'd been in low-impact email contact with about six or seven people from London (and about six or seven hundred everywhere else in the world) while I'd been away. Nothing serious, just gentle *seeing if we get on* chat.

I'd vaguely agreed to meet the friend of a friend and replied to a few people from a dating website I was on; plus I'd been asked out on a couple of regular dates just before I left on the first leg of my trip.

I'd been completely honest with everyone and explained the reason for being away. There was an unspoken agreement that if I was still available when I got back to London, we'd meet up. Inadvertently, I'd committed myself to a significant amount of home dating.

And now I was back, feeling frazzled and a bit dated-out.

```
hi there are you back? I was just wondering if
you were around to meet up for a quick coffee?
Patrick

It would be lovely to see you, either in Greenwich
or the West End if you are free/in this country!
Love, James

I can't remember when you said you'd be back?
Give us a call—can't wait to meet up. Cheers,
Chris
```

Karl was a Swiss man I'd found on an Italian dating website, when I was looking into dating in Rome. As it turned out, he now lived in Egypt, but we'd stayed in regular contact, partially because there was no reason not to go to Egypt for a date (even at this point my route wasn't confirmed) and also because we were both working away from home and had struck up a rapport via email.

But suddenly, Karl was coming to London:

```
I will probably come back around the third for a
couple of days before I head off to Cairo, will you
be around then? Otherwise I am also in London on
fourteenth for three days, how about then? How is
your quest for the perfect match going, have you
met someone special yet? Karl
```

I desperately needed a break from dating. But at the same time, what if one of these men turned out to be what I was looking for? My journey would be over and I could stay in London. I could neither afford nor bear to ignore this possibility.

Clearly, I did need time off, though. The job of keeping all my *date balls* up in the air had utilized my professional skills as I had anticipated. But whereas in the past, I'd run a department to get the job done, it was now my family and friends who were helping. And I was in danger of treating *them* like staff.

My mother observed very gently on the phone that I'd become "a bit bossy." I was mortified to hear it but knew she was absolutely right. In fact, I'd become bossier than ever. I'd had to be to make all the elements of my journey come together. But I was home now, and I'd missed my Date Wranglers as the regular friends they'd always been and wanted to hear what they'd all been up to in the time I'd been away.

But it didn't quite work out that way, precisely because I'd asked all my friends to help me with my quest. Now I was home, they understandably wanted me—in accordance with the International Girlfriend Charter—to act out the high- and lowlights of the twenty-seven dates they'd been instrumental in setting up. I was torn between my friendship and obligation to them and my need, for reasons of self-preservation, to switch off and recharge my batteries before the next big push.

I arranged to see my friends and family anyway. Belinda and I caught up as we crawled around the floor with her young daughter, Maya; Paula and I watched John Cusack films and talked about music; Eddie asked lots of questions and was as dry and funny as ever; Eleanor and I chatted as she pushed Alex along the Thames path in his pram; I did the crossword with my parents in the village pub.

It felt good to see everyone, but it was frustratingly one-sided at times. I was trying not to bore on about my journey, but it seemed that was all anyone else wanted to talk about. And as selfish as it made me feel, I did need to talk.

But it wasn't all *ooohhs* and *aahhhs*. Although interested and supportive, some had observations I found hard to hear.

Charlotte was my *other best friend,* and, like Belinda and Toz, had watched my Relationship Empires rise and fall over the years. As she fed Poppy and watched Daisy, Charlotte listened to me list the reasons why so far none of the dates had been right. "Oh, Jennifer," she said sympathetically but with characteristic bluntness. "Your problem is you've become too picky."

Charlotte didn't mean to hurt my feelings, and I think her reaction—talking with a woman who had access to virtually every single man in the world and was still complaining none was suitable—was quite understandable. But it stung. I was bossy and picky? Would I have found a suitable man among my dates if I'd been less judgmental and given them more of a chance? (*Everyone* thought I'd been too hard on Olivier in Paris.) And if this was true, was it possible my Soul Mate had been in London the whole time and it was my bad attitude that had been keeping us apart?

I gave it serious consideration, then decided, no, that wasn't the case at all: When it comes to finding your Soul Mate, there is no such thing as too picky. I wanted a boyfriend who made me happy and I could make happy in return. I didn't think I wanted children (or maybe I did? I don't know); I had my own money, house, friends, and adventures. I didn't need anything from the relationship other than the relationship itself. If I didn't like him and couldn't enjoy his company, what other reason did I have for being with him?

Being forced to examine these issues—although difficult— was incredibly useful: It helped me reestablish how important the journey was to me and my belief in the value of the search. It was another very old friend, Ian, who finally cemented my commitment to the journey I was undertaking.

I was talking to him about how hard it was to pull everything together and what if I didn't meet anyone and was my bossiness spiraling out of control and God, I looked tired and like rubbish. . . . Ian just hugged me and said calmly: "Jen, this is the trip of a lifetime and it'll be over before you know it. Stop putting yourself under so much pressure and just enjoy what you're doing while it lasts."

And I knew he was right: A bit like the Love Professor saying you had to like yourself before anyone else would, I had to enjoy the journey if I was going to get anything out of it. So I stopped moaning and got on with setting up the U.S. leg of my trip.

Out of all the places to set up dates, the States was the hardest. Although relating to my mission, Americans seemed a little reluctant to get involved. I'm not saying they weren't helpful, it's just that it rarely got us anywhere. The situation was most acute in L.A. My friend Olaf explained why:

As you know, L.A. is a very demanding city: Men already feel under so much pressure. I think perhaps they don't want the additional stress of competing with all the other men who are dating you?

I found this a worrying observation: Were L.A. men too stressed to date per se or just too stressed to date me? After I looked at the personal ads in the online papers, I started to realize just how different a culture I was dealing with:

FUN STRAIGHT GIRL SEEKING FRIENDS
Be slim and pretty, to hang out with at all the hip new clubs, shopping, movies, lunches at hip/trendy restaurants, and of course rich man hunting. Please be sincere and fun. (SFV/LA) Call Box # . . .

I assumed these ads were for prostitutes, but my friend Ellie put me straight:

Sweetie, L.A. is about what you do and how you look. Making friends is super hard, so we have Activity Buddies instead: clubbing buddies, movie buddies, gym buddies . . . L.A. is more about what you do than who you do it with.

Yikes.

But maybe because it was so hard to form any kind of relationship—romantic or social—the American online websites were full of the most gorgeous-looking men ever: all plaid shirts, strong arms, and bold smiles directly into the camera. They described themselves using words like "smart," "active" and "curious." There was a real energy and sense of manliness about them.

In contrast, the British websites were all receding hairlines, Next casual shirts, and smiles so forced they looked like they'd been photographed at gunpoint. The profiles were dispiriting too: *"I don't really know where to start . . . ,"* *"My friends say I'm caring and supportive"* (always followed with a self-deprecating *"but they would, wouldn't they?"*), *"After seven difficult years . . ."*

Going online late, after a night out with my friend Cath, I saw I had a couple of emails from a dating website. The first man looked quite normal (though he did use the phrase *open-minded* twice when describing himself), but when I looked in the photo section he was draped across the hood of a red sports car, wearing leather trousers, his shirt open to the waist.

The second man told me he liked to travel, but *"that was in the days when my knees both worked at the same time . . ."*

Happily, I had already decided to give up on London dating by then; there simply wasn't the time to date, socialize, and relax.

I did think I'd try to meet Karl, but he lost patience when I struggled to find the time. I explained:

```
It's not that I don't want to see you or you're
unimportant, it's just I won't know until the end
of the week when I'll be free.
```

Who knows, maybe I was procrastinating because I only really wanted to see him on the road, not on home turf. Either way, Karl wasn't happy:

```
For a person traveling the world dating, you seem
surprisingly afraid of committing to meet up. I
```

```
take it those you actually do see meet some crite-
ria I'm not aware of. I guess it's time to call it
quits, don't you?
```

I didn't blame him for being angry. He got back to me a few days later and said he was sorry for getting annoyed; he liked me and felt frustrated we couldn't meet. We awkwardly made up—just one example of how insane meeting through a dating website is: We'd never even met but we'd already had our first row.

In the meantime, I was still flat out trying to set up the U.S. dates. I felt I needed to approach the situation differently: Rather than have a succession of rushed one man/one night dates, I thought staying in one place with the same group of people would mean more time to get to know them.

I was going to Missoula, Montana, for a few days to date a smoke jumper (basically a parachuting fireman), a rodeo rider, and some friend of Jo's. It was a teeny town in the American Rockies and the kind of community where I thought I'd fit in. The experience of the Burning Man Festival, camping as part of the Costco Soul Mate Trading Outlet, was another strong possibility.

Costco had its own intranet site where all forty of the campers seemed to email each other constantly. Although logging on to find up to ninety emails a day from them was a bit mind-boggling at times, they seemed a really fun and interesting group of people:

"Absolutely, bring the kissing hammock," Rico had told a man called Gambo approvingly.

I chatted with Rico a lot via email; we talked about Soul Mates and work and life. He seemed a lovely man, though we did argue sometimes. He told me he was deeply in love with his partner, Rite Aid Annie, and he hoped I would meet someone who would make me just as happy:

I want to see you get your ass kicked by love.

You don't say.

What am I, some kind of a love slacker? Rico, I want to be in love too, and have taken pretty drastic steps to try and make it happen. But it takes more than just wanting and looking, you know: Fate and chemistry need to show up and play their part too.

Meanwhile, there seemed to be a strange new phenomenon at home. As word of my homecoming had spread throughout my group, old boyfriends and The Ones Who Could Have Been were getting in touch. To try to rewrite history?

Was lovely to see you. The freckles are gorgeous. Am definitely up for hot date. Not in the least worried to be one in eighty.

And Would-Be Dates (WBDs) were trying to use me to settle professional-rivalry scores.

How's your round-the-world dating going? Let me know when it's my turn! By the way, is ******** going to be a hot date as well? He wrote a nasty review of my ******* book in the *******. Cut him off your list!

The Date Wranglers were having a bit of a moment, too. Hannah rang from Budapest to ask if I thought I was going to get on with the friend she'd set me up with in Bangkok. I quite understood why she was having second thoughts, but what could I tell her? That I'd never met him, but she knew both of us and so was clearly the only person who could make that judgment call?

Posh PR Emma had set me up with Jake, her friend who worked as an A-list photographer in Vegas. Newly divorced, he lived a larger-than-showbiz life: gold bath fixtures and his last two ex-wives' implants in the fridge (cold eye-masks for reducing puffiness before a photo shoot). He sounded extraordinary. But so far his emails had been a little disappointing, more blank than bling.

Out with Jo, I mentioned my concerns about Jake and she shrieked, "Oh, God, Jennifer, he's Emma's pet project. She set me up with him too, and he's DULL, DULL, DULL. You think he'll have all these really interesting stories and he doesn't: He's just really, really boring."

I don't want to sound unkind, but I wasn't the dating arm of the Samaritans. I was looking to meet my Soul Mate and it was important I didn't get rerouted into other people's dating agendas. I know that sounds mean, but I just didn't have the energy to spare. I learned this the hard way when Paul asked me to go down to the pub.

It had been a long and trying day: trying to firm up the hotel in Vegas, work out if a tattooist two hours north of San Francisco was worth the drive, and get the New York Fire Department to take me just a little more seriously. (*Like I tell all of you ladies calling to date our boys, put it in writing.*) The dating website that based your matches on which books you read just highlighted that men and women read different books; thankfully, the site that based your matches on what you liked to watch on TV was looking more promising.

Paul rang to say that a group of our friends was going down to the pub and did I want to go? I was frazzled but thought I could do with a break, so agreed. When I arrived an hour later, Paul was the only one there.

"Oh, are we early?" I asked as I plonked myself down at the table.

"No," he replied cheerfully. I was confused but thought I must have misheard him. While Paul was at the bar buying me a drink, my phone chirped. Jo was texting me:

Let me know how it goes.

How what goes?

Paul came back from the bar and we settled down and chatted for about half an hour. He was unusually attentive, also quite tense. "Is everything okay?" I asked him, concerned he might be having a bad time about something and wanted to talk about it. "Yes," he replied anxiously, "I'm just pleased to see you."

It was then that it dawned on me. "Paul, are we on a date?" I asked, trying to sound conversational. He nodded and squeezed my hand.

I could have killed him.

He was a nice guy but there was no way I would have agreed to go on a date with him, especially at the moment when I was dated to the max. And he'd tricked me into it by pretending our other friends would be there—probably knowing it was the only way he'd get me to say yes. We walked to the railway station together at the end of the evening, and I had to execute an advanced Quick Peck and Hug maneuver to avoid his persistent advances.

· · ·

Back in my little flat, I thought how good it had been to spend time at home. But by involving all my friends in my Soul Mate quest, I'd made my home life too chaotic. And if I stayed here any longer, things would only get more complicated and out of control. My two weeks were up anyway. And in my upside-down fairy-tale world, I'd really enjoyed it: working quietly, eating nothing but toast, and living in worn-out old T-shirts and frayed jeans every day. But now the clock was striking midnight and it was time to squeeze those glass slippers back onto my feet and whirl and twirl across America, in search of my Prince.

chapter eight

U.S.A — L.A.

Date #52—All shook up in Vegas, USA

Weird, bloated stomach; indecisive and easily confused; tired and craving sugar . . . jet lag is the PMS of travelers, without the payoff of knowing you're not pregnant.

But I was in L.A., low-fat, low-sugar capital of the world, and I was determined that it would be the inspiration for a new healthy me. I was going to get back in shape, eat properly, and start working out again. I'd feel and look better, as well as having more energy for my quest.

I was staying at the Best Western on Sunset Strip, much nicer than it sounds and incredibly central, especially as my first date was with a comedian called Lowell, across the road at the Comedy Store. My friend Lizzy had given me his number but suggested I catch his show tonight and ring him tomorrow if I liked him. I knew my Date Wranglers well enough by now to know I'd live to regret not taking their advice when it was offered.

Date #28: Lowell—Sunset Strip, L.A., U.S.A.

It was open-mike night at the Comedy Store: twenty-four comedians each with three minutes to be funny. Such rapid turnover meant that the audience never got to know or care about the comedian, but looked for quick laughs instead. Faced with such performance pressure, most comedians lost first their confidence and then their audience, whose wandering attention made them chat and heckle.

Watching the audience smell the blood of a dying comedian, then finish him off with brutal indifference, was a chilling sight, like seeing a gladiator fighting for his life in front of a jaded mob.

I missed Lowell's entrance onstage: An Australian impersonator (he'd impersonated a swallow by holding the mike to his throat and swallowing) was asking me if the audience hadn't laughed because they couldn't understand his accent.

Instead of answering, I turned my attention to Lowell, who was a few moments into his act. He had an electric presence: Tall with a tense, sinewy body and short, dirty-blond hair, Lowell spoke with a deep southern drawl. There was nothing languid about him, though; his act was deeply offensive, performed with the furious belligerence of a drunk being bundled into a police van at midnight.

He did what virtually no other comedian had managed, though: He got the attention of the crowd. After telling one of the sickest jokes I have ever heard spoken aloud, his three minutes were up and Lowell stormed offstage to such howls of outrage and abuse that for a moment I wondered if *stage-struck* actually meant someone coming up onstage and punching you.

Although appalled, I actually thought he was a pretty good comedian, but there was no way in the world I was going to date him (and I suspect Lizzy knew this). I drank a beer and watched a few more of the acts, before deciding to call it a night.

Outside in the parking lot, a knot of spent comedians paced in distracted agitation, like a gang of street fighters licking their wounds after a violent clash. Lowell was among them. He didn't know I was Lizzy's friend; still, he caught my eye as I passed. "Thanks for coming," he called out.

"I admired your act," I said over my shoulder as I continued to walk.

"Really?" he asked, running to catch up. He walked a couple of paces ahead, then turned to face me. "It gets me right here," he said, hitting his fist on his chest, arrogant yet clearly stung by the reception he'd just received.

"I thought you were funny," I told him honestly.

"Really?" he asked again, his need for approval naked and demanding. "I thought it was a disaster." He looked shocked, whether at his act or the audience's response, I couldn't tell.

"You're original," I said evenly, "You weren't like the others. You weren't trying to please, you stood out."

Behind him, the strung-out comedians continued to pace, ebbing and flowing around each other as the adrenaline surge slowly abated. "Will you be coming back?" Lowell asked.

"Maybe." I shrugged as I walked off. But I knew I wouldn't: Funny was what these men did, not what they were.

Date #29: Brian—CBS TV Studios, Fairfax, L.A., U.S.A.

Brian wasn't what he appeared either.

When I'd told Ellie about my difficulties in finding a date in L.A., she promised to find me someone and, sure enough, her friend Brian was coming on a TV Date with me.

I wanted to go on a TV Date to test a theory. As I see it, once you get past the initial mutually obsessed and introspective stage of a new romance, it settles into something cozier, and that generally involves staying in and watching a fair amount of TV together. Since L.A. is where most sitcoms are recorded, I thought watching TV on a date—or, to be more specific, sitting in on the recording of a TV program on a date—would be a good way to see if we were compatible.

Sadly, my theory went untested as there were apparently two CBS studios in L.A. and we ended up going to the wrong one.

Brian picked me up from the hotel in his car and we made the short trip over to Fairfax. Tall, with short dark hair, huge blue eyes, and a body gymmed to perfection, my first impression was that he was cute . . . and gay.

Needless to say, I kept this thought to myself.

When we arrived at CBS and were told we were at the wrong studio, Brian was upset and apologized profusely: "Oh, Jennifer, I am such an idiot. I really wanted to see it, too."

He looked genuinely disappointed but rallied quickly. He grabbed my hand and we raced from the parking lot to the scariest and most fabulous secondhand clothes shop I'd ever seen. None of the genteel manners of Help the Aged; people pushed carts around the racks, shopping here because they had to.

And in the shop I discovered that Brian wasn't Brian and that he was indeed gay.

The Thrift Store had no changing rooms; instead about twenty mirrors were mounted close together on the long back wall. I modestly disrobed behind a stack of quadraphonic cartridges and a wall of Harold Robbins novels. Brian had no such hang-ups: A pile of clothes at his feet, he unselfconsciously stripped off in front of the mirrors (and a crowd of admiring young men). His stomach was so flat and his muscles so hard that, if lost at sea, you could have flipped him onto his back, gripped his nipples, and surfed to shore on him.

I stared at his buff body and blurted out: "Brian, you have the kind of body gay men would kill for." Much to the disappointment of his audience, he stopped rippling his washboard stomach and looked sheepishly at me.

He held my gaze for a moment, then said quietly, "You know, don't you?"

"Well . . ." My voice trailed off and I shrugged awkwardly (which, considering I was balancing on one leg, an apricot satin jumpsuit halfway up the other, was quite an achievement).

We left the clothes in a pile on the floor and went next door for coffee. Brian was a friend of Ellie's, and also a friend of Marc, who apparently was the man I was having coffee with right now.

"Jennifer . . ." he said with a pained look on his face. "No question, I was going to tell you, I was just waiting for the right moment. You must be really mad at me, huh?" Marc went on to explain how Brian had had to work late, but Marc—his roommate—was a huge fan of one of the actors in the program, and had volunteered to come along instead. "We figured this way, at least you'd have a Date for the night," Marc (aka Brian) reasoned wretchedly.

I'd missed my program and my Date was gay, but I genuinely couldn't have been happier. To go shopping was always a treat, but to be taken shopping by a sweet man who knew where the best designer bargains in L.A. could be found. . . . in that respect, Marc really was my Soul Mate. Brian/Marc paid for the coffee and we went right back to our shopping. It was a wonderful date.

Dates #30–50: Speed-Dating—Redondo Beach, L.A., U.S.A.

I read in the in-flight magazine coming over that 74 percent of men know after the first fifteen minutes of a date if they are interested or not.

Fifteen minutes? That long?

Women know instantly if they are interested or not. Like playing a slot machine, in those first, dense dating moments, the tone of voice, content of conversation, appearance, body language, dress sense, height, and general vibe all spin around women's heads until the barrels fall into place. They are then either predominantly cherries (put more money in and keep playing) or lemons (stop playing and leave the machine for someone else).

That's why the theory behind speed-dating—twenty dates, each lasting three minutes—makes so much sense. It might be hard on the men—whether comedians or daters—but women can learn a lot in three L.A. minutes.

My friend Ian cynically accused me of wanting to speed-date just to get my numbers up, but I was genuinely curious. Though it's less convenient than online dating—it's at a set time and you have to travel to a venue—there are real advantages. A face-to-face meeting means you quickly discover if you like someone or not, plus you see straight away if there's any chemistry between you, without feeling obligated or involved. You'll also find out how accurate their profile is—in my early online days I spent two weeks having fabulous e-chats with Martin, before meeting up and disappointedly discovering he was in fact *10 Percent Too Small Martin.*

So I went speed-dating.

As I arrived at a packed bar in Redondo Beach, organizer Styve (it's L.A.) smiled with pleasure and relief at the sight of me. "Oh, thank goodness, another woman, we're running so short." I looked around the bar and sure enough, there were five little tables with a harassed-looking woman sitting behind each one, a swarm of impatient men surrounding them, checking to see no one exceeded the allotted three minutes and edging forward in anticipation of their own.

Part of me thought I should feel intimidated by the pressure and the incredible air of competitiveness that permeated the room, but instead I was delighted. L.A. is a social barometer for the rest of the world: Was this the future of dating? Single men outnumbering women five to one?

Styve gave me a badge with my name and a number, pushed a clipboard into my hand, and told me to write down the number of any guy I was interested in. They would email me the results (like some kind of weird dating pregnancy test: *Congratulations, Jennifer, you're going to have a boyfriend*) in a couple of days.

God, I suddenly realized, I hadn't thought up a story; what reason would I give the Dates for being here? I didn't want to tell them about my quest, as that would take the whole three minutes. But if I told the truth—I was here for two days and wanted to meet someone—even in therapy-hungry L.A., that was going to scream "relationship issues."

As it turned out, I needn't have worried: With so few women and so few minutes, the Dates did all the talking.

Date #30 told me Jesus didn't mind us doing this and asked, which church did I attend? **Date #31** was an analyst of something I didn't catch because he muttered (his username was "no_talking"; I felt like replying "no_kidding"). **Date #32** worked in defense: "I can't tell you anything else until I get you security-cleared." I asked **Date #33** if he had ever been to one of these events before. "Last night," he replied. "I'm ready to have children and need to meet my wife." **Date #34** was German and desperate to talk to another European. **Date #35** was a sweet, lonely Vietnamese man: "I've decided I need to chill out and meet more people. It doesn't have to be dating—I just want some friends." **Date #36** was a management consultant who talked about how much he enjoyed Nepal. "Why?" I asked. "They floss their teeth in the street," he replied. I liked **Date #37**, though he shouted at 2 minutes 59 seconds, "I have two children," as **Date #38** dragged him away from my table by the chair.

I felt slightly overwhelmed by the time I'd completed **Date #50** and couldn't get away fast enough. Like being under the spotlight on *Who Wants to Be a Millionaire,* I thought there had to be a less stressful way of getting the prize.

As I arrived back at the hotel, Lizzy rang from London to see how it had worked out with Lowell. I told her he was a little too intense for me, but he was completely laid-back compared with some of the speed-daters I'd just met.

We laughed about it and Lizzy commented: "Jennifer, this is the first time I've heard you sound really happy in ages. I was worried it was all beginning to get to you." I hadn't thought about it, but she was right: I felt excited and alive in a way I never had in Europe.

"For some reason, I found it really hard to get under the skin of the Dates in Europe," I confessed, realizing for the first time that this was true. "I always felt like an outsider. Maybe because American culture is more like ours or everyone loves my accent here and wants to talk to me. . . . I feel part of what's going on rather than just a spectator."

It could also be that, rested from a spell at home and now with quite a few dates under my belt, I was more experienced at handling the "workload." It had felt incredibly intimidating when I'd started out, but now there seemed to be a natural rhythm and

order to events. It was easier to know what to expect and be prepared.

"You know, I actually feel excited to be here; in fact I'm even
looking forward to dating. I don't know that I ever did in Europe;
there always seemed so much of it."

We then chatted about normal stuff—how her baby Connie
was, the fabulous pair of boots I'd bought on Rodeo Drive—before saying good-bye.

Although it was late, I felt really cheery and full of energy, so I
popped next door to the House of Blues to catch Arthur Lee &
Love. It was good, simple, loud fun. Talking was impossible; I
smiled and shrugged at the guys who tried to engage me in conversation. Encoring with a scorching version of "Smokestack
Lightning," Lee removed his sunglasses for the first time and
croaked to the audience: "Hey, ya'll do me a favor: Love each
other." So different from the hard-nosed comedy crowd across
the road, the audience cheered and danced wildly.

This felt like a good omen and I cheered and danced along
with everyone else. Lizzy was right, I felt happy and flirty, and
seemed to be getting chatted up like mad as a result. I can't explain why, but for some reason I knew I was on the right path,
doing the right thing. My Soul Mate was getting closer; things
were going to change, I could feel it.

"So where are you stripping tonight?"

It took every ounce of willpower I possessed not to turn and
see who in the Southwest Airlines check-in queue had just been
asked that question.

It cleared one thing up, though: why so many big-haired, big-
boobed, teeny-outfitted blondes were walking around L.A. airport. One woman wore a small (and I mean tiny) red T-shirt and

red plastic shorts that covered just the top half of her bottom. As she bent over, struggling to lift her heavy bags onto the check-in scales, she oozed from her shorts like peanut butter out of a sandwich. The queue watched, helplessly transfixed, unsure whether we should call a porter or a gynecologist to help.

Thursday afternoon was obviously when all the strippers traveled to work: We were catching the Red Thigh to Vegas.

"You wanna see a show tomorrow, ma'am?"

The top-hatted ticket tout waved flyers energetically at the fiftysomething woman and her husband ducking into the air-conditioned sanctuary of New York New York to escape the searing heat of the Strip.

"We're going to a wedding tomorrow," she barked back in a thick Brooklyn accent. "That's the biggest show there is."

Las Vegas is famously both the wedding and gambling capital of America. You've got to wonder if there's a relationship between the two. Apart from legalities (i.e., it's quick and easy), why do so many people get married in Vegas? Is it because, a theme park in the middle of a desert and cut off from the rest of the world, Vegas brings out a *what the hell* impetuosity? Or having bet and won in the casinos, do people feel more prepared for the ultimate gamble?

And if relationships are a crapshoot, could I learn anything helpful from a professional gambler? How much was luck and how much was knowing and playing the system? I'd arranged to meet Chester through a third-generation Date Wrangler. Aware this could be a little dicey, we were having a drink in my hotel bar so I'd feel more secure on "home territory."

The problem was that my usual hotel, the Alexis Park (cheap but really homey, with three swimming pools and huge comfortable rooms), was full at the last minute, so I had to stay at the Days Inn off the Strip.

It wasn't a bad hotel; actually I grew incredibly fond of it by the time I had to leave, but it was threadbare and in a very iffy neighborhood. A dark bar ran the length of the lobby, a cluster of slot machines was behind it, and a large, basic diner was through an alcove off to the right. All was guarded by a one-armed maintenance man in his seventies called Neville.

The place was full of old people, all waiting either for the slots to pay out or the macaroni and cheese to be served up. Outside it was more lively. On the first night I was chased by a gang on chopper bikes. The second, I narrowly missed getting hit with a chain in a fight between rival chopper gangs. On the third night, a brawl between rival chopper gangs exploded onto the hotel porch where I was sitting quietly. The Days Inn was like an old people's home in a cul-de-sac off Armageddon.

And it was here that Chester came for our date.

Date #51: Chester—Professional Gambler, Las Vegas, U.S.A.

Chester, a big man in his late forties with dark hair and an expanse of Desperate Dan stubble, and I sat at the bar. He immediately became engrossed in a poker game on TV and stayed engrossed for the duration of our date.

Poker is huge in America. Not only are the games televised (including a long-running series of celebrity poker), special wrist-cams have been developed so you can see the hands of star players and follow their progress.

Chester didn't want to miss the big tournament currently under way and after several failed attempts to engage him in conversation, I resigned myself to sitting and watching with him. I set a two-drink time limit: If the program was finished and we'd talked by then, great; if not, I was going to my room to catch up on email.

The game wasn't particularly interesting, but I found the intensity of the players utterly compelling. Chester did too. "Look at his hands," he said, nodding up at the screen, "they're shaking. That means he's got a good hand."

"Really?" I asked, impatience immediately forgotten. "How do you know?"

"You can tell a lot about a player and what they're holding by their body language," he replied, his eyes never leaving the screen. "See him stare at his cards, that means he's got a good hand. When they stare at their chips, that means they've got a bad hand and they're wondering how much they can afford to lose."

This was what I had come for. "So that man tidying his stack of chips, does that mean anything?"

Chester didn't answer immediately, lost in the game again, but then with distracted impatience snorted: "It all means something. If you're going to gamble, you've got to study your opponent; you can be damned sure they'll be studying you. Man who tidies his chips? He's probably a real careful player: thinks things through, don't take a lot of risks. Man who leaves them loose, he's aggressive and harder to call. And look how they're sitting: See the guy who just sat back in his chair? He's about to fold, knows he's out of the game. . . . "

And sure enough, the man laid his cards down and the dealer swept his chips away into the center of the table.

This was fascinating. I had witnessed similar body language among the speed-daters. The mumbling analyst had leaned right back in his chair, whereas the management consultant/street flosser—presumably more confident of his hand—jutted forward, his face pushed quite intimidatingly into mine.

After the intense flurry of insights, Chester was silent again, engrossed in the game, acting as if we were two strangers at a bar (which, of course, we were). I took tiny sips of my warm beer, half watching the game, half watching Neville slowly clean the frayed carpet. Chester suddenly let out a big sigh. I turned back to the TV: The game had finished and Chester was slumped slightly, the tension he'd been holding for the duration of the game leaving his body.

You'd think gambling or comedy would be fun jobs, but so far these were some of the tensest people I'd met. Was this how I'd seemed to people when I was working?

"The thing about gambling," Chester explained, turning his stool to face mine for the first time, "is that it's not a game at all: It's a job. You've got to work at it and take it seriously. You can't put it down to luck and go in unprepared."

He was obviously very serious about it, as were all the people I'd met when it came to their professions. And where did that leave Love? Was I right to approach my Soul Mate quest like a job, or could you be lucky in Love?

"What about beginner's luck?" I asked.

"Just that," he replied dismissively. "It don't mean anything and it don't last."

"So what do you need to play well?" I asked him. "What makes a good player?"

"Well," he replied, blowing out a little more of the tension before taking a swallow of his whiskey and coke. "A good player has done half his work before he even gets to the table. Are you in the right frame of mind; have you set your limit; who's the opposition?"

Although I could see parallels, so far gambling was about winning at any cost. I didn't want a man at any cost, I wanted the right one. But being able to read my Dates would help me decide if I was on the right track.

"I know this sounds stupid, but is it always about winning?" Chester looked intrigued by my question, like I'd graduated from basics and made it through to the next—but still basic—level.

"You gotta think about what you want. I mean, obviously you want to win, but you gotta think about how much you want to win and how much you got to lose. You gotta set your limit and when you reach it, get up and walk away; never throw good money after bad."

That made sense: I'd never set a limit with Kelly, I always thought I was in too deep to go back and if I just tried a little harder, gave a little more, we'd be fine.

"That must take a lot of control," I said humbly.

"Playing is all about control," Chester observed bluntly. "You don't play angry, you don't play drunk. It's not just your cards you're playing, it's people. And at the exact same time, they're playing you. You need a clear head to think through that, then imagine yourself winning."

"Imagine yourself winning?" I repeated, perplexed. "Wouldn't that make you overconfident?"

"Not at all," Chester disagreed. "It's called positive visualization, like being a runner: See yourself making it across the finish line, you pace yourself better, run a better race too. See yourself winning at poker, you make the winning calls. See yourself as a loser, you've not got the self-belief or determination to play well, no matter how much money you gamble."

I was shocked to hear the words of the Love Professor echoed by Chester: Like yourself and you'll win; think you're a loser, and sure enough you'll end up losing.

"That's why none of these weekend gamblers got the first clue," Chester said, showing emotion for the first time. "Gambling takes patience: Before you even sit down at a table you have to watch, study, and learn. You make all the moves in your head first; you can't just rush in."

Although I thought Chester was right about being prepared, I also thought he was being overly harsh. Weekend tourists weren't professional gamblers, they were people enjoying themselves. And surely that was okay? Like all of us obsessed with our careers, Chester was assuming that everyone took gambling as seriously as he did.

"But surely most people coming to Vegas just gamble for fun," I countered.

"Yes, ma'am, they do," Chester agreed. "And there ain't nothing wrong with fun." And with that, he leaned over and kissed me.

I was absolutely not expecting this. I mean, not remotely. Not like when Frank in Holland kissed me and I wasn't expecting it, because Frank and I had spent the whole day chatting and had got on really well. Chester had hardly even spoken to me, let alone established any kind of rapport.

Horribly afraid that Neville was watching, I grabbed the edge of the bar to stop myself toppling backward off my stool and slid sideways, away from Chester's kiss. He smiled good-naturedly. "Sometimes you just gotta take a chance," he said.

In a fluster, I got up and thanked him for his time. I didn't say what I really wanted, which was: "Oh, so suddenly now you believe in luck?" It seemed when it came to romance, even professionals forgot the theory and followed their hearts (well, one of their organs, anyway).

The next day I thought about what Chester had said. The body-language tips had been useful; so had the one about setting limits (though I had learned this in Paris). What I found completely invaluable were his comments about positive visualization. This was one step on from the Love Professor's *like yourself* philosophy: It implied that once you liked yourself, you should then imagine what the lovely new you wanted and deserved.

I booted up my laptop and reread my Soul Mate Job Description:

> ... *old-fashioned enough to want to feel "ladylike" ... someone who makes me smile, lets me read them bits out of the newspaper ... tells me interesting things I didn't know ... you'll believe that life is short and you should make the most of it ... sense of fun and adventure essential.*

God, whoever he was, he sounded lovely. I concentrated on the job description and imagined us together: making each other laugh; arguing about politics; getting lost in exotic countries; curling up in front of the TV. I smiled, a little sadly, wondering if I would ever meet him, then remembered I liked myself and was meant to be positively visualizing him. He was out there and I would meet him. I would.

And suddenly I realized I actually believed it. Not because I was meant to, but because, in my heart, I truly felt it.

The next morning I came downstairs as a couple of other Days Inn-ers—Earl and Rhea—were heading off in a bus with their friends to renew their wedding vows. They were going to the famous Little White Wedding Chapel and, seeing *that cute Briddish gal,* asked if I wanted to come along. They'd been married fifty years and clearly relished each other's company (in a teasing, mock eye-rolling way). Rhea looked lovely in a peach-colored silk suit, Earl resplendent in an *"If it's got tits or tires it's gonna git you into trouble"* T-shirt.

Known as the Wedding Queen of the West, over the last forty

years Little White Wedding Chapel owner and marriage aficionado Charolette Richards had married everyone from Judy Garland, Frank Sinatra, and Joan Collins to Britney Spears and, umm, Blue Oyster Cult. Staff included ex–chorus girls and a vast array of impersonators from Sammy Davis Jr. to Dean Martin. And, of course, Elvis. I got separated from the party after they decided to hire a stretch limo and do the wedding as a drive-through. Trying to stay out of the heat, I got chatting with Roseanne, Charolette's second in command, instead.

We retreated to the cool of the staff room, and a piece of wedding cake was pushed into my hand as Roseanne told me that 25 percent of all the ceremonies were renewals. I found this, and everything else about the place, really uplifting. The room had the atmosphere of a feel-good musical: Sammy Davis Jr. laughed and spun as he showed another Sammy Davis Jr. how to do a complicated move. Flower arrangers danced around the huge fridges that kept the blooms chilled, as Elvis teased and serenaded, begging them "Don't Be Cruel."

"Is he practicing?" I asked Roseanne.

"Oh no," she replied cheerfully. "He just loves to sing. Once he starts, he don't stop." With newly married couples popping in, bursting with happy tears and heartfelt thanks, it was an emotional and joyful atmosphere. Before long I had told them about my quest and we were swapping stories and advice about love and marriage.

It was a wonderful day. Everyone hugged and kissed me good-bye, as Dean Martin prepared to drive me in a stretch limo to the Bellagio. The wardrobe mistress—a tiny Italian woman, choreographer to Michael Crawford in *Barnum,* with the unquestionable authority of a Sicilian Godmother—walked me to the car. "You wanna know the secret to a successful marriage?" she asked, poking her finger sternly into my chest. She hand-tailored fairy-tale wedding dresses and had herself been married fifty-three years, so I said yes without hesitation. "Meet the family," she said in a tone that brooked no argument. "Because when the sex is all gone, the family will still be there."

When I got back to my room, Frank had emailed from Holland:

```
i was wondering where on earth you are at this
moment, wich number of date you are dealing with,
and . . . how many guys you have been kissing untill
now. am i still the one and only lucky lips?
```

Although I had had a few kisses since Frank, he'd been the most fun, and I emailed him straight back, reassuring him that he was still the #1 Kisser.

For now.

I loved Vegas. Everything about it: my iffy hotel; the crushing heat; the incessant tackiness; the relentless beep of the slot machines. It should have been repellent, but it was the opposite. Apart from the chopper gangs, everyone was really friendly, and the tack was so well done, wandering around the imaginative air-conditioned interiors of the hotels and casinos was a real pleasure.

Over the next couple of days, I dated **Elvis (Date #52)** (real name Dean Z.), who had mesmerizing turquoise eyes and a pompadour as high and solid as a well-baked loaf. Sadly, he was too young, at just twenty years old, but he was gorgeous, clever, and extremely interesting. He'd been Elvis since he was three; his grandfather had been a drummer in the fifties with a big-name British performer.

Rob (Date #53) was nearly as good-looking as Anders without being as scary. He was determined to prove I could have gone around the world without leaving Vegas. So he took me for drinks in Venice, dinner in Paris, a stroll around the pyramids and the side streets of New York, shark-watching on the Mandalay Reef, and finally drinks again, this time in Morocco. Rob couldn't sit still for two minutes, and long-term I would have found that too distracting. But we laughed and teased each other, and at the end of the night, he stole Frank's title.

Betty's Outrageous Adventures was a funky, lesbian social club in Vegas. I'd found them on the Internet a while back and had been in regular email contact with their president, Nanc, ever since. She seemed lovely and I was looking forward to meeting her and the other **Bettys (Date #54)** at one of their regular picnics out of town:

We tend to sit around and chat, and often run off to hike because the area is so beautiful and less hot than Vegas. Feel welcome to come along. I would love to hear about your travel adventures.

Nanc picked me up from the Days Inn late the following morning, with another Betty called Elizabeth. We set off in her four-wheel-drive for the mountains, forty minutes outside of Vegas.

In her mid-thirties, Nanc was pretty, blond, and petite but also incredibly gentle and kindly. We all felt a little awkward and Nanc was at pains to make me welcome. Elizabeth, on the other hand—late thirties, slim, and very fit-looking—was a nonstop acerbic wit from the moment she opened her mouth. She was a tough and successful journalist and grilled me relentlessly as we drove through increasingly heavy rain to the mountains.

It was a brilliant drive. Not just because we were all single, so the subject of my journey was close to our hearts, but also because Nanc and Elizabeth—naturally—responded to everything from a lesbian perspective. It was a completely fresh angle for me to consider my position from.

"How do you know if they're your Soul Mate if you only have one date with them?" Elizabeth demanded.

"Oh come on," I retorted, really enjoying sparring with her. "Where's your sense of romance? Have you never just looked at someone and known they're The One?" She grudgingly admitted she had; I confessed in return that it made me uncomfortable and perplexed when men expected me to sleep with them on the first date.

"But they're men," Elizabeth snorted, "that's why they're dating you. And they only have one date, what else do you expect them to do?"

Lesbians have different priorities than straight couples, Nanc observed gently. As she spoke she kept her eyes firmly on the road, by now bouncing with huge hailstones and illuminated by the piercing forks of lightning flickering ahead. "First and foremost, we want friendship," she continued. "If that works out, the next priority is a long-term partner. Some, but very few, lesbians feel sex is their most important priority; it's way down the list."

As Elizabeth and Nanc fell into a conversation about one of the Bettys for whom sex was a priority and the mess she was in at the moment, I considered Nanc's statement. Those weren't just lesbian priorities: I was sure they were most women's. They were certainly mine. I knew I wasn't gay, so where did that leave me and my search? Trying to meet my Soul Mate in a situation where our priorities were polarized.

But now wasn't the time to be introspective. We had arrived at the spot for the Bettys' hike and picnic. On the side of a steep hill, staked by huge, shaggy pine trees, twenty-three lesbians sheltered in a five-woman tent as hail and rain thundered all around. Grabbing our potluck contributions, Nanc, Elizabeth, and I splashed through the mud and sprinted toward the tent.

It had been erected around one of those outdoor wooden picnic benches, and any surface not taken with huge bowls of tuna salad, white wine, or chocolate cookies had a drenched Betty sitting on it. Nudging our way into the shelter was like squeezing into a lesbian elevator: There was not one spare inch of room.

Under these circumstances, it was incredibly easy to make friends, and—as at the Wedding Chapel yesterday—we joined in the laughing and storytelling that were already well under way. Hearing the reason for my journey, Hettie and June, a couple in their sixties, wished me luck in my search. They were Soul Mates, June told me. Not that I needed to be told: As the Love Professor had predicted, they mirrored each other's body language and unself-consciously finished each other's sentences.

There was nothing cringy or schmaltzy about them; sitting huddled in the pouring rain in their soaked hiking jackets, they looked like they were made for each other.

"We've only been together three years," June confided. "But our entire lives were leading to our time together," Hettie added with conviction.

June smiled and squeezed Hettie's hand.

I smiled too and told them both about Chester's positive-visualization theory. "Yes." Hettie nodded thoughtfully. "You've got to believe it will happen, but just as importantly, when the moment comes, you have to be prepared to take that leap of faith."

I hugged them both, touched by their story and acknowledging the truth in Hettie's advice.

chapter nine

U.S.A.—
Black Rock
City,
Nevada

Date #55—A hot kiss
at the Burning Man Festival,
Nevada, USA

The woman motioned for me to kill the engine as she stepped from the checkpoint and swaggered through the searing desert heat toward me. Eyes protected from the harsh elements by diamanté-studded goggles, she was naked but for a pair of large graying men's briefs and a golden sheriff star painted onto each of her nipples.

Walking up to my side of the car, without saying a word, the greeter stuck her head through the open window and kissed me long and hard on the mouth.

Straightening up, she then stared at me calculatingly. Without breaking eye contact, I reached behind me into the cooler on the backseat and pulled out a six-pack of beer. In silence I handed it to her. She smiled for the first time, then, rolling the icy cans across her bare stomach, threw her head back and let out a shriek of pure joy. "You're my kind of girl," she laughed, pulling her goggles back and beaming at me. "It's a pleasure to have you in Black Rock City. Welcome to Burning Man."

At the end of every summer, the Burning Man Festival set up camp on the Playa, a blistering, barren section of the Nevada desert, two hours' drive northeast of Reno.

Started in San Francisco in 1986 by Larry Harvey and relocated to the desert in 1992, it was less a festival and more a radical exercise in personal expression and communal interdependence. Nothing grew on the Playa, there was no shelter, and you couldn't buy or sell anything (with the exception of ice and coffee). Life on the Playa was about bringing everything you needed for a week, then sharing it with a community of up to thirty thousand people.

The result was Black Rock City (BRC), a well-organized collection of theme camps—arranged in vast concentric circles— that challenged you to experience thoughts and activities ranging from the spiritual or political to the physical, artistic, or just plain silly. Feel underdressed? Walk into that tent and help yourself to a ball gown from the racks. Can't cope with your dust-encrusted body for another moment? Go to the hair-washing or the feet-washing camp, or just forget the dust altogether and go to the Picasso Painting camp and get your body *arted.*

I was here to work at the Costco Soul Mate Trading Outlet, the Playa's dating camp. As I drove very slowly along the dusty roads between the neighborhoods of tents, temples, and giant structures, trying to avoid the naked cyclists, I searched for the Costco banner to help me locate them.

"Hey, slow down," I suddenly heard someone shout. Although I was going only five miles an hour, I braked hard and peered with alarm at the group of Rangers (the volunteer BRC law enforcement) standing by their bikes (the site covers fifteen and a half square miles, so once you're parked, you cycle everywhere).

As a teenager growing up in rural Essex and attending a hippie secondary school, I've been to a lot of weird festivals, where it was the norm to stand around naked or hang out of trees at 4 a.m. playing the saxophone. But because this was an American festival, it was outside my own festival culture. Self-consciously English, I was scared I'd commit a *festival pas* and do something embarrassingly uncool.

"I'm really sorry," I called out apologetically to the Rangers. I had no idea what I'd done. "Was I going too fast?"

"No," one of the group called back, grinning. "But you're in a car so we're experiencing some difficulty in checking you out."

I rarely blush, but I did now. Deep, deep red.

They didn't notice, however, because they were too busy talking among themselves. "Oh, fuck, is she British? Hot and British?" They all nodded wide-eyed at the Ranger who'd spoken to me. "Hey, cute Brit chick . . ." he called out, handing his bike to another Ranger and walking over to my car.

Although still blushing, by now I was giggling too. "Where are you camping, sweetie?" he asked, resting his arm on the open window and leaning in, letting me admire his green eyes sparkling mischievously against his tanned skin.

"Umm, I'm with Costco," I replied, flustered and self-conscious but unable to stop laughing. "But I'm a bit lost. Do you know where they are?"

He replied that of course he did, everyone knew Costco, and pointed me toward BRC's center. "But hey, one more thing . . ." he said sternly as I started the car.

"Yes?" I asked, turning anxiously to face him.

"Just remember this . . ." he told me, and, leaning into the car, he gave me a long, lingering kiss that gently wiped the desert dust from his face onto mine.

When he finished, he raised one eyebrow and touched a finger to my cheek. "I'll be watching out for you, Hot British Chick." And, rejoining his group, he cycled off around a large group of naked people cartwheeling through the burning sand.

I watched him go and decided to take a moment to organize my thoughts. I had known Burning Man was going to be crazy—as many of the dates were in their own ways—so I had automatically slipped into my standard *whatever* traveling state of mind. What I hadn't expected was there to be so much kissing, but—do you know what?—it was nice. I was okay with this. In fact, I liked it: It was *sport kissing*, no-agenda fun. Feeling I had taken an emotional litmus test and the results had come back all clear, I started the car up again and drove slowly toward the Costco camp.

I was soon to discover this was barely the tip of the kissing iceberg: I was captain of the *Titanic,* powering full steam ahead toward a vast ocean of puckered lips.

Date #55: Garry—Burning Man Festival, Nevada, U.S.A.

Dusk settled on the cracked desert floor. The earthy scent of wood smoke mixed with the pulse of music and the sound of hundreds of camps hurrying to assemble their tents, as the long fingers of fading light brushed past them, leaving the Playa suffused in a soft, inky darkness.

As I loaded up with supplies from the trunk of the car (gallons of water, eggs, tequila) and started walking toward the Costco camp, I felt a deep and growing sense of excitement.

I'd been in contact with Rico for eight months by now and couldn't wait to finally meet him. I had a sense of most of the other forty Costco-ers too, from reading their daily email exchanges on The List (the Costco intranet).

There'd been a lot from Garry—the Seattle guy Rico had put me in contact with months ago—as he was the camp cook and had to tell The List what supplies to bring. I felt I'd left it too long to get back in contact with him after our initial exchange, but I paid close attention to any emails he posted to The List. They were always funny, affectionate, and full of energy; he sounded like a good guy, a little mysterious as well. I was curious about him, as well as feeling slightly intimidated.

There was also Annie (Rico's girlfriend), plus OB, Jennith, Kenzie, Leopard Head, Hank, Brenda and Jefe, Age, Elvis (a lovely woman called Rachel), Vanilla, Shakes, BillnotDave, Reverend Johnny, Cute Steve, Lello, Princess, Angel and Kirby, Abelicious and Boy Toy . . . and a whole ton of others, all of whom I met the moment I walked into the Costco camp.

I stepped over a guy rope, into a clearing full of dusty sofas. One of the couples draped across them looked up as I walked in and smiled at me. "Hi," I said, peering over an armful of water bottles. "I'm Jennifer, I'm camping with you guys."

It was like I had triggered some kind of Code Red security alert. As soon as the words were out of my mouth, the couple jumped to their feet, ran into an area behind the sofas where three large tents backed onto each other, and yelled at the top of their lungs: "80 Dates Jen's here! 80 Dates Jen's here!"

I jumped in surprise and struggled not to drop my supplies as people poured from the tents and ran toward me. Their faces were lit up with smiles as they exclaimed, "Oh my God, she actually came. It's 80 Dates Jen!"

I had no idea why everyone was so happy to see me (or indeed until this moment that I was called "80 Dates Jen"), but it was one of the nicest welcomes I'd ever received and I burst out laughing. "Yes," I said, grinning, accepting my title, "80 Dates Jen has arrived."

As the group gathered around me, over their heads I noticed a man standing in the tent's doorway, staring as if sizing me up. I had no idea who he was but—although looking a little harassed—I didn't mind the attention: He was tall and utterly gorgeous with bleached blond hair, startling aquamarine blue eyes, and a broad smile on his stubbly face. Shaking his head, he walked over. "I'm in the middle of cooking, but I had to come and see this for myself," he told me. "So you made it, huh? 80 Dates Jen, welcome to Costco. I'm Garry."

And he kissed me.

It wasn't a long kiss, but it was knowing, playful, and sexy. Pulling away, he grinned. "Okay, gotta get back to the kitchen," and he walked back toward the tent.

I didn't get the chance to react: As soon as he turned and walked away, every single person in the camp stepped up to introduce themselves in the same way. I felt like the U.N. of Kissing as a multitude of mouths descended on mine. About twenty kisses in, a voice shouted: "Hey, has anyone offered 80 Dates a drink?" A man with a sunburned face half-concealed by a dusty mop of curly hair and a pair of black horn-rimmed glasses beamed at me. I knew straight away it was Rico and we gave each other a big hug. "Come on, 80 Dates, let me introduce you to . . . the bar." And, putting his arm affectionately around my waist, Rico steered me into a tent.

Inside the tent, I found myself at the bar, being served cocktails from a blender by Age, the barman. Rico and I sat and chatted, too happy to see each other to be shy. He introduced me to Annie, tiny and beautiful, like a gorgeous, dusty Tinkerbell; Jennith, resplendent in a leopard-print dress, not to be outdone by Leopard Head, who was outfitted head to toe in leopard print . . . Costco staff washed in and out as over the next couple of hours I sat in the bar—too excited to eat—and finally met my co-workers at the Costco Soul Mate Trading Outlet.

As the campsite became engulfed in darkness, Rico made a speech welcoming me to the camp. "Costco staff come from all over the world, and although we shouldn't be impressed that she's traveled from England via virtually everywhere else to be here with us, we are. Welcome, 80 Dates Jen." And everyone cheered and raised their glasses to me.

"Hey, has she been welcomed *officially* with Age's chili vodka?" OB shouted from the back. I raised my eyebrows, having no idea what this welcome entailed. The doubt must have shown on my face, because Age squeezed my arm reassuringly.

"Don't worry," he said. "You can nominate someone to drink it for you."

For the last fifteen minutes, Garry had been standing a few feet away. He'd smiled at me quite a few times but hadn't yet come over to talk. I'd been dying to talk to him but had been inundated with people introducing themselves and wanting to chat; plus—if truth be told—I was feeling a little shy, so I'd contented myself with returning his smiles.

I knew this was my opportunity.

Without stopping, for fear I'd change my mind, I spun around to Age and said: "I'd like to nominate Garry to drink it for me."

Garry, who'd obviously been keeping track of our conversation, gave a groan and rolled his eyes but came straight over. Without a word, he took the brimming shot-glass from Age and, fixing me with a steady look, put the glass to his lips and downed it in one, then pulled me to him and gave me a long, deep kiss, holding me tightly against his chest. As the chili set my mouth on fire, the kiss set my heart racing. I had no idea what was going on but I didn't want it to stop.

But it did stop with Jennith, Lello, and Kenzie suddenly tugging at my shoulder and urging, "80 Dates, come with us; we're going to play on the Playa."

I felt dazed as Garry and I pulled apart, but I nodded and told them I'd love to go exploring. Turning back to Garry, I blurted: "Would you like to come too?"

Garry smiled and said, "Maybe I can organize the grand tour." He disappeared for a moment and came back with two bikes. Handing one to me, he asked: "Shall we?" and together the pair of us cycled off into the night to explore BRC.

Cycling around the festival by the light of the moon was the physical equivalent of lying in bed at night tuning a radio. Spells of intense darkness were suddenly interrupted by unconnected voices or music that suggested an incredible story you'd grasp the edge of, before the darkness sucked it away and engulfed you in silence once more.

Sharing this experience with Garry was intimate and intense since—rattling along the bumpy desert floor in the dark—we could hear but not really see each other. There was the additional danger that if you looked away for a moment, you ran the real risk of running someone down or getting knocked off yourself.

There was so much to take in, it was almost overwhelming. But this wasn't the only new experience. From the moment Garry and I had left the Costco bar and cycled off on our own, it was almost as if the chili kissing was forgotten. The focus was off us and on the wild nightlife of the Playa. We set off like wide-eyed truants, stowing away together on the first train to London.

Paradoxically, as the seething masses stripped, whipped,

danced, and paraded around the Playa, Garry and I were on a wonderfully old-fashioned date. We'd get off the bikes in busy areas and people-watch or inspect one of the many intricate pieces of art. Like the one-hundred-foot model of a chandelier that—perfect in every detail—appeared to have crashed from the sky, shattering in pieces across the Playa floor. Or the roller rink full of naked skaters laughing and crashing into each other. Or the Thunderdome, where—as in *Mad Max*—two fighters suspended from a fifty-foot metal dome by bungee ropes beat each other with padded baseball bats as the crowd roared and screamed for their champion. At the remote Temple of Remembrance, people sat quietly reflecting and remembering lost loved ones.

Garry and I shared it all.

I was really attracted to him, but I also loved the way he was always concerned for me: Whenever we rocketed over a bump in the desert or a crowd would crash into us, he would check I was okay. He was gentlemanly without being macho. And he was really good company: He talked just as much as I did and made me laugh a lot. We talked about ourselves, old relationships, family and friends, life in London and Seattle, our plans for the future. As he spoke, I was absorbed in what he was saying; I didn't feel bogged down in detail the way I had on the other dates.

We seemed to like and dislike the same things. We spent a long time with the Deities living in the base of the forty-seven-foot pyramid temple on which the thirty-two-foot Burning Man stood. Taking time out from cycling, we curled up together on a sofa and watched a rather uneventful-looking film, which suddenly turned into scary 1960s porn. The man graphically thrust his hand in and out of the woman as if searching for car keys in a glove compartment. We were both frozen to the spot with embarrassment; this was not first-date material, but we were both too self-conscious to laugh it off. Garry managed to break the tension. "Did you want to carry on watching *Bad Core* or shall we make a move?" he asked with a wry smile. I scrambled gratefully to my feet and we cycled onward.

I know this sounds clichéd, but being with Garry was effortless. It wasn't awkward or stressful; I didn't feel like I was trying to behave in a certain way or pushing myself to be more this, less that. And it wasn't just because we liked the same music and places and food. I was relaxed, like I already knew him.

Being with Garry felt like coming home.

I know, I know, it sounds completely pathetic and I don't blame you for wanting to slap me really hard, but I couldn't help it: I was smitten. Completely and utterly. And even though I'd suspected from his emails to both The List and me that I would like him, I hadn't seen this coming. I mean, in theory, Garry wasn't even a date. I had spent the last eight months cajoling and bullying the Date Wranglers into coming up with an array of the internationally available, and here I was, meeting someone on my own, just like that.

But I wasn't thinking about any of this because I was having such a brilliant and funny time. I wasn't thinking about Soul Mates or about dating or about what number I was up to and how many more I had to go. I was just here, in the desert, with a man who made me want to tell him my secrets and listen quietly as he told me his.

It had been a long day for both of us. As dawn transformed the Playa from a peekaboo playground of the twisted and the inspired into a parched wasteland of all-night revelers, we both felt the need to get some sleep.

Cycling back to the Costco camp, as we stacked our bikes against the others, Garry asked, "Did you get a chance to pitch your tent earlier?"

"Oh, I don't have a tent," I told him nonchalantly. "I'm going to sleep in my car."

Garry looked appalled and stared at me with real concern. "Jen, you can't sleep in your car. That's crazy."

I asked him why. "I've got some hotel towels to sleep under and it's pretty quiet where I parked. I'll be fine."

My *whatever* traveling attitude was so firmly in place, sleeping in the car genuinely didn't bother me at all. Garry, however, seemed to feel strongly to the contrary. He bit his lip in exasperation as if trying not to say what he was thinking, then ran his hand through his dusty blond hair. "Look," he said awkwardly, "I really don't want to tell you what to do, but I won't be able to relax knowing you are out there somewhere sleeping in your car." He frowned deeply and took my hand in his. "Jen," he said, "please sleep in my trailer."

I raised my eyebrows, but he ignored the look and continued, "You can have the bed, I'll sleep on the floor. There's plenty of space and I'm not trying to . . ." He trailed off, shrugging uncomfortably, but with a look that suggested he was going to keep insisting until I said yes.

I thought about it. I really didn't mind sleeping in the car—it was no big deal—but, for me at least, that wasn't what this was really about. I remembered Hettie's words in Vegas: " . . . when the moment comes, you have to be prepared to take that leap of faith."

I wasn't going to overthink this: I liked and trusted Garry. I felt safe with him, cared for rather than hit on. The idea of sleeping in his trailer—although a little scary—felt right. I knew it was time to take that leap.

"Thank you," I said quietly. "I appreciate the offer."

I thought I could sleep on the floor and he could have the bed. But when we got back to his trailer, it felt the most natural and wonderful thing in the world to climb out of our dusty clothes and slip under the covers together.

We were woken a couple of hours later by the sounds of the Costco crew breakfasting in the communal area outside. I felt a sudden pang of anxiety: Would they all think me a total hussy for jumping straight into bed with Garry?

Propped up on one arm, I confided my fears: "I haven't even come close to sleeping with anyone else on the trip"—I sort of glossed over Frank—"what if they think I sleep with all my Dates?"

Pulling me back down into the bed, Garry kissed me, then shook his head reassuringly. "They're not like that," he said. "Everyone will just be pleased for us. Why wouldn't they be?"

And sure enough, as we dragged ourselves out of bed and stood in the doorway of the trailer, squinting into the ferocious morning sun, the Costco-ers sitting around the breakfast tables spotted us and started clapping and cheering. Garry and I smiled at each other sheepishly. The crowd laughed and cheered even harder. By now we were laughing too and—pausing at the top of the steps to take a bow—holding hands, we joined our friends for breakfast.

The next five days were magical.

The rest of that day passed in a blur. I had to work in the Costco Store (where old Soul Mates were traded for new) and Garry had to organize dinner for forty people that night.

This was a good thing, partially as it gave me a chance to get my head around the last twelve hours and also because the desert by day was very different from the desert at night.

The heat was overwhelming. Dust storms would sweep across

the Playa, blinding and choking you. The dust was abrasive and invasive: It coated your body and hair, got in your mouth, your eyes, made your nose suddenly gush blood. You had to constantly remind yourself to drink as the heat brutally sucked moisture and minerals from your body, leaving you dizzy and disoriented. Sometimes I'd get terrible cramps. On the worst day, I was so overwhelmed by heat I couldn't remember what I was saying, and sentences would just trail off. Some people collapsed; everyone kept an eye on everyone else, alert for the first signs of dehydration and ready to share precious water.

Twice a day, trucks would drive along the main roads spraying water behind them in an attempt to keep the dust down. That was always a carnival-like atmosphere: People would stream out of their tents, running naked behind the trucks, cooling off in the al fresco shower.

Over the next five days, I'd see this all from the Store as I worked to help people find their Soul Mates.

The way it worked: People brought in a Soul Mate they didn't want and both answered questions on a form that would help us find one they did want. The forms recorded where they were camping (vital if Soul Mates were to find each other) and included questions like: What do people say is your most annoying habit? What's the one class you regret not taking at school? Are you or have you ever been a slut?

Using their answers, interviewers would further probe the applicants. They would then pass their conclusions on to the matchers, who would use all this information to identify the applicant's ideal Soul Mate from among the hundreds of other interviewed applicants on file. People would return the next day to find out who they'd been matched with and then go to their Soul Mate's camp to introduce themselves.

Costco was one of the oldest and most popular theme camps on the Playa; every day hundreds of people turned up to have a fun experience, but also seriously hoping we could help them find their Soul Mate.

And we took it just as seriously.

Working in two shifts from 10 a.m. until 6 p.m., we sat every day in the sweltering tent, literally sweating over the completed forms of hopeful applicants. Tears welled up in the heavily made-up eyes of a dreadlocked pixie as she confided how she hoped to find a man who loved welding as much as she did. A French-woman told me she had been matched with a fabulous "Playa lover," last year and wanted one just as good this year. Naked but for a Viking helmet, one man suddenly got really upset after twenty minutes of banter and told me he just wanted a woman he could trust.

I was surprised by how similar the hopes and needs of the people here in BRC were to those of the men I'd already dated on my travels.

As countless people, dressed as fairies or undressed as nudists and every possible combination and permutation in between, sat across the table and talked, I heard the same heartfelt story each time. It didn't matter that some had extreme tastes or habits; whatever the personality, the aims were the same: to find some-one who was like them. They wanted a companion who shared their interests, someone who would understand and cohabit in their world.

More than anything, people didn't want to be alone.

Listening to people talk honestly and vulnerably about what they hoped for in a Soul Mate was exhausting but humbling. Of course, I knew exactly how they felt (with the possible exception of the man looking for a Soul Mate who would lock him in the trunk of his car) and I wanted to do all I could to help.

Sometimes this worked, for example with the lovely artist guy and Welding Woman. They came to see me at the end of the week, still delighting in each other's company, and thanked me for helping them meet. Sometimes it didn't work, like the nervous mid-thirties teacher, who anxiously told me that he was always unlucky in love. I was so convinced he was gay it didn't even occur to me to ask.

As I happily told him I had the perfect man for him (a sweet scientist from the day before), his face crumpled; his chin jutted in and out dangerously, like a cutlery drawer possessed by demons.

"But I'm not gay!" he told me incredulously.

"Are you really sure about that?" I wanted to ask, but his eyes beseeched me to say I had made a mistake. I wanted to help him find happiness (with his gay Soul Mate), but seeing him look so miserable, I lost the courage of my convictions. Patting his hand, I guiltily told him I was sure we had a ton of suitable women for him.

He sniffed tearfully, still looking shocked and upset. Quickly scanning his application form in the hope of changing the subject, I hit the Talents section and started talking as I read. "Oh, that's interesting," I said heartily. "It says here, you do an extremely lifelike impersonation of . . ." My voice trailed off, ". . . a . . . ummm . . . frog?" I finished weakly, looking up to check I hadn't misunderstood.

The man looked at me steadily. Still swathed in misery, he nevertheless cleared his throat and—wobbly at first, then louder as his confidence grew—started to impersonate a frog. He sat staring at me, unblinking. Croaking. Although he still looked completely wretched, he clearly had been unable to resist the opportunity to show off his party piece. Watching, I struggled to arrange my expression into one that (I hoped) conveyed both enjoyment and admiration.

After a couple of minutes, his croaking crescendoed, then came to an end. I thanked him for *sharing* (a popular ritual in America) and told him we'd do our very best to find him his Soul Mate. Revitalized by his impersonation, he thanked me sincerely and left the tent. I reached for my water bottle and took a deep swallow. Perhaps I was suffering from heat exhaustion and had just imagined the entire episode.

The days were filled with incidents like this and interspersed with a kaleidoscope of impressions and adventures shared with the other Costco-ers.

One day, Jennith and I ended up on the Spanking Machine.

I had never tried or even been curious about S&M, but as Jennith and I came across the Bike Mistress sitting on her saddle, hard wire bristles radiating out from the front wheel, we thought, *Why not?*

I went first, standing in front of the bike, the scary wheel a few inches from my bottom. Bike Mistress demanded in a strict voice: "How bad have you been?"

Even though I'd never experienced recreational beating, I knew instinctively my reply would impact very directly on what happened next. I thought carefully before answering. "Well, on the whole, actually I've been pretty good," I prevaricated, "but . . . you know . . . possibly a bit bad toward the end?"

Hoping I'd said the right thing, I heard Bike Mistress turn the pedals over. And as she started to pedal, the wire spokes gently slapped against the back of my combat shorts.

As Bike Mistress began cycling harder, though, I could feel the wires start to sting. I let out a gasp: It hurt. Bike Mistress was in her element by now and pedaling faster and faster; the wire switches started slapping and biting hard into my skin.

As the pain increased, I opened my mouth and let out a shriek that grew louder and louder as the bike went faster and faster. By now the pain was intense, and I shrieked unreservedly, like a kettle boiling near to the point of death.

Then it stopped.

I stumbled forward from the sudden change in pressure; then, realizing it was over and how much my bottom hurt, I started laughing. I don't know why I found it so funny—maybe because why anyone would do this for pleasure was now truly a mystery to me, or because I was happy I'd tried something new. I turned around and saw Bike Mistress looking at me with respect. "That was really awesome," she said. "You did well."

I grinned and looked at Jennith, who—in complete contrast—looked mortified. "Come *on,* 80 Dates," she said, grabbing my arm and hustling me away. "You're making *so* much noise."

"But, Jennith . . ." I protested in astonishment. "You're next. You're going on too, aren't you?"

Pretending she hadn't heard, Jennith was already on her bike and cycling determinedly away. I gingerly climbed onto my own saddle and pedaled after her, shouting unconvincingly: "It didn't hurt that much. Come back, you baby. . . . "

I loved having these experiences with the Costco-ers; they were warm, wonderful people, a community I instantly belonged with.

The time we all felt this most strongly was at the communal dinners each night. Dinner was always accompanied by speeches: Rico thanking us for all our hard work; Garry and the kitcheners being told what an amazing meal they'd made; Hank sharing an experience he'd had in the Store; Elvis telling us about a fantastic theme camp she'd discovered. It might sound gushing and maudlin, but having a brilliant time in an ultra-extreme environment was only possible because everyone worked so hard as a team; sharing a good meal and making speeches was a way of acknowledging that.

And I especially loved this time of night because Garry and I were off-duty. We'd pop in and see each other during the day, but, busy as we were working in the kitchen and store respectively, it wasn't until the evening that we could spend more than a couple of minutes together.

Some nights we'd stay with the whole group, dressing up in ball gowns and going to the Prom a couple of camps down, or cycling around with OB and showing each other parts of the site that had been built that day, or watching the world go by from the dusty comfort of one of the Costco sofas.

It'd always end up just the two of us, though. Caught up in conversation with each other, we sometimes just didn't notice when the group moved on. Other times, we wanted to be on our own, to hold hands and walk through a neon maze or marvel at the people scrambling over vast granite obelisks impossibly suspended from thick iron chains.

And the whole time we'd be talking about everything and nothing, laughing at silly jokes we now shared, stopping in the dust and kissing each other with a hungry passion.

And, of course, we talked about my journey. Garry understood absolutely why I had decided to embark on it. Being a career junkie himself, he'd started to lose hope of meeting anyone he really cared about, too. "Until now," he told me as we sat by the Temple of Remembrance, looking up at the stars over the desert.

After just four days together, it seemed crazy to say that I had met and was falling in love with my Soul Mate. But that's how it felt. We'd clicked instantly, in a way that was powerful and very real.

But I was also painfully aware that I was going to have to leave soon. As well as a dating past, I had a dating future.

I couldn't quite get my head around how I was going to incorporate the fact that I had met Garry—potentially my Soul Mate—into my journey, but I knew I had to. I was committed to my Dates: They weren't just numbers, they were people I was involved with now, and I didn't want to treat them badly. And I *wanted* to meet them, as well as do all those things my DWs and I had worked flat-out to pull together. And besides, leaving here would hopefully give me a chance to think about Garry and put everything that had happened between us on the Playa into perspective. Who knew, maybe I was just in denial and marching on with a *business as usual* attitude because I didn't know how else to handle this new minefield of feelings.

Garry seemed much calmer about it all. "Don't worry, Jen," he said reassuringly, "I know you have to do this."

I think one of the reasons he was able to be so reasonable was that our experience was so intense that we weren't really able to imagine anything beyond it. Everything about *now* felt so right. Leaving Garry and the Playa seemed impossible, like this was our home and we'd stay here forever. Leaving Garry—the man I'd traveled the world to find—to go date other men seemed too bizarre for words. Like a parallel universe.

But I thought again of the couple in Vegas united through the dogged efforts of Fate: *"Our entire lives were leading to our time together,"* Hettie had told me.

Well, Fate had brought me on this journey and had led me to Garry; it would seem she had plans for our future, too.

Back in London, when I'd finally settled on my route through the U.S., I had decided to go from here to Missoula, then from Missoula on to Seattle.

Seattle was where Garry lived.

After I left the Playa, I'd see Garry again in Seattle five days later and stay with him for the duration of my visit.

We slept less as the time to leave grew closer. It wasn't that we were consciously trying to cram in as much time together as possible, it was more that the better we got to know each other, the more hours we wanted to spend together.

The morning I had to leave, we'd been up all night.

It was 5.30 a.m. I'd said a tearful good-bye to the lovely Costco-ers the night before; Garry and I walked along the dusty road to the car with armfuls of my belongings that item by item had taken up residence in Garry's trailer.

Usually when we went out onto the Playa together, we'd always be nudging each other to look at an incredible sculpture, an interesting theme camp, a crazy costume (or lack of it). But now we walked in silence. We didn't notice the pink dawn blossom around us, or the dancers or the cyclists or the art. We were both quietly wondering how we were going to say good-bye.

Over the last week, I had lived in my boots, combat shorts, and bikini; I'd almost been embarrassed changing out of them into my regular jeans and a T-shirt half an hour earlier. Here for another three days, Garry was still in his crazy shorts and a Burning Man necklace while I was dressed for the real world and feeling as if I already had one foot out the door.

We dumped the stuff in the trunk of my dusty car and Garry walked me to the driver's side, opening the door for me. I threw my bag onto the passenger seat and turned to face him.

We looked at each other in silence. Neither of us wanted to say the words, so we said nothing at all. Garry reached out and took me in his arms.

"I am not going to cry, I am not going to cry," I told myself.

But strangely, in a way, I felt sort of all right.

I'd been on fifty-four dates and met no one. What were the chances of me meeting anyone else? In fact, considering the odds, I thought myself pretty lucky to have stumbled upon Garry at all. Also, I had talked so much to Garry, I now needed to talk *about* Garry. I wanted to ring and email my friends and tell them I'd met someone amazing; give them a blow-by-blow account of how gorgeous he was, what he'd said, what he was like, how he made me feel. Girl stuff. And I'd see him in five days.

Okay, I'd talked myself around. It was all right; it was all going to be fine.

"It's all going to be fine, you know," I said gently, moving my head from Garry's shoulder and looking up at him. "We'll see each other in five days and you can show me Seattle."

But Garry didn't look fine; he looked tired and sad. I could tell he was thinking about how it was going to be when I was gone. But he forced a smile and narrowed his eyes, studying me intensely. "Yes," he said quietly. "Yes. It'll be fine." Then, determined to be strong, he straightened his shoulders and stopped frowning. "Now, you drive safely and have a good flight." I nodded dutifully. "I've got your hotel number in Missoula," he continued. "I'll call you on Monday when I'm on the way back to Seattle."

Now that he was suddenly fine, I started getting upset. The tears ran down my cheeks as I buried my face in his shoulder.

We held each other tightly as all around us BRC geared up for another hot day on the Playa. But I had a long drive to Reno and a plane to catch, so with one last kiss and one last promise to call, I got in the car, got out of the car, gave him another kiss and a hug, got back in the car. And drove away.

I kept looking up at the rearview mirror. Garry stood on the side of the road and watched for a long time as I drove out of

BRC, past the greeters and away. A part of me was saying, "Oh bugger the Dates, I'm staying," and thinking of turning back. But I knew I couldn't. And I knew I mustn't. Garry lived in Seattle, I lived in London.

If we really were Soul Mates, this would be the first of many good-byes.

chapter ten

U.S.A.– Missoula, Montana

Me with real rodeo-ers, Bill and Ramona Holt, at the Holt Heritage Museum, Missoula, USA

In the heart of the Rocky Mountains that run southeast from Alaska all the way down to Mexico, Missoula was one of those places where it was hard not to have a good time. The University of Montana's campus was here, so there was always a decent band playing, plus with all the rivers and trails dotted around, you could pedal, paddle, and promenade to your heart's content.

That was one of the reasons I'd planned to come here on my dating tour: Missoula has always been one of my feel-good places and, even before I'd met the Love Professor, I'd known that happy people are luckier in love. The other reason was a bit sillier but no less heartfelt. Nicholas Evans's book *The Smoke Jumper* was based on the Missoulian firemen who fight the huge fires that ravage the surrounding area each summer by jumping out of planes directly into the path of the blaze.

It was a classic, sappy love story full of fearless, athletic, yet imperceptibly vulnerable men doing a real and dangerous job. I was in a romantic daze as I read it and—since it was set in my beloved Missoula—wanted to see for myself if the real smokejumpers were just as dreamy.

Of course, all this was before I met Garry.

For the ten hours I'd been traveling, I could only think of two things: how much I needed a bath and how much I missed Garry. The notion that I had Dates waiting for me at the end of the journey (the smokejumper plus a rodeo rider and possibly Cam, an American friend of Jo's) was not so much unwelcome as unimaginable.

Descending the steep mountain pass from Interstate 90 into Missoula, I was struck by the eerie brown pall engulfing not just the entire town but the mountains all around it. I already knew from conversations with the Missoula Smokejumpers' headquarters that this summer's fires were some of the worst on record: over 3,300 wildfires already burning out of control across 665,800 acres, with new fires taking hold every day. It was only now I was here that I understood just how serious it was, and I felt guilty for having taken such a flippant attitude.

Parking the car, I walked up the steps of the Holiday Inn, admiring the pretty Clark Fork River and bike trails that ran behind the hotel and along the edge of town. Down in the valley it was a fabulous sun-trap, but the smoke from the burning mountains that surrounded us made the hot sun hazy. I couldn't actually see the smoke but my eyes were streaming and my throat stung; people checking in ahead of me were coughing constantly. The town really was in the grip of a disaster.

I wasn't surprised, therefore, when reading my messages up in my room, to see one from Tim Eldridge, my contact at the smokejumper HQ and the man Nicholas Evans's main character had been based on. He wanted to warn me that the date probably wasn't going to happen since all the men were working back-to-back shifts trying to control the fires. He invited me to meet him at HQ the next day and said he'd do the best he could. I left a message immediately asking him to please not worry about the date: I hoped everyone was safe and, yes, I'd love to meet him tomorrow.

I opened up my laptop. On the Playa there had been no cell-phone coverage, no emails, so I hadn't been in contact with the outside world for five days. But as AOL popped onto the screen, it quickly became clear that the outside world had indeed been in contact with me.

There were 378 emails. From Dates who had been, Dates who were to be, and friends checking the details on Dates who might be. There were confirmations from hotels; invoices for reserved flights; details for rental cars to be collected. There were also work emails: Could I do an interview about this; was I free to write an article about that; did I have the notes for a conference I was chairing next month?

My eyes blurred as I struggled to take in the details, and I finally gave up and ran a bath instead.

After five days in the desert—where I had barely washed, knowing not to waste a single precious drop—I now marveled at how freely the water gushed from the taps. It seemed an extraordinary extravagance to be able to lie in a huge tub of hot, clean water.

Undressing, I was shocked when I caught sight of my reflection in the mirror: Tanned a deep brown, my face was sprinkled with freckles and my body was caked with sand and dirt from the desert. My hair was rigid with dust, my plaits sticking out almost at right angles. It took me a moment to work out why I had angry red welts and black bruises on my bottom, until I realized I was inspecting the handiwork of Bike Mistress.

Exhausted from the last week's excitement and lack of sleep, I caught myself dozing off in the bath, and had to drag myself out and dry off. Crawling into the impossibly huge and impossibly clean bed, I slept like a dead person for fourteen hours.

The next morning, feeling stunned like I had jet lag, I walked to one of the downtown coffee shops. Armed with a couple of strong black coffees, I planned another attempt at reading my emails and getting my thoughts into some sort of order.

"A grande Americano with space please," I told the thirty-something woman busy taking orders behind the counter—a black coffee, cup not filled to the top. Starbucks has taught even us Brits the universal language of coffee ordering: *Espresseranto*.

She took my money. "I'm not sure what kind of spice you want, hon," she noted helpfully, "but we have cinnamon over there by the milk."

I looked at her blankly. "Spice?" I repeated slowly; then realizing she'd misunderstood my accent, I laughed and said: "Not spice, s-p-*a*-c-e," putting heavy emphasis on the offending vowel.

Now it was her turn to stare blankly. Another woman, making the coffee, sensed a problem and came over to the counter. "Everything okay?" she asked brightly.

The first woman turned and said: "She wants spice but we only have cinnamon."

"Oh, I'm sorry," the barista apologized. "What kind of spice was it that you wanted?"

I was a bit too tired for this, but persevered. "I don't want s-p-i-c-e," I explained, enunciating for all I was worth, "I want s-p-a-c-e." Now both looked at me blankly. I tried another tack: "Room. I'd like room in the cup, please."

Upon hearing my request, both women stiffened visibly and regarded me with open disapproval. "We don't have a license to serve alcohol, ma'am," the barista said with a sniff. "I'm afraid you'll have to go to a bar if you want to drink."

This really was too much. Putting both hands flat on the counter and leaning toward them menacingly, I hissed through gritted teeth: "Not RUM, r-o-o-m!" A caffeine-withdrawal meltdown was barreling irrevocably toward the surface, like a great white shark with a stomach unexpectedly full of cork.

"She wants a black Americano with space," the man behind me called across the counter. *That's what I just SAID,* I thought to myself. But his American accent made all the difference and the cloud perceptibly lifted from the countenances of both women. They beamed, as all anxiety over serving the alcoholic foreign lady vanished and they busied themselves with my order. I turned to thank the man, but he spoke first: "It's Jennifer, isn't it?"

That threw me. Could today be any more disorienting?

"Ummm, yes?" I replied, as if unsure myself. "Errrr, how do you . . . ? "

"I'm Cam," he interrupted, seeing my bewilderment, "Jo's friend? I swung by your hotel to ask if you wanted me to show you around a little. They said I'd find you here."

God, it was a Date. I was on a date and I hadn't even had a flaming cup of coffee yet.

Date #56: Cam—Missoula, Montana, U.S.A.
Cam was a friend of Jo's. They'd met at a Buddhist retreat in California, where he lived. Although I was grateful he'd rescued me

from my coffee debacle (it turned out to be terrible coffee, for the record), he scared the bejesus out of me right from the start.

With a shaven head and extraordinary cornflower-blue eyes (I felt like I was on *The Amazing Eyes of America* tour—all the men I met seemed to have them), he sat across the table from me, talking about kayaking but giving me a direct and unnerving look that said: *I will take all your clothes off here and now, if you just say the word.*

It was all too much. I hadn't yet mentally prepared myself: I was still loved up and back in *Garryland.*

Every year, Cam came to Missoula to take a ten-day rafting trip along the Lochsa River. He'd got back from it just the night before and was excited and energized by the adventure. "Moving with the elements allows you to harness the energy of nature," he told me, his face feverish with excitement. Apparently he'd come away believing more strongly than ever that "you can't waste that energy. You have to store it up and channel it through everyday life; channel it through the people you meet."

It was no good: I wasn't in the mood for Cam and his channeling. "Cam, it's lovely to meet you," I said, trying to stem the flow. "And I'm glad you had such an exciting trip, but . . ." And I told him all about Burning Man and Garry and how I needed a couple of hours simply to absorb and understand what had happened to me. I was sorry and was very much looking forward to our date, but could we maybe have it a little later?

Cam smiled. "That's beautiful, Jennifer," he said, taking my hand in his. "And I can feel this man has affected you deeply: I have to tell you that you are generating some very strong, spiritual energy right now." I nodded, relieved. "In fact," Cam continued, now trailing his fingers across my palm and circling them around my wrist, "perhaps there is a way that you and I can channel our energies together." Giving me *that look* again, he edged his chair closer, sliding his leg slowly and deliberately against mine. "It would be a very powerful experience for us both," he added in a low voice.

Wriggling my hand out of Cam's grip, I lurched unsteadily to my feet as I attempted to disentangle my legs from his while grabbing my laptop from underneath the table and snatching my cardigan from the back of the chair.

"So, umm, Cam, thank you for coming out to find me," I stammered, backing away from the table and pretending I hadn't understood his suggestion. "I'm pretty busy while I'm here and, actually, may have to go early. But, you know, I've got your number, so if there's time, I'll . . . uummm . . . give you a call." And with that, I fled the café and went straight back to my hotel, leaving a message at reception that under no circumstances was I to be disturbed.

Back in my room, I threw myself onto the bed and stared up at the ceiling for inspiration. What was I going to do? Where could my dating tour go from here? I mean, forget about Cam and his energetic overtures, could I carry on dating any man when all I could think about was Garry?

It felt like sitting down to dinner having already eaten: I wasn't hungry for more dates. I wanted to see Garry, pick up where we'd left off. I felt embarrassed to be missing him already—it was only a day since I'd seen him, for chrissakes—but it wasn't just that I missed his presence: I missed the way I felt when I was with him.

But what if it was just Playa Love?

What if, outside the extraordinary, emotionally live environment of BRC, we met in the real world and . . . there was nothing? No spark, no wonder?

Should I give up on my trip or should I keep dating?

If I stopped dating, Garry and I would have the time to get to
know each other and see if this was for real. But would I then feel
I'd let my Dates and Date Wranglers down? And if I didn't complete my journey, would there always be a quiet voice whispering
What if?

From a positive perspective, would continuing to date be the
test that proved Garry and I really were Soul Mates? But did I
have the confidence in me, in Garry and me, and in Fate, to believe our relationship could survive the rest of my journey? Or
was I being naïve and selfish even imagining that a relationship
could be that flexible? Would I inevitably push Garry's understanding too far and lose him forever?

Ugh! It was all going round and round in my head. I wanted
to do the right thing, but I had no idea what the right thing was.
Then it hit me. I sat up on the bed and dragged my laptop onto
my knees.

This was a question for the Date Wranglers.

My Very Dear Date Wranglers,
    I'm sorry to be so me, me, me (though you all
know me well enough not to be surprised), but, as
the inner circle of my Date Wranglers, I am in urgent need of your advice and counsel.
    55 dates in, I've met my Soul Mate and I don't
know what to do.
    I met Garry at the Burning Man Festival last
week and it was pretty much love at first sight (see
attached pic). From the moment he took me on the
moonlit bike ride through the desert—romantic and
magical—we were inseparable.
    He's my age, works in radio, lives in Seattle,
and is funny, kind, and utterly gorgeous :) I'm

going to stay with him in Seattle next week to see
how we get on in "real life."

But in the meantime, I'm in Missoula and the
last thing I feel like doing is dating the rodeo
rider or smokejumper while I'm missing him so much.
I still have loads more dates to go and don't want
to drop everything at the first sign of SMA (Soul
Mate Action), but at the same time, he's just great
and I don't seem to be able to think beyond that.

Please tell me what you think I should do.

Sorry to be so melodramatic—this has completely
thrown me. I always assumed I'd meet someone in
Fulham when I got home! Hope you are all groovy and
well. Kisses, Jxxx

P.S. Jo—we need to talk about Cam!

The moment I sent the email I felt relieved: I knew I'd done the
right thing. The DWs would give me some perspective and good
advice. The situation felt too big for me alone, and for the mil-
lionth time I was grateful to have such good friends to call on.

And, seeing that the decision was now percolating through
the system, I felt free to get on with my day. Grabbing a coffee
from reception, I jumped in the car and drove the seven miles
west out of town to the Missoula Smokejumper HQ.

Tim wasn't there, but he'd left another message saying he was
sorry he couldn't make it, he was out fielding calls. As he'd predicted, all the men were out fighting the fires, so getting me a
date (Date #57) had proven impossible.

To be honest, I felt relieved, and that was nothing to do with
my feelings about Garry. The fires were so bad, crews were being
called in from neighboring states to help. This was clearly the
wrong time for me to be turning up looking for a fun night out.

Latching onto a passing tour, I noticed a visiting crew were just finishing a tour of their own and were preparing to drill. Liz, our guide and a student volunteer, explained that drills were vital: From the time the siren sounded to being airborne, the crew had less than twelve minutes to drop everything, scramble into their 110-pound packs and suits, and be in position aboard the plane. To do this, the smokejumpers had to be fit (able to do seven pull-ups, forty-five sit-ups, and twenty-five push-ups and run a quarter of a mile in less than eleven minutes) as well as organized.

We walked through the locker room (a sign on the wall declaring STUPID HURTS), passing a couple of men at a bank of sewing machines making their own parachutes, and out into the workshop where yet more parachutes were stretched over long benches, smokejumpers hunched over them painstakingly inspecting their condition. A two-way radio sat on a shelf, surrounded by multiple containers of eyedrops and the largest collection of indigestion tablets I'd ever seen.

It was clearly a stressful life, and the room crackled with testosterone, boredom, and restless tension. The men were certainly manly, but Liz gave me a sobering insight into how life with a smokejumper would be.

Watching the visiting crew doing pull-ups on a bar, one of the women in our group asked Liz if she fancied any of the crew. "No," Liz replied, looking uncomfortable. "I know all the wives, who spend every day wondering if this will be the day their husbands don't make it home."

Back at the hotel, I logged on and was amazed to see that twenty-one of the DWs had already got back to me. All had clear and strong opinions as to what I should do. Some qualified their advice before giving it, like Paula:

I want you to know that what I know about boys can
be written on the back of a very small postage
stamp to a very small island . . . however . . .

Reading through the suggestions, I felt like a contestant on some
kind of reality game show where everyone was ringing in and vot-
ing on my next move. There were two unanimous reactions.
Firstly, thrilled I'd met someone I liked so much:

OOOOOHHHHHHH MMMMMMYYYYYYY
GOOOOOODDDDDDDDDDDDDDDDDDDDDDD!!!!!!!!!!!!!!!!!!!
    For real? He looks damn cute, that's for sure!
Grainne xxxxx

Secondly, demanding to know which of them could claim the
Date Wrangler crown, having pulled off this coup:

I'll be interested to know how the date came about
(or to cut to the chase . . . WHO gets the credit?).
Lots of love, Hec and Ang xxx
    P.S. Call IMMEDIATELY if you find yourself sere-
nading complete strangers with songs by the Carpenters and declaring yourself to be "On Top of the
World" to anyone who'll listen. . . .

However, on the dating question of should I stay or should I go,
the DWs were split down the middle.
    The No Girl—Stop Dating camp was all female, and ro-
mantic:

Wallow in it. Even if he is the one and you spend
the rest of your lives together, it'll never be the

same as it is for the first ninety days together....
I'm thrilled for you. Lots of love, Alison

inventive:

You've had 55 dates around the world, can't you do
another 25 with Garry? My advice is give it a go
and forget about the singing cowboy or whoever you
had lined up for subsequent dates. If you don't,
you'll kick yourself. Sarah xxxxx

and considerate:

No need to travel any farther. It would not be fair
on you, it would not be fair on Garry, not to mention those poor fellows who are waiting to meet
you. Malgosia xxxx

The Go Girl—Keep Dating camp was a mix of male and female,
and practical:

No matter how lovely Garry is, don't give up now.
If it's meant to be, and if he's the guy for you,
he'll wait for you. Simple as that. Lyn
xxxxxxxxxxxxxx

sensible:

when you're rolling round in the desert with exciting people, art installations, and dusty nipples at
every turn (and I'm taking this directly from you,
girl), most people look attractive/sexy/cool ...

but when you see him doing the washing up or queu-
ing to buy a coffee . . . well, that's the test. The
mundane stuff. Cath xxx

and extremely direct:

Coxy—put the relationship on hold till you've finished or do the rest REALLY FUCKING FAST!! Love, S

My advice would be to stay with your Soul Mate in
Seattle & let me carry on the dating game for you!
Okay, that wasn't very helpful, but you can't give
up: What if a month down the line SMA turns into
GOOMFYP (Get out of my face, you prat!)? Good luck,
sweetie. She MacB xx

Some brought their expertise to the problem:

Being an obsessive astro-chick—what's his star
sign/date/time of birth? If he's an Aquarian, don't
get too excited too soon: They fall head over heels
every couple of months . . . Glam Tan xxxx

Others brought their own problem to the problem:

Can't talk about Cam or anything else now . . . am
having trouble with Ryan AGAIN. Saw his ex at the
pub, who "really wants to be friends again." Of
course, we had a huge fight. Why does he get pissed
off with me when SHE'S the bitch who broke his
heart? Ah, yes, Love . . . that used to be a nice
feeling. Jo xxx

It was Belinda who gave the advice that was practical as well as romantic:

```
. . . You've worked so hard setting up this trip;
you won't be happy unless you see it through to the
end. Garry has to trust this isn't about you look-
ing for another man: It's about you having your
crazy adventure. If it's going to work, he needs to
appreciate that that's who you are and love you for
it, as we all do. Love B xxxxx
```

The jury was split.

Which actually was fine with me: They'd given me tons to think about and ultimately it *was* my decision. So I shut down the computer, put on a pair of shorts, and went and rented a mountain bike.

I think better when I'm on the move, and now, as I cycled along the trail that followed the Clark Fork River east to the university, I mulled over my situation.

I hardly noticed the football teams dashing up and down the field, their coach sweating as he shouted instructions; or the couples—also on bikes—chatting comfortably as their dogs bounded up and away; or even the early-twenties girl dressed in black, sitting strumming her guitar in the shade of a broad tree. I was pedaling hard and thinking harder.

As *I* saw it, this was my situation. I'd presented Fate with a challenge: I'd find and date eighty men around the world (okay, seventy-nine dates with seventy-nine men and one date with twenty-five women), and in return she'd give me my Soul Mate. I felt pretty sure Garry was The One, so Fate had delivered.

But of course, life is never that simple.

Rather than giving me my Soul Mate on Date #1 or Date #80, Fate had come through in the middle of my journey: Date #55. It was brutal timing, presenting no end of problems, but the fact was: Fate had delivered.

And maybe there was a reason for it happening this way. Maybe I'd met Garry halfway through the Odyssey because Fate had an additional purpose for my journey that I had yet to discover.

It might sound ridiculous, but my instincts told me that I had to stick to my plans, that if I didn't honor my side of the bargain, I'd lose Garry; if I reneged on my end of the deal, Fate would renege on hers.

I had no choice: If I wanted to keep Garry, I had to keep dating.

I'd need to ask Garry what he thought. I'd also need to tell the remaining twenty-five dates how my circumstances had changed (and accept that some might not want to see me as a result), but I'd made up my mind: I was going to keep dating.

Going back to the hotel was hard: Now that I was clear about what I needed to do, I really wanted to talk with Garry and try to explain my reasoning. I wanted to talk to him anyway; I missed him, and now that the pressure of *the next step* had lifted, I wanted to hear his voice and know I hadn't just imagined the whole thing (and that he hadn't changed his mind!).

The message light was flashing as I entered my room. My heart leaped: Even though I knew Garry was still at the festival, was it possible he'd found a way to call me?

But the message was from Chip, a friend of Tim's and a fellow smokejumper. He was getting married this weekend, had heard my story, and did I want to come and have dinner with him and his fiancée tonight? They lived a ways out of town. I checked my watch: I'd been cycling for four hours and it was now too late to go over. I rang Chip to explain.

He was incredibly friendly and down-to-earth. The wedding—a barbecue in the paddock overlooking the river, everyone drinking and dancing to a local band—sounded fantastic and I was sorry I wasn't going. Chip in turn was fascinated by my journey and the lengths to which I had gone to meet a Soul Mate. "You shoulda done what I did," he told me over the phone.

"Oh, what's that?" I asked, intrigued, imagining a barn-raising or a moonlight hike through the forests, or maybe even a dramatic rescue from the heart of a ferocious fire.

"Go on the Inner-net," he told me, breezily shattering my fantasies. "That's the way we meet our Soul Mates in these parts."

Cheered by my conversation with Chip, I took my book down to the hotel bar. It was full of petrol-heads from the Mustang Car Convention, which was currently making parking impossible outside. Aware I was a date down, I let one of the exhibitors buy me a beer as a sacrifice to the Numbers God. But my heart wasn't in it: I felt guilty and all I could think about was Garry.

The next day was the day I was going to hear from Garry, and time wouldn't pass fast enough. I wanted him to be the one to call but feared I'd be weak and ring him first (which, as much as I liked him, was obviously out of the question). I needed a distraction: It was a good day to get back on the Dating Wagon.

First, I sent an email to my Seattle Dates, letting them know that there had been a change in my date status: one to Jason, the president of the Ukulele Association of America, and the other to Ted, a friend of Posh PR Emma's.

```
Ted! :)
   Hey there, matie, how are you? How's it been
since last we spoke? I'm good, really well thx.
   Now, I have some good and bad news! The good
news is I'll be in Seattle from Thursday. The
bad news—I've met my Soul Mate and he lives in
Seattle!
   I'd still really love to meet you, though—finally
put a face to the typeface!! Let me know what you
think.
   Take care, Jx
```

I know, I know: an insane amount of punctuation and far too hearty and fake-cheerful. But let me ask you this: How do you tell a man you've never met—but have been in contact with for two months because you're dating eighty men around the world—that you've met someone else but, hey, did he still want to meet up and go on a date?

And then have to do it another twenty-four times?

And I still had to tell Garry about popping across to Australasia and completing my dating tour.

I'm not asking for sympathy. Just observing that, for some, the course of true love ne'er runs smooth. For me, the course of true love had not so much failed to run smooth as mounted the central median of the highway and taken out three lanes of oncoming traffic, and was now burning out of control on top of a hot-dog stand on the hard shoulder opposite.

Or maybe it just seemed that way to me.

Next, I rang Sandy. She was my local contact and would be able to tell me where I was meeting Cleete, the rodeo rider (**Date #58**). He had apparently thrown himself into rodeo riding after his wife had left him, and I was curious as well as slightly nervous to hear more about his life.

"Oh, I was just about to call you," Sandy said as soon as she heard my voice. Apparently, the date was off. "Cleete's recovering from surgery," she told me apologetically. "It's an occupational hazard when you ride those bulls. He punctured a lung and broke his back in seven places."

I murmured my sympathy; clearly Cleete had thrown himself into rodeo in every sense of the word.

"He's been quite depressed," she continued in a motherly tone, as if explaining why little Billy couldn't come out and play football, "and really isn't up to dating at the moment."

Reassuring Sandy that I understood (which I did; why he would choose to do something so dangerous was what I was struggling with), I noted her suggestion to visit Bill and Ramona Holt. They ran a rodeo museum on their ranch out of town and had been in the business themselves for over forty years.

The Holt Heritage Museum housed a huge and fascinating collection of wagons, saddles, and folk art from the Nez Perce Indians (who developed the Appaloosa horse) and the cowboy ranchers who settled here alongside them. It also celebrated rodeo riding, a sport with a following as big and fanatical in the western States as soccer in the U.K.

For years Bill Holt was one of the sport's top announcers and Ramona Holt, his wife, one of the country's leading barrel racers (where tiny women hurtle at breakneck speed on horse-back around a course of barrels).

Ramona let me inspect the wagons, rescued and restored from the turn of the twentieth century. Cowboy life looked organized but hard: Families were isolated and forced to be self-sufficient (noting my squeamish reaction to hearing that people sewed up their own wounds, Ramona told me she'd sewn up all her children's wounds: "When you live in the country, that's just how things are," she said with a shrug).

Cowboy ranching—close-knit families tending cattle on horseback—was at the heart of rodeo. Like ranching, rodeo was a family affair. Rodeo riders weren't contracted to a team; they mostly came from ranching families, the parents and wives acting as their support units (driving the horses across the country, maintaining the equipment, etcetera).

Rodeo was divided into five major events: steer wrestling, team roping, tie-down roping, barrel racing, and bull riding. Showing me around a barn full of intricately tooled leather saddles, Bill told me rodeo was a serious business. "It's a professional sport and the competitors are professional athletes," he said gravely.

Bill stressed that the sport had standards. A heritage, too. "It's the only sport that's grown out of an industry," he said proudly. "The cattle industry. Rodeo represents ranching and the Old West."

It made sense that rodeo had evolved from ranching. Like being a turn-of-the-century-cowboy's wife, life with a rodeo rider sounded like a hard, extremely full-time job. I doubted that I— riding skills limited to cycling to Starbucks every morning; animal-wrangling skills limited to a pet hamster when I was eight—would be a natural fit. I explained to Bill I'd been due to date a ranch cowboy, but he'd been too damaged (something I generally didn't discover until the date) to make it.

"When you say he had a punctured lung," Bill said, waving his hand dismissively and snorting with contempt, "well, he wasn't wearing a protective vest. You're telling me straight away he's not a professional." Like a father comforting his stood-up daughter on prom night, he patted my arm reassuringly. "I'm sure he's a wonderful guy, but, sweetie, he's just an amateur."

Amateur date promptly dismissed, Bill and Ramona showed me around their collection of cowboy boots.

It was fabulous: a vast array of boot couture featuring the cream of C & W instep royalty, from John Wayne, Johnny Cash, and Clint Eastwood to Patsy Cline, Dolly Parton, and Loretta Lynn. I teased Bill when he showed me Tom Selleck's boots. Shiny and showy, they were the cowboy boot equivalent of a Porsche.

"They're surprisingly small," I taunted mischievously.

"No, ma'am," Bill replied firmly, without hesitation, "I think you'll find you're wrong there."

I left the ranch in no doubt that—from head to toe—rodeo men were Real Men.

As I walked into the hotel lobby, one of the receptionists called me over. "Ms. Cox, you have a visitor. He's waiting outside on the terrace."

A visitor? My heart sank. *Oh, please, don't let it be Cam.*

With a huge sense of dread and trepidation, I walked through the side doors onto the terrace that looked out across the river. But I didn't recognize the man sitting quietly on the bench, his eyes closed as if asleep. He wore a cowboy hat and leather chaps. He also wore an extremely uncomfortable-looking corset, which reached from his waist up to his neck, holding him in a rigid upright position.

Oh, no. This had to be Cleete, the rodeo rider.

As he heard my feet on the path, Cleete turned awkwardly, winced, tried to stand up, winced again, and miserably eased himself back into a sitting position on the bench.

"Oh, my God, Cleete, is that you?" I asked, sitting carefully next to him, fearing he'd try to stand up again.

"Yes, ma'am, it is," Cleete replied through gritted teeth, sweat trickling down his face, either from the heat of the corset or the pain of his injuries.

"Cleete, whatever are you doing here? Sandy said you were recovering from surgery," I asked, horrified.

Unable to turn, Cleete wiggled the fingers on his left hand, as if they were doing the talking. "Couldn't have no Enger-lish lady thinkin' rodeo riders let a little biddy bit o' pain git in the way o' their datin'," he wheezed, clearly in agony.

This was crazy.

"Cleete, how did you get here? Did Sandy bring you?" He wiggled his fingers. I took that to mean yes. "Is she here now?" Again he wiggled his fingers. Asking Cleete to excuse me, I ran into reception, borrowing their phone, and called Sandy on her cell.

She answered straight away. "I know, I know, Jennifer," she told me in a fluster. "But he just wouldn't listen to reason. He insisted on coming to meet you."

"Sandy, you've got to come and pick him up," I told her sternly. "The man should be on anti-inflammatories and pain killers, not on a date."

"I'm just pulling into the parking lot now," she said, sounding more harassed than ever. "I'll be with you in two minutes."

Four minutes later, Sandy and I were loading Cleete into her truck.

"Don't be leavin' on my account." Cleete winced as Sandy gently buckled the seat belt over his surgical corset.

"It's not you, it's me," I lied, wanting him to get home but with his pride intact. "I have a bit of a headache."

Rigid with pain, Cleete was clearly having trouble focusing.

He stared vaguely from the backseat as if a hundred miles away. "Ma'am, I sure am sorry to hear that," he mumbled politely. "I have some pills here that'll git rid of that problem for you real fast."

But Sandy had started the truck and was shouting her good-byes. I thanked Cleete for coming to see me and waved them off.

That poor man: If bull riding was helping him forget the pain of a broken heart, his heart had clearly taken quite a thrashing.

Back in my hotel room, and still no message from Garry. Like a plate, I couldn't spin forever; my resolve not to call wobbled precariously.

I mean, it was fine: I knew he would call and it was still only 5 p.m. But in the meantime, waiting for the call was like needing to go to the toilet really badly: Until it had happened, it was impossible to do or think about anything else.

I turned on my laptop hoping to distract myself with Date Traffic. I thought Ted and Jason might have got back to me. I felt curiously guilty: almost as if by meeting Garry I'd cheated on them. I wanted to check that they were okay with my change in date status and that their feelings weren't hurt.

Scrolling down the emails, I caught up with the news from my world around the world. Things were calmer (for now) between Jo and Ryan; Cath had just got back from Antarctica; Belinda's baby daughter Maya was walking; my Thai date was happy I'd met someone but still wanted to go ahead with our date. I opened an email from a woman whose name I half-recognized:

Hello, Jennifer—How are you? Things are excellent though extremely busy here: We are setting up another conference and I wanted to ask Kelly to

speak. I bumped into him and his girlfriend at a
party last week but don't have his email address.
Could I trouble you for it? All the best, Sue

My heart started to beat really fast as I read the email. I felt my
mouth go dry and I put my hand up to it, as if fearing my heart
was going to leap right out.

Kelly had a girlfriend.

You never know how much you're really over your ex, until you
hear he has another girlfriend. Yes, I know I was dating stacks of
people, I had met Garry, and I know it was now nearly a year and
a half since Kelly and I had split up. But the shock of someone casually talking to me about him and his girlfriend was still immense.

I forgot to turn the computer off; I just scooped up my sunglasses, grabbed my bag, and went straight out into the smoke-
hazed, late afternoon heat. In a daze, I got on the bike and cycled
across town to the Iron Horse microbrewery. I needed a drink.

I found a table in the corner of the terrace and sat staring
out across the other drinkers without noticing a single one of
them.

Kelly had a girlfriend.

I hated that it hurt so much. And the fact that it did took me
by surprise. For me, he was an appalling boyfriend; I was glad we
weren't together anymore AND I'd just met the most amazing
man ever. So why did it hurt that Kelly was with someone else? I
thought I'd got him completely out of my system; why was there
still undigested Kelly clogging up my emotional colon?

All these thoughts jostled around my head, fighting to be the
one that made me feel the worst. I took a sip of my honey ale and

pushed my sunglasses up my nose to hide the tears that were threatening to spill over my lower lashes.

Not wanting to cry in front of anyone made me more aware of the people at the tables around me. Two women in their late twenties sat close by. Both had huge manes of bleached blond hair, billowing magnificently out like breaking waves sculpted from cotton candy. They leaned close together, talking and smoking furiously.

They had boyfriend problems. The woman on the left stubbed her cigarette out, keeping on stubbing long after the glow was extinguished and the cigarette crumpled into the filter. ". . . I mean, I was only out of town for a week," she said bitterly, "it really pisses me off."

My heart sank further as I eavesdropped. Comparing their cheating boyfriends' misdemeanors, they complained it was hard to be a woman, yet both were standing by their man.

Two more women singing in Tammy's choir.

Was this the course of all relationships: starting out thrilled that you'd found your Soul Mate; ending up hating yourself for being a doormat? And if that was the case, did I really want to be in another relationship? Was Garry going to turn into another Kelly? Could I trust him, or would I always be bracing myself, waiting for the telltale signs it had all gone wrong?

I took a long sip of my drink and thought hard. Suddenly I felt a surge of irritation with myself for being so melodramatic. *Oh, get over it, Jenny,* I told myself crossly.

If I'd come all this way only to get cold feet, well, I didn't deserve the support of my friends, let alone to meet someone as lovely as Garry. Not everyone was a cheater. I mean, I'd cheated on poor Peter with Philip when I went to Australia, but I'd never been unfaithful again.

Let Kelly have a girlfriend (poor woman); I didn't want him back. I didn't want to keep looking back, either. I wanted a better boyfriend, and I could stay here and keep brooding about it, or go and find out if I'd just met him.

Jumping up and resisting the temptation to tell the women to dump their loser boyfriends, I headed for the door. Bugger being cool: I was going to the hotel to call Garry.

I cycled across town like a maniac, weaving in and out of traffic. I shot through two lights that stayed red far too long. Dumping my bike in the hotel reception, I paced agitatedly as a crowd of new arrivals slowly tried to work out the best way to fit all their luggage into the lift. Too impatient to wait any longer, I ran up three flights of stairs to my floor.

Hurtling into my room, the first thing I saw was the message light flashing on the console.

YES!

Snatching up the phone, I dialed into the answering service. An automated voice thanked me for calling and gave me the news that:

You have two messages. First message, left today at 5:23 p.m. Message one:

"Hey, baby, so I finally made it off the Playa. I am totally tired and dirty. Make me jealous: You're clean and sleeping in a real bed, huh? That'll be me in another seven hours. Call me when you get this message, I want to hear your news."

As soon as I had heard Garry's voice, I sank down onto the bed, a huge smile taking up my entire face. God, he sounded gorgeous: American accent, voice gravelly from the desert dust and lack of sleep. Ummmmmm.

Second message, left today at 7:09 p.m. Message two:
    "Five crazy days on the Playa and you've got me thinking about you. You're really something, British Girl. Call me."

And I did.

I curled up on my bed in Missoula; he lay on the bed in his roadside trailer somewhere between Reno and Seattle. And we talked and talked. For two hours we talked about the Deities in the base of the Pyramid; the Booth of Bad Advice telling people not to apply sunscreen and drink less water; we talked about what our Costco friends had been up to after I left. . . . We talked about my continuing to date and what that meant for us. He was supportive and understanding, leaving me reassured that I was doing the right thing. And we also talked about Seattle and the time we would have together in his city.

Meeting in the desert had been magical and dramatic; it had been larger than life, like something out of a film. But now, as we talked and laughed and teased each other over the phone, I realized we could have met at a bus stop or a bar or on a blind date and I still would have found Garry intriguing and entertaining. It wasn't the Playa or BRC that had captivated me: It was him.

You know, I blame Hector for putting Carpenters lyrics into my head, but I had the strongest feeling that Garry and I . . . *had only just begun.*

chapter eleven

U.S.A.— Seattle, Washington, & San Francisco, California

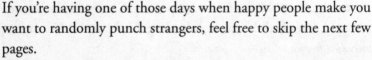

Garry's folks' boat in the Bay area

If you're having one of those days when happy people make you want to randomly punch strangers, feel free to skip the next few pages.

I was excited but extremely nervous when I arrived at Seattle airport two days later. One look at Garry told me he was just as nervous, though, and I immediately felt relieved: It wasn't just me that needed a little time for romance reacclimation.

But we had too much to talk about and got on too well to stay self-conscious for long, and the days that followed (. . . I warned you this was coming) were complete and utter bliss.

I'd never been to Seattle, and although I expected an interesting city, I hadn't expected such a beautiful setting. Seattle is actually a rash of islands, with the city sitting on a lick of land between Puget Sound and Lake Washington. Mountains run around three-quarters of the horizon like a mandarin collar: the Olympic Mountains to the west, Mount Rainier to the south, and the Cascades to the east.

Although a native Californian, Garry had lived in Seattle for seven years and made an excellent guide. He took me to all the funky areas, buying me drinks in the coolest bars, waiting outside as I ran riot in the clothing boutiques and cosmetic stores in Fremont and West Seattle.

At Ballard Locks, we made up stupid stories about each of the salmon trying to work out how to use the fish ladder. The sun was hot as we walked along Lincoln Beach holding hands, constantly stopping because we were laughing or kissing.

Incidentally, I know this sounds sugary and sentimental, but I want to make it absolutely clear that we weren't one of those slobbery, big-tongue-action-in-public, "hey, get a room!" couples. We were electrified with newly minted romance—it pinged out of us like static from nylon sheets—and we couldn't get enough of it or each other.

Garry had a comfortable house in a quiet, forested area overlooking Puget Sound. He was an incredible cook and happiest when creating impressive gourmet meals as I perched on a stool with a glass of wine, chatting or rifling through his CD collection. Other than perhaps toast or spaghetti, I'd never had a man cook for me before. Once Garry finally managed to persuade me that he enjoyed making barbecued pizza with red onion, pesto, and goat cheese or baked snapper with chili and mango salsa and I didn't need to keep offering to help, I was surprised by how much I liked it.

It did take some getting used to, though. Garry was clearly

someone who liked to be a gentleman: He insisted on paying for everything, holding open doors, giving me his jacket if I was cold, and generally being kind and considerate. As much as it thrilled and amazed me (I felt like I'd picked the best ride at the Relationship Theme Park), I struggled with it, a little at first and more so as time went on.

It was really the *paying for things* part. Although I knew Garry enjoyed treating me, I was extremely conscious of not wanting to take advantage of him or cruise along on his generosity. Plus, I had little experience of being treated this way: I had my own money and expected to contribute. I genuinely didn't know how to deal with it. So I kept trying to pick up the bills and Garry kept saying no.

On the third night, it came to a head.

We'd spent a lovely afternoon wandering around the touristy but entertaining Pike Place Market, and were now having early evening drinks at Anthony's on Belltown Harbor. As the sun set, we drank martinis and watched a sleek, chic, sixty something couple confidently moor their boat (elegant, opulent, and the size of a small city), looking every inch like an advertisement for the wonders of Viagra.

Garry looked up as the waitress came to take our food order. "Jen, I know you don't like oysters," he said, prodding tentatively at the minefield of my dietary foibles, "but they're so good here, why don't you try one?"

I hate oysters. They have a hellish texture and aren't even vaguely filling; eating them has always seemed a pointless exercise in combining the traumatic with the superfluous. He asked so sweetly, though, so two cocktails later our perky waitress ("Ohmigosh, are you Briddish? Oh, man, I just love your accent!") brought us half a dozen Kumamoto oysters, served on a

bed of pink champagne and cracked-pepper sorbet. Garry
showed me how to fork a tiny amount of sorbet onto the oyster,
and top it with a squeeze of fresh lemon.

I was determined not to think as I popped the oyster into my
mouth and chewed gingerly. The rich, creamy, salty flavor filled
my mouth and wrapped itself around my taste buds. I was
amazed to find I loved it. And glad. Not just that Garry had
talked me into trying them, but also that for once I'd been un-
dogmatic enough to say yes. But when the bill came, things took
a sudden turn. As we tussled as usual over who was paying, Garry
suddenly sat back, thought for a moment, and then took my
hand in his. "Jen," he said slowly. "I know you're used to paying
your way and that's why you keep offering to pick up the tab. But
here's the thing: You're only here for a few days and you're my
girlfriend; can you please just accept that I want to take care of
you and let me do it?" He looked both firm and sincere, but I was
too scared to say anything for fear I'd burst into tears. It was the
most romantic thing anyone had ever said to me in my whole life.

As the sun set across the bay and the early evening crowd
strolled across the boardwalk next to us, I felt lost in my emotions. Was he for real? Was this for real? Did Garry have a wife,
twenty-seven children, and a job in a lawnmower repair shop in
Iowa and that's why he could say and do the things he did? Also,
I don't want to sound contrary here, but much as I wanted to
make changes to my life, could I allow someone to give what felt
to me like so much and not feel weird or diminished by the loss
of control?

I looked at Garry, still sitting quietly waiting for my answer.
He looked incredibly handsome: those crazy, deep blue eyes
fringed by dark lashes so long they made me jealous, his face
tanned and smooth from the desert heat. I loved being with him

so much: He was funny, generous, a good storyteller, and with just enough self-doubt to make him seem a little vulnerable and utterly lovable.

And he seemed completely smitten with me.

It was no good; I'd held off for as long as anyone could possibly have expected me to. The tears started rolling down my cheeks.

Garry, of course, had no idea what was going on. He just knew he'd challenged me and now I was sitting here silent and in tears. He looked completely mortified. "Oh, God, Jennifer, I didn't mean to upset you," he said, the anxiety clear in his voice. I sniffled, one hand rifling through my handbag for a tissue, the other still in his. "No, no . . ." I spluttered between tears. "You haven't upset me at all. Quite the opposite: It's the most wonderful thing anyone has ever said to me. I'm crying because I'm happy."

Garry looked unconvinced, but gradually his expression changed from one of horror to one of *never try to understand women* instead. I wiped the last of the tears from my cheeks and gave a wobbly smile. "Thank you, Garry, it's a deal: You're buying."

I extended my ticket so we'd have ten days together in Seattle. I was flying back to London out of San Francisco, so we decided to spend three days on his parents' boat in the Bay Area, too (Anders's floating sauna had begrudgingly opened my mind to the possibility that maybe *some* boats were okay).

As time sped by, real life started to reassert itself. Garry had to go to work, doing audio for the Mariners baseball games on TV, and in theory I was meant to be seeing Ted and Jason.

Turning on my laptop, I spotted emails from both of them among the deluge. I was surprised and happy to see one from Nanc in Vegas as well and I opened it straight away:

Well, he sounds very interesting. Maybe you should
get us his driver's license identification and Eliza-
abeth can run his background for us (just kidding).
I am very happy for you. But I still think Elizabeth and I should interrogate him. Seattle isn't
far from Vegas. Send him to us and we'll take
him to dinner and let you know. Miss you kiddo.
Nanc xx

I laughed when I read the email: Nanc might have been joking
about the background check, but Elizabeth would be completely
serious. I was incredibly touched that Nanc and Elizabeth were
looking out for me and thought—not for the first time—how
many unique and genuinely special people I had met on this trip.

I replied to my old friend Eddie, who'd emailed asking for my
phone number in Seattle (another subtle vetting ploy as he could
easily have called me on my cell). I then got to the emails from
Jason and Ted to check they were still okay to meet up now I had
met Garry.

So . . . are you serious? You've actually met your
Soul Mate and he lives here? That was fast! What
happened? Okay. I'll admit that I'm a little disappointed but I'm obviously very happy for you. Of
course we can still go hang out. I'd love to finally
meet and hear all about Burning Man, too. I'll be
around this week, is there any time that's good for
you? Take care, Jason

I felt relieved: The last thing I wanted to do was upset anyone.
And I was pleased that Jason still wanted to meet up. Although
I'd suspected he wasn't The One, I'd enjoyed e-chatting with

him—mainly talking about music—and could tell he was a good person.

I'd got Jason through the usual network of relationships maintained via email. Randy was a second-generation Date Wrangler. He knew my friend Paula from the time he worked in Amazon's British office, but before that he worked at their head office in Seattle, which was how he knew Jason. Randy now lived in New York but was still in regular email contact with both Paula and Jason (neither of whom knew each other). When Randy had got my Soul Mate Job Description, he'd emailed Jason, who in turn—as I was in the middle of *A Date for Europe*—emailed me.

The other Seattle date, Ted, was a friend of Posh PR Emma's. He ran a thriving dot-com company and warned me from the start (nearly three months ago) that although he had *no time to email, wait until you get to Seattle, then I'll impress the hell out of you.*

Well, here I was in Seattle, though admittedly under different circumstances from those Ted and I had originally anticipated. When I opened the email, instead of impressing, Ted *scared* the hell out of me:

Jennifer, you are kidding, right? I have had Saturday marked off on my calendar for two months. I sent my director of operations to the Tokyo conference in my place because you and I had this engagement. This is not acceptable. Meet me and I will change your mind (I am considering the possibility that defaulting on your promise constitutes the breaking of a contract between us, the honoring of which on my part could subsequently result in the loss of earnings for my company). Please call

```
Janelle my secretary to confirm on telephone
# 206- . . .
```

I read it and reread it. The first half was bad; the second half read like some loan small print where the company reserved the right to eat your parents should you miss a payment. Ted had to be joking; he couldn't be serious. But what if he was serious? What if America had become so litigious and work-obsessed, you could be sued for wasting someone's time and emotional energy by falling in love with a third party?

I hit reply, then closed down the empty email about five times, each time wanting to get back to him but each time being at a loss as to what exactly I should say.

In the end, I decided to forward it to Posh PR Emma. Much as I was grateful to the Date Wranglers for all their hard work and support, it was like a dinner party that was a guy short at the last minute. If the guy you brought as a favor went on to get drunk and threw up in the hostess's fish tank, favor or no favor, it was your job to sort out the mess. Whether she liked it or not, Emma was going to have to get Ted's head out of the tank and give him a good talking to.

Meanwhile, Garry was upstairs in his office getting on top of his own life. I could hear his fingers clatter across the keyboard as he emailed and talked on the (constantly ringing) phone. People called to talk about work, catch up after Burning Man, and find out about his new British girlfriend (I heard the term *New British Girlfriend* so many times I started feeling like some political initiative).

He was very sweet, and as he talked I couldn't help but overhear how proud and happy he sounded. Most people were clearly delighted for him, a few less so. When Garry told one woman in particular about us, she was so upset I could hear her reaction

(*"NOOOOOO!"*) from where I was sitting down in the kitchen. ("Don't be like that," Garry reasoned, clearly taken aback by her response.)

But I was soon to meet the female who would pose the biggest challenge to our relationship. She was called Hal, and she was so much a part of Garry's life, she was already in the house.

Garry had to work the Mariners baseball game but—worried I'd be bored on my own—suggested I drop him off and keep the truck for the rest of the day.

I was touched and slightly overwhelmed. That he trusted me to drive his huge truck was kind but a bit of a responsibility. That he thought I would make it home without ending up in Vancouver was lovely but possibly expecting too much from my navigational skills. That I would be able to make my way back to where he worked, from the house—twenty minutes of twisting and turning roads, in the dark—felt like madness.

But, whatever, I'd make it or I wouldn't.

When we arrived at Safeco Field, the Mariners' home ground, OB and some of Garry's other workmates came out to say hello.

It obviously wasn't just my friends who were vetting for suitability: Garry's clearly wanted to make sure I was good for him, too. And don't forget, they all knew Garry and I had met because I was traveling the world dating eighty men. That made them doubly protective of him and doubly curious about me. (In the likelihood I was an International Hussy, what guy wouldn't want to come and take a look: *Step right up, step right up, Ladies and Gents, see the freakishly loose woman* . . .) They teased Garry mercilessly and made me feel really welcome. I was touched they cared about him so much, and it felt good to have their seal of approval, because no matter how we met, Garry was my boyfriend and I wanted his friends to like me.

I did end up getting hopelessly lost trying to find my way back to Garry's house, but I didn't mind as I ended up in Alki Beach. Full of pert in-line skaters and deal-breakers walking their dogs and barking into their cell phones, it's a little corner of L.A. in Seattle.

I managed to make it home at last, intending to spend a quiet evening catching up on emails and American sitcoms. It was all going well until I started to get cold.

I mentioned Hal. She was the Home Automated Living (HAL) computer system that allowed Garry to operate lights, heating, and burglar alarms remotely when he was on tour. Garry had shown me a couple of days ago how to operate Hal through his computer, also by speaking to her via a microphone wired into the system.

I was sitting in front of the Hal program now, trying to turn the heating on. But as I scrolled through the various options, I couldn't for the life of me remember how to make it work. There was no way I was going to ring Garry and admit that, though, so I had to figure it out for myself.

As I drummed my fingers in irritation, I jumped in shock as, out of the blue, a woman's voice queried: "Yes?" The microphone on the desk had picked up the sound of my tapping fingers and activated Hal's listening program. "Yes?" she asked again, sounding imperious and resentful, like a beautiful cat left cooped up too long.

The Hal program allowed you to select a male or female voice for the system. It also let you pick the pitch and attitude of the voice (polite or curt). Garry had made Hal sound like a sexy woman, who, in my opinion, also sounded high-handed and high-maintenance—I hoped that wasn't how he saw me . . . apart from the sexy bit: I could live with that.

Picking up the microphone and trying to remember how

Garry had given voice commands, I addressed the computer: "Hal, turn the heating on." Nothing happened. I waited for a moment. Nothing continued to happen. I tried again, this time a little louder, my voice echoing around the large, open-plan, increasingly chilly house: "Hal, turn the heating on."

Again, nothing. Hal remained willfully silent.

Don't tell Garry, my new hi-tech audio-guy boyfriend, this, but I thumped the microphone down on the desk in exasperation. It was too frustrating: Why wasn't there just a switch on the wall I could turn on, like in a normal house?

The mike was obviously a better communicator than I, though: The sound of it clunking onto the desk got Hal's attention. "Yes?" she asked again in a bored voice, calculated to inspire impotent fury in the listener (or maybe just this listener). I snatched up the mike from the desk, refusing to admit defeat; perhaps the problem was I'd been speaking too quietly. The advancing cold concentrated my mind; I spoke loudly and clearly: "Hal, turn the heating on."

"Did you say, 'turn the lighting on'?" Hal shot back snootily, her tone suggesting, "There really is no need to shout: it's quite vulgar and impolite."

Thank God, the damn thing had heard me. "No," I replied, feeling a little flash of triumph, "I said, 'Turn the heating on.'" I made a point of exaggerating the word *heating*, hoping Hal would feel the humiliation she'd brought upon herself. "Lights turning on," Hal chimed smugly, ignoring my contradiction. And with that, every single light in every single room in the house snapped on.

Right.

This was an open declaration of war. That Sim-sucking bitch was wrong if she thought she was going to get the better of me;

she was about to discover the hard way that she'd chosen the wrong woman to play computer games with.

Ignoring the house lights, which now blazed as harshly as a fridge opened at 4 a.m., I fixed the monitor with a steady look. In a tone as clear as it was cold (actually, by now freezing cold), my voice rang out in defiance. "Hal!" I commanded, "turn the heating on."

"Did you say, 'Turn the heating up'?" Hal asked bitchily, by now clearly reveling in my discomfort. Had I asked that? Could the heating be turned *up*, if it wasn't actually *on*? Was this a trick; was she trying to outmaneuver me? I wasn't sure, but didn't want to be caught out on a technicality, so I said evenly, "No, I said, 'Turn the heating *on*.' "

"I am turning the heating up," Hal declared, a withering glance at my poker face as she slammed down the winning hand.

For a moment there was only silence. Then, a faint whirring noise stirred in the basement. It grew louder and louder, and as it did the walls of the house started to shudder gently. I looked around nervously, trying to work out what was causing the noise. Then, CRASH: With a terrifying roar, air—hot as a breath from Lucifer himself—blasted out from vents and ducts all over the house.

The noise was deafening, and, moments later, the house became unbearably hot. Pausing instinctively to admire the system's efficiency, I yelled, "Hal, turn the heating off, turn the heating off," over and over. Maybe she couldn't hear me over the fans as they powered the atmosphere of the Serengeti around the house; maybe she was ignoring me on purpose. Either way, Hal refused to answer.

The house got hotter and hotter, the lights dazzled overhead: I was being cooked to death by a crazed computer-generated housekeeper, unwilling to tolerate another woman in Garry's house.

I shouted and shouted until the heat made my throat too dry to shout anymore, but nothing seemed to be working. If I was going to get around Hal, I clearly needed a different strategy. Staggering downstairs to get some water, I threw open the doors and windows to let some cool air in. And then I had an idea. I ran back upstairs through the blasting heat and resumed my position in the computer hot-seat.

Hal obviously wasn't going to do what I asked her, but I bet she'd listen to Garry.

It was tricky. Much as I adored Garry, I didn't really know his voice that well, plus there was the whole accent thing. I rang the house number three or four times to listen to his voice on the answering machine, then took a swallow of water and cleared my throat. "Hal, turn the heating off," I said in a deep American accent.

Nothing. Okay, it had been a dodgy accent. I tried again: "Hal, turn the heating off." Still nothing.

I tried a variety of pitches; I experimented with placing the stresses in different parts of the sentence; I truncated and elongated vowels. In short, I went deep undercover and immersed myself, blindly navigating the twists and turns of another gender and another culture.

"Did you say, 'Turn the heating off'?" Hal suddenly inquired sweetly.

Oh my God, I'd done it; she thought I was Garry. "Yes," I replied succinctly, not wanting to blow it now I was getting somewhere. "I am turning the heating off," Hal replied coquettishly. And with that, the roaring from the vents stopped dead.

The house was filled with silence.

It was like someone had been pointing a hairdryer in my face for twenty minutes and the relief of it stopping was immense. Taking a moment to recover, I took a deep breath; then, trying to recall the winning pitch and accent, I attempted to cajole Hal into turning the lights off, too. Three tries later and off they went.

I sat in the dark, quiet, cooling house and let the silence wash over me. Until Garry got home, there was little I could do without lights or heating. Settling back onto the sofa as comfortably as I could to recover from the ridiculous pantomime, I started pondering for the first time what I was actually doing here. I was besotted with Garry and I thought he felt the same way about me, but, seriously, where would we go from here? How was our hothouse relationship going to survive outside in the real world?

We both lived full and demanding lives a continent apart. I couldn't bear the thought of a permanent long-distance relationship, so where did that leave us? Would I be willing to move to Seattle? It seemed insane to be even considering the question so soon (or perhaps it seemed insane not to have considered it sooner), but if my answer was *no,* for both Garry's and my sake I had to end it now before we got in any deeper.

But there was no way I could do that. The more I got to know Garry, the more I liked him; even after this short time together I'd miss him too much.

Wrestling to find an answer, I gradually realized that I was expecting too much too soon.

Being with Garry had taken a giant leap of faith. Maybe I was like Neil Armstrong and my giant leap had catapulted me so high I'd be up bobbing around in orbit for a while yet. It was pointless agonizing about it all now. I wanted to be with Garry and it felt amazing. That was what was important; anything else would just have to wait until I came back down to earth.

Damn Hal: It was her nonsense that had forced me to think

about all this stuff. She was a pretty formidable housekeeper; had all this been her doing? Turning up the heat and putting me under the spotlight—I think she'd been vetting me like the rest of Garry's circle.

"Did you have a good night, sweetie?" Garry asked when I arrived wrung out and exhausted at Safeco Field to collect him.

"Yes, thanks," I replied dishonestly. Tonight's events were going to stay between Hal and me. And, whatever else our differences, I suspected this would be the one thing we'd agree on.

The next morning was busy. Posh PR Emma had replied immediately:

Darling, Ted can be a frightful bully sometimes but his bark is far worse than his bite. I've told him he's got to stop being so silly if he ever wants to meet a nice girl, but you know men: love to talk, hate to listen. If you can bear it, do pop in and see him; he's a total sweetie really. Let me know. Oh, loved the piccy of you and Garry—what a hunk! You lucky old thing. Ciao ciao, Ems xxxx

There was no email from Ted (maybe he was out chasing the postman up and down his street). As a sacrifice to the Numbers God I'd probably see him, but I'd make him wait a bit first. I was in the middle of emailing Jason when Garry shouted down from his office that there was a phone call for me. I picked up the extension in the kitchen, half expecting it to be Jason and feeling more than a little awkward, as Garry had been talking to whoever it was for quite a while. But it was Eddie, my old friend from home. Somehow, I seemed to be the kind of person who—based on no good reason or track record—people came to for advice.

Eddie was the person *I* always went to—he was tough and smart and he was also concerned and protective of me, like a big brother.

Eddie had been talking to Garry and I instinctively held my breath, hoping, for Garry's sake, he'd passed muster. "So, you've found your Soul Mate?" Eddie teased as I picked up the phone.

"Yes," I replied happily, "I have. I hope you were nice to him?"

"Tolerably so," Eddie replied sardonically, then suddenly becoming serious: "So, apart from fancying the pants off him, is everything okay?"

I took this to be code for *Have you picked another loser?* And I smiled, touched by his concern. "Honestly, Eds," I replied. "He really is wonderful. And if you hadn't liked the sound of him yourself, you'd be telling me so by now."

Eddie never gave ground: The fact he wasn't arguing was his way of agreeing. "Well," he said finally, "I'll meet him when he comes to London so I'll tell you what I think of him then."

Come to London? When was that happening? "Oh, I don't know that he is," I replied, a little defensively.

"Why wouldn't he?" Eddie demanded.

I didn't really have an answer for him: I hadn't even thought about Garry visiting me, let alone talked to him about it.

Eddie and I caught up on news from home before finally saying good-bye. Garry came downstairs. "Your friend Eddie's very funny," he said, hugging me and noting my smile.

"Yes, he's a good man. Did you get on with him okay?" I asked, pulling back a little so I could see his reaction.

Garry told me they had, then added unexpectedly: "He asked when I was coming to London."

I shrugged awkwardly. "Yes, Eddie asked me that too. Don't worry, it's fine."

Garry looked nonplussed. "Why? Don't you want me to?"

Now it was my turn to look blank. "Well, yes, of course I do," I replied. "But I know how busy you are and . . . you know, it's expensive and . . . a long way . . ."

As I said it, I realized how pathetic I sounded. I trailed off.

Garry looked a bit cross. "Jenny, London is where you live—of course I'm going to come and see you there. Why would you imagine I wouldn't?"

I was taken aback by how exasperated he sounded, and also by the logic of what he was saying. Garry was right: I was happy to fly halfway around the world to be with someone I cared for, but didn't imagine for one moment he'd be prepared to do the same for me. And that's not all. I was probably being pretty controlling, too. I was the one who waltzed in and out of the Dates' lives, deciding when and how they got to see me. It was in their territory but always on my terms. And I kept London for me: a barrier behind which I went *off-duty*, to relax and recharge.

Garry, in London, seeing me on my home turf, meeting my friends, experiencing my life, would break down that barrier. But Garry was different. Shouldn't I be giving him the same kind of Access All Areas into my life that he was giving me to his?

God, why was I suddenly in the House of Questions?

It would be good to ask the Date Wranglers their opinion about all of this, but comforting as the thought was, I knew this was something Garry and I had to work out for ourselves. There was a point when new lovers stopped being public property and made their own world in private (and this was especially true of our *cast of thousands* relationship).

"So?" Garry asked, obviously getting used to the long silences that inevitably accompanied me furiously debating sticky issues with myself.

I snapped out of my inner turmoil and answered him imme-

diately. "Yes, come to London," I replied with complete conviction. "I'd really like you to see my home."

So, over the next week and a half we settled into a comfortable
rhythm of going out, eating in, and falling in love. Sharing a
space felt easy and natural, uncomplicated and companionable,
not like we had to constantly be on our best behavior.

And when Garry went to work, so did I.

I'd relented and had Janelle schedule me into **Ted's (Date
#59)** diary for a coffee. He actually was far nicer in real life and,
tall with short black hair and deep brown skin that at times
seemed to shimmer golden, he was very good-looking. But he
was a complete workaholic: His phone rang constantly throughout our coffee date and although Ted never took the call, each
time he frowned furiously, checking to see who it was. That was
my old life, and I felt a twinge of guilt remembering the many
times I'd done exactly the same thing.

Still, date done, at least Ted couldn't sue me now.

Jason (Date #60) was just as much fun as I had hoped. Both
huge music fans, we talked nonstop over margaritas at a little
Mexican place in Belltown. I loved the sound of his life: both that
he knew and was so involved with the Seattle music scene, also
the more niche activities revolving around his love of the ukulele.
He wasn't my Soul Mate but he was very entertaining and we had
a fun night out.

Relaxed and comfortable as Garry and I were with each other,
as the time approached to go to San Francisco I became increasingly preoccupied. Only three more days together, then I'd be flying back to London. And although I missed London and was
looking forward to seeing family, friends, and my flat, leaving
Garry and going back to my old life filled me with a kind of
dread.

. . .

Too soon it was time to fly down to San Francisco.

We picked up a rental car at the airport and drove to Androni-co's, the upscale supermarket in Walnut Creek, for boat provisions. We browsed among the aisles of soft fruit, glossy like multicolored cricket balls; rich rounds of ripe, pungent cheeses; broad loaves of crusty bread, knotted like muscular arms; cakes as fussy as Easter bonnets. But as we pressed the spongy flesh of the portobello mushrooms and piled feathery fronds of dill and fennel into our baskets, I was jittery and distracted. And this was nothing to do with flying home.

I was about to meet Garry's parents.

I wanted to buy them something but found myself getting increasingly worked up as I dithered between the walls of unfamiliar wines and the banks of endlessly exotic flowers. Of course, I wanted to make a good impression, but never having met them, I didn't know what they liked.

Garry was no use. "You don't have to get them anything." He shrugged.

I narrowed my eyes and sighed in exasperation. "Garry, your parents are letting us use their boat for three days; there is no way I'm going to turn up empty-handed."

We left the supermarket and drove to the Bay Area marina where the boat was moored. I was very quiet as we started unloading the provisions, and Garry put the groceries down on the ground, wrapped his arms around my waist, and kissed me. "Jen, don't be nervous," he said, stroking my hair reassuringly, "my parents are really easygoing. And after tonight, it'll just be the two of us on the boat. It'll be relaxing, you'll see."

I knew he meant well, but I couldn't keep it in any longer. Trying to keep the snippiness out of my voice, "Garry," I said tersely, "I really appreciate you organizing this and I know it's what you find relaxing. But I have a long and well-documented history of seasickness and the thought of spending three days on a boat scares the bejesus out of me. And as for your parents: They're your parents, so I'm sure they're absolutely lovely. In fact, I already know they're lovely because they've given us their boat. But the fact remains any minute now a conversation will take place where you say: 'Mom, Dad, I'd like you to meet my girl-friend,' and they'll be like, 'Oh, how nice, how did you two meet?' and I'll have to say, 'Well, funny you should ask, because I'm going round the world dating eighty complete strangers. Garry was . . . number fifty-five, wasn't it, darling? But no need to worry: only another twenty dates with men I've never met, then I'll be all done.' "

Maybe I was being a little melodramatic, but, let's face it, it was the truth and it didn't look good. I was genuinely horrified at what his parents must think. Garry looked at me in astonish-ment. Okay, maybe I should have said something sooner rather than waiting until, one, I was completely freaked out about it and, two, we were moments from boarding the boat.

Garry took it all in his stride, though. He was calm (which was good because I clearly wasn't) as he pulled me to him, giving me a long, slow kiss. I don't know which stress-management school taught that particular technique, but they deserved a medal: I immediately felt calmer and more secure. Pulling away, Garry smiled affectionately. "My parents are going to love you as much as I do, Jennifer Cox," he said.

"Really?" I whispered, crinkling up my face in concern.

"Yes, really," Garry replied softly.

Hang on. Had Garry just told me he loved me?

Is that what he meant? Or did he mean it in another way? Did he mean he loved—as in was *in love* with—me, or did he mean, he liked me and . . . you know . . . *loved* liking me, and his parents would like me and love that, too? Or did it mean something else altogether?

Like a crying child having a stuffed toy thrust in its face, the distraction worked brilliantly. As we walked down the ramp onto the jetty, with armfuls of food, flowers, and wine, I was blissfully preoccupied and not in the least bit nervous.

And, of course, Garry was right: His parents were completely wonderful. And the boat, forty feet of beautiful wood, fantastically restored and outfitted by Garry's dad, was delightful. And most importantly, very still.

Garry's parents seemed to be one of those couples who enjoyed each other's company, so were relaxed and easy to be around. They went out of their way to make me feel welcome and I liked them immediately. In their early sixties, Gerry and Judy complemented each other. Both fit and energetic, they mirrored each other's body language; instinctively reaching from a shelf what the other was looking for or interrupting each other's stories with gentle teasing.

They clearly were Soul Mates, which felt like a good omen for Garry and me.

Garry busied himself preparing salmon for the barbecue and making some kind of complicated marinade for the mushrooms. So Gerry, Judy, and I took our drinks up on deck and sat out in the heat of the early evening sun. We chatted easily about family and work and life in the Bay Area, and life in London.

I didn't know whether to talk about my journey or not, but Judy, perhaps sensing my discomfort, made it easy for me. "So, Jennifer," she said in a tone so neutral the Swiss would have begged for the recipe, "Garry's told us a lot about you; your journey sounds very interesting."

And with that the floodgates opened. I told them about London and how, although I'd been happy with my job for years, my priority had become finding the relationship that would make me just as happy. The journey had been to find my Soul Mate but also to understand why I made the choices that had stopped me meeting him sooner.

I told them about the Love Professor and his theories; I told them about the Vegas Bettys and their insights; I told them about Davide and his dead love in Verona; I even told them about Anders and his amazing floating sauna. As the sun set over the bay, I told them about my whole journey and how it had brought me into their son's life.

Judy had lots of questions. She asked as a woman as well as a mother, curious about the lengths I had gone to and the people I had met along the way. "Judy, quit interrogating the poor girl!" Gerry said after a while. But I was glad of Judy's questions: I wanted to tell them my story, but mostly I wanted them to know that Garry was safe with me. And much as it made me hot with embarrassment, I knew the only way was to come right out with it. I checked my glass to make sure I had enough wine for what I was about to say.

But just as I opened my mouth, Garry came up on deck, a beer in one hand, barbecue tongs in the other. Flushed from cooking, he looked relaxed, happy, and extremely sexy. Perching on the back of my chair, he draped his arm across my shoulders. "Hey, what's with all the talking?" he teased. Gerry raised his eyebrows in an *I already tried telling them that* way. Judy and I smiled conspiratorially at each other. "Are you ready to eat? Dinner's a couple of minutes off," Garry announced, taking a lazy pull on his beer and watching with Gerry as a powerboat cruised slowly by.

I wished Garry had been just three minutes longer in the kitchen. Pausing to take a gulp from my glass, I started nervously. "Look, before we eat, can I please say something really quickly?"

Judy nodded encouragingly.

"Judy, Gerry, it's really nice to meet you. It's very kind of you to invite me onto your boat and I'm having a lovely evening. Thank you," I told them by way of a preamble. Garry's parents seemed a little nonplussed by my speech and looked over to Garry, whom I felt shrugging behind me as if to say: *What can I say, she's British, they're very formal* . . .

Judy reached over and patted my arm. "Well, dear, you really are very welcome—"

"No, no . . ." I interrupted. "Sorry, I didn't mean to be rude, what I'm saying is—Garry is an extremely special man and I feel blessed to have met him and have him in my life. And although I have to keep traveling and dating . . ." Out of breath, I trailed off. ". . . I just want you to know, I'm in love with your son and I'm not going to do anything to hurt him or mess it up."

Garry looked self-conscious but touched. Gerry beamed as Judy hugged me and said: "Oh, aren't you, darling. Thank you, Jennifer, and don't you worry. We know how happy you make Garry and that makes us very happy too."

Garry got to his feet, clearly desperate to change the subject. "So, if everyone's finished *saying what they have to say* . . ." He gave me a pointed look ". . . can we eat?" And, picking up his beer, he led the way into the cabin. Judy and Gerry stood up and followed.

Feeling emotional and light-headed, I was a little slower. Today I'd flown to San Francisco. Today Garry had (possibly) told me that he loved me. Today he'd brought me to meet his parents. Today I'd told his parents I was dating eighty men and loved their son.

Yes, sitting down to a nice dinner and a number of very large drinks was probably the best way to cope with days like today. I got up and followed them all into the cabin.

· · ·

The rest of the evening, like the three days that followed, was perfect. As usual, it was an extraordinary meal, and we all talked and laughed until around 10 p.m., when Judy and Gerry left. "We have so enjoyed meeting you, Jennifer," Judy told me as we hugged and kissed good-bye. "You two look so happy together; I do hope it's not too long before we see you again."

I agreed wholeheartedly.

San Francisco was like a holiday—neither of us worked and we didn't check email once. We had plans to visit some of the Costco crew: Rico and Annie, Brenda, and Jefe all lived about half an hour away. Lonely Planet's U.S. office was also in the area and I'd let some of my old friends from the company know we were in town.

But, in the end, we saw no one: We stayed in bed late; lazed on the boat in the sun; drove around with the convertible roof down, singing to Johnny Cash and Def Leppard's request to *"Pour some sugar on meeee . . ."* at the tops of our voices. And, of course, we talked.

We talked about Garry coming to see me in London next month. And Garry was traveling to Japan with Seattle's basketball team, the Sonics. Russia had fallen through but Hector had some dates for me in China; could I go via Tokyo? We got out our diaries: The timing would be tight and I'd have to scramble to set up dates there, but it could work.

These were not always easy conversations to have; we didn't know what would happen after this point, plus there was the business of my ongoing dating. Plus we were both a little frazzled from our relationship being so fast and intense: It was as if we were *speed-learning* each other, knowing that, for the foreseeable future, this was all the time we had together. "We've fitted three years of relationship into three weeks," Garry observed as we curled up on deck together under the moonlight, drinking wine. We felt the same way about the situation: incredibly grateful to have met each other, but at times overwhelmed by the pace at which the relationship was forced to run.

And to think I'd initially imagined I'd meet my Soul Mate and simply drive off into the sunset, the road straight and easy to navigate.

But, whatever the pressure or complications, I didn't regret it and wouldn't have changed it for the world. And even more perfectly, any time I got scared and thought I was in too deep, Garry would say or do things that made it clear he felt the same way.

We were in this together.

In the end, it was Garry's dad who made the last day easier than it might have been.

He rang to ask if Garry minded giving him a hand with a boat he had to move from a harbor nearby. I think Garry was a little worried I'd get upset since we'd planned a trip into downtown San Francisco, but I was pleased. Gerry was fun, and messing around with fast boats rather than thinking about leaving was exactly the distraction we needed.

So we spent the rest of the morning tinkering with boats (they tinkered, I sunbathed), then roared around the bay for a couple of hours.

After saying good-bye to Gerry, we had an entertaining afternoon in San Francisco. We watched a large transsexual shoplifter get chased down the road by police on bicycles; we played tourist and rode the cable car from Union Square, via Chinatown and trendy North Beach, out to Fisherman's Wharf. The sunset stained the ocean orange and purple, and as we queued to catch the cable car back we held hands, listening to a soulful street musician sing "Georgia." Then we drove to Lulu's, a trendy but low-key restaurant, where we ate oysters and made up stories about the old moguls who hungrily watched the starving starlets at their tables.

We got back to the boat late, and got to sleep even later. Knowing it was our last evening together, we didn't want it to end.

Early the next morning, tired from the lack of sleep and a little hungover from the excess of Oregon pinot, we found a diner in the airport and ordered a huge breakfast. Slumping next to each other in the laminated booth, we stared at the taxiing planes as we sipped scalding black coffee from chunky china mugs.

Airports are famously awful places for saying good-bye: busy and anonymous, they have no room for what's been, only what's coming next. It's one big Hello and Good-bye factory: pairing and parting busy people the length of its production line.

That I was off somewhere new was what I always loved about airports. But not this time. This time I didn't want new: I wanted what I had. I wanted to be with Garry.

Feeling upset and tired, though, neither of us wanted to dwell on what was to come, so we ate instead. I can't speak for Garry, but I wasn't even hungry. That didn't stop us. We ate our way through an insane amount of pancakes and eggs and coffee and toast and French toast and home fries and more coffee. When the time came to say good-bye, I felt unbelievably full and unbelievably sick.

At the departure gate, our arms wrapped around each other with my face buried in Garry's shoulder, I could smell the sour odor of fried food in my hair. We stood for about ten minutes, partially because we were too stuffed to move but mostly because we knew the moment we pulled apart, it would all be over. But we'd had our time together, until the next time; we had to accept this was good-bye.

We stroked each other's faces, trying to absorb and memorize every freckle, every lash. "Thank you for everything, Garry," I told him. I know that sounds like something from a bland greeting card, but in truth I was grateful for everything. That I'd met him; that he had been so willing to let me into his world, share his house, his truck, introduce me to his friends and family. The fact that he'd let me see so many different parts of his life meant I was leaving not only feeling like I knew a lot about him, but also reassured and optimistic that he wanted me in his life. It wasn't just that, after Keep Your Distance Kelly, being with someone who wanted to be with me was very welcome. I also believed Garry and I were similar people, alike in what we wanted and needed, for ourselves and each other. To have found someone like that, who was cute as hell to boot, was truly something to be thankful for.

Even if he lived in America.

When Garry looked up at the monitor and said with a sad smile, "Jen, they're calling your plane," I started to cry. I knew it wasn't fair—we were both trying to be brave and get through this in one piece—but I couldn't help it.

I wanted to tell him that I loved him, but I stopped myself. Nothing had been said since the half-declaration on the boat, and a part of me felt it was still too soon. We'd only known each other for three weeks. "I'll see you soon," Garry said, looking distressed as he wiped away the tears that now streamed down my cheeks, ". . . London or Tokyo, I'll see you soon."

"Garry . . ." I said, looking up at him through the fresh tears that clung to the ends of my lashes, ". . . I love you."

And the tears shook themselves free from my lashes as new ones rose up to take their place. The tears glistened in Garry's eyes too as he pulled me to him, cradling me in his arms. "I love you too, baby," he whispered.

chapter twelve

37,000 feet (on the way to London)

Back in London, I got ready to give Garry the grand tour.

Exhausted from the lack of sleep and the excess of emotions, I fell asleep as soon as the plane took off.

I slept lightly and my mind flitted around the events of the last few weeks, plucking individual moments from memory like rosy apples from a tree. Garry drinking my chili vodka shot in the Costco bar at Burning Man; last night on the boat, curled up quietly on deck, his hand stroking my hair, Frank Sinatra on the radio singing "I Left My Heart in San Francisco."

I hated that these were now just memories, that I had to look back to what had happened rather than forward to what was ahead of me. Before too long they would become like gum that had been chewed and chewed until all favor was gone. They'd become stories and set pieces rather than the rich jumble of sensations, emotions, and experiences I could still so vividly recall.

I dreamed about Garry visiting me in London; cutting through the back alleys of Soho; walking along the South Bank from the National Theatre to the Tate Modern and Borough Market . . .

But as I dreamed, pleasure turned to fear and I woke up: What if it didn't work in London? What if our relationship only worked on his home ground, when I was happy and uncomplicated, not distracted by the demands of my London life? Was I going to slide back into old habits and end up a dull workaholic again?

I gave up trying to sleep and slouched tiredly in my seat. I knew it was pathetic, but I missed Garry already. Instead of us being together with our *what nexts?*, I was now alone with my *what ifs?*

Arriving back home took the edge off my worries as, once again, the welcome flood of friends, family, and a variety of wardrobe options washed over me. And funnily enough, even though he was in America, Garry became part of my London life too. In the morning when I logged on, there'd be an email from him, and most nights (eight hours ahead, so his afternoons) we'd sit on the computer and instant-message each other or sit on the phone for hours. I loved hearing how his day had gone, what JR had said, where he'd gone for a drink with Doug and his girlfriend Bette. And, in turn, I loved to tell him where the Sonar Sisters (Lizzy and Grainne got so excited hearing about Garry that their voices would get higher and higher until eventually their conversation was only audible to bats, dogs, and whales) and I had been the night before; what had happened during my bike ride to Starbucks that morning. I missed him, but technology made it possible to still feel close to each other.

And, as ever, we both had work to do: Garry was preparing for the start of the basketball season and his trip to Japan; I was nailing down the final leg of my journey through Australasia, as well as trying to find some dates in Japan. Fortunately, my friend Kylie worked for the tourist board, plus by lucky chance I was on a radio program with a journalist based in Japan. I emailed him after the interview and he got straight back, saying he'd be delighted to date me, though warned:

```
I've only been here a month, so don't expect me to
know anything! Will, emailing from Tokyo
```

For the first time since I'd made the decision to undertake this adventure, I felt calm and content. Possibly because I'd met my Soul Mate and was now on the home stretch of my journey, but also because it seemed that my theory of working your way to your Soul Mate was valid after all. I felt a real sense of satisfaction and achievement and—I have to admit it—All-Purpose Flirty.

This isn't a type of bathroom cleaner, it's one of the side effects of falling in love. I felt so happy and good about everything, I think I must have been exuding a sort of cheerful, uncomplicated energy. I don't know which way round it happened, but total strangers were smiling and saying hello, holding doors open, and generally being lovely. And I was doing it all right back.

It was like the Love Professor said: You get back what you put out there.

Of course, it was all because I'd met Garry. I was aware of the irony: that falling for him seemed to have made me more notice-able and, possibly, more attractive to other men. This came in handy, as I still had another twenty dates to go, but at the same time I didn't want to do anything that was going to threaten my relationship with Garry.

I'll be honest, I really didn't understand how he was managing to cope; it must have been a nightmare for him. If the tables were turned and he told me he was dating twenty women, I can tell you now, I would have completely lost it. Maybe it was because he'd known all along that this was what I was doing, or maybe he was just choosing not to think about it. Whatever the reason, I wanted to help by making it as painless for him as possible. I tried to get the balance right between telling him what I was doing (whether going swimming with Cath or securing a date in Mel-bourne) but being sensitive to his feelings and not telling him in a way that would hurt or distress him. It was important I didn't keep things from him: Honesty was one of the few straight lines we had in this hall-of-mirrors situation. But I didn't want to make him jealous either, a strong but ultimately useless bond that would foster nothing good. I wanted him to choose to be close because he liked me, not because I was driving him mad and he was scared of losing me.

So I got on with my job.

I dated Robert (or Irritating Robert, as I was soon to think of him), one of the website dating people who'd been the most per-sistent. Every couple of weeks or so for the last three months it had been:

```
Hello Jen, Rob here again!!!! So where are you
now?!! Still traveling or are you back in old
Blighty? Any chance you might have time for a lit-
tle drinky?!! Rob xx
```

The abundance of punctuation was unnerving, but it was the excessive use of animated *smilies* that had me on red alert—reading an email peppered with flashing grins, waves, winks, and blinks was like sitting in front of a short-circuiting traffic light.

Whether I saw myself as the Patron Saint of Single Souls, dispensing *mercy dates* among the *relationship needy,* finally giving in to Robert turned out to be a bad idea. **Robert (Date #61)** asked me to dinner at the Dorchester. Not my kind of place, but I went, only to find he'd invited me to his office Summer Ball and told everyone I was his girlfriend.

Robert worked at the head office of a national courier company and the party was like going to the wedding of someone you've never met (including, in my case, your Date): a room full of people talking animatedly about things you didn't understand and couldn't contribute to.

It was a long night, made longer by the sit-down meal where I accidentally bonded with *the loud, drunk wife* who then tried to give me a head massage during the awards ceremony. There was also a Brotherhood of Man tribute band (though, who knows, maybe it was the real thing). Robert led me onto the dance floor and proceeded to throw some moves reminiscent of the scene in *Diamonds Are Forever* where the man has a scorpion dropped down the back of his shirt. Not that I did much better. Accepting that resistance was useless, I gave it some Travolta. Assuming the position, hand on one hip, I energetically flung the other hand out, rapping the old man dancing next to me very hard on the back of the head with my knuckles.

My final sight of Robert, as I mouthed I was *going to the loo* and fled the building, was him doing the funky chicken with *the loud, drunk wife*. I vowed no matter how much the Numbers God needed appeasing in the future, I was never doing a mercy date ever again.

. . .

And then Garry rang to say he'd booked his flight to London.

I had a million emotions, all of them good. In the time I'd been back, I'd realized how much I loved London. I wanted Garry to see the city, but also to see me in my hometown. He was the reason I felt good about being here—when you're happy and in love, London is a wonderful place. In fact my newfound All-Purpose Flirty wasn't just for the people I beamed at walking down the street; I was flirting with the city too. And from the red of the double-decker buses, the white of the Brick Lane bagels, and the boys in blue on the beat, the city was flirting right back. Eros had shot his arrow from Piccadilly Circus; the London Eye was giving me a big, cheeky wink.

God, I needed to stop being so cheerful: Any minute now I was going to break into song and the entire street would join in, dancing like a scene out of *Mary Poppins,* singing: *"It's a jolly holiday with Garry."*

And it would be good to have a break from having a long-distance relationship: emailing, Instant Messaging, and chatting on the phone were an important part of both of our days, but this was also frustrating at times. Not just that we weren't face to face, but because of the logistics of being an ocean apart. The time difference meant there was always one of us sitting up until 2 a.m. or getting up at 6 a.m.

I loved our marathon conversation today. I feel bad, though, that it is on the wrong side of the clock for you. Next marathon, we can do it on the wrong side of the clock for me. (gotta keep things fair!)

We rarely talked for less than two hours (after the terrible shock of the first phone bill, we'd renegotiated phone plans to get the cheapest international rates), so we were both constantly exhausted from broken sleep patterns and harassed that we were always late for work or meeting friends in the evening.

One good thing, though: The stress and excitement of the situation meant that the weight was finally falling off me. I might have become clinically insane by the time Garry got here, but at least I'd look good in a pair of shorts.

Eleven p.m. at Heathrow airport and I was sitting in a grim, smoky café waiting to meet Garry.

Not that I was particularly aware of my surroundings: I had so much adrenaline racing around my body, I was concerned I might actually start astral-planing. I was drinking herbal tea to try to calm my nerves, but that and the nerves were making me want to pee constantly. Every time I popped into the loo, I'd worry I was going to miss him arriving, and then I'd catch sight of myself in the mirror, see how anxious I looked, and get nervous all over again.

But the moment he walked through the gate, all nerves vanished instantaneously. I suddenly didn't feel awkward or nervous about seeing him at all, just really, really glad he was here.

Looking amazing (he'd had a long flight and looked great; I'd had a short drive and looked like crap—where was the justice in that?), he cut through the barrier, finding the shortest possible route to my side. Walking up with a huge smile on his face, he said, "Hey, baby," dumped his bags on the ground, reached out, and pulled me into a close embrace.

I buried my face in his neck and silently hugged him right back. I was just so happy to see him, I couldn't say a word, I couldn't even kiss him. I just stood wrapped in his embrace, pulling my fingers through his hair, trying to absorb the fact that after the last few weeks of emailing and phoning and waiting, he was actually here in London.

We must have looked like the poster for *Lovers Reunited at the Airport,* but I didn't care. I felt only relief. Like arriving back from a school trip late at night and sleepily spotting your parents waiting to collect you, a sense of *all is right in the world* washed over me.

It was now my turn to play tour guide, and I really enjoyed it. We explored the huge Buddhist temple by Wimbledon common; watched the herds of deer roaming wild in Richmond Park; wandered wide-eyed around the cornucopia of Harrods' food hall; and annoyed everyone as we sang *"I don't want to go to Chelsea,"* jumping on and off buses in Chelsea and along the King's Road.

I explained the mysteries of roundabouts, Marmite, Teletext, the *Telegraph* crossword, clotted cream, and night buses. Unable to find a pub serving food after 2 p.m., I tried (and failed) to make a case for English licensing laws. I also tried to explain why Garry couldn't find anywhere serving decent cocktails. That British people drink beer to be sociable, wine to be sophisticated, and cocktails to be insensible. Cocktail names did seem to indicate the drinker's intent: Americans were moderate, elegant drinkers, and they had the Manhattan and the Cosmopolitan. As night follows day, so the Brits had the Slippery Nipple and Sex on the Beach.

Garry loved my flat and by being there made me realize how much I'd missed living with someone, cooking together and listening to music in the kitchen or content to do our own thing in separate rooms.

There was an ongoing fuss about coffee. Garry had brought his favorite coffee, Peet's, with him but my coffeemaker broke on the second day. As Garry tinkered with it, I confessed that I'd bought it at a garage sale thirteen years ago for fifty pence.

"There was a reason it was being sold cheap," he said dismissively.

"Oh, you mean there was a chance it would stop working a decade later?" I replied smugly.

In the spirit of Access All Areas, Garry was meeting my parents. I was nervous because I knew Garry would be nervous; I thought maybe my parents would be a little nervous too. As the pregnant woman eats for two, the woman introducing her boyfriend to her parents eats anxiously for four. I bought my body-weight in ciabatta from the Italian bakery round the corner, and we set off.

But, as invariably happens in these situations, from the moment my parents opened the front door and slightly awkward introductions were made, everyone immediately hit it off. Garry was charming and funny, and my parents clearly liked him straight away. My dad had spent quite a bit of time working in the States, and since my mother has long followed international politics, they were both full of questions about Garry's life, American domestic policy, the NBA, and "Do you know that bar in Vegas . . . ?"

Relieved of the role of community liaison officer, I was free to advance steadily up Mount Ciabatta, washing it down with cup after cup of strong, black coffee. After half an hour, bloated with excess wheat but caffeinated to the hilt, I could barely sit still. I bounced up and down, contributing nothing but constantly interrupting the conversation: *"Does anyone want more coffee . . . that's in today's paper, isn't it, let me see if I can find it . . . was that someone at the door . . . did you see that bird in the tree . . . oh, that's in my bag, Garry, I'll get it . . ."*

In the end I went upstairs to my old room and lay on the bed reading my old childhood comic books until I was calm enough to return to the group and enjoy the rest of the morning.

Hugging and kissing my parents good-bye, we drove on to Cambridge. It was a perfect autumn afternoon; both of us were impressed and slightly awed as the city unveiled itself from the shroud of chilled mist that swathed the buildings and streets.

We peeped into the beautiful fifteenth-century inner courts of Trinity College and Queens' College. We walked hand in hand along the paths of damp autumn leaves that lined the banks of the River Cam, watching the boaters elegantly punt their way along the chill, still water.

We drove home via my sister Toz's and spent a boisterous evening with her and the kids. Zack, Tabs, and Michael were adorable as ever and raced around showing off their toys, clambering over Garry trying to tickle him. We set off for home at 10 p.m., leaving poor Toz to put three overexcited children to bed.

Collapsing on the sofa with a glass of wine at the end of our long day, Garry looked very thoughtful. "You know, it meant a lot, seeing you with your family today," he told me seriously.

"Why's that?" I quipped. "Are you starting to realize anything involving parents turns me into a nervous wreck?"

He laughed. "No," he said gently. "It's that seeing you with your family makes me realize how much they love you."

I smiled shyly. "Yeah, they think I'm okay," I said, trying to make light of it.

But Garry refused to be distracted. "It's made me realize," he continued, "when you come and stay with me in America, how important it is that I make you feel just as loved and special." He put down his glass and sat close so he could kiss me. "I really love you, Jen."

When I come to stay with him in America . . . ? I looked at the china cats next to the chimney as if checking to see if they'd heard it too. If they had, they didn't let on, just stared back sphinxlike, keeping a dignified silence, their feelings firmly under control.

You can learn a lot from cats. I wasn't going to cry this time; I could easily have done so but I'd decided it was time to find a better way of showing my happiness. So I kissed him back instead and we went to bed.

Apart from the time passing too quickly, Garry's visit was completely perfect. Things took a bit of a downturn, though, the day before he left.

I had to chair a one-day conference in the city. It wasn't how either of us wanted to spend our last full day together, but there was no way around it. So we'd agreed: Garry was going to wander around sightseeing, then he'd come and join me and the speakers for drinks at the end of the day. Paula, Posh PR Emma, and Jo would be there too and were all very excited about meeting him.

It was a miserably cold, wet day, but the conference was well attended, and after the wonderful but busy and intense week together it felt almost relaxing now to have a straightforward day of work.

Midmorning, I was up onstage going over some points for the delegates before the coffee break, when someone walked in at the back of the hall.

It was Kelly.

It was nearly a year since we'd seen each other, and that had only been brief, me dropping off some of the things he'd left at my flat at his office. The shock of seeing him now felt just that, like a harsh jolt of electricity slamming into my body. He looked over in my direction, but was too far away for me to know if he could see me staring incredulously back. He took off his jacket and leaned against the wall.

I'd forgotten what a presence he had; I hate to use the word *smoldering*, but unfortunately I have no choice.

All credit to me, I have to say, I kept talking as if the man who'd broken my heart hadn't just walked into the room. Instead, I reminded the delegates that the coffee break lasted only fifteen minutes and please remember that phones had to be switched off as soon as they came back into the auditorium.

Experts at precisely how many calls they could make and how many chocolate cookies they could get through in the fifteen minutes allotted to them, three hundred people looked at their watches, then stampeded out of the hall in unison. Only two remained.

I stepped down from the stage and walked over to the end of the aisle from where Kelly was now casually watching me.

"Hi," he said in a friendly, relaxed way as I walked up. "Seminar going okay?"

"It was until you turned up," I felt like retorting, but I didn't. I just nodded and said: "Hello, Kelly, how are you?"

He was fine, apparently. Work was going well; he'd just got back from a job in Algeria and was off to China at the end of the month. I watched him as he talked. I watched the way his mouth moved, the way he tugged at his dark curls to process a thought, the way his head tilted slightly as he listened. It was all very familiar. And that it was so familiar triggered an almost forgotten sensation inside me. Over our five years together, we'd gradually grown into a certain *shape*. I could feel my part of our shape forming now: the *girlfriend shape*. But even as it developed, and even as we talked, and even as I looked at the handsome face and strong body of the man I had loved so much, a far more powerful feeling grew alongside it: one of impatience. Growing together and learning each other's ways and worlds had been for nothing—Kelly had never wanted a serious girlfriend. And I had never wanted to seriously admit that.

I now knew that to be the truth. I recognized the role I'd played in my own deception. But I'd known that for a while; I'd done the work and was a long way past that insight. I wasn't angry anymore, I just wasn't interested.

Another bond between us flexed, stretched, then shattered into a million pieces.

I stood up. "So, it's lovely to see you again, Kelly," I said, really meaning it. "I'd better get on with all this, but thanks for dropping by. I'll see you around."

In my head, I stood in the center of the Coliseum, Kelly's broken body crumpled on the ground before me. My bloodied arms held aloft, I acknowledged the cheers of the crowds and saluted as they threw flowers and bags of Kettle Chips at my feet in exaltation. My female friends poured into the arena, stamping their feet and clapping their hands, chanting: *"Jen-ny, Jen-ny . . ."*

But the body got back up.

"I'll see you tonight," Kelly said. "Jo's asked me to the drinks."

Crowds stopped cheering and an eerie silence filled the arena. Bags of Kettle Chips rolled like tumbleweeds across the dusty ground.

"Ummm, Kelly, well, that's nice," I replied weakly, my thoughts freefalling in shock. ". . . But you don't have to come to the drinks. . . ."

"I know I don't." He shrugged. "But I'll be in town anyway, so why not?"

This was very, very, very awkward. "Kelly . . ." I said tentatively, groping for the right way to phrase this. "You know I'm seeing someone?"

He nodded and shrugged again, as if to say *what of it?*

"Well, he's over from America at the moment and is coming along to the drinks tonight."

"Yeah, I heard something about that," Kelly replied nonchalantly. "Well," he said, picking up his jacket and fixing me with a lazy grin, "I don't mind if he doesn't." And, kissing my cheek and gently squeezing my shoulder, Kelly turned and walked out the hall.

I watched him go in amazement. *If he doesn't mind* . . . What about if *I* sodding mind? Had Kelly done this on purpose? Did he know Garry was in town and was checking him out? Was this some kind of macho guy thing? And how would Garry feel about meeting a load of my friends *and* Kelly?

All around me, delegates were flooding back into the hall, chancing one last hurried phone call through a mouthful of cookie crumbs. They took one look at my expression and turned off their phones guiltily, mouthing their apologies.

Was this going to be okay? Was Garry going to be okay? Was *I* going to be okay? One thing I was sure about, Jo was *not* going to be okay. In my head, I was back in the Coliseum, Jo peering anxiously out from behind the rump of a nervous-looking lion. The crowd held their breath as I grimly crunched over flowers and Kettle Chips toward her, hands on hips.

The rest of the day passed quickly. And juggling a busy seminar packed with high-maintenance speakers, I actually managed to forget about pretty much everything but the task in hand. For once I didn't mind work monopolizing my attention.

After the final speaker had delivered her presentation, I gave a summary of, then conclusion about, the day's key points, thanked everyone for coming, and with that we were finished. As I stood in front of the stage with the organizer, fielding individual questions from the delegates, I saw Garry walk in at the back of the hall. Although I was happy to see him, I also felt quite anxious: I really had no idea how he was going to react to the news that Kelly was here. Garry came down to join us—windswept but very upbeat after a day spent exploring—and I introduced him to some of the speakers. Twenty minutes later we all managed to escape to the pub.

The whole time we were walking through the driving rain to the bar, I tried to get Garry on his own so I could tell him about Kelly. Whatever his reaction was going to be, for both our sakes I wanted to give him the chance to have it now, rather than in a room with my friends, colleagues, and ex. But it was impossible for us to break away from the group, and as we walked into the smoky bar I could see Kelly over on the far side of the room talking to Posh PR Emma.

Paula (who had set up the date with Seattle Jason) was right by the door, and as soon as she saw me she broke off from her conversation to come over and give me a big hug. She hadn't met Garry yet and on being introduced to him gave him a warm hug, too. She clearly wanted to make him feel welcome, but the whole time she was hugging Garry she was also looking at me and frantically wiggling her eyebrows and gesturing with her head in the direction of Kelly.

"I know, I know," I mouthed helplessly. *"Bloody Jo invited him."*

Paula rolled her eyes and we both looked over at the bar where Jo was standing, rifling through her handbag for her purse while shouting exasperatedly into her cell: ". . . but Ryan, you promised you'd be here . . ."

The bar was crowded, but as Paula (one of life's wonderful people) engaged Garry in an animated conversation, I fought my way across the bar to Posh PR Emma (Kelly had moved on and was now lost in the crowd). I pushed past a ton of people I vaguely knew, but all of whom seemed to know me. As I *"Excuse me, please . . . can I just squeeze through here . . . ?"* -ed my way around them, I was relentlessly quizzed: "Jennifer, did you know Kelly's here . . . ?" "Is it true you met your Soul Mate on your 80 Dates trip . . . ?" "Has your Soul Mate really come over from America to see you . . . ?" "Ohmigod, are Garry and Kelly both here *now?*"

The chatter seemed to grow from a mutter to a rumble, until it swelled into what felt like a soccer chant reverberating around the stadium. Any moment I expected to see people waving scarves and blowing on their hands to keep them warm, singing to the tune of "Blue Is the Color": *"Garry's her boyfriend, Kelly is her ex, they're here together, and Jennifer is stressed . . ."*

I fought my way through the inquisition and finally made it to where Emma was standing: "Ohmigod, Jennifer, did you know—?" I held up my hand to stop Emma saying any more. She squeezed my arm sympathetically and signaled the barman to serve us. "I just couldn't believe it when I saw him," she said, shards of incredulity splintering from her cut-glass accent.

"Ummm, me neither," I said grimly. We both turned in synchronized disapproval to glare at Jo, who was now deep in conversation with Kelly about ten feet away. Kelly's body-language said *Get me away from this madwoman,* but I had no intention of rescuing him.

Emma frowned and gave a little huff of irritation. "You know, darling, this nonsense of hers over Ryan really has been going on far too long. That Jo is making a mess of her life doesn't give her the right to make a mess of yours, too."

I smiled at Emma fondly and gave her a hug: "I got Garry . . ." I whispered in her ear, and we both looked over to Garry, chatting easily with the organizer and a couple of the delegates. ". . . my life has never been less messy." She smiled, happy for me.

Jo and Kelly had spotted us and started making their way over. But in the crush, Jo ran into another friend and fell into conversation. Emma's phone started ringing (PR people are never off phone duty) and she took it outside to talk. Kelly arrived on his own and stood next to me at the bar.

"Can I buy you a drink?" he asked. I shook my head politely and pointed to the wine Emma had just bought me. "You're looking well," he said.

I smiled graciously. "You too." It was true: He never looked anything less than amazing. I was tempted to ask about his girlfriend but decided against it.

"It didn't work out with that woman I was seeing," he said, as if reading my mind. I nodded neutrally. I wasn't going there; I didn't want to have any opinion about his love life, or any other part of his life. He was in my past and that's where I wanted him to stay.

But before I consigned him to Another Country, there was one last thing I needed to do: introduce him to Garry. I felt awkward about it but for some reason compelled to, not for Kelly's sake, but for Garry's. I didn't know what the etiquette was, but if he found out (or indeed already knew) Kelly was here and I hadn't introduced him, he might read something into it. I left Kelly talking to other people and fought my way back to Garry. "Kelly's here," I told him quietly, linking my arm through his. "Do you want to meet him?"

Garry looked a little surprised and an expression I couldn't read flickered across his face. He shrugged (it really was my day for shrugging men). "Sure," he said. "Why not?"

I could think of any number of reasons *why not*, my friends and peers having front row seats at the premiere of *When Garry Met Kelly* being one of them. I raised my eyebrows. "Are you sure?" He nodded.

I had such a bad feeling about this.

On my way back to find Kelly, I bumped into Jo. I gave her a look but didn't say a word.

She burst into tears. "I know, I know," she blubbered. "Ems has already told me what a despicable person I am. I didn't mean it," she cried miserably. "I bumped into him and he told me he'd split up with whatshername and I wasn't thinking and I just . . ." She faltered, looking at me wretchedly, then, "Sorry, Jennifer," she whispered plaintively, looking down at the floor.

What could I do? I gave her a hug. "You are such a twit," I told her exasperatedly as she continued mumbling apologies. "Go and introduce yourself to Garry; your punishment is to be there when I introduce him to Kelly!" She looked horrified and I gently shoved her in Garry's direction.

Back at the bar, Kelly was talking to Paula. I asked him if he wanted to meet Garry and we pushed back through the crowd to Jo, now animatedly talking with Garry. It was the moment of truth, and I could tell people were watching.

But when we got there, something completely unexpected happened: Garry ignored us. Jo chatted and laughed and fluttered her eyelashes. Garry smiled, asked her questions, and generally paid her a ton of attention that kept Jo—delighted to sparkle for a change rather than be miserable about Ryan—spinning like a top.

Kelly and I stood waiting for them to stop talking and acknowledge us, but Garry kept talking and Jo kept spinning. After waiting like idiots for a couple of very long minutes, Kelly turned to me with one eyebrow raised. "It seems your man is busy," he said, the sarcasm clear in his voice. "I'll be at the bar if you fancy a drink." And with that, he walked off.

I was mortified and furious, furious, furious.

I instinctively looked over at Emma and Paula, who were

looking back with expressions of disbelief. This wasn't right. What the hell was Jo doing, inviting Kelly here, and then hitting on Garry in front of everybody? And why was Garry chatting up Jo? And doing it in front of the man who'd broken my heart being unfaithful?

And all this on Garry's and my last night.

Suddenly it was all too much. I grabbed my coat and marched over to where Emma and Paula were standing. "Sorry, but I have to go." On the way out, I stopped by Garry and said: "I'm going home, I'll see you later." And without stopping to see his reaction, I stormed out.

Outside, the weather was cold, wet, and miserable. It fitted my mood perfectly as I whirled down Upper Regent Street toward the tube. I hadn't got far before I heard someone run up behind me and then grab my shoulder. It was Garry.

"What the hell are you doing?" he shouted in exasperation.

"What the hell am *I* doing?" I shouted back. "*I'm* going home so you can stay and ignore my ex and flirt with my friend," I exploded.

"What are you talking about?" Garry retorted, his coat flapping in the wind that blew wildly all around us. "I wasn't flirting with your friend, I was trying not to get in a fight."

Not get in a fight? Whatever was he going on about? "Garry, I'm tired and I can't be bothered to talk about this. You have a key, stay or go, the choice is yours, but I'm going home."

And now, although at the entrance to the subway, I marched straight past it: I needed to walk off my anger.

Garry next to me, we walked together in silence. It was the Misery Walking Tour of London. We tramped furiously down Oxford Street; angrily around Piccadilly Circus; heatedly down Haymarket; bitterly past the National Gallery and speechlessly around Trafalgar Square; irately along Whitehall; unhappily past Downing Street; and miserably over Westminster Bridge to Waterloo.

About halfway over the bridge, I'd walked off enough of my rage to be able to listen when Garry tried to talk to me. We descended the steps onto the promenade along the South Bank and sheltered under a tree as the rain grimly lashed the marble lions stoically waiting it out.

I knew I was punishing Garry for something that ultimately Kelly had done, but at the same time, I didn't understand why Garry had ignored us and got so wrapped up in Jo.

"Jen, I'm sorry if I hurt your feelings or embarrassed you in front of your friends," Garry said. "But seriously . . . Kelly? What did you think I was going to do?"

I looked at him in surprise. "What do you mean?" I asked in spite of myself.

Garry suddenly looked as angry as I'd felt moments earlier. "All I know about this jerk-off is that he cheated on you and treated you really badly. I love you and I think you're the most beautiful, kind, loving, and giving person I've ever met. He totally fucked you over and you think, what . . . ? That I'm going to stand around and make small talk with him? How did you think that was going to go?"

Now it was my turn to look amazed. I hadn't even considered that.

But Garry, who had just been forced to march across London in the pouring rain, was not happy and had not finished. "And as for your friend Jo . . ." he continued heatedly, ". . . she said some guy called Ryan had just walked in and could I look like I was having a good time talking with her to make him jealous." He shook his head as he talked. "I thought it was weird, but she's your friend and you'd been over at the bar for ages talking to that

jerk. . . ." Garry looked at me exasperatedly. "It's our last goddamn night: I had dinner reservations and was trying to get you
out of there, but I didn't want to take you away from your
friends. . . ." He spread his hands in a gesture of frustration and
looked out across the river, clearly trying to control his temper.

I listened quietly as Garry talked. When he finished, I
scrunched my face up in a half-smile, half-frown. "Really?" I
asked. Garry didn't answer, he just looked off into the rain with
an impenetrable expression.

Oooops.

Ryan *had* walked in. I'd seen him but hadn't paid any attention to him. And it was exactly the kind of stunt Jo would pull—
their relationship thrived on drama and make up sex.

I sighed. I didn't want to be a doormat again, but what Garry
said made sense. I'd dropped him into the middle of a really difficult situation; finding a clear path through tonight's social minefield would have been virtually impossible. But he'd tried anyway.

It seemed I wasn't the only one blasting off on an intergalactic
leap of faith.

I shuffled closer to Garry on the wet bench and tried to work
my hands into his, which were clamped down hard on his wet
legs. "I'm so sorry, Garry," I told him penitently. "I can only
imagine what tonight must have been like for you. I really, really
appreciate you sticking it out."

Garry continued to stare out at the water for a few more moments, then, breathing out slowly, let me slide my hands under
his. We looked at each other and both smiled wryly.

And so the moment passed. It was too late and we were both too
cold and wet to stay out any longer, so we went home and curled
up in front of the fire with a pizza, happy to watch TV rather than
talk any more. But in among the pizza and sitcoms, there was a

strange feeling of closeness, having resolved and survived such a bizarre, emotional evening together.

By the next morning, our first row was not so much forgotten as one more thing we'd shared and experienced. Garry had an early afternoon flight back to America. Although seeing each other soon in Tokyo made it slightly easier to say good-bye, I was still in such a daze afterward I had to text him from the parking lot to ask if he remembered where I'd parked the car.

So Garry went back to America and I finalized the Australasian trip. We quickly fell back into our emailing, instant messaging, and two-hour-phone-call pattern. But this time as well as being able to ask about Garry's friends I'd met in Seattle, Garry asked how my family was; what Paula was doing . . . if Jo and Ryan were still up to their old tricks?

And three days after Garry left, a huge box arrived from Amazon. Mystified, I opened it and laughed out loud as I pulled out a brand-new coffee grinder, a coffeemaker, and a note from Garry:

"Coffee in the house!"

I was thrilled and very touched, so putting some beans in to grind, I went into my little office to email him a thank-you. But in my befuddlement, I hadn't put the lid on properly, and as I typed the coffee beans rattled against the blades and fresh grounds whizzed out the top of the machine, spraying every surface in the kitchen.

Coffee in the house indeed.

chapter thirteen

Tokyo, Japan

Tokyo love charms

And now, final dates lined up, accompanying logistics locked in, I was ready in all senses to embark on the concluding leg of my journey. One Soul Mate and nineteen dates in nine cities and six countries, spread across Japan, Indochina, and Australasia.

It was the final stage of a long journey and, mission partially accomplished, I was setting off on my Date Odyssey facing a completely new set of challenges and experiences.

I'd needed to go to the Date Wranglers one last time to ask for their help rounding up the remaining Dates. I was slightly nervous about approaching them since I suspected they might be ambiguous about helping me. Not with my decision to complete the journey. All big travelers themselves, the Date Wranglers would feel the same way I did: that to end it now would be like

Jason and his Argonauts heroically battling through to Colchis, then, on finding the Golden Fleece, checking it as hand luggage and flying home with British Airways from Tbilisi.

No, what I expected to be the sticking point was me still needing their single friends to make up the rest of my dates. I braced myself for a reaction of: *"Well, great, Jennifer, you've met The One and I'm happy for you, but what about my friend? He's still out there looking. Why would he get his hopes up and go to the trouble of dating a woman who's not even available?"*

In fact, worse than unavailable: newly and—almost certainly annoyingly—in love.

But, as it turned out, I couldn't have been more wrong. The Date Wranglers were actually even more into my journey than before.

This was partially due to the fact that they'd been emailing regular progress reports to the Date *Wranglees,* including the fact that I had now met The One. And as a result, rather than being put off meeting me, Wranglees now *really* wanted to meet me. It seemed they saw a date with me as the chance to learn the mysterious secrets of Soul Matery, presumably so they could use this hard-won knowledge to track down Soul Mates of their own.

I also got the impression they believed once I turned up for their date, I'd take one look at them and realize I'd got it terribly wrong: Garry wasn't my Soul Mate after all, *they* were.

If you don't apologize for having met "your man," I won't apologize for trying to change your mind when you get here. . . . Daniel, emailing from Kuala Lumpur

And, in a strange way, I think the Date Wranglers encouraged this kind of thinking. I'd picked up little undercurrents of displeasure in their ranks—they seemed a bit piqued that after all their matchmaking efforts, I'd found Mr. Right almost by myself.

It's not that the DWs didn't want me to meet The One—they did—but they wanted just as much to *be* the one who found The One for me. They loved a challenge, and appeared determined to have one last shot at winning the Date Wrangler crown. Like supermarkets tailoring special offers to your buying patterns, the DWs seemed to be operating on an *If you liked that . . . you might also be interested in these . . . ?* policy. There was the journalist in China, the environmentalist in Kuala Lumpur, the Chief of Sydney Harbour Police in Australia, even a *mystery date* in New Zealand:

```
I've been working on it for a while but he's been
out of the country. Clues: handsome (Julia says a
knockout), single, well-off, very exciting profes-
sion (but dangerous), interesting, good company,
works with a famous film producer...etc, etc.
Chris, emailing from Marlborough
```

But that was fine, I wasn't worried: I loved Garry and felt confident in our developing relationship. That's not to say I wasn't expecting the journey to throw all sorts of unexpected surprises at me. I was, but I was sure whatever it was wouldn't be in the hands of the Date Wranglers, it would be in the hands of Fate.

But although Fate may shape your life, she doesn't book the airline tickets or arrange the visas.

As ever, the task of tying all the unconnected strands of the journey together had been an exercise in logistical gymnastics. I was meeting Garry in Tokyo, but wanted to go via India because I had the chance of a great date in Calcutta.

As a member of the Laughter Club of India, I believe in the curative power of joy. We meet each
week to laugh health and happiness into our
lives. . . . Bhaskar, emailing from Calcutta

After Tokyo, I was flying to Beijing, where I hoped to make a little detour to Shanghai:

Jennifer, remember me? Tom. I emailed in March from
Hong Kong after the article in the *China Daily*. I
am now living in Shanghai and—as expected—my Long
Distance Relationship didn't survive the journey.
I'd love to show you around if you make it over
this way. All the best, Tom

And although it was still mind-bogglingly stressful trying to pull
it all together, I felt incredibly energized and enthusiastic about
both the traveling and the dates. Out from under the *God, am I
ever going to meet anyone?* yoke, I was free to do what I did best:
travel the world having adventures, meeting lots of interesting,
entertaining people along the way.

But there were limits to what could be achieved in the time I
had left, and trying to work Bhaskar and Tom into a trip that already jumped from Tokyo to Beijing, Bangkok, Kuala Lumpur,
Perth, and ever onward, was—despite my best efforts—impossible. Reluctantly I crossed their names off my dance card.

But that was fine—there were so many things I was already
looking forward to and, best of all, it would be summer again. I
was flying to Tokyo, hitting the Southern Hemisphere just as the
weather had gone to hell in a handbasket here in London.

The Seattle SuperSonics basketball team was in Tokyo playing a
couple of preseason games against the L.A. Clippers. Although

not quite as big as baseball, basketball is a very popular sport in Japan and the games were long sold out.

It was all new to me: basketball and Japan. So as the shuttle bus inched for two hours through traffic, solid from the airport to the Four Seasons in Chinzan-so, my eyes scoured the people, buildings, and streets outside, taking in as much information as possible. The elevated expressways were built what felt like mere inches from the housing complexes and office blocks that sprouted up from every inch of ground. You could virtually read the computer screens in front of row after row of office workers—a unisex uniform of black hair, white shirts, and a black jacket hanging from the back of every chair. The offices were full even though it was close to 9 p.m. With working hours notoriously long in Japan, I wondered how the staff unwound in the small window between one working day ending and the next beginning. I hoped for their sake it wasn't by hanging out in the café-pub we passed, neon sign advertising DANCING AND FRUIT.

Although flying in separately from London and Seattle respectively, Garry and I arrived at the hotel within moments of each other. It felt a little odd to be in a hotel, but we picked right up from where we'd left off in London.

Rather than succumb to jet lag, we joined Garry's co-workers JR, Jon, Doug, Bob, and Bobby (all of whom I remembered fondly from Seattle) for a night out with JR's Japanese friend, Toshi. We piled into two cabs and fought to get the best views out the windows as we inched through Tokyo by night.

Miniskirted teenagers chatted in private huddles as they waited to cross the road. Their bodies flickered with light from the billboard video screens and neon signs suspended from every building around, giggling mouths hidden modestly behind cupped hands and long fringes. A couple of feet away, tired-looking businessmen—shoulders drooping, suits crumpled, briefcases held limply in their slack hands—stared off into space, seemingly aware of nothing but the red crosswalk light that stood between them and the remains of their evening. Behind them all, in brightly lit alleyways, streams of people disappeared into bars that seemed too small to contain the numbers pouring in.

In Tokyo, it seemed *packed* was the norm, whether in the office, traffic, or bar.

We arrived at our destination, a teeny noodle place in Shibuya. The waitress led us three short paces from the door to the bar and gestured that we should sit on the stools squeezed in front of it. Heads bent low over their steaming bowls, all around us locals scooped soba noodles into their mouths, chopsticks swooping rapidly and efficiently from bowl to mouth in a movement that was both graceful and (to our Western eyes, at least) a bit greedy. Jet-lagged, disoriented, and bigger than all the other diners there, we clumsily clashed knees and prodded elbows as we swiveled around on our stools and gulped down every movement and moment being served up around us.

The next morning Garry and I had a couple of hours to explore a little of Bunkyo-ku—the ward or district the hotel was in—before he headed off with the rest of the broadcast crew to the arena where the games would be played, two days from now.

After Garry left, I lost no time heading back out into the city on my own: My traveler's instincts were tugging—like a dog on a leash—to be free to explore. The first thing I liked to do in a strange city was to find my bearings; I didn't feel comfortable until I knew where I was in relation to everything else. Also, I wanted to know as soon as possible what was out there to see and do. Tomorrow there was the date with Will the journalist; three days from now I had a date with Kylie's friend Rob, a Brit working out here for one of the big airlines.

So today I wanted to explore Bunkyo-ku.

I peeked into rice cracker bakeries, watching old ladies deftly wrap long, pungent strips of seaweed around little bricks of puffed rice, or lay hand-lacquered wafers on yards and yards of bamboo mats to dry. I braved the deafening racket of the pachinko parlors, where businessmen sat for the duration of their lunch break compulsively feeding ball-bearings into slot machines: a dexterous and addictive mix of hard concentration and soft porn.

After a long day, Garry and I arrived back at the hotel again at the same time. Too jet-lagged and weary to do much, we lay in the hotel's spacious steam room and caught up on each other's day. Garry had never seen me with my Road Head on and was eager to hear my stories of the world around the hotel, as he'd been working in the arena for twelve hours. Swathed in towels and steamed near insensible, we lay in the sauna and sweated companionably together.

And the next morning, like an old married couple, we had breakfast, kissed each other good-bye and went off in separate directions to work: Garry to continue setting up for the broadcasts at the arena, me to date Will the journalist.

Although I'd walked as far as the subway station at Edogawabashi, I hadn't yet traveled on the subway.

The first cut may be the deepest, but the first hurdle for solo independent travelers in a new country—whatever it may be—is always the highest. Until you have a sense of how routine things operate, a city remains frustratingly inaccessible. Today was no exception. All the ticket machines were in Japanese, and although countless locals were kind enough to stop and ask *"Can I help you?"* since it turned out that that was the full extent of their English, I remained stuck on square one.

In the end I just randomly bought a ticket. Through the barrier, I stood in front of the huge wall-mounted subway map to work out which lines would take me to Shibuya-Ku. Although the color-coded lines meant I could easily figure out where I had to go, it was going to be a complicated journey and I spent a few minutes looking for the shortest route. A student stopped and asked: *"Can I help you?"*

Thinking it was another well-meant but ultimately pointless offer, I gave the briefest answer, only to be surprised and delighted when she replied: "Ah, Shibuya-Ku is on my way. Come with me and we will travel together."

I didn't discover her name, but the young Japanese woman was a fascinating guide and we chatted all the way to my destination. She worked hard: In her fifth year of studying to be a doctor, she was also working in a bar to pay her tuition fees. I asked if that was how she had learned such good English.

"No," she replied earnestly. "I spent last summer studying in New York."

"Oh," I said curiously. "On a medical program?"

"No," she answered gravely. "I was training to be a cheerleader."

As my eyebrows shot up in surprise, she gave a little moue of alarm, instinctively covering her mouth as she did so. "Here is your stop," she said, bowing her head urgently as she gestured toward the closing door. "I hope you have a good stay here in Tokyo."

I thanked her and jumped off the train, joining the crowd heading for the exit onto the street.

I was in Harajuku ward and was meeting **Will (Date #62)** here, at the entrance to Yoyogi Park. It was next to the square where the Japanese teen fashionistas bused in from the surrounding towns to show off their *look* (running the entire subcultural gamut from Ninja nurses to Goths and skate punks). Although curious about the phenomenon, we weren't meeting here for that reason: Will wanted to show me the Meiji Jingu shrine.

Will was very much the boy next door; tall with floppy, light brown hair, he looked a little warm in his thick blue cords and long-sleeved shirt. But he was good company, chatty and obviously pleased to see someone from home. As soon as he'd spotted me, he'd rushed over, given me an awkward hug, then bombarded me with questions about album releases, soccer results, and the progress of the repairs to the Central Line on the London Underground.

When moving overseas, there is a transition point at which the enthusiasm and excitement of being somewhere new has worn off but the routine sense of comfort and familiarity with your new home has yet to kick in. The result is homesickness, and Will was clearly at that point. I tried to answer all his questions as we walked along the peaceful, tree-lined path to the Meiji Jingu shrine.

The building was a faithful reconstruction of the prized Shinto shrine, simple but imposing, built here with dedication and reverence in 1920, then destroyed by incendiary bombs during World War II. Monks in deep green robes and tall black headdresses sat in the shrine's inner courtyard. Although they sat perfectly still, their eyes sternly followed the white-robed acolytes humbly sweeping the ground between them and the altar.

Although Will wasn't my type, he was a nice man and it was a charming date. Quite literally, actually—we were both fascinated and tickled to see the stalls outside the shrine selling charms and offerings. They were extremely specific and covered everything from health and happiness to passing your driving test, having a good visit to the dentist, and getting a university scholarship. As a little offering to Fate, I bought one of the many charms dedicated to meeting your Soul Mate and was intrigued to see they were far more expensive than all of the others. It would seem that even in the more spiritual world, falling in love was big business.

I was already asleep when Garry got back from the arena that night, but at breakfast the next morning we had a chance to catch up. "How did it all go yesterday?" Garry asked in a tone that seemed—to me, at least—to indicate concern for my well-being rather than anxiety over my fidelity. "Was everything okay?"

I told him all about it: how frustrating the underground had been; how I'd been saved from aimless wanderings by a cheer-leading doctor; how interesting the shrine had been; and how Will was like a million people I knew from home.

Without dwelling too much on the date, we talked on, about Garry's day and the progress they were making over at the arena.

"You know," he said, grabbing a bottle of water and dropping it into his bag, "it looks like we'll have all of tomorrow off. What have you got planned? If you like, we can go exploring." A smile blossomed on my face, then just as quickly froze and died.

Tomorrow I had a date with Rob.

The thing was, after this week I didn't know when I'd see Garry again. If he had a day free, I wanted to spend it with him. But at the same time, I was here to date and committed to doing it thoroughly and to the best of my ability.

And, of course, there were Rob's feelings to consider, too. Even though we hadn't had much contact, I still felt a great sense of responsibility toward him. I couldn't drop a date because I'd got a better offer from my boyfriend (not for the first time, I wondered if *anyone* knew what the rules were in this situation). But if I said all of this to Garry, I knew his response would be: *"Baby, you've gotta go on the date: It's what you're here to do."* And that would be our only day gone.

Oh, this was tricky. What to do?

Garry gave me a ticket so I could go to the basketball game that night; then he left for the arena and I for our room.

In the lobby, I jumped into one of the lifts just as the doors were closing. As I tumbled in, I belatedly realized that the lift was already full of people. And not just *any* people: It didn't take me long to recognize that I had inadvertently crashed in and was now *going up* with the Seattle SuperSonics basketball team.

Although I'd seen some of *the wives* around the spa, it was the first time I'd actually seen any of the players. And they were really quite a sight, like long ladders of muscle, propped up against the lift's interior. I wasn't sure what the protocol was, so I didn't introduce myself, just stood quietly as they discussed their training session. It was surreal, being stuck in a lift with a group of seven-foot athletes. I looked up instinctively as they conversed in the air a foot above my head, and it was like gazing up into the muscular branches of a forest of bench-pressing oak trees. And when they did complicated handshakes and talked in completely incomprehensible slang, I felt myself getting smaller and smaller.

"We're not in Essex anymore, Toto," I observed to myself sagely.

Up in our room, I sat distractedly on the toilet and wondered what I should do. I didn't actually need to go to the toilet, but it had a thermostatically controlled, five-setting heated seat, and after all the walking around yesterday the hot seat on my aching thigh muscles was bliss.

These bathrooms were the Rolls-Royce of the peeing world. If the hotel had charged for each of the facilities the toilet offered, like, say, the minibar or the pay-per-view TV, it would have made a fortune. In addition to the hot seat, it sported two bidet-esque water jets, both with fully adjustable water pressure and temperature settings. There was also a hot-air fan (for drying), an air extractor, an air freshener, and a panel with built-in sound effects including that of a toilet flushing and waves crashing on a shore (both presumably to cover the sound of what you'd shortly be needing the air freshener for).

But unfortunately, all the fluffing, flushing, and freshening didn't seem to be helping today, so I decided to call Rob and take it from there. He was in a meeting when I rang, so I left a message on his voice mail explaining my situation.

The phone rang virtually the second I hung up. Snatching up the receiver, I found not Rob but Garry on the end of the line. "Hey," he said busily, "just wanted to check you're okay to get out to the arena tonight."

"Ummm, yes, there's a bus going from here," I told him a little distractedly.

"Cool," he replied, "and if you're up for it, we'll go out with the boys after the game tonight. I'm definitely not working tomorrow, so we'll be able to stay up late tonight and sleep in tomorrow."

Okay, now I really had to sort this out.

As I put the phone back in the cradle, the voice mail light started flashing. I punched in the code: Rob had called. Could I either ring him back in the next few minutes or email him, as he was in meetings the rest of the afternoon. "I've been thinking about the date tomorrow," he continued in the message. "There's an incredible fish market called Tsukiji-shijo, it handles the seafood sales to most of the restaurants in the country. It's an early start but absolutely worth it: I thought we could meet at, say 5:15 a.m., then have a sushi breakfast afterward. Let me know if that suits."

What was it with men, that the dates always seemed to include boats or raw fish?

But more to the point, I'd just managed to arrange a very late night out drinking, immediately followed by a very early morning eating raw fish. It would be full-on, no question, but that was my fault for not coming clean with Garry.

But there was one more twist. "Oh, and as for Garry," Rob continued in a winding-up-the-message voice, "why not just bring him along?"

I looked at the phone in amazement.

Bring Garry on our date? How would that work? Was Rob serious? Did he really think that was a good idea?

I shook my head and blinked hard as if trying to dislodge something blocking my logic circuits. No, it was still there. I sat in front of my laptop for about half an hour trying to compose my response. I had no idea if Garry would want to come along or not. He was certainly a huge fan of Japanese food; a fish market and sushi breakfast was definitely his thing (in fact, far more so than mine, probably). But would he agree? I sighed heavily as I typed:

```
Rob, you are an amazing man! Thank you for being so
kind and understanding. I'll find out if Garry can
make it tomorrow. Either way, I'll be coming, so
can you please let me know where I should go? I'm
really looking forward to meeting you. Take care,
Jennifer x
```

I then went to the hotel gym and ran on the treadmill like a woman possessed for the rest of the afternoon.

Just before I left for the game, I checked my emails and Rob had got back to me with the details of our rendezvous:

```
Let's make it 5:15 a.m. at Shintomi-cho station
(Yurakucho line), on the platform as you get off
the train.
```

Well, so far so good. And with that, I picked up my coat and my ticket: After a day of jumping through hoops, I was glad to now have the distraction of watching a group of men shooting them instead.

When I arrived at the game, I didn't see Garry or any of the crew, as they were in the broadcast truck behind the arena. But both JR and Bobby waved to me during the break from their camera positions courtside.

I loved watching the game; it was easy to follow and the enthusiasm of the crowd was infectious. I was lucky—my seat was next to Mimi and Missy, wives of the team doctors, friendly and funny women who had been going to the games together for years. They knew all the rules and all the players and they entertainingly explained everything that happened on court.

The Sonics won, and later, back at the hotel, I joined Garry and the crew for drinks. The broadcast had gone well and everyone was boisterous and upbeat, chatting animatedly and drinking steadily.

Suddenly it was well after 3 a.m. and I was quite tipsy. Garry put his arm around me. "Ready for bed?" he asked. I'd had a lovely evening and I couldn't wait to see the next game, plus the guys were all so much fun to be with.

But I still hadn't got around to telling Garry about the date that was, in fact, happening two hours from now.

Back in our room, as we stood in front of the bathroom mirror brushing our teeth, I knew I had no choice but to bite the (minty) bullet. "Garry . . ." I started.

"Ummm?" he replied sleepily through a mouthful of toothpaste.

"Garry . . ." I said, spitting out the toothpaste and going for it. "I know I should have told you earlier . . ." Garry continued to brush his teeth, but raised one eyebrow quizzically. "You see, the thing is . . ." I continued, ". . . I actually had a date lined up for later today, but when you said you'd be free, I really wanted to spend the day with you."

Garry had stopped brushing his teeth. I looked at the clock on the wall: 3:45 a.m. I had to meet Rob in an hour and a half.

I spat it out. "So I rang Rob—he's my Date—and he's invited me to look around a fish market and go for a sushi breakfast afterward . . ." Words tumbled out of my mouth; Garry frowned in concentration. ". . . and he said why don't you come too?"

There was a brief delay as Garry made sense of the sentences I'd just rattled out. He smiled unexpectedly, then laughed. "That's really funny," he said, apparently genuinely amused at the prospect of coming on a date with me . . . and my Date. "There's never a dull moment with you, is there?"

I smiled weakly; if Garry was okay about this, I didn't want to change that by saying the wrong thing.

"Sure, I'd love to come," he said with a broad grin. "In fact, it sounds like fun. But let's go to bed now, huh, I'm pooped."

Ahh, I'd forgotten one vital piece of information. I looked up at the clock again: 4 a.m. "Right," I said with a *the show must go on* smile. "That's good, I'm so pleased you want to come. But here's the thing . . . we have to meet him in an hour and fifteen minutes. . . ."

Garry's smile gently fell from his face like a balloon deflating after a party. "An hour and fifteen minutes . . . ?" he repeated incredulously. I grimaced and rolled my eyes, spreading my hands feebly as if suggesting *who would have thought it?*

He looked at me carefully, as if trying to decide whether to waste any more of the very small amount of time we had left asking why I was only telling him this now, then deciding against it. "Okay," he said. "Half an hour's sleep, then we'll get a cab." I nodded meekly and we went to bed.

A little over an hour and twenty minutes later, I was running down the steps of Shintomi-cho station, ten minutes late for meeting **Rob (Date #63).** He'd said in his email we'd have no problem spotting each other and he was right: In a sea of Japanese, we were the only Westerners. We towered over them, just like the basketball players had towered over me in the elevator yesterday.

Rob was a little shorter than me, with close-cropped brown hair and pale skin, and I immediately had a good feeling about him. He looked relaxed and cheerful, not at all worried about the tandem date.

He looked up, smiled, and started walking over, as he saw me fighting my way down the stairs that the crowds of disembarking commuters were all surging up. We met at the bottom of the steps and gave each other a big hug. "Is Garry not with you?" Rob asked. I shook my head. Rob frowned.

"No, no, sorry," I protested. "He's upstairs, waiting for us outside, trying to come to terms with how little sleep he's had."

So Rob and I went upstairs, slightly awkward introductions were made, then the three of us set off together to walk to Tsukiji-shijo market, for my date with Rob.

All was fine: We chatted generally about Tokyo and what we thought of it. Rob had just got back from Beijing and I said I was going there in two days; Garry talked about his love of Japanese cuisine and the places he'd eaten.

We arrived at Tsukiji-shijo market and spent a couple of hours making our way through the crowds. I'd been to a lot of food markets in Asia, and they were invariably the *Apocalypse*

Now of the culinary world. Tsukiji-shijo was no exception. Twelve million people came here every day to buy over four thousand tons of seafood: It was an incredibly busy place with porters racing around, trucks piled high with dripping boxes and wilting fins. The vast warehouses were dark and noisy; we waded through blood and melting ice as all around us band saws screamed through huge tuna carcasses and octopuses lay on their sides, one dark eye sadly following us from shallow plastic trays as we walked by.

The conversation got a bit bogged down. I'd ask Rob a question, as per my dating MO, but Rob, being polite, would address his reply to Garry as well as me and then they'd end up disappearing into a big chat together. I wanted to make good on my plans to date Rob, but, slightly hungover and surviving on thirty minutes' sleep, it was too complicated. I walked a few paces ahead and left Garry and Rob to their own devices, sensing that before I could get anywhere with Rob, the guys needed to scope each other out.

And, without my input, they did this in no time at all. Thankfully, Rob then suggested coffee and food.

We found a tiny sushi bar—about eight by four feet—in the outside part of the market (fresh air, thank God) and crowded in around the counter. Rob spoke excellent Japanese—he was one of those people who spoke any language you could think of—and Garry was delighted to be able to quiz the sushi chef with Rob acting as interpreter. Just as we'd finished ordering the food, Garry fell into conversation with two Canadian women, and I could finally get on with the date.

We talked about living overseas and the chance it gave you to reinvent yourself. We also talked about Japanese culture, the subculture of the Burning Man Festival, and, of course, love and how sometimes it's easier just to work harder and forget all about it.

Three hours later, we stood on the steps of Rob's office, saying good-bye with real affection. It had been a unique and special morning. But just as Garry and I turned to go, Rob called us back. "Come with me," he said in an almost guilty whisper. "There's something I think you should see."

He took us into the building, through the lobby, and into the lift, and forty-five floors later we stood in front of a vast panoramic window surveying the Tokyo cityscape.

It was a clear, sunny morning and both Garry and I gasped in awe as we looked out across Tokyo: built-up and bustling as far as the eye could see. But, looking more closely, we realized that that wasn't quite true. Beyond the landmark Tokyo Tower, Fuji TV buildings, and a jumble of greater and lesser structures, rising up from the horizon, marking the limit of the city's relentless urban ambition, Mount Fuji loomed majestically over the city, its roots seemingly in another world.

I looked out across the cityscape to the mountain and was struck powerfully, not for the first time, by what an incredible experience this all was. Time and again, the dates had given me a perspective that was unexpected and poignant. As I looked over to Garry shaking hands with Rob and thanking him once again, I knew today was no exception.

The next three days passed quickly, but in between the basketball games, where Mimi and Missy once again schooled me on play and players, we crammed in as much as we could.

We walked through the serene gardens of the Imperial Palace and watched a delicate geisha girl in traditional dress walk in tiny steps over a wooden bridge, hand cupped to her mouth as she talked into her cell phone. Late at night we ate at one of the small, anarchic yakitori stalls under the arches of the Yamanote subway line. Then, going into the station, we watched in amazement as scores of businessmen dropped dead-drunk onto the floor. They collapsed on top of each other and gathered in drunken piles, like an impromptu flea market, on the entrance steps.

It was wonderful to be able to share this time and I was thrilled to see Garry curious and energized by the surroundings. One of the main reasons Kelly and I had stayed together for so long was our compatibility as traveling companions. It wouldn't have been the end of the world if Garry hadn't been enthusiastic about traveling, but that he enjoyed it so much was great: Like showing him my life in London, this was another important part of who I was.

Because although it sometimes exasperated me, made me tired, meant I missed my friends, and liposucked all the money out of my bank account, leaving it svelte and lean, I loved traveling. My mother had traveled solo through Europe in the fifties (unheard-of then); my father had worked in China and Russia when they were closed to most of the world.

For people of my parents' generation, travel was a hard-won opportunity. My generation just assumed we would do it, we saw it almost as a right. But I cherished it anyway. It might make no sense to some, but it spoke to me and I couldn't be without it.

It was the reason I'd met Garry. And—as I prepared to go to China, Garry back to the States—now it was the reason we had to say good-bye again.

"So, let's see how we get on, but maybe there'll be time after New Zealand for me to pop in and see you in Seattle," I told him, a brave stab at nonchalance as we stood in front of my packed bags in our hotel room.

I had a round-the-world ticket and was flying east all the way. The grand finale of my International Tour of Shame was in New Zealand, so I'd fly over the U.S. on the way back to the U.K. But time was tight: I was godmother to Toz's son Michael and needed to get back for the christening.

"And you'll email me when you get to Beijing?" Garry reiterated.

I was staying with Hector and Ang and didn't really know how easy it was going to be to phone or email from there. Also, two days ago they'd had a baby daughter, Grace (or Haixin, her Chinese name), and I was anxious not to get in the way of their parental learning curve.

Suddenly it all seemed very tentative. Every other time we'd said good-bye, we'd known when we were going to see each other again. This time we didn't, and I felt unsettled and a little scared by that.

Walking down to reception together, Garry carried my bags out to the shuttle bus as I hugged and kissed all the Seattle guys good-bye. Then Garry reappeared in the doorway and we held each other close one last time.

"Thank you for inviting me out here," I told him.

"Thank you for inviting me on a date with your Date," he replied with a cheeky smile.

For some reason that made me tearful. "I'm saying good-bye now," I told him firmly, "or you're going to have to put up with me crying again, and, for once, I'd really like not to."

Garry smiled and walked me to the bus, his arm tight around my waist. We kissed good-bye and kissed good-bye, then I boarded the bus and found my seat.

"Call me from Beijing," he mouthed as he stood on the pavement below my window. *"You want to hear me sing?"* I mouthed back teasingly. He smiled, then took a step back as the bus started up noisily. Looking back up at me, Garry pressed his fingers to his lips. Then the bus pulled away and he was gone.

chapter fourteen

Indochina— Beijing, China

Date #66—Paul in Beijing
...it all started so well

Hector was an old friend of mine. I'd known him originally through work: He was news editor on one of the papers and used to interview me whenever a travel story came up. He'd traveled a lot himself and he was a huge music fan, too. We quickly became close and had stayed that way ever since.

Another thing we had in common was a suspicion that hard work had taken over our lives and that travel had the power to put things back into perspective. In some respects, Hector had achieved by chance what I was trying for via my complex geo-social engineering. He'd left Britain for a job at *China Daily* in Beijing and met a gorgeous Chinese woman, Ang, virtually the day he'd arrived. They'd dated and fallen in love, and now they were married.

In the early days, as the romance had developed, Hector had emailed pictures of them both to us back at home. He was clearly besotted with her and you could see them growing closer and closer with each new photo. Instinctively I felt protective of him: When you see a good friend wholeheartedly fall for someone, there's always a part of you that's anxious on their behalf. You hope it really is as good as it looks and something isn't about to happen that will make it end badly.

But as soon as I met Ang at their wedding, any worries I had vanished completely: She was great and they were perfect for each other, total Soul Mates. Ang had a witty yet shrewd attitude that I particularly liked and respected. Whenever I emailed Hector as a Date Wrangler, I always asked for Ang's opinion and advice, too.

And they had both more than lived up to their responsibilities as Date Wranglers. I was arriving in Beijing, ready to go to work.

After the balmy sunshine and techno-opulence of Tokyo, Beijing was a shock to the system. China seemed everything that Japan wasn't. It was freezing cold and snowing; cars were full of dents and rust. They rattled down potholed streets at night with headlights switched off, bicycles pelting past them in their hundreds, equally unilluminated. Crossing the road was a perilous affair; it took the courage and faith of a fire-walker. Everything seemed chaotic. Tokyo had been busy, too, but there had been a sense of order and serene dignity to the place. Beijing seemed poorer, dirtier, and louder by far.

It was brilliant.

I flew into Beijing quite late, so after a meal at a local café, Hector and I spent the remains of the evening at their small apartment on Huixin Dongjie, in the northeast of the city. Like most of the expat journalists, Hector's accommodation was provided by the newspaper he worked for. He lived in an apartment building in a compound, the offices and cafeteria just a few steps away across the forecourt.

It was good to see him. The two of us sat and caught up on everything: the new baby, Garry, work, friends, obscure Scottish bands . . . As we chatted, Hector noticed I was cold. He apologized and got up to fetch me another sweater. "The good thing about living in Communist China is that it's cheap," he explained mildly. "The bad thing is that the government doesn't turn the city's heating on for another three weeks."

Ang and baby Grace weren't at home. As is common with new mothers, they were both staying at her parents' house about an hour across town. Hector had been staying there as well and I felt bad that he was forced to play host to me rather than be with his family. But first thing the next morning, we went visiting.

Ang's parents lived in a development over in the northwest of the city, although, as Hector and I walked to the subway, it quickly became apparent that the entire city was a development.

China had been a closed economy to the West for years, but winning the bid to host the 2008 Olympics was confirmation that both China and the West wanted that to change. Although fifty years of Communist rule had kept China isolated from the financial and social growth the West had experienced, China was grabbing it now with both hands. International money was pouring into the country, and rural Chinese were moving in their millions into the cities (354 million over the next twenty-five years, according to the experts), where work, opportunities, and a better standard of living would, theoretically, be found.

But there was no infrastructure to support them, not enough housing, roads, shops, restaurants, schools, or utilities. There wasn't enough to support the 2008 Olympics, come to that, so China was working at fever pitch trying to get it built in time.

Consequently, Beijing was a building site: Deep ruts of dried, frozen mud ran through the city like streetcar lines. The noise of jackhammers and cement mixers, like industrial elevator music, was persistent, irritating, and intrusive. On the way to the station, Hector and I constantly shielded our eyes against swirling eddies of dust and grit kicked up by the drilling and digging going on all around us. On construction sites, men dressed in nothing more protective than slippers and suit jackets hacked at the frozen earth with spades.

Ang's mother spoke no English but managed to make me feel very welcome anyway. She retreated to the kitchen to prepare a big meal for us; she'd never met a western woman before and was shy but extremely curious. When I saw her again later in the week, she got Ang to ask if—since they were *so long*—my eyelashes were real. I put her fingers to my lashes and let her gently tug them, which caused no end of giggling. Despite being kept up all night by the baby, Ang was obviously pleased to have company. Grace was cute as a button and we cooed over her.

It was funny hearing how much of each other's language and phrases they'd adopted in everyday conversation. Hector's English (Scottish) was now peppered with Mandarin; Ang's English was excellent, and even more authentic now that she was using an increasing amount of slang. The baby had a cold that was giving her some difficulty breathing. It was clearly a worry and Hector had been to the pharmacist. He gave Ang the drops he'd bought. "Grace's congestion is caused by snotters," he said gravely.

"Ah, yes," Ang said, peering up Grace's nose. "I see snotters too."

Ang's favorite word seemed to be *dodgy* (in the sense that the subject was suspect or unreliable). She pronounced it *dodtchy* and it always made me smile. Suddenly missing Garry with a sharp pang, I thought how our language had started cross-pollinating too. He loved the British *cheers* but, like Ang, also seemed to enjoy saying that things were *dahgee*.

Promising we would meet up the next day, I managed to persuade Hec that I'd be fine on my own and he should stay here with Ang. I'd be perfectly happy spending the rest of the day exploring.

It was easy to find my way back to the station, which was just as well since no one would have spoken English had I needed directions. This was a Chinese residential area and not a place tourists would ever come to. There were no other westerners around, and everyone stared at me quite openly. People had done the same in Japan, especially as I was so tall. On more than one occasion, someone had reached over and touched my face or arm, wanting to know if my skin felt the same as theirs. It wasn't frightening or hostile. Clearly, foreigners were still a relative oddity here and everyone was just curious.

I was curious too.

I poked around shops and food markets; walked thoughtfully around Tiananmen Square, watching clouds of ornate kites skate across the air in front of the Mao Mausoleum; explored the Underground City, where volunteers had built a secret city under Beijing in the 1960s, scared of a Soviet invasion.

It was dark by the time I took the cold, dusty walk from the underground station back to Hector's flat. Street traders sold potatoes and apples from huge mounds laid out on cloths on the irregular pavements; a woman sat before a sewing machine in the middle of the street, a pile of repairs and alterations folded neatly in a plastic sack by her feet. In the doorway of a DVD shop, the owner was engrossed in an American workout program blaring out of one of the TVs. As he watched the perfectly toned, heavily made-up, lightly dressed Californians stretch and jump in time with the music, he jumped and gyrated along with them. Completely absorbed in what he was doing, he kicked his leg out and one of his slippers shot off his foot and lay unnoticed in the road, only to be run over a few seconds later by a stream of bicycles. His body might have been in Beijing, but his pounding heart and mind were pure Beverly Hills.

I popped into another of the countless CD and DVD stalls that lined the road and browsed through copies of pirated films yet to be released in the cinema. As I flicked through the racks, I half-listened to the old woman behind the counter talk to a young man I guessed to be her grandson, busy taking cases from cardboard boxes and arranging them on the shelves.

The cadence of their conversation seemed to jab and twang sharply, rising and falling atonally like a Japanese lute. I've often noticed how the singsong sound of certain Asian accents could make a perfectly ordinary conversation sound like an argument. And as I thought this again now, there was a loud crash. To my astonishment, the old lady came careening out from behind the counter, brandishing a long stick like a samurai sword over her head. Her face brick-red with rage, bellowing and swinging wildly, she proceeded to chase her grandson around the small shop, flailing as she ran.

But she couldn't catch him. And as grandmother and grandson ran around the shop shouting angrily, with each dodge the stick whizzed past the agile grandson and smashed instead into the racks of DVDs. They went flying off the shelves, skidding across the floor and scattering their contents under boxes and life-size cardboard cutouts of Jackie Chan. There were three Chinese men in the shop along with me, and we all stood frozen in disbelief as the scene unfolded around us. But as an airborne DVD caught one of the men painfully in the neck, we exchanged a quick look of *No DVD is cheap enough to be worth this,* and all made a beeline for the door and dashed out into the safety of the street. I walked briskly away without looking back, the sound of people shouting and DVD cases splintering clearly audible all the way down the street.

Happily, both my cell phone and email worked in China, so as I walked, I rang Garry and told him what had just happened.

"What's all that noise?" Garry shouted a few seconds into the conversation.

"That's China!" I shouted back, as all around me the sound of drilling, driving, sewing, and shouting filled the air.

We talked on the phone all the way back to the apartment, then—fearing my phone bill—spent another hour instant-messaging after that. I had so much to tell him, there was so much going on. I really wished he was here; I missed him terribly. He would have loved this.

The next morning Hector and I met early and ambled along the painted corridors and temples around the vast Kunming Lake in the grounds of the Summer Palace, before heading back to Huixin Dongjie. We were having lunch with a group of Hector's fellow journalists at the Great Wall of China, a landmark restaurant just down the road from his flat.

The restaurant was fancy, friendly, and insanely cheap. Hector's friends—Siobhan, Marta and Paul—were already seated when we arrived, so introductions were made as the waitress passed the menus around. These were huge: over thirty pages of dishes, each with accompanying photo and description in Chinese and English.

We randomly ordered so we could talk. All his friends loved living here, though it could clearly be quite challenging. Marta had broken her hand that morning when a bike had pedaled straight into her on the road. We talked about running to de-stress; Siobhan got up at 5 a.m. to run on an outdoor track. But there was no lighting; she had to shine a flashlight in front of her as she ran so she wouldn't fall down the potholes.

Paul was an early-thirties Australian. He was tall and handsome, also quiet and a little shy. I chatted with him, asking how long he'd been here, where he'd worked before, where he'd lived in Australia. . . . These were actually highlights from my *don't worry it'll all be fine* warm-up date questions; and as if reading my mind, Hector leaned across the table and said: "Jen, you do know that it's Paul you're dating tomorrow?"

God, was it? Why hadn't he told me sooner? I was appalled.

Okay, I'm exaggerating. I was actually very pleased: He was sweet and I already felt so comfortable and curious that I knew he'd be a good date. But I'd been asking him *the date questions* already. What would I talk to him about tomorrow?

"Paul, I'm really sorry," I told him, in a tone that almost certainly sounded like a guard telling passengers they couldn't board the train even though it was standing at the station with the doors wide open. "Do you mind if we don't talk until tomorrow? I don't want to peak too soon."

Hector rolled his eyes and sighed. Paul was too much of a gentleman to show any of the misgivings he now had about dating me; he merely smiled and nodded.

As it turned out, though, everyone talked nonstop, including Paul and me. It was an entertaining and companionable meal— Chinese food is sociable and made for sharing, quite the opposite of Japanese food, which is either in *meal for one* bento boxes or means bending low over bowls of *no eye contact* ramen noodles— and the food was extraordinary. Dish after sumptuous dish arrived: salted fish in black-bean sauce; shredded potato with chili; aubergine in sour sauce. It was piquant with attention-grabbing flavors and textures. I was amazed at how much I loved it.

I think of myself as being pretty open-minded, but there are two things I've always been sure of: I get really seasick and I hate Chinese food.

Clearly, this journey was playing havoc with my sense of self.

After lunch, Hec and I embarked on a series of crosstown buses—the subway might be fast and easy, but it was the buses that gave you a true sense of what a city was like—to go and meet Les.

It was funny: Virtually every date I'd been on, I'd dressed up and gone off on my own like the modern woman I was. But Hector seemed to be acting as an old-fashioned chaperone: arranging dates with people he knew and coming along with me for the introduction. Hector had always been considerate and courteous; I smiled to myself, wondering if in the back of his mind he was steeling himself for the day he'd meet his daughter's beaux.

Les (Date #64) was an expat journalist who had worked in London's journalistic hub, Fleet Street, during its notorious heyday. We met him in a tea shop in the foreign embassy district near Silk Alley (and Starbucks).

Meeting Les—although not obvious date material—was a wonderful encounter. He was a seventy-one-year-old Brit and larger-than-life character. He'd spent the last twenty-odd years stacking up adventures throughout Africa and Asia, writing for and running a variety of newspapers and magazines.

At the height of his career in Fleet Street he'd lost his leg through illness, but he refused to allow this to compromise the quality of his life. His old colleagues in London had had trouble making the same adjustment, however; so rather than accept their pity and the loss of his career, he'd moved to Asia. As he said: "In Britain people can kill you with kindness; in Asia, they may seem a harder people but at least they don't write a man off who wants to work. They don't look at a man with one leg and see a cripple."

It was yet another reminder of how travel revitalizes you and allows you to, if not be reincarnated, then to focus on the parts of your life you value and don't want to lose. It was enormously entertaining and refreshing listening to Les. And I did a lot of listening. In some respects, he actually reminded me of my maternal grandfather, who had run away to sea when he was fourteen and kept us all rapt with the stories of his adventures on the high seas.

That night, Hec went back to see Ang, and I sat at the computer trying to work out where I was going to stay in Bangkok. I was flying there the day after tomorrow and everywhere seemed to be full. I was just about to get a bit stressed about it and moaned on instant message to Garry, when he suggested:

Sounds like you're super busy, just tell me where you want to stay and I'll sort it out for you.

For some reason, his offer made me stop short. I'd been setting up stuff for months now and my standard operating procedure was: Leave it too late, make a fuss about it, get stressed, then—somewhere in the middle of boring everyone rigid about how demanding everything was—get over it and make the booking.

That Garry had taken my complaints seriously, to the point where he actually wanted to do something to help, was incredibly kind. But to have my boyfriend help with the logistics of dating a score of other men felt just a bit weird. Plus, I was committed to the journey, and *sucking up* the logistics hassles was part of that. I just had to tough it out and stop being such a baby.

Nonetheless, I was touched and IM-ed Garry back my appreciation:

```
Thx that's kind of you. I'm fine, though: I'm just
being a drama queen, please ignore me.
```

I slept badly that night: I dreamed that Garry, Paul, one-legged Les, and I were all wandering around Bangkok trying to find somewhere to stay. Hotel after hotel turned us away; they all had rooms, but when we came to book we could never agree on the number of rooms we needed and it'd end up with us shouting at each other and the manager kicking us out into the street.

When I woke at dawn I felt rattled and bedraggled from the unsettled night. As I lay there feeling uncomfortable and out of sorts, my stomach made a strange noise, like water gurgling down a sink. I looked at it, perplexed: What was that all about? Thirty seconds later in the bathroom, as I threw up what felt like every meal I'd eaten since 1986, I realized I must have picked up a traveler's tummy bug. Damn, on the day of my hot date with Paul, too.

Sometime later, crawling from the toilet to the sink, I ran the cold tap and splashed freezing water onto my burning face. Steadying myself against the edge, I slowly pulled myself upright. Catching sight of my reflection in the mirror, I let out a long groan. My hair was lank and stringy, like a dog left out in the rain. And under my right eye was a mosquito bite the size of a pebble big enough to skim clear across the English Channel.

My stomach heaved. It was officially a disaster.

I crawled back to bed and fell into a deep sleep, getting up just once more to be violently sick. But by the time I finally woke at 11 a.m. and was well enough to sit at the kitchen table gingerly sipping bottled water, my temperature was back to normal and whatever had made me so ill seemed to be out of my system (in every sense).

As I stared dully out of the window, I was jerked out of my numbness by the shrill ringing of my cell phone. I fumbled for it in my bag.

"Hello?" I answered scratchily.

"Jennifer, hi," a man's voice replied. "You sound terrible, are you okay?"

"I'm fine, thanks, just a little groggy. Who is this?" I didn't mean to be rude, but there was nothing like a tummy bug to dull your social skills.

He laughed. "Sorry, it's Will. . . ."

Will . . . ? Will who? I wondered silently.

". . . your date," he added, picking up on my hesitation.

My date. My date? I'd dated sixty-four people, and more than one of them had been called Will.

". . . from Tokyo, four days ago," Will finished, his voice trailing off, clearly hurt.

Oh, that Will.

"Will, hi, I'm sorry," I apologized quickly. "I just had a bit of a bad night and I'm not quite awake yet. How are you? How's Tokyo?"

"Well, that's why I'm ringing," he replied, sounding more cheerful. "I'm over in Beijing covering the economic conference and I wondered if you'd like to meet up. I don't know anyone here and I thought we could go exploring together."

He knew I was in Beijing staying with friends near *China Daily*'s building, but it was still a surprise to hear from him. I tried not to show it—I'd been rude enough already. And besides, he was a nice guy. If there had been time, I probably would have met up with him again. "Will, that's really sweet of you and I really hate to say this, but I don't think I'm going to have time. I'm out tonight and I'm flying to Bangkok tomorrow."

I heard nothing but silence from his end of the phone. I waited; still no response. I thought maybe the connection had been lost (he was, after all, ringing on a British cell phone in China to another British cell in China). "Hello, Will, are you there?" I asked.

"Yes," he said quietly. "I am."

My instincts were immediately primed and on full alert. Why was he being so intense? He answered that question in his next sentence. "Jennifer, when we had our date in Tokyo, I was worried that I possibly didn't make a good impression."

"Oh, Will," I replied without hesitation. "You were lovely; it was really good to meet you. Why would you think that?"

He was silent for a moment, then said dejectedly: "Oh, you know, I just really enjoyed meeting you. It was so good to meet someone I could really talk to."

"And I enjoyed talking to you too, Will," I replied, trying to reassure him, but at the same time thinking how unexpected it was to be having this conversation. I knew he liked me when we met, and we had got on well, but I hadn't picked up any indication he was really keen on me.

"Well, that's how I felt," Will said firmly. "And I don't want to make you feel uncomfortable, but I just thought if we could have another date . . . I'd be more prepared and we'd really hit it off this time."

Another date?

"Will," I said, trying to sound reasonable rather than panicky. "I promise, you made a really good impression. I really enjoyed our afternoon together. Honestly, you don't have to worry about going to all that trouble. And anyway . . ." I said kindly but firmly, ". . . I hate to say this, but I'm going to be flat-out right up to the time I fly."

"I've just been in at *China Daily*. I'm in the café across the road," Will blurted out. "You could come and have a coffee with me. It wouldn't take long."

I shut my eyes and opened my mouth to let out a long, silent shriek.

Living overseas can be an intensely lonely experience, so I didn't take what Will was saying as a sign he was necessarily a scary stalker. But the fact was I looked and felt like crap, I still had a lot to do, and I really wasn't in the mood for a Date Addendum.

Will must have sensed my reluctance to meet. "Please, Jennifer," he asked sadly. "Let me have another date. I just want the chance to prove to you that I can be fun."

I wanted to shout: *"It's not fun I flipping need; it's more sleep and some quality time with www.hotels.com."* But I didn't. I felt sorry for him. And the fact was, he'd gone out of his way to meet me when I needed to see him, it was only fair I did the same now he needed some company.

So I went across the road and had a Coke (my stomach rebelled at the thought of anything else) with **Will (Date #65).**

And he was exactly the same as he was before: chatty boy-next-door, full of talk of London and the life he'd be having over there if he wasn't over here. After an hour talking about politics and our favorite bars, I looked at my watch. "I am so sorry, Will," I told him gently. "I really have to go."

He smiled happily. "Please don't apologize, Jennifer," he told me cheerfully, clearly restored by having a chat. "I really appreciate you coming to meet me. It was good being able to talk like this."

As I nodded amiably, my heart went out to him. He hadn't wanted the chance to prove he was The One, he'd just wanted to talk to someone from home. And because we had a lot in common and could talk easily, I helped him believe he wasn't sad and anxious but happy, with friends, opinions, and good times ahead. Will was clearly desperately homesick and struggling with the sense of isolation he felt over here. But he was right: I was glad I'd met him; no one deserved to be lonely and on their own in a foreign country.

Hector was back at the flat, getting it ready for Ang and Grace's arrival tomorrow. He smiled as I walked in the door. "Hello, Dater Girl, how's your day going? Or, more to the point, how're your Dates going? Got them under control?" I rolled my eyes and told him it was most assuredly *they* who had me under control. But I didn't want to think about it, so instead I helped him carry furniture into the spare bedroom.

Paul had said he'd ring before he picked me up for our date, so relying on having a good half hour to get ready (twenty-nine minutes of which would be spent putting concealer on the bite under my eye), I lost track of time helping Hector get the flat straight. I also (finally) feinted left and dodged right around the obstacle of my indecision and booked a hotel in Bangkok.

But Paul lived in the compound, too. I'd forgotten how living somewhere akin to a student hall of residence can blur the social boundaries and create a sense of informality between residents.

So, instead of calling, Paul just turned up. He knocked on the door and let himself in, looking far more dressed up—black trousers and shirt, with nicely gelled hair—than he had yesterday at lunch.

I was unprepared for his arrival in every sense, no makeup and wearing an old pair of jeans. As I scurried around the flat frantically getting changed, Hector teased Paul about wearing aftershave. The two of them sat down at the kitchen table and chatted over a beer while I got ready.

Hector's flat was small, and although I could disappear into the bedroom to change, I also needed to go to the bathroom. Only a glass door separated the small kitchen from the small bathroom, and the kitchen table was about two feet away from it.

I hate it when people can hear me pee. Even more so when I'm about to go on a date with one of them. But I had to go, so, avoiding eye contact as I passed in front of the table, I went into the bathroom and pulled the glass door shut behind me.

From my vantage point on the toilet, I could see Hector's and Paul's outlines through the frosted glass and I could clearly hear every single word of their conversation about soccer.

I couldn't go.

Five minutes passed. I could make out the sleeve being pulled back on a shadowy arm, as Paul checked his watch to see what the time was. We were obviously running late. I still couldn't go.

In the end I did what I am certain all women do in these situations: I dropped some paper down the toilet and peed really slowly and very quietly. It took forever and was excruciatingly painful, like an instant case of cystitis.

I'm sorry if that seems like too much information, but you don't get a second chance to make a first impression: I didn't want Paul to spend our entire date thinking about . . .

Okay, I'll move on.

Paul (Date #66) and I finally left the flat and caught a taxi to a Chinese foot-massage place five minutes away. I was absolutely delighted: I really love having reflexology (based on the belief that each part of your foot is linked to a part of your body, so massaging your feet can relieve anything from an upset tummy to tension in your shoulders). Paul had chosen a perfect date (and there wasn't a boat or raw fish in sight).

When we arrived at the center, there was a moment of slight confusion as Paul tried to explain to the manager what type of treatment we wanted. ("My Chinese isn't that good," he confessed with a self-deprecating grimace.) But the situation was resolved by using Travelers' Semaphore (basically a lot of pointing and nodding). We were then led down a white corridor to a small unadorned room, two large wing-back chairs in the middle, a low table between them, two footstools in front. Up on the wall, a television belted out a Chinese soap opera at a deafening level. The place felt less curative, more geriatric: I wondered if we'd come to a local retirement home by mistake.

But then a Chinese man and woman in their twenties walked into the room. Each was holding a footbath and a pitcher full of scaldingly hot water. They gestured we should remove our shoes and socks and immerse our feet in the baths they had laid at our feet.

That neither of our reflexologists spoke English didn't stop them from gamely trying to engage us in conversation. They gave up after a few minutes, though, and settled on chatting animatedly with each other instead. They clearly enjoyed each other's company; crouching over our feet washing them vigorously, they talked and teased each other nonstop. It was almost as if they were on a date, too.

"So I hear you have some dating questions for me," Paul teased good-naturedly.

I gave a rueful smile and blushed slightly. "It's survival of the fittest out there in the dating world," I told him in mock seriousness. "A girl's gotta be prepared."

He laughed. Graciously accepting the two beers the manager

had just popped in to offer us (just a thought, Western Masseurs: less Enya, more alcohol), Paul opened both cans and handed one to me. I smiled and raised it in a toast: "Here's to Hector, Ang, and Grace," I declared.

"Hector, Ang, and Grace," Paul echoed and laughed.

We clunked cans and drank. Then, leaning back in our chairs, we put the cans down on the low table between us and relaxed as the young man and woman expertly worked our feet.

And, of course, we chatted. Paul was lovely and as he told me about growing up in Perth and we talked about the places we both knew there, I wondered how he could still be single. He was really sweet, good-looking, and gentle, entertaining company. I thought of Garry and felt a bit guilty that I was enjoying myself so much.

Apart from the occasional moment of excruciating pain when the masseur probed a tender part of my foot (*I bet that's the bit linked to my tummy,* I thought each time), we were so engrossed in conversation that I almost forgot there was someone working on my feet.

Until suddenly I was jolted back into reality by the sound of my masseur gasping in shock. His fingers were pressing painfully into the sole of my right foot. I froze in horror: I knew exactly what he'd found and I cursed myself for not having thought about this sooner.

There was a huge, horrible wart on my right foot and the masseur had clearly just spotted it. To my humiliation, he was pointing flamboyantly, trying to bring it to my—and in the process everyone else's—attention.

Okay, I had a terrible wart. He knew it and I knew it; for God's sake, couldn't we just leave it at that?

I felt my cheeks grow scarlet with embarrassment. My masseur didn't speak English, so thankfully wasn't able to come out and say what the problem was. And, mercifully, although Paul did speak a little Chinese, he'd obviously been off the week the class had covered *diseased feet,* and his vocabulary didn't extend to the word for wart. So as my masseur gesticulated urgently, and as Paul's masseur scolded my masseur furiously, and as I sat there red-faced and mortified, Paul was the only one who had no idea what was going on.

I badly wanted to keep it that way.

"Is your foot okay?" he asked in his Australian drawl, clearly concerned for my well-being.

"Ummm, yes," I replied brittlely. "It's . . . err . . . a blister from running. I did a bit of training with the NBA in Tokyo." (Well, I'd chatted with the Sonics' assistant coach in the gym, that was like training, wasn't it?) I was desperately trying to sound ladylike and dignified. I was also trying to ignore the completely appalled expression on the face of my masseur, who continued to point animatedly at the sole of my foot.

"Mate, must be a pretty bad one," Paul observed in a mixture of sympathy and awe.

The pantomime continued.

At the end of my leg, my masseur had given up pointing and was now miming a vigorous chopping motion with his hands instead. The girl working on Paul's feet rolled her eyes and hissed at him angrily. I think she'd picked up on my fervent and increasingly desperate wish that he would please, for the love of God, shut up about my foot.

But he wouldn't. He continued to energetically act out the chopping motion.

I guessed however bad the wart, it was unlikely my masseur was recommending amputation as the most appropriate course of action. I wondered if perhaps he was advising some light pumicing. I would have agreed to pretty much anything at this point, so like a secretive bidder at an auction, I gave my masseur a discreet but definite nod to proceed with whatever he had in mind. The man immediately jumped to his feet and dashed out the door.

In the face of such sustained drama, all pretense that everything was fine was abandoned at this point. Conversation stopped dead as Paul, his masseur, and I sat silently watching the space in which the man would soon reappear. Thirty seconds later, he did. He burst theatrically through the door, dropped to his knees, and with much ceremony took a long roll of black cloth from under his arm. Laying the cloth reverentially on my footstool, my masseur unfurled it slowly. And as he did, one by one, fifteen deadly silver scalpels came terrifyingly into view.

That would explain the chopping motion then.

There was a collective intake of breath. *"Jeez,"* Paul breathed out, openly horrified as we watched the light fall and die on the cold edges of the pitiless steel. "I hope he knows what he's doing."

I know this sounds ridiculous, but I was genuinely in a quandary at this point. Of course, I didn't want the masseur to hack out my instep, but at the same time this was excruciatingly embarrassing and had gone on for what felt like forever. I wanted to go back to the happy chatting of ten minutes ago; I wanted us all to forget about why my hideous feet had become the uneasy focal point for the entire room. If my masseur's plans kept him quiet and happy, let him get on with it; I was willing to take my chances with the consequences.

Paul's masseur had lost patience by now and resumed her work on his feet. But both Paul and I watched mutely as my masseur trailed his fingers gently over the handles of his scalpels. They came to rest on a knife whose broad blade resembled a flat chisel. Untying the ribbons that secured it to the pack, my masseur carefully plucked it from the cloth and oiled the blade lovingly. Lifting it high, then pausing for a moment to admire its wicked edge, he plunged it down dramatically on the sole of my foot, again and again and again.

I let out a gasp and braced myself for the terrible pain, but, surprisingly, there was no sensation at all. I felt nothing. The knife was so sharp it sliced effortlessly and painlessly through the skin (or the whole thing was a cruel joke and he wasn't chopping at all).

Mortification turned into irritation. I was meant to be on a date; this had now taken up more than enough time. I turned to Paul and, stuttering in an unstable, high-pitched voice, demanded: "So, Paul, why did you decide to move to China?"

And incredibly, the dating questions worked their magic.

As I asked and Paul answered, gradually we forgot about the stupid drama that had distracted us and instead focused on the task at hand. Our date. We chatted about loves we'd had and lost; places we'd visited; how work can absorb and make you feel good about yourself. We lost ourselves in conversation, talking easily and comfortably. All was as it should be once more.

Until, from outside the cocoon of our conversation, a sound jolted us back into our surroundings: We were having our feet massaged and the man working on mine was clearing his throat, trying to get my attention. Paul and I stopped midchatter and I instinctively reached forward as my masseur held something out for me to take. He dropped it into the palm of my hand and I retracted my arm so I could inspect it more closely. Paul looked over curiously.

As I unclenched my fingers, Paul and I looked in. Nestling in the center of my palm was the large, yellowing, blood-encrusted lump that up until very recently had been my wart. Like something out of *Reservoir Dogs,* the masseur had cut it off and given it to me. Paul and I both looked at it open-mouthed. We turned to each other, our eyes wide and blank in surprise. We looked back: I was still holding a wart.

It's easy to know in hindsight what the correct response to a given situation should be. And, looking back, I can see clearly mine was *not* the correct response. But it was a very difficult situation; I didn't know what to do. I have to admit, I panicked.

I put the wart in my pocket.

Looking up, I could see this was the wrong thing: Even the man who'd been unsqueamish enough to cut it off was now regarding me with an open look of horror and disgust.

The date ended pretty much there and then. Paul was good enough to last through the end of the massage and the taxi back to Hector's. He didn't stay long once we got there, though.

"Did the date go okay?" Hector asked curiously as soon as Paul had left. I watched him dropping into a chair, exhausted from a frantic evening of getting the flat ready for Ang, the baby, and his new life.

"Hector, do you have anything stronger than beer to drink?" I asked him in a tone that suggested it possibly hadn't gone well at all.

Hector and I sat up all night drinking. I stayed long enough the next morning to see Ang and Grace arrive home. Then, hugging and kissing everyone, wishing them luck and thanking them for their help and hospitality, I caught a taxi to the airport.

I was ready to move on.

chapter fifteen

Australasia

Date #71—Surfer Steve,
Perth, West Australia

As I flew out of Beijing, I curled up in my seat thinking about the date with Paul. Every now and again a primal whimper escaped, as I replayed the action lowlights of the evening again and again in my head.

It had all been going so well, too.

But even as I beat myself up with the shame of it all, I wondered if—apart from the embarrassment, the humiliation, the *can't get out of here fast enough* good-bye, and the subsequent all-night drinking with Hector—it would have ended any differently. I mean, I had liked Paul, and I'd really enjoyed meeting him, but he wasn't The One; there wasn't the instant attraction and solid sense of connection I'd felt on meeting Garry.

I felt relieved, since it meant that I hadn't really messed up anything with Paul after all, but also a little disingenuous. Was I going on the remaining dates just to check that no one else matched up to Garry? Was this like shopping for a new style of clothes, but in this case it was suitors I was trying on for size?

I hoped not: It was cold and cynical and not fair on the dates or Garry. But at the same time, how could it be any other way? And, perhaps more importantly, if in a twist of Fate, I actually did meet someone who measured up to Garry . . . what then?

Bangkok, Thailand

I felt a little troubled as I flew southeast from Beijing across the Chinese mainland and down over northern Vietnam, Laos, and into Thailand. But I've never had a bad time in Bangkok, and during the drive from the airport to the city, the excitement of being there chased away any lingering anxiety.

The hotel turned out to be perfect: La Résidence was a boutique property near Silom. It was cool, quiet, and easy walking distance from Chong Nonsi Skytrain station, Bangkok's life saving monorail that allowed you to bypass the city's notoriously gridlocked traffic and pollution.

The weather was over a hundred degrees and insanely humid; I felt like I was being poached in my own perspiration every time I stepped out of the hotel. But Bangkok was not a place to stay in your room and watch MTV. With the gilded curlicues and ornate carvings of the Grand Palace, Wat Phra Kaew and the Emerald Buddha, the seven-thousand-stall consumeropolis that is Chatuchak market, selling everything from snakes to milkshakes, you didn't have to go far to find something amazing.

In fact, Thailand in general was an incredibly easy, friendly, forgiving country to travel around. Asia 101: Wobble up the first-time-traveler learning curve here and you'll find it much easier than, say, India or Cambodia.

But it would be a mistake to stereotype Thailand as a living museum of tradition and culture, as special as these features were. Bangkok in particular was an educated, affluent city with sophisticated urban tastes.

This was clear the moment I walked into the lobby of the Conrad Hotel for my next date. Endless marble columns rose up from oceans of gleaming marble floors; tiny, beautiful women floated across the surface in sparkly, diaphanous outfits, like jeweled dragonflies. I was meeting my date in the Diplomat Bar at 9:30 p.m. and, depending on how it went, I would take him along or go on my own to meet my friend Joe at the ultra-hip Club 87 at 11 p.m.

Andrew (Date #67) was a friend of my Australian friend Lorna (the one who'd set me up with her *he ain't heavy metal, he's my brother* William in Stockholm). I hadn't had any previous contact with Andrew because—and this shocked me almost more than the incident with Paul, Lorna's brother, Garry meeting Kelly, and every other crazy thing that had happened on this trip—he wasn't on email.

Imagine.

Andrew was a wine importer and was clearly nice, but a little bland for my tastes. Or, to be more specific, there was no chemistry; he just wasn't my type. He made a bit of a fuss about ordering the right wine and then spent a long time telling me how if it was more *this* and less *that,* it would have been superb. He had very fine blond hair which he fiddled with constantly. He'd sweep his bangs across to the right, smooth them into place, then once they were perfectly neat push them back off his face and start all over again. It was mesmerizing, like watching clothes in a tumble dryer go round and round and round.

I didn't take him to see Joe, and as it turned out, I didn't get to see Joe myself: Popping into the toilet on the way down to the club, I managed to *misfaucet* (as in Japan, Thai toilets favored water over paper and had little extendable hoses for that purpose). A combination of high water-pressure and poor coordination meant that at the vital moment, a jet of water shot up from between my legs, soaking the front of my skirt and drenching my fabulous Rodeo Drive boots. The look on the faces of the beautiful women around the mirror (who'd probably never peed in their lives) as I emerged confirmed my worst suspicions regarding how bad it looked, and I decided to call it a night.

I stopped for a drink in a laid-back bar round the corner from my hotel on the way back, wanting to take a moment to review how everything was going before I went to bed. It was time to face something I'd been trying to ignore but couldn't any longer. I was developing a bit of an attitude problem regarding the journey—my attention was beginning to wander and I was in the grip of Date Doubt.

"You've come so far," I told myself sternly. "You have to focus. Your job is to stay in the Date Zone; the reason for what you're doing will become clear when the time is right."

In truth, I was struggling to see where all this was leading. I mean, I loved dating and I wanted to give the Dates my very best. But acting as a counselor to Will, then the drama with Paul, then the so-so date with Andrew just now, made it hard to see what purpose these dates served in the larger scheme of things. And the less I was absorbed by the Dates, the more I missed Garry (which, of course, made me wonder anew why I was still dating). I wished he was here with me now.

But, I told myself severely, Garry *wasn't* here now. I was, though, and so were my Dates. I needed to keep to the course, navigating from Date to Date, as planned and plotted by the Date Wranglers and me.

I had to take another leap of faith: to believe there was an important discovery still to be made on my quest, and that the course I was on would lead me to it. I had to trust in that now, as I had when I'd been "looking" for Garry.

Giving myself a talking-to must have worked, because the next date was brilliant.

My friend Katia lived in Bangkok, but bad timing meant she was in London when I was there. "I don't know how you expect to find a date in Asia if you won't date anyone shorter than six foot. Tall Asian men aren't exactly the norm here, you know," she'd remonstrated earlier that month. But Katia was one of the Date Wranglers who seemed to think that the belief I'd met my Soul Mate needed to be tested:

```
I have an absolute corker for you, though. I've set
you up with my friend Toi. He's a model. Half Thai,
half Italian and wholly gorgeous. Date him at your
peril . . . then tell me how it goes. Kat xxxx email-
ing from Bangkok
```

This, of course, reeked of The One Who Could Have Been, but that was fine. As Katia had rightly observed, my height requirement had made Asian dates thin (and short) on the ground. And **Toi (Date #68)** turned out to be the perfect cure for my severe case of Date Doubt.

There was no doubt that he was a model. Tall and slim, with high cheekbones and beautiful soft brown eyes, he was as striking as he was elegant. People stared as he passed by. Not that any of this was the reason he was the perfect cure (in fact, good-looking and confident, he should have been the perfect nightmare), he was just lovely. Full of energy and enthusiasm, Toi was completely unaffected. He was also really into music, and we twit-

tered on about the Asian and European music scene for ages. He
was also fascinated by my journey and couldn't seem to hear
enough about it.

Toi took me to a traditional Thai festival for our date.

Loi Krathong took place during the first full moon in Novem-
ber. Across Thailand, people gathered at rivers and floated boats
made from banana palms as an offering to the river goddess. It
was a huge occasion, and in Bangkok thousands of Thais came to
the banks of the Chao Phraya river by the Shangri La hotel, all
looking for the best spot to launch their krathongs from.

In Bangkok, krathong-making was a thriving cottage industry since people buy rather than make their own. The stall-
holders that lined the street were doing brisk trade in what
looked like colorful cakes, but were in fact huge lotus flowers.
Their green outer petals were folded neatly back, creating a frame
of little green triangles around the flower's center, which was then
studded with marigolds, orchids, candles, and incense sticks. I
exclaimed they seemed far too beautiful to float. "Ahhh, but we
float them for love, and what is more beautiful than that?" Toi
replied.

I laughed, thinking how Toi's head may have been Thai, but
his heart was pure Italian.

There must have been five thousand people on the street
around us, pushing their way down to join the thousands already
on the riverbank. We stepped out of the crush to buy krathongs
of our own.

"You see," Toi explained, "krathongs are an offering to the
river goddess, but they also tell the future of your love."

I stopped trying to choose from the stall's array of krathongs,
each more beautiful and delicate than the next, and listened more
closely. But Toi shooed my attention back to the stall, clearly intending I should listen as I chose.

"When single people place their krathong on the water, it represents the baggage of old relationships. It floats away, leaving them free to find someone new." Toi sounded very serious as he described the ritual. "And then when you've met someone new, you come back the next year and place your krathong in the water as an offering of thanks, and to ensure a happy future together."

I inspected the krathongs even more closely on hearing this; I wanted to say the best possible thank-you for finding Garry.

I looked up to tell Toi this, but then suddenly thought maybe he didn't know about Garry. I wondered if he'd mind that I'd already met someone. I could tell he liked me, but, now I came to think about it, the vibe I was picking up from him was one of preoccupation rather than of interest. I watched him as he talked and wondered what could be the reason.

"When you meet someone, you should bring them here," he continued, "and you both launch your krathongs into the water. How far they float downstream together tells you how long you can expect the relationship to last."

It was a beautiful story and one that felt extremely pertinent to me. But I was now also intrigued by Toi. Maybe because I knew of his Italian connection, there was something about his tone that reminded me of sorrowful Solimano in Verona, weighed down by the thought of playing Romeo in perpetuity.

But the stall-holder had no time for our poetry-of-the-soul moment; she was in the business of selling krathongs, and so far we were all talk, no action. Growing impatient with my distracted dithering, she grabbed the nearest krathong, shoved it into my startled grasp, and held her hand out to be paid.

I was too shocked to be polite. I shoved it right back at her in indignation: I was picking the krathong that was both the thanks for meeting Garry and the down payment on our future together.

Was she mad? One wrong krathong, and that was my love life sold down the river, gone forever, thank you very much.

But fair enough, it was time to make up our minds.

Toi and I picked out—to our eyes anyway—the nicest krathongs and once again joined the dense crowd of families, couples, teenagers, and pickpockets squeezing over the bridge to the water's edge.

There was such a crush we could hardly move, so as we inched along, we chatted about my journey and how much traveling Toi got to do as a model.

Impetuously, I suddenly asked: "Toi, is everything okay?" We couldn't move much because of the crush, but even so, Toi jerked around involuntarily at my question.

"Why do you ask?" he demanded, not angrily, more intrigued, as if I could see something he couldn't.

"I don't know." I shrugged neutrally. "It was just a thought."

I'd learned two things on this trip. One, my dates always seemed to be at a crossroads and therefore thought (probably rightly) that I was too. Two, they agreed to date me because, in my role as *pair of ears today, gone tomorrow,* they wanted to talk to someone outside their circle about the cause of their crossroads.

Toi sighed, turned to face me, and assumed an expression of *you asked, so . . .* (Mentally I checked all the aforementioned boxes.)

Apparently, he wanted time out from modeling. He'd gone into it because it was easy: He'd been spotted by a scout when he was twenty and had worked regularly ever since. "But you know, Jennifer," he said without a trace of irony, "I keep thinking to myself, 'Is how I look all I amount to? Am I really just a face and a pair of shoulders?' "

It would have been easy to tease Toi but I didn't; my conversation with International Correspondent Will in Beijing was fresh in my mind, and I didn't doubt that glamorous jobs could be lonely.

We were over the bridge by now, but Toi and I walked slowly, resisting the surge of the crowd that pressed all around us. He seemed disoriented by his confession and I was waiting to see if he had anything to add. But he remained quiet and troubled.

"So what are you going to do about it?" I asked. He looked up and studied my face. I thought instinctively how beautiful he was; if people had said that his whole life, I could see how it could get on his nerves after a while.

"What do you mean, what am I going to do about it?" he asked slowly, suggesting he knew exactly what he wanted to do, but was too scared to come out and say it.

Suddenly, a chill hit my stomach: I had the most awful premonition. *Oh no,* I thought, *he's going to tell me he wants to be a priest and give up this life of vanity.* I forced myself not to roll my eyes, imagining all those poor women looking at this exquisite man's face and having to confess to impure thoughts every time they clapped eyes on him. Every day there'd be queues around the confessional box, like the first day of the Macy's sale.

Toi took a deep breath. So did I. "I want to be . . ." he started. I was still holding my deep breath. ". . . a foreign-aid worker in Africa."

My breath shot out like I'd been given the Heimlich maneuver. "Great idea, do it," I shouted, almost before he'd finished the sentence.

Toi raised one perfectly shaped eyebrow, like a rainbow made of black silken threads. "Really? Wow. Jennifer, I wasn't expecting such encouragement. You really think it's a good idea?"

Actually, now that the shock of thinking Toi was going to be a priest had passed, I did think it was a good idea. I mean, why not: Why shouldn't he follow his heart and do some good? We talked about various schemes I knew; the type of experience and training he'd need; the reality of life in a refugee camp. Toi borrowed my notebook and wrote down all my suggestions. He listened carefully to what I said and asked a lot of questions; he'd obviously been thinking about this for some time.

All around us people pushed and squeezed, carrying krathongs carefully in front of them, or in some cases over their heads out of the way of the crowds.

As we joined the throng, Toi whispered in my ear: "I really want to thank you for taking me seriously, Jennifer. It means so much to be able to see a way forward."

I smiled and squeezed his arm. "You're very welcome, Toi. If this trip has taught me one thing, it's that, however freaky it feels, sometimes you've just got to take a leap of faith."

"Like you meeting Garry?" Toi stated. He'd known all along.

"Yes." I nodded firmly. "Exactly like me meeting Garry."

And maybe more than that besides? I thought, realizing that the Date Doubt I'd experienced earlier was—as for Will and Toi—a feeling of isolation, a sense of momentum without connection. Talking with Toi had helped me feel connected again.

And with that, we both went down to the moonlit river. Standing on the bank, we lit the candles and joss sticks in our krathongs, and, reaching down into the dark, placed them carefully in the water.

I didn't ask Toi whether he was letting go of old baggage or wishing for new. Instead I watched my krathong gently bob on the water's inky surface. It was soon joined by another krathong, then another, then ten more, then fifty. They were all swept into the current and glided like swans into the center of the river and gradually out of sight. They were joining the thousands of wishes and dreams, launched in hope and carried by Fate, in the current under the moonlit sky that night.

· · ·

At times, the dates appeared to me like pieces of a jigsaw, helping me build a picture that, although tantalizing me with glimpses, would remain obscured until I had completed the whole puzzle.

Toi was **Date #68,** and there were twelve more pieces of the jigsaw to find.

Daniel (Date #69), Mr. *I'll make you change your mind about Garry when you get here* in Kuala Lumpur, turned out to be a non-event: He had been forced to go to Bali on business and wasn't able to take me on the elaborate date he had planned. He insisted we meet at the airport for coffee, though, and after a long time spent to-ing and fro-ing with airline schedules (I was off to Perth afterward), we managed it. Daniel was stressed and apologetic. "Jennifer," he said wretchedly, "I had it all planned. I was going to take you sailing."

Of course you were, I thought with a little smile (boats and fish, boats and fish—the man may vary, but the date remains the same), as I nodded sympathetically.

Perth, Australia

I'd flown into Perth when I'd come out to Australia in the eighties for my three-month visit that turned into six years with Philip. I'd spent my first year here, and although I'd been back to Australia at least once a year since I left (Lonely Planet's head office was in Melbourne), I hadn't spent much time in Perth, and I couldn't wait to see my old and very dear friend Jude, whom I also knew from my puppet-theater days.

I was also dating one of the puppeteers I'd vaguely known from that time. It was years since I'd seen **Toby (Date #70)** and I was looking forward to catching up. But the date ended up making me rather uncomfortable. I'd met Toby roughly the same time I'd met Philip. He was convinced that I'd made a mistake marrying Philip and spent the whole date quizzing me as to why our marriage had broken up.

When Jude came to pick me up from the Esplanade Hotel that night, I was still irritated and slightly perplexed by his behavior. "I mean, honestly, Jude, Philip and I got divorced over ten years ago," I told her exasperatedly, as we sat on the sea wall watching the sun disappearing into the Indian Ocean in a blaze of red, orange, and purple, "but Toby was going over it all like it was just yesterday. And what the hell does it matter to him anyway?"

But I was too happy to see Jude, and the night was too beautiful to waste getting agitated. We talked about more recent relationships, one that Jude had just ended and the one I had just found. And Jude listened carefully as I talked about the reasons behind my journey and the adventures I'd had since leaving Britain. "Had you ever really thought about who you wanted to be with before this?" she asked thoughtfully. I admitted I hadn't: Thinking about who you wanted either seemed too calculating or just impossible to achieve.

Wistfully, Jude said she hadn't either, and she really wished she had.

"But, Jude," I said with some feeling, "even if I had given it some thought back then, it wouldn't have made any difference: I would have assumed the man I wanted didn't exist, or if he did, that I wasn't pretty, smart, or lucky enough to get him. That's why I needed to go on this adventure: I needed to feel good about myself before I could meet the right man. Also, to realize the right man wasn't someone so different from me he'd be out of my reach and I might as well settle for less."

But for now, though, the man of my dreams really was out of my reach: Garry was touring the States with the Sonics, and as both his and my time differences constantly shifted, trying to catch up with each other was proving harder and harder. And I was forced to admit that, although now back in tune with my journey, I still missed him horribly.

Seven a.m. the next morning found me on the edge of my bed nursing a scalding cup of black coffee and an evil hangover. The coffee was too hot to drink, but the pain of holding the cup was forcing me to focus my attention on that rather than on how desperately I wanted to go back to bed.

And I couldn't go back to bed: I had a date with a surfer at 8 a.m.

Surfing Western Australia was a school based about forty-five minutes north of Fremantle. They gave lessons to members of the public, but since surfing was on the school curriculum, they taught students as well. (Can you imagine being taught surfing at school? When I was a student, we thought we were lucky if we got to hold the school guinea pig.) Jude knew someone, who knew someone, who had a friend who taught there. He'd agreed to date me as long as it was a surf date.

Steve (Date #71) was an ex-champion and looked incredible. With a rock-hard body, he had short, sun-bleached hair, luminous periwinkle-blue eyes, and a rugged, handsome face, etched deep with lines from a lifetime spent in the sun. He looked uncannily like a young Samuel Beckett, so much so that I dubbed him *Salty Beckett* (but not to his face).

I struggled into a full-body wetsuit (imagine putting on rubber gloves that've got water in them, on your entire body, with a hangover), and after the rudiments of surfing had been explained and demonstrated, we plunged into the ocean.

I quickly discovered that I loved surfing. As the waves crashed over me and the board—tied to my ankle—dragged me back into the surf and ground me into the sand, I felt invigorated and energized (and discovered a new beauty treatment cum water sport: Extreme Exfoliating). With Steve's patient encouragement I finally figured out how to snatch my feet out from underneath me and spring from a lying position to standing upright on the board riding the wave to the shore. I was completely euphoric.

And then utterly exhausted.

We collapsed onto the sand afterward and chatted. Steve talked about his life surfing and how, although it had knocked out his teeth, wrecked his knees, and destroyed his shoulder, it made him feel alive and he couldn't live without it. As he talked, my sinuses endlessly and uncontrollably emptied the gallons of saltwater I'd sucked up through my nose. It wasn't a good look, but no amount of sniffing would keep the water from coming out.

At that moment, one of the young girls having a lesson walked past, three of her girlfriends crowding in concern around her. She had possibly the worst nosebleed I'd ever seen in my life; blood streamed from between her fingers as she held them protectively around her face. Steve watched carefully as they all disappeared inside the office.

"Board to the face," he observed sagely.

I had a suspicion I was far too vain to be a surfer chick.

Melbourne, Australia

From Perth I went on to Melbourne to stay with my closest Australian friends, Linda and Dale, and their children, Grace and Patrick. It was wonderful to see them all. Dale brought Patrick and drove me down to Phillip Island, seventy-five miles southeast of Melbourne, where I was dating one of the Penguin Rangers.

Phillip Island was home to a colony of wild blue or fairy penguins. Each night at sunset the penguins, around forty-five hundred of them, waddled in from the sea and scurried for the safety of their burrows. Over dinner, **Jervis (Date #72)** told me that as a ranger, among other things, his job was to gather on lookout posts along the beach and count the penguins as they came in each night. I thought he was joking, but after dinner we went and counted penguins.

Dale and Patrick joined us and we all stood in the observatory tower, watching the penguins emerge from the fog-shrouded sea. They were tiny, vulnerable things and there was something incredibly heroic about the way they waddled drunkenly from the cold sea; then, suddenly alert to danger, scuttled in terrified huddles from clump of grass to clump of grass, peeping little *the coast is clear* messages to the ones still sheltering one clump back.

Jervis was actually extremely cute and we had a wonderful evening. He clearly loved his job and was devoted to the penguins, though I wasn't sure how he or any of the rangers would have time for forty-five hundred penguins and a woman (unless the woman was a ranger, of course).

I felt really lucky to be able to have this time with Linda. She was my best friend in Australia; we'd both lived in Brisbane and had managed to see each other regularly and stay close even when I'd moved back to England and she'd moved down to Melbourne. It had been good to see Jude, too.

At the same time, though, I was starting to feel pulled in all different directions. In Australia, I was seeing friends who'd known me when I was married. Logging on to my computer, I found my friends at Lonely Planet's Melbourne office had heard I was around:

Don't you dare leave town without coming to see me: so much has happened since you've left I'm dying to talk to you about and I reeeeaally miss you. Lisa xxxxx

Plus friends in London had (not unreasonably) lost track of my travels and assumed I was at home:

Not sure where you are, Jen, but James and Ian and everyone else are going over to play table football at Exmouth Market tonight. We're meeting at 7 p.m., do you think you'll drive or take the tube? See you there, Love Glam Tan xxxxx

There were also the rest of the Dates:

Hi, Jen, I'm really glad you'll be arriving in Queenstown a day late: I've got something very special lined up and it gives me more time to take care of details! Sorry to be personal, but can you please tell me how much you weigh? Love David, emailing from New Zealand

Talking to some people about my long-divorced ex-husband, to others about what was going on at a company I didn't work for anymore, and to another set arranging a social life in a country I'd just left or was yet to arrive in was a real juggling act. Every group felt or assumed I was *around* and available because technology made it so easy for them to get hold of me.

I could never have contemplated organizing this journey without modern technology, from emailing the Soul Mate Job Description around and recruiting ranks of Date Wranglers to setting up the Dates themselves and carrying all their details and emails with me on my laptop. It also made researching dates possible, as well as booking flights and hotels, and of course doing all this when on the road via email, cell-phone calls, and text. Modern technology had made this journey possible.

But technology is just a tool. And one that didn't seem to be working for me and Garry at the moment. Although we communicated constantly—texting, emailing, and leaving messages on each other's home and cell phones—all the technology in the world didn't seem able to connect us.

We wanted to be together. Trying to find a brief space to share in each other's ever-changing time zones and schedules was a constant battle. All we seemed able to share was our frustration.

I'm really missing you Jen

Garry said simply in a text.

And I knew it to be true.

It was late when I read the text. I was packed and ready to fly to Sydney early the next morning, but I lay awake for a long time after I got the message. For the first time I felt really scared. What if Garry forgot me? What if he forgot what I was like and why we were so good together? Forgot why it was worth putting up with this. Forgot why he'd agreed to be boyfriend to a girl living in England and currently traveling across Australia dating other men.

What was I doing to him? And to us? I had no answer, only a sense of dread.

Sydney, Australia

I was happy to arrive in Sydney. As ever, I hoped the change of scene would, if not improve the situation with Garry, at least distract me from it. Not that we really had a *situation,* more an intangible and unsettling sense of being dislocated and drifting. It was hard to put my finger on it and—now that the demands of my long journey were starting to take their toll—I couldn't work out if it was just me being overtired, the inevitable powering

down that couples default to when apart, or something more serious altogether.

I didn't know, so I got back to what I did know: dating.

Early the next morning I dated **Terry (Date #73)**, com-
mander of the Sydney Harbour Police. Terry was a charismatic,
fascinating man, who was clearly loved and respected at the station. ("Morning, boss," everyone chimed as we walked from his
office to the quay.) He asked one of his men to take us in a patrol
boat from the police headquarters over to Balmoral, a slight delay
as they tried to hide a dead body they'd fished out of the water
moments before I arrived.

It was exhilarating to motor through the harbor (at least I'd
been *expecting* a boat on this date). The sun gleamed on the water
that sprayed out behind us as we cut through the water past the
Opera House and the Harbour Bridge.

Disembarking in Balmoral, we walked across the beach and
into the ultra-chic Bathers' Pavilion for brunch.

It was great to walk anywhere with Terry: He looked fabulous
in uniform, and people touched their caps or just smiled. He was
lovely to talk with, a really nice man. He'd carried out close protection for all the big politicians who visited (he'd been out with
Prince Harry just the day before) and had me wide-eyed and rapt
at his stories. Divorced, he talked about how being a policeman
was very hard on relationships. We agreed, inevitably, that sometimes it's easier just to stick to your work.

Terry and his sergeant dropped me at the Rushcutters Bay
Yacht Club, which was a short walk from my hotel in Dar-
linghurst. Waving them off, I switched on my phone and a message popped up from my next date, Nathan.

Nathan (Date #74) taught Bikram yoga: the Indian discipline of yoga in a room heated to 100 degrees (the idea being that
it relaxes your muscles, releasing trapped toxins and allowing you

to efficiently sweat them out). I'd been put in touch with Nathan through my friend Kate at the Australian Tourist Commission in Sydney.

Our date was tonight, but in his message Nathan suggested I come to his class that afternoon, then we could go straight on to our date afterward.

Unfortunately, I'd had my phone switched off. Date Protocol: I felt it was bad form to take a phone call from your next Date while the current one was still in progress—and now it was already afternoon. I stuck out my arm and hailed a cab downtown.

I arrived at the Bikram center with five minutes to spare. As I dashed up the steps, I caught sight of a completely gorgeous man disappearing into a room, steam already condensing madly on the windows. He was followed by a group of star struck women (and a couple of men). If that was Nathan, I could see why the class was so popular . . . and why the classroom was hot and steamy (I'm always happy to embrace my *inner shallow*).

But I'd been in such a rush I hadn't given any thought to what I was going to wear. The bra I had on was okay, but no way was anyone going to see me going lotus wearing a thong.

I went careening over to the woman sitting at the reception (so far, yoga was proving anything but relaxing) to see if they had a spare pair of shorts I could borrow. No, but "go to Gowers on the corner," she told me shortly, looking with disapproval at her watch, "they're real cheap and you'll pick up some shorts for nothing. Once the class has started, you can't go in, though, so quick, go, go," she shooed.

I raced across the street to Gowers, but all I could find cheap was a nasty pair of men's gray Y-fronts. I held the packet at arm's length and examined it speculatively. Nathan was gorgeous and these men's briefs were ugly, ugly, ugly. But I'd never wear them again and they were only nine dollars, so sod it, I was in a hurry, I shoved some cash at the sales clerk and dashed back to the center. In the changing rooms I ripped the knickers out of the packaging, and, without stopping to inspect them, shoved them on, pulled my top off, grabbed my bags, and bolted for the yoga room.

I got to the doors just as they were locking them. There wasn't time to introduce myself, so I quickly walked into the class, past mats full of limbering ladies to a free spot at the front of the class, and sat down.

Nathan stood before us, lithe and muscled to the point of being edible. As he walked us through the first positions, I attempted to bend my upper body down over my extended thighs. As I strained downward, I caught sight of my pants for the first time. The thick gray flannel was so stiff that the Y flap at the front was poking straight out in a disturbingly suggestive manner. Embarrassed and trying not to draw attention to it, I quickly reached down and pushed the flap back into place.

But it was having none of it and sprang straight out again, veering purposefully like the rudder on a sailboat.

It was horrible. I tried another tack: Leaning into my stretch, I surreptitiously attempted to pin the protruding piece of material flat with my elbow. But it was impossible to concentrate on both this and the yoga, and the front of the pants sprang straight out again, wagging from side to side, like the tail of a dog happy to see you.

The room was as hot as a furnace by now, and soon the pants were thoroughly soaked in my sweat, turning the dark gray flannel an even darker gray—apart from the flap at the front, which, since it wasn't in contact with my body, remained free from sweat and light gray, sticking out in lewd shamelessness.

After what seemed like an eternity, the class ended. And—all credit to me—I was brave enough to stay behind and introduce myself to Nathan. But as I hadn't thought to bring a towel for the shower or any clean clothes, our date ended up too *yin and yang* for comfort: He was serene and self-aware, I was sweaty and self-conscious. I stayed for one drink, then went back to the hotel, lay on the bed, and watched *When Harry Met Sally* on TV, using biscotti as spoons to eat a tub of ice cream.

chapter sixteen

New Zealand— Auckland

Flyboy Gene swept me off my feet in Blenheim, New Zealand

New Zealand was the last leg of my journey and involved a complicated itinerary of dates dotted around the two islands. It was very much an all-singing, all-dancing grand finale—one last blaze of dating glory—rather than the gentle coast to the finish line that would have been more sensible to aim for.

I was dating Frank in Auckland, then flying into Blenheim for Chris's mystery date, and two more flights, a four-hour train journey, and a two-and-a-half-hour bus journey would put me into Middlemarch, where I was dating their Bachelor of the Year ("He's as good at changing diapers as he is at changing tires," one of the female judges had observed approvingly). Then it was a three-hour bus journey into Queenstown to *speak your weight* Date David.

And I was waiting to hear back from Justin, another Queenstown date who was currently leading a rafting trip somewhere around Wanaka but had promised to *take you to Paradise and back when you get here.* (According to my guidebook, Paradise was a trail.) Whatever time I could meet Justin would decide when I'd fly back into Auckland, meet Nick, my eightieth and final date, and from there catch the plane back to London.

I really hoped there'd be time to visit Garry on the way back to London.

We hadn't managed to speak for three days now. After months of staying up till 3 a.m. or waking up at 6 a.m. for a common chink of time across the time zones and the phone satellites, we were both exhausted. It was a struggle to find energy to put into our schedules and conversations, as well as keeping up with the demands of the lives we led separately.

I trusted Garry (which felt good: I was glad Kelly hadn't destroyed my ability to believe in faithfulness) and I'm pretty sure he trusted me. Neither of us lacked the desire or commitment to make this work, but we'd been apart longer than we'd ever been together and logistics didn't seem to be favoring us.

Dammit, I was going to call him. I looked at my watch, did some mental gymnastics—2 a.m. his time, the poor love would have just arrived in Texas—and dialed his number. I heard the connections leap across the satellites before getting through to . . . his voice mail. I drooped disappointedly, but tried not to let it come across in my voice: "Hello, love, this is your wandering girlfriend. I've just got to Auckland. I'm staying at the Hilton, you've got the number—give me a call and tell me what the weather's doing in Texas when you've got a moment. I miss you."

Doing a double take at my watch, I realized I was running late for my next date. I threw open my case and rummaged around, desperately trying to find anything I could wear that was clean and presentable.

Frank (Date #75) was actually Posh PR Emma's The One Who Could Have Been from when they'd both lived in Sydney. He and I had missed meeting up there, as he was over here on business. But our stay in Auckland overlapped by one night, so we'd arranged to meet in the hotel bar for a drink.

The bar had extraordinary views across Freeman's Bay and ultimately the South Pacific, and we admired them now as we chatted. We talked about mutual friends; how *Yes, Emma worked too hard* and *Yes, how she absolutely deserved a decent boyfriend.* We also talked about my dating. Since he was obviously interested in Posh PR Emma rather than me, I talked about the situation with Garry. I confided that I was worried that, although we were both working hard at including each other in what we were doing, we still seemed so far apart.

Frank looked sympathetic. "Jen, your schedule sounds exhausting, and from what you've said about Garry, he's working and traveling like crazy too. You just have to accept that that's the way it's going to be for a while; it's very demanding traveling for work, inevitably relationships suffer."

Frank was head of PR for an upmarket hotel chain. Posh PR Emma had told me he'd got divorced a couple of years ago because he spent so much time on the road. I nodded in agreement; Frank obviously knew what he was talking about.

But even so . . . "That's true, Frank, but I am trying. I'm still putting energy into our relationship," I countered a little defensively.

Frank looked at me over the top of his martini glass. "Right, Jennifer," he said with one raised eyebrow. "You're putting energy into your relationship with Garry. So how is it you're in a bar, in Auckland, out on a date with me?"

He did have a point.

And I don't want to sound like I'm changing the subject here (okay, maybe a little), but he obviously had a thing for Posh PR Emma, and I wondered if I should put aside my dating for a moment and do a little freelance Date Wrangling instead. He talked about her constantly, wanting to know everything going on in her life at the moment. ("Work, Frank," I told him honestly. "She's in a relationship with her job, like everyone we know.") I was glad I didn't fancy Frank, but I really liked him, and I think he would have been perfect for Ems. They seemed less like a case of Could Have Been and more one of Still Might Be.

Blenheim, New Zealand

New Zealand is made up of two islands, one above the other. Imaginatively, the top one is called the North Island and the bottom one the South Island. Auckland is two-thirds of the way up the North Island, and I was flying down to Blenheim, which is at the top of the South Island. (Got that? I shall be asking questions later.)

The area I was flying into is called Marlborough, New Zealand's famous wine region, where some of the world's best sauvignon blanc and pinot noir come from. I love Marlborough's Cloudy Bay wine, so when I'd been thinking about where in the world I might find my Soul Mate, coming here had seemed a good idea. Who I would meet here was now down to Chris and his much-hyped *single, well-off, interesting, good company* Date.

Chris was a friend of my friend Susie, who did PR for the New Zealand Tourist Board in London. Chris and his wife Julia ran the Hotel D'Urville, a charismatic property made from a converted bank in the middle of Blenheim and my home for the next two days.

Chris met me straight off the twelve-seater plane at Blenheim's tiny airport and wasted no time planting a big wet kiss on my cheek and enveloping me in a huge hug. With his curly hair, ruddy face, and thick-knit sweater, he looked just like a Cornish fisherman. But Chris was sharp as a tack and very much in demand; he wheeled and dealed via his constantly ringing phone as we drove to the hotel, stopping at a couple of notable wineries on the way.

The town itself wasn't impressive. A wide main street of half-empty shops, Blenheim reminded me of depressed outback farming towns in Australia or the American Midwest. The hotel was fabulous, though: gourmet cuisine and luxurious, themed rooms. I was very happy at the thought of spending some time here. In fact, I'll be honest, I was happy at the thought of getting through whatever Chris had cooked up date-wise and whiling away the rest of my stay by lying in the huge freestanding iron bath in my room, applying a face mask, painting my toenails, and soaking the knots out of my muscles.

So, over dinner that night, as Julia buzzed around the busy restaurant checking all the diners were happy, Chris joked with me about finally meeting my Date tomorrow morning.

I'd long since learned not to react to his teasing, but I did think it was funny that he was displaying all the classic signs of what I now recognized as a Control Dater. This was someone who liked to hold all the cards, enjoying the sense of power over you. Chris did it nicely, but it was still there. And he was a second-generation Date Wrangler, he wasn't even a Date.

While he talked on, a wave of tiredness suddenly washed over me. I'd dated seventy-five men. There were just five more to go.

The journey had been incredible and I felt lucky to have had all these experiences, but at the same time it felt like I had been doing nothing but dating forever. Seventy-five dates—that's how many applications of mascara? How many *"oh, you must be"*s? How many life stories confided over drinks and dinners? As I said, there are far worse things in life, but the fact was that going on this many dates had slowly turned into aversion therapy. I never wanted to go on another First Date as long as I lived. If things didn't work out with Garry, I swore, I would go back to London, get 102 cats, and never leave the house again.

Trying (and failing) one last time over breakfast the next morning to get a rise out of me, Chris then drove us out to Marlborough Air Club, a private airstrip and hangar on the edge of town. *It would seem the date has something to do with planes,* I thought to myself limply.

We got out of the car and walked toward a tiny hut with a sign over the door identifying it as the reception. A man in pilot's uniform was leaving as I approached, and he stood politely to one side, holding the door open so I could go in. But I wasn't at my most alert and I remained outside so he could come out. We stood gazing at each other, waiting for the other to make a move. Chris pushed past us both. "Come on, kids," he said mischievously. "That's no way to greet your Date."

Chris was having fun, that much was clear.

As he marched off into a large aircraft hangar, the man and I looked awkwardly at each other. So this was the mystery Date. He looked nice: about six feet two, broad shoulders, slightly wavy brown hair, and an easy smile. He must have been about my age, with the air of someone sure of himself, but in a capable rather than an arrogant way. There was also something boyish about him; his green eyes crinkled playfully as he smiled, as if we were already sharing a joke. He was smiling now. "You must excuse Chris," he said with an American accent and a resigned yet affectionate expression that led me to believe he was Chris's friend. "He means well! My name's Gene, by the way. I'm a pilot; I think I'm also your Date?" Gene smiled reassuringly at me. "It's good to meet you." And with that he held out his hand.

I put out mine and we shook. "My name's Jennifer," I said, smiling back at him. "I think I'm your Date, too, but I'm afraid that's all I know at this point." We both laughed.

As it turned out, Chris had kept both **Gene (Date #76)** and me completely in the dark about each other, so rather than being intriguing and exciting, meeting Gene was just a blank. That would have been fine—I had immediately warmed to Gene and we could easily have filled in the spaces by talking to each other now—but Chris had other plans and shouted for us to come over.

He was out on the runway, next to a small vintage plane (a Provost, in case you care). He held out a flying suit (nothing glamorous—shapeless green overalls) for me to wear while tapping his watch theatrically. "Come on, Young Lovers," he teased, making my toes curl with the inappropriateness of the remark, "it's time for you lovebirds to fly away."

Obediently, Gene and I clambered into the plane. Checking that I was strapped in securely, Gene then systematically checked the gauges on the panel in front of us, fired up the engines, and off we went, taxiing bumpily down the short runway. I held my breath as the little plane picked up speed, then rose unsteadily into the air, like an old man stiffly getting up from his armchair at bedtime. Slowly climbing up through the clouds, we leveled off after a couple of minutes and headed out across the patchwork fields and valleys of Marlborough.

Gene and I still hadn't said more than ten words to each other, and I felt quite self-conscious to be in such intimate proximity—wedged close to each other in the cockpit, sharing this incredible view—without really knowing more than his name.

But it was a spectacular sight. I craned my neck to look around at the mountains, vineyards, and fast-flowing rivers we were flying above. "I was rafting down that river on the weekend," Gene shouted into his headset microphone over the thundering of the engines. He looked really happy when he said it, and I immediately wanted to know more: What had the day on the water been like; how often did he do it; could I do it in the short time I had left here; what else did he do in his free time . . . ? But when I tried to answer by shouting back into my microphone, it kept breaking up and Gene couldn't hear me.

So I gave up trying to talk. Sitting back in my seat and looking down into the coves and islands of Marlborough Sound and the shimmering waters of Cloudy Bay, it was wonderful not to speak: I felt like I had been talking forever. I could now speak First Date so fluently I was in danger of suffering from the first-ever recorded case of RSI (Repetitive Speech Injury).

But even as I enjoyed the breathing space and the chance to soak up the views, I felt the first telltale signs of travel sickness suddenly grip me. The smell of the hot engines and the way the small plane banked and bobbed in the air was making my mouth grow dry and my stomach crawl (oh, the irony: not a boat in sight and here I was having my first bout of motion sickness in a long time). Gene must have picked up on the change in my demeanor, and I was extremely grateful that he decided this was a good time to gently and smoothly take the plane back to base.

We touched back down on the runway. And as soon as the engines had been turned off and we could hear each other talk, I congratulated Gene on his flying and thanked him for giving me the chance to enjoy the magnificent scenery from the air. I then scrambled out of the plane as fast as I could and savored the relief of being back on the still, flat earth once more.

Chris was waiting excitedly for us on the tarmac. "Wasn't that knockout?" he said with a huge, excited grin. "Wasn't it exciting? Did you think you were going to crash?" he demanded, hopping from foot to foot in glee.

I felt more than a little irritated: Why would I want to go on a date where I thought I was going to die? (Though God knew, I thought grimly, remembering the date with the wart . . . the gray men's briefs . . . moaning Lars in Christiania . . . there'd been more than one where I'd wanted to kill myself.)

I wanted to take Chris aside and tell him: "Look, that was a boy's date, not a girl's. Girls don't care about going up in planes where it's too loud to talk and all the flipping around makes you want to throw up." Instead I nodded graciously and told Chris it was wonderful.

It was a shame about Gene, though; from what I could tell, he seemed funny, charming, and definitely the type of person I would enjoy getting to know. But I was saying this based purely on instinct; we hadn't been allowed to fall into a conversation that would have strayed and wandered naturally, opening random windows of our personalities and experiences to each other. If Chris had involved us a little more, or himself a little less, I'm sure we would have got on well, but we'd both held back, waiting patiently for an opportunity to talk that had never presented itself.

"Great," Chris said, rubbing his hands happily. "So let's move on to the next part. We're running late."

Late? *Next part?*

The date wasn't over.

Gene and I exchanged weary and wary glances as we were bundled into Chris's car and driven halfway up a mountain to the

Tohu winery, a local Maori-owned vineyard run according to tribal values.

Parking in a small gravel drive, Chris led Gene and me into a tiny hut that looked out across a dramatic glacial valley. The wind ushered puffy white clouds in and out of the glare of the sun, which alternately shot long shadows and blazed white light across the rocks and hillocks. Chris gestured for us to take a seat at a table facing the view. He brought the head of the winery in to meet us. We all chatted for a while, then were joined by the Wine Master and her assistant for a tasting. After a little while, Chris's chef arrived with his assistant to cook us a gourmet lunch in the corner of the hut while Chris stayed to keep an eye on things. There was standing room only by the time the eight Maori singers squeezed in with their guitars and pom-poms to serenade Gene and me as we self-consciously ate.

I'm sure the intention was that the meal, eaten overlooking this beautiful valley, would be romantic. But the room was so crowded and Gene and I were under such intense scrutiny, it felt more like we were day-release prisoners from a maximum-security penitentiary, expected to escape at any moment.

Gene was an attractive, interesting man, but after five hours in his company, I knew nothing whatsoever about him.

Finally, the busiest date in the world came to an end.

Gene and I shuffled past the singers, the owners, the Wine Master, the chef, and half a dozen other people assembled in the hut, thanking them for their efforts, like the Queen backstage after a performance of *Cats*. Shell-shocked, we climbed into the rear of the car and Chris took off down the track, retracing our route along the roads that twisted back through the vine-strewn countryside to Blenheim.

In the back of the car, finally out from under the tyrannous dating yoke, Gene and I both became giggly and rebellious. We teased Chris for being controling and bossy. Chris, now off-duty and able to relax, rolled his eyes at us in the rearview mirror and joined in the fun.

The whole atmosphere changed and we started enjoying ourselves. And Gene and I, now able to act like adults, chatted easily, getting on with each other every bit as well as I'd suspected we would.

Chris dropped me back at the hotel and we all bade our farewells. I felt fond of them and a little sad it was only now that we were able to enjoy each other's company.

Early the next morning I arrived at the airport feeling groggy but with my traveling head firmly on. This was going to be a long day of planes, trains, and minibuses. I could hardly believe my eyes when I saw Gene sitting over by the window of the teeny departure lounge reading a newspaper. I went straight over and tapped him on the shoulder. "Hey, what are you doing here?"

Apparently he'd been on the 6 a.m. to Wellington, but there'd been a problem with the plane. ("I bet someone turned their cell phone on and messed up the plane's navigation system," he joked dryly.) "And now I'm wait-listed on your flight," he told me as he rose to his feet, asking politely if I would care to sit down and join him.

So for the first time since we'd met, and despite all the hours we'd already spent in each other's company, Gene and I were on our own. Unsupervised. We joked how scandalously improper it was; it was as well we were flying in an hour, otherwise we'd be run out of town.

Gene was relaxed and funny. He had a wry sense of humor and made me laugh as he told me all that had been going through his mind the day before. "Chris said you were four foot tall and weighed two hundred eighty pounds," he said. "It's just as well flying suits are one size only: I'd spent a sleepless night wondering how you were going to fit into the one I'd brought for you, not to mention the cockpit of the plane."

I laughed and explained that Chris had made a point of giving away nothing whatsoever about him, and how I'd hoped we could have talked over lunch but had just felt too scrutinized. Gene agreed. He'd bumped into Chris's chef later that night, who'd apologized for crashing our date.

Gene suddenly got to his feet. "Allow me to introduce myself," he said with mock formality. "My name is Gene and it's my pleasure to meet you. You are . . . ?"

I laughed and got to my feet too. "It's a pleasure to meet you too, Gene," I said with a little curtsy. "My name is Jennifer and I have traveled far, through the Land of Many Dates. Please tell me how it is that you came to be upon this fair isle."

And sitting back down, we settled into our chairs and talked. Gene was in his late thirties, divorced, and a pilot from New York. He lived in Blenheim for about six months of the year, designing flying sequences for the blockbuster films everyone seemed to be shooting in New Zealand these days. The rest of the time he traveled around the world restoring and flying planes, catching up with friends, and hanging out.

It was ridiculously glamorous, but the way he described it was more self-deprecating and down-to-earth. "Besides," he said, "flying is not to everyone's liking, as I think you demonstrated yesterday?"

I grinned ruefully, remembering the motion sickness. I explained to Gene that—although I had appreciated it—I thought the plane had been a bit of a *guy date.*

Gene agreed. "If it had been down to me, I would have taken

you to a gorgeous old lodge I know on that lake we flew over, the other side of Nelson. I would have brought some great wine and made you lunch by the water."

Mmmmm, I agreed that sounded far more appealing.

We talked about travel and relationships, jobs and friends.

"You know," Gene said suddenly, looking at me very seriously. "I wish I'd organized the date yesterday."

"Yes, I do too," I agreed wistfully, instantly feeling a twinge of guilt about Garry.

I hadn't actually told Gene about Garry. Yesterday, I'd barely had the chance to tell him my name; going into details about the minutiae of my love life would have felt completely incongruous.

But then I heard the boarding call for my flight. Although it seemed like only five minutes, Gene and I had been sitting there deep in conversation for over an hour. Gene got up and went to confirm at the check-in desk that he had a seat as well, but he returned minutes later with a grim expression.

"The flight's full," he told me flatly, sitting back down next to me.

"Oh no," I said, dismayed, instinctively putting my hand on his arm. Gene took my hand in his and looked equally distraught. It was as if after all the false starts, we'd finally begun our date, only to have it stop just as it was getting going.

But even in the middle of all this, I thought of Garry, and felt I had to tell Gene.

"You know I've met my Soul Mate, don't you?" I told him gently.

Gene looked away for a moment, then, moving closer and making eye contact again, said gruffly: "Well, I heard you were spoken for."

"He's an American too," I said, as if by way of consolation.

Gene looked very serious. "How do you know when you've met your Soul Mate?" he asked, watching my reaction very closely.

"You just know," I replied evenly.

It's a trite, annoying answer and it's what people always say, but it's true. You do just know. Like a key fitting in a lock, it feels right and natural, you don't have to force it.

"This is an announcement for Miss Jennifer Cox. If Miss Jennifer Cox is in the airport, can she please make her way as quickly as possible to gate number one, where flight 2454 to Wellington is boarded and ready to depart."

"Gene," I said, startled out of the intensity of our conversation, realizing I hadn't even heard them give the final call, "I'm going to miss my plane, I have to go."

I felt like a World War II soldier's sweetheart; I knew that once I got on that plane, I was never going to see Gene again. And in that moment, the reality of it seemed both intense and tragic, with an underlying sense of loss and sadness.

It was also confusing: I could hardly wait to be with Garry, but at the same time, and out of nowhere, something was happening with Gene. I felt I had to say something.

"Gene, apart from Garry, you're the only man on my entire journey that I've really connected with," I told him truthfully. "I know this has all been very strange, but I want you to know I'm really glad I met you."

We rose to our feet together, looking into each other's eyes the entire time. "I'll be in touch," Gene said, pulling me toward him and holding me tightly. "You can count on it," he whispered. Then he kissed me.

He kissed me on the cheek. Which was probably just as well; the tension between us was so electric by now that if he'd kissed me on the lips, the release of pressure would probably have taken out the coffee shop, if not the entire air-traffic-control navigation system for a week.

But even in the eye of the storm, I thought of Garry. I pulled back and looked into Gene's eyes. I felt torn: knowing nothing could happen, but at the same time sensing something already was. And liking it.

I gently broke away from the embrace. I had to go. Now.

I didn't even say good-bye to Gene. Picking up my bags, half walking, half sprinting, I stumbled away from him and out of the building across the tarmac to the tiny aircraft waiting on the runway.

I felt light-headed, like I was in a film where every moment and action was charged with purpose and significance. As I handed my pass to the *so there you are* attendant, I paused at the bottom of the aircraft steps and looked back across the runway to the airport building. Gene was standing where I'd left him, meeting my gaze head-on.

We stared at each other, steadily and unflinchingly, neither of us looking away even for a second. Then we smiled. It was an intimate and private smile, acknowledging the deep, still waters we had both dipped our toes into, and on whose bank Gene still stood, holding a towel out for me to join him.

I blew him a kiss and boarded the plane.

As we taxied down the runway, I felt thrilled and excited at the intense and romantic scene that had just unfolded. And at the unexpectedness of it, too. Yesterday I was thanking my stars that my dating days were nearly at an end; today a handsome pilot had waved me off from a tiny airstrip in a remote part of New Zealand.

It seemed the only two who had a handle on the big picture of my Dating Odyssey were Fate and Chris. Dammit.

. . .

So I flew to Wellington, made my connection, and flew on to Dunedin, where I was going to pick up the Taieri Gorge steam train. This would take me as far as Pukerangi, from where I would travel a further two hours by bus to Middlemarch. I was dating Bachelor of the Year there tomorrow but having dinner with one of the judges at the Kissing Gate Café tonight.

But I was having trouble focusing. When I'd woken up this morning, I'd prepared myself mentally for a very long day of scenic traveling. What I wasn't ready for (and frankly didn't know that I could have been if I'd tried) was a Date I'd pretty much written off, reappearing and making the remaining *straightforward* days of my trip suddenly seem anything but.

I just had to tell someone before I burst.

Across the road from the railway station was an Internet café. Although I'd pretty much disbanded the Date Wranglers now (my trip was in the homestretch, and foolishly I'd imagined I wouldn't be needing them anymore), they were still my friends and there would be just enough time before I boarded the train to get an *ohmigod* message off to one of them. Whether to the Sonar Sisters, Lizzy and Grainne; my real sisters, Mandy and Toz; or Belinda, Charlotte, Cath, or even Jo, I needed to talk to someone about what had taken place in the airport this morning.

I found a free terminal, and as AOL flashed through its paces, I suddenly really hoped there'd be an email from Garry.

There wasn't.

But there was one from Gene.

I sat and stared at the screen. Which should I do: Get advice from one of my girlfriends, or open Gene's email and get in deeper?

I dithered for a second.

Then I opened Gene's email.

And it was light and fun. An uncomplicated and undemanding message, saying how much he'd enjoyed meeting me and embarking on our slightly surreal adventures together. Also how—like me—he wished we'd had more time to get to know each other:

I had a whole bunch of questions for you, he wrote. And proceeded to ask me twenty fun, silly questions, like Does every cloud have a silver lining? I smiled as I read them: His tone was just right—conversational but with a hint of confidences.

But as I scrolled down to the bottom of the message, the last question was very different from all the others:

20. When can I see you again? Wondering, Gene

I pressed my fingers to my lips as I read the question, as if trying to suppress any emotion that might show on my face. Gene was raising the stakes with question twenty. I read and reread it; what was the best way to handle this? Reading Gene's email was one thing; replying, and replying to *that question,* was quite another. There'd been a real sense of *connection* at the airport this morning, both spontaneous and unexpected. But to reply to his email was different: It would nurture an intimacy—currently budlike and innocent—that would inevitably develop and grow. And however much I tried to pretend to the contrary, it would be the start of something between us.

I couldn't help being flattered, though, especially since the memory of our morning in the airport was still so fresh and real. In the end I opted to reply, but in a way that was light-hearted—friendly but not flirty—and I chose to ignore question twenty for now. As I finished typing, I hovered over the keyboard for an instant. Was this a good idea? Should I just delete it and not reply to him at all? But, stealing a quick glance at my watch and realizing I was running late, I impulsively hit *send,* and then, grabbing my bags, ran for the train.

The Taieri Gorge is rightly known as one of the world's classic train journeys. Nearly forty miles of track was painstakingly and gruelingly laid across the beautiful and remote center of the Otago Peninsula at the end of the 1800s. It connected out-of-the-way towns like Cromwell and Alexandra to the coast, allowing trade in and out of the otherwise isolated communities there.

The cargo the train now transported across the region—like steam trains everywhere—was tourists. Over the summer months the wooden carriages were full of Japanese and European visitors *oohhhing* and *ahhhing* at the dramatic gorges that dipped beneath the rails, falling steeply away to end in fast-flowing rivers lined by spiky clumps of yellow gorse and broom.

Today was no exception.

I love steam trains. My paternal grandfather worked on the Great Western Railway, and as kids we spent many happy afternoons either traveling up front on the trains with him or going with my parents on lines like the Bluebell in Sussex or the Lappa Valley in Cornwall. The Taieri Gorge train transported me back to my childhood, the plumes of acrid smoke streaming back to us from the engine's funnel, the soprano whistle echoing urgently through long, dark tunnels.

The whole journey had a homey feel to it. The staff all seemed to be old steam enthusiasts, volunteering out of their love for the trains. The guard gave an on-and-off commentary over the train's PA system, an introductory *"Righteo, folks"* alerting us to each upcoming point of interest. He had a butter mint in his mouth, and as he described each new feature, the mint clicked comfortably against his teeth, keeping time with his words like a spun-sugar metronome.

But as much as I was enjoying the journey, I was increasingly preoccupied by a creeping sense of wrongdoing. The heady excitement of this morning's encounter with Gene and the subsequent email exchange had dissipated slightly, and I was now able to think more calmly about what had happened and put it into a larger context.

Or, to be more specific, a *Garry context*.

I'd been attracted to Gene, no question, but why? I adored Garry and—although missing him and going through a bit of a weird spell at the moment—I genuinely didn't want to be with anyone else. So why had Gene made such an impression?

I could blame it on being tired or feeling neglected or even *survivor bonding*, the way hostages unite to get through their ordeal. But where there might have been elements of truth in all these explanations, they weren't the real reason. The real reason was less noble and more basic, and it was that Gene—like Garry—was completely my type, so I'd been attracted to him and we'd clicked, instantly and powerfully.

A while ago, back in Europe before I'd met Garry and was struggling to maintain faith in my quest, I'd speculated on what my Soul Mate odds might be: one in how many dates before I met Mr. Right? Then I'd met Garry and had learned—using the Soul Mate Formula—that my Soul Mate odds were 1 in 55. Well, perhaps I should have asked what the odds of meeting *two* of my Soul Mates were, because sticking to the same formula, I'd inadvertently come up with the answer: 2 in 76.

Because I believed that Gene, Date #76, was my Soul Mate #2.

As the train puffed up hills, and grazing sheep, balancing unnecessarily on rocks, watched us pass with startled but lazy expressions, I tried to put aside my feelings of guilt to understand the chain of events that had led to them.

But no matter how much I tried to rationalize and explain away what had happened, I couldn't argue with how I felt. Gene, Date #76, was a man about whom my Soul Mate Job Description could have been written. And what did that mean? I'm no good at math—and do feel free to shout out the answer if you know it—but surely there must be some kind of Soul Mate Formula here, which, I figured roughly, would mean if I kept on dating, I would meet Soul Mate #3 by around Date #100.

Apart from all else that was going on, this was actually an incredibly reassuring and exciting discovery: that with the right attitude and effort, meeting your Soul Mate was a demonstrable and calculable proposition. And the longer you applied the formula, the shorter your Soul Mate odds became.

But my Attraction Fraction calculations were suddenly interrupted by a tugging on my sleeve. "You're for Pukerangi, aren't you, miss?" the guard was asking me urgently. He sounded slightly concerned, as well he might: I'd been staring out the window wrestling with my thoughts for four hours and hadn't even noticed the train pull into Pukerangi station. This was my stop and I had a connection to make.

Hurriedly thanking the guard, I scrambled to my feet, grabbed my bags, and in my dazed state almost fell off the train as I rushed to make the Middlemarch bus before it left without me. I found the bus, a small ten-seater minivan, easily: It was the only vehicle in the exposed, windswept parking lot.

Lloyd, the driver, noted my panic as I bustled up. "No need to worry, miss," he said calmly. "Just you and two others getting on. We're not going anywhere without you."

I smiled my thanks and, realizing I must be radiating a

slightly manic air, attempted to get aboard in a manner that denoted both composure and dignity. But as I found a seat and dumped my bags on the floor, I realized that in my hurry to get off the train I'd left my laptop behind. My laptop, with my files, photos, emails and itineraries—my *life*—on it. *Count your bags on, count your bags off* is the first lesson any traveler learns.

Furious with myself for being so distracted and disorganized, I hurtled off the bus past Lloyd and sprinted across the gravel toward the train, which was slowly shunting out of the station. Shouting up at the driver, I asked if he could stop so I could jump on and retrieve my computer.

I scrambled on and off the train; then, laptop safely back in my possession, I meekly returned to the bus. Lloyd had the measure of me after that little display and there was no point in trying to persuade him otherwise.

All four of us—plus bags—safely aboard, Lloyd then drove the bus out of the station parking lot. And as we started our journey across the scrubland plains and stoic, weather-beaten granite of Otago's barren interior, once again I became lost in my thoughts.

So, if I'd uncovered the Soul Mate Formula, and my Dating Odyssey—leading me first to Garry, now to Gene—had been such a resounding success, why was it that I felt so confused?

The question was rhetorical, really: I already knew the answer. I was Garry's girlfriend and I shouldn't be accepting romantic overtures from anyone else. Garry trusted me. He was my Soul Mate, for chrissakes: I'd literally traveled the world to find him. And so what if Gene was my Soul Mate, too? I didn't need any more Soul Mates—it wasn't like I was looking to collect a set of them. I just wanted one, and Garry *was* that one. But by responding to Gene's email, I ran the risk of starting something I couldn't finish with Gene and having Garry finish with me altogether.

With a flash, I suddenly realized that this was why Fate had wanted me to keep traveling, to force me to realize that the journey was about more than just finding my Soul Mate. That was just the first—and, in a crazy way, the easiest—stage of my adventure.

Fate had shown me conclusively that the Soul Mate Formula worked: The right effort and attitude could and would lead to Mr. Right. But unless I wanted to keep on meeting Mr. Rights forever, I also had to have faith that I'd met The One, stop applying the Formula, and move on to the *next* stage of my journey *with him*.

And the truth was, deep down, putting my heart on the line and running the risk of being hurt again felt like a gamble for this *gotta catch a plane* girl. Safer just to keep traveling.

But the journey I'd undertaken hadn't only led to my Soul Mate; it had also led to people wise about relationships and with faith in love. Having met them, I now had the tools to help me through the scary minefield of actually *being* in a relationship—if I could find the courage to use them.

Or I could just carry on hedging my bets and travel forever.

Well, as Chester, the professional gambler in Vegas, had told me: "Think about how much you have to lose . . . set your limit and when you reach it, get up and walk away." I'd reached my limit now, and I had too much to lose. I had bet all the way up to Date #76, and I didn't want to play anymore. Garry was The One and I didn't want to hurt him, I didn't want to deceive him, and I didn't want to lose him.

It was time to fold. It was time to close my Date Wranglers' Little Black Books. The challenge wasn't playing the Soul Mate Odds from country to country, date to date anymore; it was taking that leap of faith and placing all my chips on Date #55.

I'd really liked Gene, and in other circumstances, who

knew . . . ? But I knew one thing for sure now: The answer to
"When can I see you again?" question twenty, would be a tactful
but unequivocal *"Never."* I was hanging up my dating shoes and
calling it a day.

I love New Zealand and—even in the midst of my dilemma—
was enjoying Lloyd driving us along the deserted roads that
crossed the bleak plains and skirted the desolate foothills of the
dramatic Taieri Ridge. But I'd just made the decision to end my
dating tour; this was a huge deal and I wanted to get the hell out
of here as soon as possible. I contemplated my date escape route.

Middlemarch is a lick of a town—a petrol station and a general store—in the middle of nowhere. But I knew a bus went
from Middlemarch to Queenstown. I had no idea how often it
went, but if I could catch it, I'd be able to fly from Queenstown
on to either Auckland or Wellington, and from there out of the
country and away.

I walked to the front of the bus and sat on the seat behind
Lloyd. "Excuse me, but do you know how often buses go from
Middlemarch to Queenstown?" I asked him.

"Just once a day at 5 p.m.," Lloyd replied in a mildly alarmed
way, as if I'd just asked where in Middlemarch I'd be able to buy a
Ferrari after 10 p.m.

"Oh, it's okay," I reassured him, "I'm booked onto it tomorrow. I just wondered if there was more than one a day."

"No," Lloyd said apologetically, as if personally troubled
he couldn't provide more frequent service. "I'm afraid that's all
there is."

I thanked him and made my way back to my seat. Glumly
staring out of the window, I could see we were the only vehicle on
the only road for miles. I watched a cinnamon-colored colt race
exuberantly around the grass, radiating an absolute joy at being a

horse and alive on the side of this desolate mountain. I suddenly felt trapped and more tired than I'd ever felt in my life. *Please don't make me have to do any more dating,* I thought earnestly. I had to find a way out. I just had to.

Going back up to the front, I apologized for interrupting Lloyd again. "But I was just wondering," I asked him, "will we make it to Middlemarch in time for the 5 p.m. bus to Queenstown?"

"Madam," Lloyd replied solemnly, "we *are* the 5 p.m. bus to Queenstown. We go right the way through."

I could have kissed him. Lloyd must have sensed this and, seeking the protection of his steering wheel, hunched over it defensively. This wasn't going to make me popular, but I sensed an escape plan. "Lloyd," I said (he was my getaway driver, I had the right to call him by his first name), "I might need to do some explaining, but if I wanted to ride all the way to Queenstown with you tonight, would that be okay?"

"Yes, that's fine by me," he replied gravely.

So we pulled into Middlemarch.

I'm ashamed to admit that, when the bus came to a stop, I hesitated in my seat. If my cell phone had been working, I could have just rung and canceled all the arrangements, but we were miles from any phone reception so I was going to have to do it in person. For a moment I was tempted to just stay on the bus, keep going, and sort it all out when I got to Queenstown.

Lloyd had other ideas, though. "Barry and Lorna run the B&B you're staying at, he runs the garage, too. You could go over and tell them you're not stopping, but I thought I just saw Barry drive off."

I felt rightly chastised by Lloyd for thinking of taking the cowardly way out. I got out of the bus and walked across the road to the neat bungalow Lloyd had pointed out to me. Two old men were standing talking outside the general store, but they broke off their conversation to watch me cross the road. This was a small village: If Lloyd knew where I was staying, he—and—everyone else—probably knew what I was doing here, too.

But, whatever. I was more concerned about how I was going to explain to Barry and Lorna why I wasn't staying at their house tonight: *"I seem to have overextended myself romantically and need to leave the country as soon as possible."* I felt so overwhelmed, I barely understood what was going on myself; how I would explain it to Barry and Lorna was anyone's guess. Or, I suddenly thought, hope erupting like a volcano in my heart, was I going to be lucky enough to find them out and escape having to make any explanation at all?

As I opened the gate and walked up the path to the front door of the bungalow, an intense feeling of guilt and fear washed over me, as if I were a burglar who could be caught at any moment.

Arriving at the net-curtained front door, through a side window I could make out a neat single bed, covered with a candlewick bedspread, a towel folded tidily on the pillow. My room. "Please be out. Please be out," I whispered over and over again as I rang the doorbell.

The seconds ticked by. *Please . . . please . . .*

I let a full thirty seconds drag endlessly by before breathlessly thinking, *Right—no question, they're out!* and bolting back down the path and out onto the street, slamming the front gate shut behind me.

Running back across the road to the petrol station, "Is Barry in?" I asked the young mechanic behind the counter as I hurtled into the office. He stopped wiping a silver wrench with an oily cloth and looked at me suspiciously. "No. He's at home," he replied shortly, as if fearing to engage me in conversation.

My heart was beating really fast now. *Please don't let him be home when I turn around, please don't let Lorna and Barry and the Judge and the Bachelor be sitting in the car outside their house waiting for me,* a voice gabbled wildly in my head.

"No, he's out," I replied with more certainty than I felt and without turning around to check.

"Oh," the mechanic replied dully.

He studied me through half-downcast eyes. He almost certainly knew why I was here. It was as if he was refusing to make eye contact with me for fear I'd leap over the counter, rip the wrench out of his hand, and ravish him where he stood.

Well, frankly, if he wanted ravishing, he'd have to take a ticket and wait his turn.

"Can you please give him a message?" I asked politely in my best *I am respectable, you know,* posh English accent.

"Sure," the mechanic replied, though clearly he was anything but.

"Please tell him Jennifer came by and she's very sorry, but something came up and she's not going to be staying. Please tell him I'm very sorry," I repeated. "Tell Lorna, too," I added guiltily.

"Okay," he said, making full eye contact for the first time and looking surprised.

"You got that?" I checked. He nodded, looking down again now as if I'd already left.

Suddenly elated, I rushed out of the garage and jumped back onto the bus that was waiting on the forecourt, engine running.

"Everything okay?" Lloyd asked as I collapsed into my seat. I nodded, too wired to talk.

"Want to use the restroom before we go?" he inquired. I looked at Lloyd in wide-eyed amazement. Was he insane? I could be dragged off the bus and made to date the Bachelor of the Year at any moment. We didn't have time for me to go to the toilet. We needed to leave this very moment.

I shook my head and the automatic doors whirred shut. And without being pulled over by the police, sirens blazing, giving me the choice of dating the Bachelor or serving a long stretch in jail for wasting police and everyone else's time, we quietly drove out of Middlemarch. After fifteen minutes, we started climbing up into the mountains. And Middlemarch was lost in the distance.

It was over. I couldn't believe it. My journey was over. All those dates; all those adventures; all those people; all those places. It was over. I was going home.

It had been quite a journey: the skaters; the Vikings; the midnight-sun sauna; the festival in the desert; the fires in the mountains; the Elvis impersonators; the surfer; the ravers; the Romeos . . . all those bloody boats.

It had been an emotional journey, too: learning to trust my instincts and know that because I'd made stupid mistakes in the past didn't mean I was going to make them forever.

And realizing how wonderful my friends were and how lucky I was to know them. I go on about how technology made the journey possible, but, really, it was my friends (and their friends) who had made it all happen. And I'm not just talking about their contacts; accepting my friends' and family's support and realizing the value of their advice had been an important lesson in itself.

Just at that moment, from inside my bag, my cell phone gave a little cheep. Now down from the mountains and driving through lush green valleys where farms were fringed by wide rivers, their water cold and fresh from the mountains, I finally had a signal on my phone. Phew, I was back in the world again.

I took it out of my bag, and there was text from Garry. I knew he'd be packing up after a basketball game, with Jon, Doug, JR,

OB, and the rest of the crew. *sorry I've been so busy: I want u 2 know how v important u r 2 me,* it read.

I gave a wobbly little smile and felt the tears sting in my eyes. I blinked hard and texted him straight back with my news: *dating tour over. thank u 4 being so loving and trusting. am so lucky 2 know u.*

u've finished? he texted back immediately.

chosen 2 finish, I replied carefully.

How u feel—exhausted, victorious . . . ? he asked.

Feeling a little ashamed and very emotional, I texted back: *v long story, will tell all when c u. 4 now feel drained but happy. love & miss u. flying to Seattle 2MORROW if okay?*

I had to see Garry. And I wanted to tell him everything that had happened: He deserved to know the truth. But I was going to tell him in person, not over the phone or email or instant message or text. In fact, much as I loved technology, I was sick of having a relationship through it. I was going to try to have our relationship face to face from now on.

I had no idea how it would all work. Would I move to America? Would he move to London? Would we commute between the two?

I had no plans. And that was fine: We'd make them together.

Looking out the window at the soft chocolate-colored mountains topped by the purple clouds at sunset, I felt utterly spent. But I also had a sense of absolute certainty about this. I'd made the right decision. I was sure of it.

Another text popped up; *YES! It's about time u came home.*

I smiled and shut my eyes. That's how it felt to me, too: like coming home.

one year later . . .

Happily ever after. . .

What comes after *happily ever after?*

I mean, once we close the book and sigh happily, do the Prince and his Princess drive on unobserved, holding hands and cuddling up in their golden carriage? Or does the Princess wriggle away from her hero, snapping: "You're ruining my dress, for chrissakes, stop sitting on it" as the Prince, engrossed in the latest issue of *Men's Health,* dreams of buff bodies and tunes her out?

I suppose what I'm saying is, it wasn't until I was flying from New Zealand to Seattle that I stopped to consider the small print of my *happily ever after.* And was completely terrified. I mean, no question Garry and I were in love and were meant to be together, but how exactly was it going to work on a daily basis?

Arriving in Seattle, I was relieved to find Garry in a similar state; so, agreeing we'd take it one day at a time, he gave me a key to his house and I moved in.

Real life caught up with me almost immediately. I'd been traveling for ages, and deadlines for long-overdue articles circled ominously overhead like hungry vultures. But since—as I'd just proven—technology meant that wherever I lay my Mac, that's my home, we hatched a plan. I'd spend the rest of the winter with Garry in Seattle, soldiering through my U.K. deadlines, and Garry would carry on as usual, working the busy basketball season. This was the perfect solution, since it meant that straightaway we were forced to get on with our *normal* lives without being daunted by the big picture. And as a result, building a life together simply happened.

Gradually, my life in Seattle took shape. I was with a man I adored and adored being with; but I also instinctively recognized that my Soul Mate couldn't give me everything I needed. Good friends; Seattle Athletic Club; KEXP, XM, and NPR on the radio . . . I went about finding the equivalent essentials to my life in London, and that made Seattle feel more like home.

But as much as I needed elements of my London life, being with Garry meant much more to me. Being around him seemed to bring a part of me to life that I'd almost forgotten about; for the first time in ages, I was someone's girlfriend and didn't feel on my own anymore. I don't mean that to sound quite as self-pitying as it possibly does, or to imply that I didn't already have special people in my life (if I were one of those people who drop their friends at the first sign of Love Action, I'd be the first to call myself a total cow). Finding your Soul Mate isn't about having someone who *replaces* your friends; it's a different relationship altogether. Now at the end of the day when I turn my computer off, I'll go downstairs and Garry will be there, cooking dinner or lighting the fire. I'll mix us a cocktail and find some good music, and another part of the day begins. Another part of me begins.

It's a more intimate and private part of me that grows out of sitting across the table from my super-cute boyfriend, sharing a wonderful meal and catching up on the day, and falling asleep in his arms, knowing he'll wake up wanting me, even though I haven't brushed my teeth or combed my hair. I can be *me*. And no matter where Garry is, I feel a deep sense of peace from that honest and loving bond.

Look away for a minute when I say this, since it's a bit embarrassing, but . . . my relationship with Garry makes me feel more attractive, too. And that feels a-m-a-z-i-n-g. Not because I'm looking to catch the attention of other guys (trust me—if I never go on another date again, that'll be too soon), but because, deep down, I'm actually quite shy. I need to be with a man I really love and trust before I'm ready to explore the fun and power of being a woman. Garry reached in and gently drew out a part of me that had been shut down for ages. He does it with the tiniest things: always holding my hand when we walk down the street, letting me leave a silly outgoing message on our answering machine, going for walks when I know he'd rather drive, talking about feelings when I know he'd sooner eat broken glass . . . In relationships, the smallest things underpin the biggest. And, yes, it's crazy that I had to travel literally to the ends of the earth to discover such a simple truth: that falling in love with a *good* man makes you happy.

But I *did* have to travel to the ends of the earth. It's taken me this long to understand that I had to keep traveling to prove to myself that my instincts about Garry were right, and also to give Garry the chance to back out. I didn't want to date another *commitmentphobe,* nor did I want to give up the things in life I loved, like the freedom to travel. I wanted him to know me for who I was and still want me. I set us both a tough test because I was scared and I needed to be sure. I needed us both to be sure.

And all that traveling and testing brought me here: to the man I always dreamed of, but never dared hope I'd find. And part of what makes being with Garry so *right* is that, for all its glorious magic, our relationship is really very normal. He can't fathom how I can spend hours wandering around stores and come away at the end of it empty-handed; I fail to grasp the allure of NASCAR or *Iron Chef*. But it works. We're matched, and that's the essence of a Soul Mate: someone who's like you to a point, and someone you like enough beyond that point to be open to their ideas and interests. You'll probably laugh to hear that this summer Garry and I, the famously seasick woman, bought a little sailboat called *Date #55*.

Everyone else seems to have picked up on what a perfect match Garry and I are. In fact, it's quite extraordinary how thrilled but totally matter-of-fact all my friends seem to be about the outcome of my quest.

Darling, you look like you've been together forever.
    Posh PR Emma emailing from Sydney

My parents, who'd been understandably anxious that I was dating my way around the world, have become very fond of Garry (as I am of his parents):

It's a long time since I've seen you looking this happy. . . .

My mother emailed after my last visit back to England (making me realize, not for the first time, that mothers see far more than they ever let on).

Now a year has passed since I ended my Dating Odyssey, and as I look back over the incredible adventure that led me to Garry, I feel a sense of wonder and pride. Did I really travel around the world in eighty dates? Did Garry really say he was okay with me continuing after I met him? Now that it's all over, it seems a crazy thing to have done; yet at the time it felt like the most logical and practical course of action.

I think of my Dates often. I honestly hope I didn't hurt anyone's feelings: They are good people and deserve to find their Soul Mates and happiness, too. I don't want to be the only person who benefited from my Dating Odyssey. In fact, I'd like to think some of them will try aspects of it for themselves. You, too. Like the Relationship Résumé or the Soul Mate Job Description. And although I suspect my solution isn't for everyone, I did learn a couple of things that possibly are. Firstly, that before I could find my Soul Mate, I had to be brutally honest about how much room there was in my life for him, and be prepared to rearrange my priorities accordingly. Secondly, that I believed that with hard work, I would find an exciting job, lovely friends, and a body that didn't wobble too much when I walked—yet, strangely (or perhaps because I'd been hurt and disappointed before), I had no such expectations of my love life. When it came to *earning* a decent boyfriend, I lacked the same confidence and ambition.

My journey around the world in eighty dates changed all that and gave me reason to take a huge leap of faith. I am indebted to those friends, both old and new, who allowed me to see what total nonsense it is to believe (with apologies to Nat King Cole) that *"When I **fail** in love, it will be forever."*

—Jennifer Cox
December 2004

acknowledgments

This book would not have been possible without the help and encouragement of a huge number of people. For any I now fail to thank, sorry, but you know what a thoughtless cow I can be.

Firstly, I owe a huge debt of thanks to my agent and dear friend Lizzy Kremer from David Higham Associates; such a rock throughout the entire researching and writing process, she made granite look positively flighty. Also to Grainne Fox at Ed Victor Ltd., who had an unerring knack for buying me strong cocktails at just the right time. I would like to thank all at Random House for their tireless support, enthusiasm, and hard work, in particular my editor Nikola Scott, who did a brilliant job while resisting the temptation to shout *Do you know what a deadline is?* Also Susan Sandon for her open door and desktop Mr. Right.

My family and friends deserve some kind of an award for making not only their address books but also their time and patience available throughout my obsessive *soul searching.* I lost track of the number of *"No it wasn't you, it was him"* and *"You are KIDDING—if it was me, I would've called the police"* emails, phone calls, and cups of coffee/glasses of wine moments that kept me going. In particular I would like to thank: my sisters, Madeleine and Rosalind Cox, for late-night chats and afternoons at the Sanctuary, and my best friends, Belinda Rhodes, Charlotte Hindle, and Cath Urquhart, for helping me remember boyfriends I'd managed to forget, for my Relationship Résumé. For never mentioning the times when my cookie eating spiraled out of control, thank you to my special friends: Paula Shutkever, Eddie Mair, Ian Belcher, Hector and Ang MacKenzie, Linda Ferguson, Jude Espie, Sheena MacBain, Eleanor and Adam Garland, Jeannette Hyde, Sarah Long, Sara-Jane Hall, Malgosia Czarniecka, Simon Calder, Jilly Mead and Stevie *Bee* Benbow, Lyn Hughes and Paul Morrison, Tania Cagnoni, Paul and Jude Mansfield, Nigel Tisdall, Steve Bleach, Sue D'Arcy, Rob Ryan, Alison Rice, Dea Birkett, Sally Shalam, Sophie Campbell, also Anna Cherrett.

Not to mention all the people who helped with the *Is there a plane that leaves later than 5:30 a.m.?* logistics of the trip itself. Fujifilm for the S300 digital camera that captured my dating high- and lowlights, Karin Hop at the Netherlands tourist board, Ann-Charlotte and Emelie at the Swedish tourist board, as well as Madeleine Meech at Travel PR. Catherine Raynor at VSO, Allesandra Smith at the Italian tourist board, Elena at Il Club di Giulietta, all at Berlin Tourismus Marketing GmbH, Nim Singh at the Canadian Tourist Commission, Jill White and Wendy Burns at Yukon tourism, Erika Brandvik at the Las Vegas CVB, Susie and Anna at Cellet PR, Jenni at First PR, Wendy King and Olaf Kaehlert at the LA CVB, all at Missoula CVB, Kylie Clark at JNTO, Abi and Khun Lilly at the Tourist Authority of Thailand. And in particular, a huge thank-you to all who helped me with the very end—therefore at the apex of my *Ummm, it might be Friday, it might be Wednesday—it's hard to say at this point* wavering. In particular Fiona Reese, Viv Kessler and Emma Humphreys at BGB and Associates, Rae White, Jac and Belinda at WATC, Kate Kenward at the ATC in London, Kate Bailey at the ATC in Sydney, Karen Reid at Random House Australia, Susie Tempest at Saltmarsh PR, and all at Tourism New Zealand and Air New Zealand.

I am extremely grateful to all my Dates for taking me out and showing me a good time, as well as the Dates who would have taken me out if only things had worked out differently. In particular, David O, Per, Beaver, and the VSO man working as a yak cheese farmer on the Chinese-Mongolian border.

When I arrived in Seattle at the end of my adventure to write this book, there were some people without whom it would never have felt like home: Bette "Burien" Allen, Terri Bassett, and Ann Anderson, as well as Judy and Gerry Greth, Hank and Rachel, JR, Doug, Jon, and OB.

And talking of adventures, I'd like not only to thank Lloyd, my getaway driver, but also to thank and apologize to Louise Kiely at Queenstown House B&B in New Zealand. The first person I spoke with following the dramatic final forty-eight hours of my journey, she made the mistake of innocently asking over breakfast how my visit was going.

At various points I have changed names and blurred the edges of personalities and events in the telling of my story. I wanted to spare people's blushes but also to emerge with my social life vaguely intact.

I would like to thank everyone for helping me with my quest, but none more so than Garry Greth, who took it all in his stride and made his home my home.

A sincere and heartfelt thank-you to you all.

THE HUNTER EQUATION

Secret Whisperings

From God & The Universe

D0674927

Also By Brian Hunter,

Heal Me is a powerful and touching book that will pull at your heartstrings, give you practical advice on overcoming a variety of life traumas, and will put you on the road to recovery and healing. *Heal Me* examines such issues as the death of a loved one, loss of a pet, suicide, anxiety, addiction, life failures, major life mistakes, broken relationships, abuse, sexual assault, self-esteem, living in a toxic world surrounded by toxic people, loneliness, and many other issues. This is a self-care book written in a very loving, practical, and informative way that you can gift to yourself, family, young people, and friends, as a gesture of love, support, and hope.

Rising To Greatness is a self-help book that takes you on a step by step transformation, from the ashes of being broken and lost, to the greatness of self-empowerment, accomplishment, and happiness. This book includes such topics as developing your sense of self, eliminating fear from your life, mastering your emotions, self-discipline and motivation, communication skills, and so much more.

The Walk-In takes you on a personal life-long journey, from childhood, through coming of age discoveries, successes, failures, and deep depressions and struggles. The book describes paranormal events, resulting in the development of psychic abilities.
This book is a very raw and honest adventure, which is not for the faint of heart, and is very hard to put down once you have started.

www.brianhunterhelps.com

THE HUNTER EQUATION

Secret Whisperings
From God & The Universe

By Brian Hunter

Published by
Rainbow Wisdom
Ireland

ABOUT THE AUTHOR

Brian Hunter is a well-known American psychic counselor, author, and Life Coach based in Los Angeles, California. Brian grew up highly intuitive, but after a major paranormal event chronicled in his book *The Walk-In*, his abilities increased, and he shortly thereafter became a professional psychic.

Brian has been a member of Best American Psychics, and was listed as one of the top 50 psychics in the world. He is the author of *The Walk-In*, *Rising To Greatness*, and *Heal Me*. Brian has worked with people from all over the world, including celebrities and captains of industry. Brian was an original cast member of the TV series pilot "*Missing Peace*," in which psychics worked with detectives to solve cold cases. He has also worked as an actor in Hollywood, featured in various movie and TV productions unrelated to his psychic work.

Brian's current work consists mainly of life coaching and counseling, but he also does psychic readings and work as a psychic Medium, Healer, and Energy worker.

www.thehunterequation.com

CONTENTS

CONTENTS

spiritualist who specializes in life coaching and counseling. I am an Empath, Psychic Medium, and Healer. I am also a teacher, advisor, consultant, and fixer. I have some experience and knowledge in the areas of psychology, medical, business, management, real estate, law, banking, working with children, adolescent counseling, hospice counseling, relationships, career development, and many other areas.

I started to realize my psychic abilities when I was 6 years old. I became lost in the woods and used my senses and communication ability with wildlife to find my way back home. Growing up, I was an excellent student, earning awards for my academic achievement. I have always been a self-starter and entrepreneur since my teens. I started mentoring young people at risk for suicide, and then counseling people of all ages and backgrounds. It was not long before I was listed by a publication as one of the top 50 psychics in the world. My primary interest remains my desire to improve people's lives through my life coaching work.

The reason I wrote this book stems from my responsibility to pass on all the knowledge and insights the Universe has imparted onto me. Most of the concepts in this book are from a higher power or source. I am merely presenting to you what I was shown directly by Source and the Universe. I also feel a compelling desire and responsibility to contribute toward human evolution any way I can. As teachers, that is what we do. My dream is for humanity to evolve and ascend to a higher state where all humans from all different beliefs, cultures, and backgrounds, can live in peace and prosperity. I believe this is possible with human evolution, as people develop a higher education, empathy, and moral values.

But the question remains, what makes me qualified to write a book like this? How would I even know any of the concepts I am about to present?

I have experienced intense paranormal events that have changed me as a person, deeply and forever. Among other things, I have had an "entity walk-in event," as chronicled in my book *The Walk-In*. This essentially gave me knowledge and insights from an outside source, which I never would have had. I also believe I have been subject to contact with life outside of our Earth realm. While some of these paranormal events were traumatizing and damaged me, they have also given me deep insights into all that surrounds us.

After my paranormal events, it was common for me to have lucid dreams where I was shown certain concepts of the Universe. I also have waking communications with higher Universal powers. You could say, "The Universe whispers into my ear." I believe I also have had various Spirit Guides trying to teach me and show me things. I have literally been on my exercise run and had mathematical equations or concepts come into my mind from nowhere. Sometimes I have words or thoughts pop into my mind randomly, which serve as hints of concepts to work on. I have been living for years like this, and thus have been exposed to many interesting ideas and pieces of knowledge, which I am about to pass onto you.

I consider myself very close to God, as I define God. I belong to no particular faith or religion, but am highly spiritual, and closely tuned into spirit guides, angels, and all that exists within the heavens and the hereafter. I believe Jesus existed as a historical figure and I look up to him for his love, inspiration, and mentorship. But with that said, I want to make it clear that I favor no particular religion, or even the concept of religion itself. I embrace all my Christian, Islamic, Hindu, Buddhist, and Jewish brothers and sisters, as well as those from all other faiths and beliefs, and embrace those with no faith at all. Thus, I mean no disrespect to any of the above, as I present in a very forthright way all the concepts that have been shown to me by the Universe. Please consider me a loving neutral party as I attempt to objectively present to you what I believe, and what I have been shown to be, the ways of the Universe. My hope is that the concepts and insights I am about to speak of, aid in human evolution, as well as each of you living a healthier, happier, and more successful life of your choosing.

CHAPTER 2

God And The Universe

Who is God, and what is the Universe? First, let me preface this by saying that I am not a scientist, astronomer, or physicist. Also, this is not a physics journal or textbook. My goal is to present my information and theories in a plain, linear, easy to understand, simple format. So, I am not going to get deep into the weeds, and I am not going to footnote everything I say. This book is about presenting my views and theories in a way everyone can understand. So, I will oversimplify everything, and use layman's terms and explanations.

Wikipedia defines "God" as: conceived of as the Supreme Being and the principal object of faith. The concept of God, as described by theologians, commonly includes the attributes of omniscience (all-knowing), omnipresence (present everywhere), omnipotence (unlimited power), and as having an eternal and necessary existence. Depending on one's kind of theism, these attributes are used either in way of analogy, or in a literal sense as distinct properties of the God.

Wikipedia defines the "Universe" as all of space and time and their contents, including planets, stars, galaxies, and all other forms of matter and energy.

Now for my own view and definition of God and the Universe, which has been whispered to me by higher sources greater than myself. I truly believe that God and the Universe is the same thing. They are two different words describing the same thing, and they are interchangeable.

I do not think the Universe is a dark space, and I do not think God is an old man with a white beard. I believe humans have been incapable of comprehending the Universe; thus, they have created a symbol or character for it. They have created "God" as a way to humanize, personalize, and clearly define "the maker" in human terms. The Universe made itself (will explain in a moment), and therefore is "the maker." The name God, or calling the Universe God, puts a human face onto the Universe. But the Universe is God, and God is the Universe.

I have always thought it weird, arrogant, and small-minded, how humans feel justified in "owning" everything in the Universe. In an infinite Universe with undoubtedly countless solar systems, planets, and life forms, humans are convinced God is a human man. I think it is embarrassing to think like that. It is almost proof that humanity is very underdeveloped to be thinking in such short-sighted terms.

If God were actually a living being, he/she/it would most certainly not be human. God would likely be some other alien life form much more powerful and intelligent than a human. "He" would most certainly have to be an alien of some sort. God would also likely have no gender. But I do not think God is a living humanoid being. I believe God is the characterized human face we put on the Universe.

Science says the Universe was created 13.8 Billion years ago via the "Big Bang Theory." The Big Bang Theory indicates the Universe was formed from a Singularity, or single "event," or "explosion." Simply put, the Universe started as nothing from nothingness, such as from a black hole, where matter is infinitely dense inside a hole of nothingness. In a sense, everything is combined with nothing. I believe this push-pull may have collided with a random event or condition, which caused an explosion, releasing the infinite amount of matter out of nothingness, and into everything, which we call the Universe. Think of it as dropping a single pebble into calm water. Nothingness becomes an "event" (Singularity), where the water is hit, and then creates a wave of action which then emanates or spreads outward infinitely in the form of a wave of "something" (as opposed to calm nothing).

So, the big question really is what caused the nothingness to explode into everything. Physics has been desperately trying to determine this. In my own view, it was a Random Event, which mixed with the Singularity to cause the explosion, which resulted in the Universe. Math and the world of Physics will tell you that there is always a mathematical or scientific reason for everything. I disagree. I think there is a Random component to the Universe that cannot be quantified. Sometimes stuff just happens. No rhyme or reason. Humans are always desperate to have an explanation for everything because human nature requires it. But just because humans will not accept random events does not mean random events are not factually true. I think they are.

My Law of Randomality states: Events and circumstances exist within the Universe that cannot be predicted, explained, or quantified, by mathematics or science.

Let me give you an example of Randomality. Let's say there is a herd of zebras being hunted by a lion. The lion will indeed have a tendency to go after the smaller weaker zebras in the back of the zebra herd. However, there are usually several smaller weaker zebras on the fringes of the herd. What makes a lion decide to go after a certain zebra at a certain moment? Well, the lion is an organic thinking being. The lion has moods, urges, and compulsions. Due to these organic conditions, the lion's actions can be random. Based upon the random organization of the lion's thoughts, moods, and urges at that moment, the lion may attack at any given time of his choosing or instinct, or for reasons even the lion does not know. When he does attack, he will attack a certain zebra that happens to randomly be in a weak position at that moment. It is "bad luck" on the part of the zebra for being in the wrong place at the wrong time. This "bad luck" is random. If the lion was in the mood to attack a few minutes earlier, that zebra may have been in a different position and not been the one attacked. The positioning, timing, mood of the lion, and so forth, makes the event random. Thus, the lion randomly attacks one of the zebras he considers a prime target. The choice the lion made could have been easily changed by its mood, urge, or if the timing had the zebra in a different position earlier. Thus, the whole event is random. That zebra did not have to scientifically or mathematically be the obvious target of attack. It was just a random set of unfortunate circumstances which made that zebra the target of attack in that moment.

Also, no, I do not think the zebra signed a soul contract to come into this life to be eaten by a lion at that moment. It makes no sense and would serve the soul of the zebra no purpose. We have to apply some common sense to our situations, even if it would be tidier to just say the zebra signed a soul contract to be brutally eaten by a lion because he thought it would be fun and interesting to provide that important lion with sustenance.

There are many other examples I could give, such as why tornadoes destroy one home, but leave the home next door untouched. Had the slightest condition been different, a different set of homes would have been destroyed. I will not fill this book with random examples, but I am hoping you understand my point that randomness exists, thus my Law of Randomality. So therefore, Randomality also affects the Universe and all within it. As with the lion, Randomality is more common when involving organic forces. Organic forces would include anything living or any intelligent energy or matter. The Universe is full of energy and intelligent matter in my opinion. It is this organic intelligence and energy which causes random behaviors, such as with the lion. I will be describing this organic intelligent energy and matter later on.

Anyway, my larger point is that I believe some random event interacted with the Singularity, which caused the explosion, releasing all matter outward like an ever-expanding ripple in the water.

So, picture an infinite amount of matter exploding outward from a single point. Like the ripples from a pebble, the matter continues to expand outward. Thus, the Universe is ever expanding. The Universe is ever growing, constantly expanding outward. Therefore, if you asked me how big the Universe is, I would not be able to tell you because the size of the Universe changes from second to second, since it is always expanding and growing.

This is where we come to my next concept. I believe everything is round. Everything is a sphere. Everything goes in circles. Everything comes around. Everything has a cycle that repeats in circles.

Everything I describe to you, whether it be the Universe itself, or the life cycle, it is all is based on the fact that everything is a sphere, round, and goes in a circle. It is a specific way of thinking, and you will see this theme in all my theories, views, and thoughts.

With this in mind, I describe the Universe as the inside of an ever-expanding balloon. Firstly, this means I believe the Universe, from our perspective, is concave. Meaning, we are looking at the inside of the balloon. All the contents of the Universe where we exist are inside the balloon. Outside the balloon is nothingness. The Universe is an ever-expanding balloon that never pops. The infinite amount of matter from which it originates guarantees that the balloon will never run out of matter or motion to continue expanding. The waves created by the pebble falling in the water will continue infinitely and will always be filled by an infinite amount of matter that came from the Singularity.

Therefore, I do believe there is a finite limited amount of space (volume) within the Universe, within the balloon. However, it is so huge and expansive, and ever growing (thus always changing volume), that it cannot be quantified, and will never limit us in any way. The

16

inside of that Universe/balloon gets bigger with every moment.

Thus far we have covered what the Universe is, how it formed, and what its actual structure is. Before we get any further, let me revisit this idea that God is indeed the Universe and that they are one in the same thing. If you read the Wikipedia definition of God, you will see it talks about the attributes of God being omniscience (all knowing), omnipotence (unlimited power), omnipresence (present everywhere), and as having an eternal and necessary existence. These attributes given to God are identical to attributes the Universe has. This is because God *is* the Universe. People of faith have simply put a face on the Universe, so they can more easily relate to it on a personal psychological human level. It is the equivalent of calling the Earth "Mother Nature." There is no such person called Mother Nature. But humans wanted to put a relatable face on the Earth environment that they can relate to on a personal psychological level. I see nothing wrong with this, by the way. But it is important to point out these facts as a reality, so we see things clearly from a factual scientific point of view.

Now that we know what the Universe/God is, how it was formed, and that its structure is the inside of an ever-expanding sphere, let us discuss the contents of that sphere. Scientists say the Universe contains Space, Matter, Time, and Energy. We will look at each of those items.

Space is all of the volume within the sphere we call the Universe. It can also be thought of as all the distance between the edges of the sphere, and the distance between the objects within that sphere. So, space is real, and we see it and know it. It is the volume of all the area around us and beyond.

Matter is all the "objects" within the Universe. These would be anything constructed with atoms, which is everything. So, Space is the volume of area, and Matter would be all the objects within that space.

Time is more interesting and complicated. Time is a concept, rather than a thing. Time has to do with distance and is a unit of measurement between one moment to the next moment. Moments do not all happen at once. Moments happen at different times, different intervals. *Time* is how we measure the different intervals. But here is where it gets interesting. Most humans think of *time* as linear, meaning a straight line from one point in time, to the next point in time. The timeline between January 1st to December 31st is a straight line. We move along this straight line through all the days, weeks, months.

With all this said, I believe *Time*, like everything else, is a sphere. What I mean is that I believe *Time* is little lines that wrap around the inside edges of the sphere. If this is true, then the lines of time must be round, because if you follow along the inside of the balloon, then you end up bending into a circle since the balloon is basically round inside.

I also believe that because the Universe is ever expanding, Time is also adjusting and bending to account for this expansion of the balloon, and growth of the balloon. Therefore, we will have some instances of time being imperfect. Time might bend. Time might also end up back where it started eventually since it is essentially a sphere.

So, on a micro level time is a very useful tool of measurement. Time is very accurate and reliable for measuring the passing of moments from last year to this year. It does not bend or alter. It is fixed. However, time on a macro level is very unstable and not fixed at all. On the grand universe level, time is always growing, expanding, and bending along with the concave insides of the balloon. Therefore, time can have imperfections and unexpected results we humans never consider.

For example, if we were to find one of these bends in Time, or irregularities in Time, we would be able to "travel" in time instantaneously. We could be in different Times, or maybe even more than one Time at the same time. I believe this is why humans on a deep intuitive level, realize that time travel might be possible.

Also, when people talk about traveling to different dimensions, or being in different dimensions, what they are actually saying is that they can be in a different Time within space. A different dimension is simply a different reality as defined by being in a different "time and space." So, if I can identify and exploit an imperfection or bend in *Time*, then I could certainly instantaneously be in a different dimension. Being in this different dimension puts me in a different time and space. It does this because being in a different time automatically means you are in a different space within the Universe.

I believe as we continue to explore the Universe, we will find such bends in *Time*. We already know Black Holes exist, and we know to stay away from them. We will also find bends in *Time* and we will know to stay away from them, or risk never being seen or heard from again.

The final content within the Universe is *Energy*. For our discussions in this book, *Energy* is the most important item, and the one we will be focusing on most. *Energy* has different meanings and there are different types, such as waves, etc.

Energy can be defined as a force, such as the energy (force) required to move an object. But Energy can also be defined as a collection of atoms forming an organic intelligence. This is the type of Energy we will focus on.

We psychics always talk about "energy," and "reading energy." We talk about this because as psychics, we actually feel, see, sense, and touch *Energy*. It is real to us, and consists of actual *matter*, made of particles. But what makes this particular *matter* interesting, is that it has a "life" to it. It has intelligence. We can sense feeling, thought, intention, and intelligence within this Energy. Somehow, this "object" of Energy is "alive." It is living Energy. It is a collection of waves, particles, and atoms that has organized into a mass of intelligence that we call *Energy*.

This *Energy* has life to it. What I mean by that is that it seems to contain life, intelligence, random movements, and intention. It seems to have some self-determination. The Energy behaves in forms of frequencies that can be sensed by psychics, or those who are sensitive enough to tune into the Universe or nature.

I believe this *Energy* is the "brain" of the Universe. I believe this

Energy IS God. This *Energy* is also what gives the Universe its random factor. Why? Because the Energy is somehow organic or alive in some way; and just like the lion, what is organic and alive, can behave in a random way.

Whereas the *Space* is the vast darkness, the *Energy* is the light. *Matter* is the body, and *Time* is the movement and distance. But I believe it is all controlled by the brain, which is the *Energy*. I believe the Energy consists of the souls and intelligence of all organic beings, or all intelligent life. But we will get into all this later, when we discuss *Souls* in depth.

I believe this Energy, which is the light, is what people talk about when they have near death experiences and "go toward the light." When people talk about "going to God," they are talking about their soul reuniting with the light. They are reuniting with this collection of *Energy*, which I call the *Universe Energy Collective*. This is another reason I believe the Universe and God are the same thing. The *Energy* component of the Universe is what all of us go back to eventually. We go back home to God. We go back to the Universe Energy Collective.

Energy is the collection of Universal intelligence. It is the light. It is the brains of the Universe. It is the soul of the Universe. It is God.

I promise the rest of the book will not be this technical or complicated. Hang in there with me, as the fun is only beginning.

CHAPTER 3

Life Forms And Aliens

What life forms exist in the Universe? There are many. I challenge anyone to accurately define "life," and have that definition stand up to the test of time. Science is always making advances and I would guess things we do not consider "alive" now, we will consider "alive" or "life" in the future.

Let me give you one great example of this. Soul Energy. Soul energy from the Universe is something that does not require food, water, or sustenance, and never dies. Yet, I consider Soul Energy "life" because it is intelligent. Any entity with intelligence and self-awareness would have to be considered a "life form."

Conversely, let's look at grass. Grass is not thought to have any intelligence or self-awareness. Yet, grass is certainly a life form because it is alive and takes in sustenance, and eventually dies.

So, you can see trying to define "life" is a sticky wicket. Someday someone might say that rocks are life forms because they contain stored Universal Energy and can be unpredictable in how they move or react to certain conditions. I am kidding. But I'm not. So, I am not going to define "life" or "life form." But for the purposes of this book, I am going to consider "life forms" as anything organic *or* intelligent in nature. Examples would be Soul energy, Universal Energy, Plants, and animals. Obviously included as life forms would be humans and extra-terrestrial aliens.

I hope that last mention got your attention. This is not a book on biology, so we will not spend time discussing plants and animals. We have, and will again, discuss Soul Energy and Universal Energy. The book is really mostly about humans. But for this chapter, we need to discuss Aliens, or Extra-terrestrials. I do not want to seem politically or socially insensitive in how I refer to them. I apologize if any aliens reading this are offended at how I refer to them or terms used.

Now getting to the point, I find it arrogant and short sighted how humans always consider themselves the supreme beings at the top of the food chain, so to speak. If you read about the Universe, many would come away thinking that Earth is the only planet with life on it, and humans are the only highly developed life forms. Religions are all based on "God" being human form and serving only humans.

Are we really that underdeveloped that we believe this for real? Not about God or religion, but the fact that the Universe is all about humans, and only humans?

Scientists believe there are at least 100 billion galaxies in the Universe, with each galaxy having 30 billion planets. Notice I said "billion" in those numbers. The numbers are too big to comprehend. I cannot comprehend them. Humans cannot comprehend them. But the point is that surely any life form with an IQ better than a blade of grass, can deduce that there are advanced life forms out there other than just humans.

Thus, there must be aliens, extra-terrestrials. Fact.

So, the question is not about "if." The better question is "have aliens had contact with Earth yet?" I can say yes. You could say,

"Prove it." I might say "no," or "I can't," or "I won't." So, it is a debate we can have. Although you realistically cannot claim no aliens exist in the Universe, you could claim humans have not had contact with aliens yet, if you so desire to remain in that state of denial.

However, I personally am going to suggest that not only do aliens exist, but also that they have had contact with Earth; have had contact with humans and are among us already in some fashion. How do I know this? Well, I do not have an alien carcass to show you, if that is what you require. But I have had personal experiences which have led me to believe in their existence. Furthermore, I remind you of certain mysteries, such as the Egyptian Pyramids and other structures, which suggest more advanced life forms could have been on Earth in the past.

Anyone who knows me personally will tell you that I am a very logical, pragmatic guy that does not believe in bullshit. In fact, I have always been somewhat of a cynic when it came to psychic abilities and aliens. But life events and experience has taught me differently. I will give you some examples.

Firstly, I feel I have had direct contact with humans who have an alien component to them. What I mean by that is I feel there are humans who have been born with some alien interference or even alien DNA introduced into them.

Various children, teens, young adults and older adults, have told me stories of dreams they have had which are alien in nature. Meaning, they have had dreams that are not based in terms of Earth or humans. They are based on locations which are not Earth-like, and that include beings that are not human or Earth-like. In addition, some of these people exhibited some strange physical characteristics such as partial webbing of toes and bone ridges on their scalp. Skeptics could easily explain away such physical features, as well as the dreams. All I am doing here is sharing my personal observations and experiences. You can form your own judgments and beliefs.

Furthermore, I have had sessions with clients who claim to be alien

23

know it's not English. Over half the people on Earth do not understand English, let alone animals, aliens, and perhaps some Energy. So, what is something all living or intelligent beings respond to?

LOVE

Show me anything that is organic and/or intelligent that does not respond to Love. It does not matter if it is a squirrel, cat, dog, human, alien, or energy, all of them would understand love.

What is love? Love is strong positive feelings and concern. If you show love, you also show compassion. If you love, you are willing to give of yourself for someone or something else. If I love, I give.

If I show love to an animal, I am peaceful and give food, comfort, and safety. If I show love to an alien, I would give something to them as a gesture, plus show safety, respect, and comfort. If I show love to Energy, I show it space, respect, and concern for its existence. Showing respect for existence can apply to anything. Anything and anyone, wants to see you will not harm it, that you are willing to let it exist, and that you are willing to give something of yourself.

So, if I run into an alien from the other side of the Universe, I need to immediately start communicating in the language of the Universe, also the language of God. Which is love. So, I will immediately respect its safety and right to exist. I will then give it something to show I am willing to give of myself for its benefit. These two acts would immediately show my intent to communicate peacefully.

I would act this way, no matter what. Maybe it is not an alien creature, but a blob of Energy, or invisible Energy, or sound. I would act the same in an effort to communicate in the Universal language of Love.

There is a caveat. The caveat is that this will not always work (snicker). For example, if I try to communicate with an angry bear this way, it is probably not smart. The same goes for a mean dog about to bite me. This is why we proceed slowly and gently. We are showing our peaceful intent, but we are also able to pull back quickly if needed. Communication with anything is always a risk. Sometimes we are hurt or rejected. But most of us agree it is worth the risk.

Hopefully I have now adequately prepared you to face an alien should you meet one. Communicate with Love. However, there are also some more sophisticated methods of communication that are worth mentioning. Music is a good method. Surprisingly, or not, most intelligent and organic beings respond to music. Sound organized in a harmonic way can convey organized thought and feelings. The only problem is that what one being thinks is great peaceful music, might be terrible aggressive music to another being. Symbols are also a method suggested. However, the obvious problem is that different symbols would mean different things to different beings.

Mathematics is a commonly suggested communication method. This would work for basic communication, but it is believed that humans are developed at such an inferior level, that our mathematics ability is only a fraction of what other alien beings, and Universal Energy itself, understand. So, speaking to the Universe or aliens with our mathematics might be the same as knowing only a few words like cat and dog.

In fact, I believe that Universal Energy operates under a very advanced and sophisticated system of mathematics, frequencies, and other things we do not even have words for yet. This is because Energy is not organic like humans and plants. Energy is eternal. With Energy, there is no organic matter involved that breaks down and dies, limiting its life. Therefore, Energy has had eternity to develop into highly advanced forms, which likely operate under highly advanced systems.

Many psychics feel communicating empathically (via telepathy) would be effective. This form of communication requires no words or sounds. It is communication using feelings and thought. This could work, unless different beings interpret feelings differently. For

29

example, in human culture, we have something called "pleasure pain." So, the feeling is one of pain, but we humans like it anyway because it might be leading to some sexual arousal or other rewarding end. So, showing an alien "pleasure pain" might be interpreted as showing them "pain," harm, and aggression. Not good.

However, in most cases you will be communicating with humans. In your communications, perhaps keep in mind the Universal language of love. Practice communicating with the language of love. Even if you are angry about something, try communicating with love. A Master is able to communicate with love, regardless of the message being put forth.

Everything has its caveats, but most definitely the language of the Universe and the language of God, is Love.

CHAPTER 5

What Is Your Soul?

Everything in the Universe is related. Why and how? Because the Universe (everything) started as a Singularity. It started as one point of infinitely dense matter, which then exploded outward. So, *everything* relates back to that one single infinite collection of matter from the Singularity.

Therefore, as the Universe consists of space, matter, time, and energy so does the human being. The space is your volume and size, the matter is your actual physical body, the time is your aging process, and the energy is your soul and collective of your intelligence.

Some people might say, "I thought the human brain was the collective of the intelligence." Well sort of, but not really. The human brain is the organ that allows the body to function and live. The brain is also the collection of knowledge that a human learns through education. But the Soul of a person is the true essence of a person. The Soul is the collection of a person's eternal Energy.

Eventually, the body dies. With the body dying, the brain dies as well. But the Soul lives on because it consists of Universal Energy, or Energy from the Universe. The brain can die, but the Soul is eternal. This is the important point to remember.

We discussed in the previous chapter how amazing and magical the Energy component of the Universe is. The Energy of the Universe is amazing because it provides that organic living intelligence factor, which is also eternal.

So, what is your Soul? Your Soul is the collection of eternal Universal Energy within you. What does this mean? Well, it means many things. It means you literally have part of the Energy from the Universe inside you. You will recall I called Energy "the light" of the Universe. So, this means you also have "the light" within you. I also inferred that this intelligent Energy is also the essence of God, since it's the intelligence of the Universe. Therefore, you also have God within you.

You should begin to notice that most of what I have been saying does not conflict with many religious views. I am describing God in much the same way, and I am using many of the same terms used in religion, such as "God is the light," "Going back to the light," "going back to God," "God being with you or within you," and so on.

In summary, at this point of our discussion, your Soul is defined as the collection of Universal Energy that is within you.

The implications of this are very complex and far-reaching. Primarily, it means you have a part of the Universe's magic within you. You have a part of the Universe's intelligence and life within you. The fact this Energy is eternal makes it that much more interesting and amazing because it never dies and exists forever.

But next, there is a concept called "Soul Splitting" I want to discuss. This was a concept first introduced to me by famed psychic Andrew Brewer; and I have done my own work on it since, and in addition. Bear in mind that your soul consists of Energy particles from the Universe. This means your Soul as a whole consists of many separate particles. It is my view that these particles do not always stay

32

together in one place.

Let me give you an example. Let us say we have a bucket of water. The water is your collection of Soul energy particles. Let us say we dump out all the water and set the bucket aside. Indeed, most of the water will be all together exactly where we dumped it. But there will still be some trace amounts of water inside the bucket that we set aside. As you know, the bucket will not be bone-dry inside. The bucket will still have some drops or a film of water in it. Thus, all of the water that was once together as one, is now separated somewhat.

I believe the Soul energy particles may work the same way. Although most of the Soul energy might make it into the human body you are inhabiting, some amount of your soul energy particles, remain in the Universe with the larger collection of Energy we call the Universal Energy Collective. So, in a sense, some of your soul may actually be up in the Universe with the Universal Energy Collective at this moment. This would explain why some people feel a connection to some greater power outside of themselves. It could be they are tuning into, or sensing, their soul energy particles that are still with the Universal Energy Collective mass.

It is also possible part of your soul could be in another human as we speak. Let us go back to the bucket of water. We dumped out the bucket in one place. But maybe we noticed there was still a little water left in the bucket. So, we dump the bucket again, except in a slightly different location. Now your soul energy is in two different locations at the same time. Perhaps in two different humans at the same time. Not only that, but even after dumping the bucket a second time, there will still be trace amounts of water left in the bucket. Thus, you will still be partly with the larger collective of Universal Energy, in addition to being in two different places, and or people, at the same time. This might explain why some people feel a deep personal connection to another place or person. It could be that place or person is actually a part of you in the sense that part of your soul energy may be in that person.

From this point, we could even hypothesize that our Soul Energy

33

The Soul is Universal Energy, and therefore is connected to the Universe and all the information the Universe contains.

CHAPTER 6

What Has A Soul?

In the last chapter, we talked at length about human souls. What I wanted to do here is expand upon the topic of souls a bit. Humans are arrogant self-centered creatures, and it is easy to forget that there might be other beings in the Universe who also have souls. So, let us ask, what has a Soul other than humans? I believe that any intelligent being has a Soul. By "intelligent," I mean a being capable of thought, feeling, and self-determination to some degree.

So, a robot that can "think," would not qualify to have a Soul since it cannot "feel." A robot also has no self-determination capability since it is controlled by its external programming. However, a squirrel has a Soul because it can think, it has at least some level of feeling regarding pain and urgency certainly, plus it has self-determination in that it can decide which tree it wants to climb first.

An alien would have a Soul because it likely has similar capabilities as a human, and then some.

Cats and dogs have a Soul because they are similar to a squirrel, except even more advanced.

Does a tree or plant have a Soul? Well, can a tree and plant think, feel, and have self-determination? Perhaps we do not have the answer to that. Science at this time would have a tendency to say no, because there is no brain or nervous system capable of thought. If science one day proves that trees and plants can think, feel, and have self-determination, then I will be the first one to claim they also have a Soul.

So, if something has a Soul, does this means when their body dies, their Soul Energy re-joins the Universe Energy Collective with all the other Soul Energy? Yes indeed. So essentially, in religious terms, does this mean all animals go to heaven? Yes, they do.

Does this mean an alien from another galaxy has Soul Energy within the Universe Energy Collective? Yes, it does. There are some of us who feel we have connected with such alien energy. Most humans do not consider such possibilities because humans in general only consider themselves within their limited human perspective.

Is the Soul Energy of cats and dogs up in the Universal Energy Collective? Yes. This is one reason why I and others believe that when we die, we can actually re-join our pets in the form of our Soul Energies reconnecting with our pet's Soul Energy.

Can Soul Energy from a human become Soul Energy of a dog? In other words, can human Soul Energy reincarnate into a dog? Yes, I believe it's possible. The reason why is because our Soul Energy has some self-determination. Our Soul Energy is on a mission and journey to have experiences, so that it may learn, grow, and evolve. If our Soul Energy determines that living a life of as a dog would be a great way to learn, grow, and evolve, then that reincarnation would be justified. I am not sure this actually happens all the time. Most likely, our Soul Energy desires to reincarnate into the most advanced beings it possibly can, in order to maximize the evolution process.

Can Soul Energy from an alien reincarnate into a human, and vice versa? Yes, it can, and I believe it does. When most people ask for a past life reading, they expect to be told they used to be some famous person, or that they remain the same gender in all past lives.

A woman wants to hear that they were Marilyn Monroe. A woman does not want to hear they were Charlie Chaplin. So, gender itself is an issue in doing readings for paying clients. So, imagine if you told a paying client they were an alien in a past life. They would freak out and want their money back.

When I do past life readings for people, I see many lives. Some lives as a human male, some as a human female, and some as an alien. I see them all. What I give the client is the one that comes through with strength, detail, and one they can mentally and emotionally accept. So, this means I almost always skip the alien past lives. But that does not mean they are not there.

When it comes to the question of what or who has a Soul, humans really need to start stepping back from themselves, and realizing they are not the only amazing creatures in the Universe worthy of having a Soul. There are many creatures and souls out there.

CHAPTER 7

The Cycle Of Life

Now that we have covered The Universe, God, and your Soul, let us drill down and begin to examine the Human Being. Certainly, the Cycle of Life could apply to any organic living thing. But for simplicity sake, we will just focus on Humans.

As I have said earlier, everything is round. Everything goes in circles. Let me first give you the example of the life cycle of water, since we have used water as an example before. We will begin our example by saying water starts in the clouds as vapor. When the water vapor gets dense enough, and other weather conditions permit, it then rains. The water vapor is born into water drops, which fall from the sky. The rain hits the ground and starts to soak into the ground or run off into the watershed. This means the water starts its long journey. The water might drain into some cracks and low-lying areas. Then the water drains into a small creek. Then it drains into a large stream. Then it might drain into a river. From there it drains into the ocean. Once in the ocean, with the sun heating it up, it starts to evaporate and turn into water vapor again, where it returns to the clouds, where it all started. So, the water began in the sky, was born into rain, had a very long journey on Earth, and then went back up into the sky. It is a cycle that repeats over and over infinitely.

Let's begin our human journey the same way. We start with our Soul Energy particles up in the light mixed with all the *Energy* of the Universe in the Universe Energy Collective. That is considered "home." It is home with God, and home in the Universal Energy Collective from whence it/we started.

Our Soul Energy is intelligent and has shared all of its prior information with the Akashic records. Our Soul Energy still mingles with its prior soul contacts, and with other Universal Energy, but our Soul Energy is ready for another adventure.

Why would our Soul Energy be ready for another adventure? The answer is because the purpose of life is to learn, grow, and evolve. The only way anything can do those things is by gaining more experience. So, if our intelligent Soul Energy wants to learn, grow, and evolve, it must gain more life experiences. One way to do that is to enter into another human life.

Meanwhile, back on Earth, we have two humans having intercourse and creating a new organic life through pregnancy. Two human life forms can create new organic matter, a new body, a new person, in this way. But it is just a body. The body still needs a soul.

A Soul can only come from Soul Energy. Soul Energy is found in the Universe, in the collective of Universal Soul Energy. So like rain watering a new plant to allow for it to live, Soul Energy finds its way down into a vacant organism (fetus), so that it can live and be a whole person.

I do not know when exactly this happens, just as I do not know exactly when a little seedling has enough water. In this book, I am not

41

those around them than they are in themselves. There is a special reconciliation that happens within a dying person. There is a reconciliation between the body which is decaying and in pain, the mind which does not want to die but knows it is dying, and the Soul which is still in perfect condition and almost yearns to continue its journey in a more viable body.

If you look carefully, you can see this reconciliation within the dying person. They are clearly in pain and disrepair with a body that just cannot continue. That is easy for everyone to admit. The dying person is most often fed up with their body and does not want to deal with it anymore. The person is often accepting of the fact the body cannot continue and needs to die. However, this conflicts with the person's mind. The person's mind often does not want to leave, and feels concern for those being left behind, as well as business left undone, regrets, and challenges not completed. The mind is the one factor usually not wanting to die. The body is ready to die, but the mind is not. Then finally there is the Soul. The Soul wants to continue the journey, but in a body or host that can live fully in order to provide the maximum life experience. A body lying in bed for days is not of much use to a Soul wanting many experiences. The Soul also has its own intelligence remember. So, the Soul has mixed feelings of wanting to continue with the journey they have been on, but also wanting to "go back home" to the light of the collective of Universal Energy. The Soul also may want to start a new journey that is more vibrant. Therefore, the soul may feel reminiscent, but also ready to move on. All of these reactions and emotions can be observed within a dying person.

Eventually, the body goes into the end stages of death. The organs start to shut down. The mind starts to die along with the body. I believe there is a moment when the mind turns over all control to the Soul.

I have personally witnessed a person's death in detail. As a psychic, I was able to sense the person's emotions and thoughts during the entire process. I witnessed the body coming to a halt. Before that, I sensed plenty of brain activity. The mind was dreaming and reaching out. The mind was communicating with higher powers and spirit guides. The mind was receiving instructions and comfort on how to proceed. Then at a certain point, I no longer sensed any brain activity. However, I felt a strong sense of "being" as the Soul Energy was still intact and within the body. But very shortly thereafter, I saw and sensed the Soul Energy leave the body. I "saw" it in the form of an actual visible flash of light. I sensed it also, because after it was gone, the person felt totally dead and gone to me. Yet the person was still breathing. But not long after that, the person stopped breathing.

So, what I witnessed, was the body coming to a near stop, then the mind dying, then the soul leaving the body, then the body coming to a total stop.

In my opinion, death actually occurred the moment the soul left the body, because a body without a soul is not viable. This is why there is great debate as to whether or not discontinue life support for those who will not recover. As a psychic, my question would be to evaluate the state of the body, the state of the mind, and the state of the soul. By figuring out the status of those three things, I would have an opinion as to whether life support should be continued or not. Maintaining a body with no mind or soul is pointless and cruel. But I really do not want to digress off our current discussion too much.

So, the mind and body dies. The Soul Energy releases from the body. For me, the release is actually visible in the form of a flash of light. So again, the soul energy, the Energy of the Universe, is indeed "the light."

The Soul Energy travels up "to the light," "to God," "to the collective of Universal Energy." which could be called "Heaven." The Soul goes back home. The Soul Energy is now back where it started. The Soul Energy can intermingle with all the other soul energies and with the Universe Energy Collective from whence it came. The Cycle of Life is complete.

CHAPTER 8

Death: A Closer Look

I know we covered Death in the previous Cycle of Life chapter. However, there is always such intense interest regarding death, and many questions. In the Cycle of Life chapter, I really wanted to keep a clear balanced flow of the entire cycle without getting you lost in the forest or the weeds. Thus, I did not want to create an imbalance with an over-emphasis on Death, which is only one part of the Life Cycle. So, in this chapter we will take a closer look just at Death and hopefully answer some questions that were left unanswered when we discussed the Cycle of Life.

Birth and Death have many similarities. They are both well described by science. Birth takes Soul Energy from the Universe Energy Collective and puts it into a body, and Death gives Soul Energy back to the Universe Energy Collect from the body. They are both bookends to the Human Experience. However, when it comes to the Human Experience, one is the beginning, and one is the end. Humans do not seem as afraid of beginnings but are terrified of endings. Thus, most humans find Death terrifying. Why is this? Two reasons probably. First, because many see death as "the end." Secondly, because of the "unknown."

Death is the end of one particular life cycle. Human bodies only last so long, and eventually the body dies. The Soul never dies. Your Soul is eternal and jumps from one body to the next, to the next, or remains in the Universal Energy Collective. But organic bodies always eventually die.

So, when we say death is the end, we are only meaning the end of that particular human body. Plus, Death is only one part of the Cycle of Life. It is not "the end." It's one dot in the circle of "connect the dots." It is only one "item" in the process as a whole. Thus, I really only look at Death as being the end of a particular human body in one particular lifetime.

This seems a good time to insert a conversation about *Reincarnation*.

REINCARNATION

Reincarnation is the theory that we live more than one lifetime, and perhaps many life times. We keep coming back for more. Reincarnation makes perfect sense because our Soul Energy is eternal. Everything in the Universe is a sphere, because the Universe itself is a sphere. Everything is a circle. Everything runs in cycles. Plus, due to the principle of "Conservation of Energy," we know that Energy does not just vanish into nothingness. Energy disperses into other forms or places, but it still exists. Therefore, when a body dies, and the Soul Energy is released, that Soul Energy will still exist. So where does it go? When water evaporates back up into the atmosphere, where does it go? Does the water just vanish into nothingness? Or does it condense into clouds and once again fall to the Earth in the form of rain?

Soul Energy is like the rain. It has a journey on Earth, goes back up into the atmosphere (Universe), then comes back down to Earth. Everything in the Universe is recycled. Under the principle of "Conservation of Matter," matter never just vanishes into nothingness. It only changes form. What you bury in the ground either stays in the ground, or it turns into compost. But it still exists. It remains. So, everything is recycled eventually. Something might turn to dust quickly and end up helping to grow a tree. Or something might sit for hundreds or thousands of years before it composts and helps grow a tree. But eventually all matter is recycled in some way.

Soul Energy is recycled. Soul Energy leaving one life form, will end up as Soul Energy in another life form eventually. Granted, some Soul Energy may remain in the Universal Energy Collective. But even that energy plays a function and is being utilized somehow, and thus recycled. Reincarnation is simply the word used for the recycling of Souls. The recycling of Soul Energy.

Do we have a choice in whether our Soul is recycled? Yes and no. Our Soul consists of Universal Energy. That energy is intelligent. It learns, grows, has experiences, downloads to the Akashic records and interacts with the other energies of the Universe. Like most intelligent "life," Soul Energy has a factor of self-determination to it. This means Souls have some power of decision.

Remember, the purpose or goal of a Soul is to gain experience, grow, and evolve. The only way to do that is through experiences. A big way to get experiences is through living out a human life. So inherently, a Soul will at some point want to gain more experiences and will want to be recycled and reincarnated.

Does the Soul really have a choice? Ultimately, eventually, everything in the Universe is recycled or goes through a cycle of some kind. So, like it or not, Soul Energy will eventually be put to use somehow in some way. So, in that macro view, Souls have no choice but to be recycled or reincarnated. It is very similar to how humans have no choice but to eat. However, humans can choose when to eat

48

and what to eat. Humans can even choose to fast for a period of time. I believe the same type of choice exists regarding reincarnation and recycling. Some Souls may wait a period of time before reincarnating, while others may enter back into life form immediately.

Which is more enjoyable for Soul Energy? To be within the Universe Energy Collective, or inside a life form living out a lifetime? Well I am sure it is a matter of opinion but consider this. The Universe Energy Collective is certainly considered "home." It is where Souls begin and where Souls end. So, I can imagine "home" is where it is most comfortable. But like most of us, after we have been home a long time, we start to get bored and we get cabin fever. We lust for adventure and something new. This would be when a Soul would yearn to be within a life form living a lifetime. So, I think the ultimate answer is that a balance of both is best. "Balance" is usually a good answer to many questions involving the Universe and Life.

It is hard to talk about Reincarnation and not talk about Past Lives.

PAST LIVES

A Past Life is what the phrase suggests. Past Lives are the collection of lives, or lifetimes, we have had in the past. Our Soul Energy has been jumping from life form to life form since the beginning of time, except for any time it has remained in the Universal Energy Collective.

Usually we have very little connection or thoughts regarding Past Lives. Why is this? Well, our Soul is inhabiting a human body which only knows itself. Our body and mind only know the experiences they are having in *this* lifetime. Our brain was born with this body. Our mind is our intelligent word for our brain. They only live in this lifetime. However, our Souls have lived many lifetimes. But our Souls do not control our thinking. Our minds control our thinking. Our brains control processes and speech. So, everything our Soul knows, does not come out in the form of thought or speech. Therefore, most of us do not think about our past lives, nor can we talk about them.

49

With all that said above, our Souls do makes us feel things. Our Souls have a memory. Our Souls remember, and they feel. We can often feel our Souls deep inside on a spiritual level. As humans, we know what our heart feels is superficial but powerful. We know our brain sometimes rejects or embraces what the heart feels. But what we feel on a spiritual Soul level is never superficial. It is separate, deep, and permanent. This is how we know the Soul is separate from our mind and heart. Obviously, you will accept me using the term "heart" in a figurative way, meaning the sensitive emotional side to our mind.

Souls are able to make us feel or remember things in a vague way. Therefore, Souls can sometimes give us vague clues of past lives. Most people can relate to some of these weird vague feelings of familiarity with places, people, or events. We do not know where it comes from, but we know it evokes real feelings within us.

I personally have very deep and heavy familiar feelings regarding the Vietnam War, Vietnam itself, and music from that time. I have nightmares about it, dreams, feelings, and impressions. Yet, I was not a living functioning person during the Vietnam War. I have never been to Vietnam. I have had very little education or connection to the Vietnam War. So why are my feelings so intense on a Soul level? The explanation is that I could have had a past life that lived during the Vietnam War, and participated in it.

As a matter of fact, I am convinced I did have a past life in the Vietnam War era. I have had recurring dreams for years about my death. I have seen over and over in the same dream through many years, how I was wounded and then stabbed to death by the enemy. The meaningful part of the dream for me is how I knew I was going to die, and I was hoping they would stab me again and finish it quickly. It is horrible. I live it out with such detail and feeling each time I have this same dream.

Others have similar experiences and dreams. Others have unexplained fears about certain places and things. These illogical fears are likely a response to a deep Soul memory that we cannot explain.

While we have these vague feelings, memories, impressions, or dreams from time to time, for the most part we live out our current lives with little interference or knowledge of our past lives. It is probably best this way since we are supposed to be focused on gaining experience in this lifetime, rather than suffering from trauma due to our past lifetimes.

Why is it that so many people claim to be someone famous in a past life? For example, how many thousands of people claim to be Marilyn Monroe in a past life, right? Well first off, not all those people were Marilyn Monroe. Perhaps they wanted to be, or wished they were Marilyn Monroe, but clearly, they were not. However, let us not forget about our discussion regarding "Soul Splitting." Under the Soul Splitting theory, some of our Soul Energy could be scattered in more than one place or more than one body or life at a time. So perhaps Marilyn Monroe's Soul consisted of a collection of many different Soul Energies. So yes, it is possible more than one person could legitimately claim they were once Marilyn Monroe.

How does a psychic do a past life reading? Well of course, every psychic is different and has their own techniques and style. But in general, just like all psychic readings, a psychic will read your Energy. If a psychic can tune into your Soul Energy, they can access those feelings and memories contained within your Soul. This means the psychic can get impressions on the Energy they are reading. Through these impressions, a psychic might "see" an image, description, or feeling, of a past life. The psychic can then describe to you what they are "seeing." It might not be perfectly accurate, but indeed a good psychic can get impressions into your Energy which are revealing and interesting on a past life scale.

Is it possible some people have more past lives than others do? Yes. The reason for this is two-fold. Firstly, some Soul Energy may have spent more time in the Universal Energy Collective and less time in organic life forms. Secondly, some Souls may have had more lifetimes due to increased Soul Splitting. Thus, in effect, some souls are living two lifetimes while you are living one.

Obviously, entire books can be written on Past Lives, as well as Reincarnation. But let's move on and discuss in more detail the process of death itself.

I talked about the process of dying in the Cycle of Life chapter. So, let me jump ahead right to the moment of actual death. Let us say we have a human, who for whatever reason, is dying. The body is dying, and the Soul is transitioning back to the Universal Energy Collective.

I have seen this happen. As a psychic, it is fascinating to watch a person transition. Obviously, it is permanently traumatizing on the highest level if it is a family member or close loved one. But as a professional who works with clients and associates, I was able to witness it from a more detached third-party perspective. I alluded to this story previously, but I will tell it in its full detail now.

His name was Larry and he was someone I had worked with on a professional level, so I knew him fairly well. However, we had fallen out of touch and I went months without any contact with him. One day I received a message from a close friend and associate of Larry. She informed me that Larry had been diagnosed with terminal cancer and she thought I should know. She told me he was presently in hospice, and where. The next day I made a trip up to the other side of town to see Larry. It was indeed a hospice facility. The front desk told me which room he was in. I found the room and walked in. Larry was lying in bed half unconscious, with oxygen and tubes coming out of him. I was horrified and shocked. I was obviously way too late for a proper visit.

But when I walked closer to him, he woke and saw it was me. He seemed really surprised and I said, "Hey Larry." He responded, "Hey Brian, how are you doing?" There was something funny about it because he was acting like everything was normal and totally fine, as if we were meeting on the street or something.

I told him I had only heard about his situation recently and that I was sorry. I knew he had bone cancer and clearly, he was very end stage. Then Larry said something under his mask. He said, "Heal me. Try." I gulped because, um, it looked a bit late for that. But I took his hand and focused. What I "saw" in my mind was a body completely littered and covered with tumors and cancer cells. There was seriously no way. But I acted as if I was giving it a good college try as a way of showing Larry I cared enough to try. I knew he was dying. So, I thought to myself that if I cannot save him, maybe I can help him with his passing. I became determined and looked at Larry and said, "You won't have to do this alone." "I will come back." "I will come back in a few days." "You need to hang on until then." Larry nodded and motioned to me goodbye and I left.

In my car on the way home I contemplated when I should return. The psychic message came in very clear. "Thanksgiving Day." Thanksgiving was about a week away and I actually had no plans for Thanksgiving that year. So, I waited until then.

The morning of Thanksgiving I drove up to Larry. I was hoping he would still be there, if you know what I mean. Sure enough, he was. I walked in, and he seemed both surprised and relieved I was there. By this time, he could no longer speak. I could tell he knew it was me though, and he could understand when I spoke to him.

I told him it was good to see him and that I was honored to spend my Thanksgiving with him. I am not a touchy-feely guy, but I took Larry's hand and just held it, as if praying with him. I was trying to tune into him and determine where he was at with his process, and how close. I could tell he was very close to the end. So, I started talking to him. I told him it was going to be Okay. Then I just started launching into my "instructions" on how to "do this." I told him to relax. I told him that if at some point he felt an urge to just "push off," that he should gently "push off." I told him I would be with him and guide him to the light. He seemed to truly focus on what I was saying and be determined to follow my instructions. That day Larry fell in and out of consciousness. I could tell when he was in pain, and I would get the nurse for more morphine. I also had to have his oxygen turned up regularly all day until it was on full blast.

During my day with Larry, his daughter showed up, who I had never met. I introduced myself to her and explained what I was doing. I told her that if she preferred privacy and wanted me to leave, that I would do so with no hard feelings. She enthusiastically asked me to stay. We visited and got to know each other, and we bonded.

I monitored Larry all day and into the evening, making sure he got his morphine shots. I observed him closely and stayed tuned into him. He woke up momentarily when his daughter was there, and they had a moment together, but then Larry was out again.

Eventually I could tell Larry was fading. I could sense he was seeing things and interacting with someone, or some presence. I could sense he was very close, and he was "talking" to whoever was basically "meeting him" at this point of transition, is what it felt like to me. My senses were much heightened, and I even told his daughter that I thought it was close.

Larry got "quiet" psychically, and I watched him. I am pretty sure I sensed the "push," or he was trying to push up. For some reason, I felt like I was intruding, and I looked the other way, almost as a way of giving Larry some privacy. A minute or seconds later, I turned my head to glance over at him, and I saw this huge flash of light. I was a bit startled by it. I immediately asked his daughter, who had been watching TV in the room, if she had just seen that flash of light. She indicated she had not. But I was sure of what I saw. I got closer to Larry and looked at him. I tried to sense him. Nothing. He was still breathing slowly, but I could not sense any brain activity. He was gone to me.

I explained to the daughter what I felt just happened and I told her I felt he was gone. We kind of had a moment and I just stared at him. We had a nurse come in and check on him, and he was still breathing, but he was totally cold and barely had a pulse. I stayed another hour, and then I really felt I should leave. I really felt Larry was gone. I felt Larry no longer needed me because he was actually gone. I felt him push off, I saw his soul leave his body, and I sensed his soul meet the light in spirit world or the Universe Energy Collective, or in religious terms, Heaven. It felt complete to me. I asked his daughter if she needed me to stay. She indicated it was okay if I left. I said my

54

goodbyes to her and left. Shortly after I returned home, his daughter texted me saying "He stopped breathing and it's over. Thank you, Brian."

I want to acknowledge Larry in this book and thank him for allowing me the gift of witnessing his transition. Larry always liked being the star of the show and I think he would approve of us all learning from his experience of transitioning from human life back into Soul Energy within the Universe.

Let's talk about some of the points of the process I witnessed with Larry.

How did I know which day Larry would die? I read his energy. As a psychic, I received the message and impression of "Thanksgiving Day." You can call it a guess or a hunch, or a good psychic read. But to me, it is about reading energy and listening for psychic messages.

Did Larry have some choice in which day he passed? Yes. Certainly, a person can choose to "fight on," or "let go." Larry was dying for sure, so there was a limit to how long he could wait. But as long as I showed up in a reasonable amount of time, Larry was able to "hold off" his transition by choice. It is a matter of remaining engaged and fighting, as opposed to "letting go," and "pushing off" when the opportunity arises. Life is full of stories about how elderly couples both die within a short period of each other. The human mind, along with the Soul can conspire to have an influence on such things.

Who was Larry talking to in his mind shortly before he passed? I believe our Souls can communicate with other Soul Energies. I discussed previously how during death, the brain/mind ends up yielding control to the Soul as the mind shuts down and dies. Therefore, the Soul is in control of the brain and can communicate with other Soul Energies in such a way that the person can for the first time "see" and "hear" these communications which previously could only be "felt." Larry was communicating with Soul Energies that he felt very close to, and perhaps were going to comfort him or even "accompany" his Soul Energy back to the Universe

they are able to receive your messages. They would have to be somewhat psychic and open to recognizing, tuning into, and listening, to the frequencies of your energy.

Can you be in more than one place at the same time after you die? Yes, you can. This is because of Soul Splitting. You can be in as many places at one time as you have particles of Energy. If I had a million particles of Energy, I could be in a million places at once by splitting up all my energy particles to go separate places.

Being dead sounds amazing and wonderful, so why would I want to be alive? Read the chapter later in the book called "The Human Experience." Despite all the limitations of being human, there are amazing experiences and sensations that can only be enjoyed as a human. I could also say being a collection of Energy particles also has its limitations. That is why the Universe offers diversity and balance.

I mentioned at the beginning of the chapter that the second reason Death was scary to people was because of the "unknown." I am hoping I have addressed that part of the equation by making the death process less unknown.

CHAPTER 9

The Hunter Equation

I just spent a lot of time talking about Death. I think now it's time we talk about how we live. Much of the remainder of the book will be discussing the various philosophies by which humans live and exist.

Humans like to think they live in their own bubble they entirely control. There are many philosophies and books written on how a human can get anything they want by thinking or doing certain things. All humans by nature want to have total control over their environment, their circumstances, and their future. Humans will buy anything and do anything, which they believe will give them this magical power to control their fate and get anything they want.

The "Law of Attraction" is a perfect example of a philosophy millions of people have bought into thinking they can bring positive outcomes into their life simply by thinking positive thoughts and bring negative outcomes into their lives if they think negative thoughts. Can a person really control their outcome by what they think? Is it that simple? Have you tried it?

Or is there more? Is the Universe more complicated than that? Is life more complicated than that? Like many people, I spent plenty of time contemplating all of these questions.

When I was a teenager, I read many motivational books based on the power of positive thinking. I was very interested in becoming wealthy and successful back then. I was young, full of energy, and highly motivated to do anything I needed to do in order to achieve "success." The books I read all preached how I must think positive 100% of the time and "fake it until I make it," meaning "pretend" I am successful even if I am not. Or in other words, live a fantasy in my mind that I already have what I want, even though I do not have it yet.

I did find these books to be motivating. They made me feel better. They made me feel like I was already successful and already made it to the Promised Land. They made me feel like I would achieve all my dreams. I enjoyed them a great deal. But did the books make me successful? Did I achieve all my goals and dreams from thinking positive thoughts and having wonderful fantasies in my mind?

No. I ended up achieving a certain level of success mostly from keeping my goals in mind, staying focused, working very hard and persistently for many years, and by leveraging my contacts I met along the way. I also took full advantage of opportunities offered and found. Finally, I must admit I also got lucky in some things.

Honestly, it was not easy. By the time I had achieved anything, I had long stopped reading all those motivational and positive thinking books. I was exhausted and too busy juggling all the aspects I mentioned above. No one thing worked. Even just working hard was useless. A person can work hard for years and accomplish little. A person can think of their goals every minute of every day and still accomplish little. A person can try to use their contacts and coat tails to succeed, but without some substance behind them, they will not get far. Then there is always the luck factor that brings both good luck and bad luck. We have all heard of and seen people get lucky in business. It happens.

So how does a person succeed? How should a person live? How should a person think? How can a person survive in this world of endless complications and problems? Why can't life just be easy, where I think what I want, and I get what I think?

Well first of all, humans have to get off their high horse and get over themselves. Humans are but small creatures within the Universe. We do not control the Universe. The Universe controls us. More accurately, we as humans are all part of the Universe. We are one cog in the machinery.

I have talked about how I see the Universe in structure and in operation. I have shown how humans have a cycle within the Universe and are a part of the Universe. It seems to me that the most logical approach to success is for humans to better fully understand their place in the Universe and how they can best interact with the Universe.

I am trying to say in a very polite way that humans do not exist in a bubble. Humans exist as part of the Universe, and with the Universe. Humans do not control everything, however much we wish that were true. Humans do not control the world just by using their wishful thoughts. Sorry to break that to you. Grab a tissue if you need one. Instead, humans play a part in the Universe and are free to react with the Universe and everything within it.

Do not worry, I am not here to simply debunk everything you thought you knew and leave you more confused and discouraged than when you started. As a reminder, ever since I experienced my traumatic paranormal events that changed me forever, resulting in accelerated psychic abilities, I have had whispers from the Universe coming into my head for years. I am that guy at the grocery store buying fruit, and all of a sudden have an epiphany about how the world works. I have equations, ideas, and concepts constantly streaming through my head out of nowhere. I literally think that way and live that way most every day. But some epiphanies are bigger or more significant than others.

One day, I had one such epiphany while out for my run. At the time, my regular run included running up to the top of this holy mountain. You might not consider it a holy mountain. It is not on the map of the most holy places, or on any map for any reason actually. But it is a place where I have done lots of energy work. It is a magical place to me. I have felt the energies up there and tuned into them. I have been inspired up there. I have performed healings and other miracles for people up there. It is holy to me.

But anyway, one day I was running up the mountain and I had one of my epiphanies. I had been wondering for a very long time "how the Universe works," in connection to how humans can successfully engage with it. I had long become cynical of the positive thinking books and the Law of Attraction. I was looking for the real answer. I was not looking for something that sounded clever and easy. I was looking for the Truth. What is the True Truth on how things work? Please tell me the Truth even if it is not good or easy. I asked this of the Universe.

Finally, I received an answer on this one day. I was shown a written equation by some higher power of the Universe. It was like a whisper in my ear, along with a visual in my mind. Therefore, I cannot claim that I sat down writing equations and one day I figured it out myself. I was given this by a higher power, so I am not going to claim full credit.

Keeping that in mind, please forgive any perception of arrogance as I introduce to you what I call "The Hunter Equation."

The Hunter Equation states that a person's Future Outcome is determined by four elements: Intent, Actions, External Forces, and Random Luck.

The Hunter Equation:

Future Outcome =
(Intent + Actions + External Forces + Random Luck)

Let's discuss each of the elements.

Intent: Intent refers to your intentions, attitude, goals, and thoughts. The Law of Attraction people should at least be happy with this element. Clearly, your future does indeed depend somewhat on what you intend to do. This, therefore, could be considered a Free Will element. You must clearly decide what you want to do and put some thought to it. Some persistent positive thought does not hurt. But I do not even think it has to be positive thought, as long as it is a strong intended thought which you remain fixated on while you work to achieve it.

Actions: Actions refer to actions you actually take toward a certain goal, outcome, or future. Just thinking something does not make it happen. A person must take actions to physically make it happen. Of course, actions can also be bad things. If a person performs bad actions, then that will contribute to a bad result and bad future outcome. Actions are very powerful. Actions can very quickly result in very bad things. Actions can also result in very good things. I have observed that bad actions seem to have more immediate results than good actions though. Again, life is not easy. So, Actions are critical. Actions are obviously considered another Free Will element.

External Forces: External Forces refer to all those pesky environmental or circumstantial limitations, people, or events that are outside our control that affect our outcomes. Regardless of our Intent and Actions, External Forces will always be there to provide obstacles or total blockages. External Forces tend to limit us and cause us problems. However, External Forces can also help us. For example, a good External Force might be a mentor or powerful person who actively helps us achieve something that we could not have achieved on our own. Therefore, a clever person will find a way to use External Forces as positive leverage in helping themselves. External Forces are often limitations and road blocks, but they are also short cuts and opportunities. The key point on External Forces is they are outside our control. External Forces are things we mostly have to react to, rather than plan and control.

Random Luck: Random Luck is that element I introduced earlier into our discussions of the Universe that make life interesting and scary. Random Luck acknowledges that some things are truly outside our control. If I am trying to get a certain job, it truly does depend on what day and what mood the boss is in when he reads my resume. I cannot control what day, what hour, or what mood the boss is in when he happens to pick up my resume. It depends on total dumb luck. It's random. Sometimes people, companies, or the Universe, simply has to flip a coin to see which person gets something. and which person does not. It's random and luck. It has nothing to do with what you deserve, what you think, what you did, or your circumstances. It just depends on random luck. Some days it goes in your favor, and other days it does not. Anyone who has won a huge prize in a lottery understands random luck. They know they did not earn it, or even deserve it, or even do much to get it. All they know is they got lucky and were randomly chosen. Hopefully they are at least grateful. So fortunately, or unfortunately, random luck will partly influence your outcomes and your future.

A melting pot of these four elements is what I think determines a human's outcome and future.

Does one element have more power than others do? I do not know. I wish I had a definitive clever answer for you. But I would be lying if I said with authority that I knew. Again, I can only profess to know what I have been shown by the higher powers of the Universe. I was shown the equation. I was not told if the elements had different weights. Personally, I live my life assuming they all have equal weight. Realistically, for the most part, they do I would say. I say this because each element is so critically important, that one element can easily throw off all the others. So, for that reason, I would personally theorize that all elements have equal importance.

Not to make this more complicated, but it is slightly more complicated. I was shown there is another layer to the equation. The equation repeats itself under each element. This means that under each element, all four elements exist again. Perhaps it is easier I show you this way below:

Future Outcome =
(Intent + Actions + External Forces + Random Luck)

Intent	Intent	Intent	Intent
Actions	Actions	Actions	Actions
Ext Forces	Ext Forces	Ext Forces	Ext Forces
Luck	Luck	Luck	Luck

So, what I am saying above is that under each element, also lies all four elements again. Let's take Intent for example. The element of Intent includes Intent, Actions, External Forces, and Random Luck. To drill down on this example, let us say for a moment that you are creating an intent of achieving a certain goal. While you are creating that Intent, you need to consider the literal Intent, obviously. But you also need to consider the actual Action of creating the Intent, plus any External Forces affecting your Intent, plus the fact that Random Luck will play a role in your Intent.

Hopefully that is not too confusing, but now let us use the element of Action as an example to hopefully provide more clarity. Let's say you are deciding on Actions to attain your desired Future Outcome. While you are considering what "Action" you are going to take, you need to consider the Intent of each Action. This adds another layer of validation that the Intent of your Action make that Action correct. You also need to clearly define the Actions required behind the general Action you are taking. Then you need to consider all possible External Forces that might affect your Action. Finally, consider what part Random Luck may play in your Action.

In short, the four basic elements determine your Future Outcome. Additionally, when constructing your plan for each element, you must also consider all four elements for each.

Nobody said the Universe was easy. Nobody said life was simple. Nobody promised you a rose garden. But if you take the time to truly understand The Hunter Equation, and truly understand each of the four elements, and how to apply each element, you are very close to the Truth of how your Future Outcome is determined. Once you understand and accept this, it becomes easier to use this equation and its elements to your greatest advantage. Do not worry, I will talk more later in the book about how to apply the equation to your life for maximum desired results until it is crystal clear.

CHAPTER 10

Destiny Vs. Free Will

Spiritualists argue over the question of Destiny vs. Free Will. Do we sign some contract before birth to live out some predetermined destiny? Or are we born to do with our life whatever we decide? Do we have total control over our future? Or is our fate sealed and there is very little wiggle room? What is Destiny? First, let me preface by saying I may use the words Destiny and Fate interchangeably. The two words might have different connotations to some people, but for the most part, they can be used interchangeably. Wikipedia defines Destiny as: Destiny, sometimes referred to as fate (from Latin *fatum* – destiny), is a predetermined course of events. It may be conceived as a predetermined future, whether in general or of an individual.

Destiny means we have a set future that we cannot change. Some Spiritualists say we agree to a life contract or soul contract, before we enter a new life, and we agree in advance to everything that is about to happen to us. These Spiritualists claim that if I step in front of a bus at age 10, it is because I chose to do that in advance of being born, and it was meant to be.

Spiritualists defend and support their views by the fact that many people define the Akashic records as including everything that will happen in the future. Meaning, the Akashic records not only contain everything that has happened, thought, and learned, but also everything that *will* happen. This would infer that the future is already decided, and is already written, and just needs to be played out. Our culture is full of references to the fact that many believe our futures are about Destiny.

In how many films and books have you seen or heard the phrase "It's your Destiny." The first thought in my mind is Darth Vader standing over Luke Skywalker proclaiming, "It's your destiny." Of course, he is referring to how Luke is supposed to join the Dark Side, overthrow the Emperor, and lead the Dark Side.

But *was* it Luke's destiny to do this? Or were these just the words of an evil narcissistic father trying to brainwash Skywalker? If I tell you "It's your destiny," perhaps you will believe me, and do what I say because you are convinced you have no choice, since your fate is sealed? I do not know about you, but Destiny is starting to feel more like a "tool" someone would use to manipulate another person into doing something.

It is hard to imagine that an unpredictable organic living being could have a set Destiny. That this freethinking being could have a set future that cannot be changed no matter what they do. Does that make sense to you? If this were true, then why would we bother doing anything? If our fate is sealed and future destiny laid out, why would I even bother going to work? If my destiny is sealed, then I can just lay on the couch and eat cookies instead of working.

Plus, I have already talked about how there is a random factor to the Universe. If this is so, then a pre-determined future would be impossible. You cannot have a set future if random things are happening as you go. This is the reason I disagree with the official definition of the Akashic records. You will recall the Wikipedia definition of Akashic records to be: The Akashic records are a compendium of all human events, thoughts, words, emotions, and intent ever to have occurred in the past, present, or future. It is the part of the definition indicating that the Akashic records contain records of what happens in the future, that is a problem for me. Clearly, since the future is not fixed, it is impossible for there to be records of everything happening in the future. So, I am suggesting a revision to the Akashic records definition to remove any reference to Akashic records knowing everything that will happen in the future.

Additionally, why would a Soul want to live, grow, evolve, and experience things, if it already knew the end of the story? What would be the point of the Universe entirely if the end is already written? Why would the Universe be expanding if the future is determined already? Also, how can a future already be set in stone while the Universe is ever expanding?

There are too many variables and constantly moving parts for there to be a set ending, or pre-determined future. It is logically impossible. Physics and Mathematics would say a set ending is impossible with constantly changing variables and exponentials in effect. It also goes against common sense.

So, what about Free Will? Wikipedia defines Free Will as: Free will is the ability to choose between different possible courses of action unimpeded. Basically, it is pretty clear that Free Will means a human has complete full control over all events. Notice the word "unimpeded" is used. That definitely means no limits, exceptions, or caveats.

Therefore, under the Free Will theory of life, Spiritualists say that a person has full control over their lives. A person can decide what they think and what they do. A person can create any outcome or any future by actively choosing it. Now we are getting into "Law of Attraction" territory.

A Free Will Spiritualist would say you first decide what you want your future outcome to be. They would say you have full control over your future, so tell me exactly what you want your future to be. Then, you would set that intention clearly in your mind. You would only think positive thoughts focused on that intention. Then you would take actions that support that intention. They claim if you did all this correctly, you would eventually get your desired outcome. Or, in other words, your future would turn out exactly as you intended it. Or, in other words, you just had full control over your future and created your own future from entirely your own Free Will.

The only problem with this inspiring motivational theory is that reality and real life gets in the way. Darn it, don't you hate it when that happens?

What happens is things do not turn out exactly as you had planned or hoped. The narcissistic Spiritualist that guaranteed this technique would work, then blames its failure all on you. They will say that your intention must have been unclear, or weak, or not specific enough. They might say your focus must have been too weak. They might say that a negative thought must have slipped into your mind at some point, thus destroying your mojo. They will have 100 reasons to say it is all your fault, and that the Law of Attraction and Free Will method is still absolutely true and correct.

Are we really going to buy into that? It sounds like snake oil to me. Do not tell me a certain method is God's truth, when in fact it is impossible to follow, and when I fail, you are just going to blame it all on me, and still declare victory for yourself.

The truth is that nobody has total Free Will. You already know this. Anyone over the age of 30 knows this. Anyone who has fought like hell for something and done everything possible to get it, yet failed to get it, knows what I am talking about. Sometimes things just don't work out despite our best efforts. If Free Will were as easy as deciding what we want, thinking positive thoughts, and taking action to get it, then we would all be doing it and succeeding, yes? I mean come on. Most of us reading this have busted our behinds for things and failed. One important lesson we teach our kids is that we do not always get what we want. That does not mean we should not try. It just means failure and disappointment is part of life. Accept it, brush yourself off, try again, and never give up. Life is not easy. Why is life not easy? Life is not easy because none of us have absolute Free Will.

We all have limitations. We are limited by being human, first of all. Some of us have academic limitations. I suck at math, so it is not likely I could use Free Will to become a rocket scientist. Others are blind, so it's not likely their free will would allow them to become a brain surgeon. We all have physical and mental limitations as a result of being human.

We also have environmental limitations. We have circumstances that limit us. It would be hard to use my Free Will to become President of the United States when I am a poor child born in Africa. We all have these environmental and circumstantial limitations that prevent Free Will. No amount of intent, positive thinking, or actions are going to eliminate all human, environmental, and circumstantial limitations. Limitations are part of the Human Experience. Due to limitations, Free Will is impossible. So Free Will is not happening. Sorry.

To sum up, we live in a world where philosophers and Spiritualists argue whether we live a life of Destiny or a life of Free Will. In reality, both Destiny and Free Will are impossible and debunked. I am going to go under the assumption I have done a fair job of invalidating both Destiny and Free Will. You are free to disagree, but under the circumstances, and my supporting evidential arguments, I have to move on assuming Destiny and Free Will is not an option. Neither of them is a Universal Truth.

So, what now? Should I just leave you hanging here? Should I leave you with more questions than you had before you started reading this chapter? Of course not! From the previous chapter, you probably already know where I am heading with all this. Neither Destiny nor Free Will is the answer, because neither of those are based on all four elements of the Hunter Equation.

As a reminder, here is the Hunter Equation again:

The Hunter Equation

Future Outcome =
(Intent + Actions + External Forces + Random Luck)

You cannot just throw your hands up and leave everything to Destiny. Nor can you have the arrogance to think you decide and control your fate. Your future actually depends upon the four elements of the Hunter Equation, which are your Intent, Actions, External Forces and Random Luck.

Does this mean there is no such thing as Destiny or Free Will? No, actually both still exist. However, they exist with less importance, as only a part of the whole. Destiny can certainly be confused with what will happen to you through Random Luck. Free Will certainly has plenty to do with the Intent of what you decide, and the Actions you take. So, elements exist, but they are not the entire picture, and therefore not complete Universal Truths or Laws.

Your future outcome relies on The Hunter Equation.

CHAPTER 11

Synchronicities & Soul Mates

So, what is a Synchronicity? Wikipedia defines a Synchronicity as: a concept, first introduced by analytical psychologist Carl Jung, which holds that events are "meaningful coincidences" if they occur with no causal relationship yet seem to be meaningfully related. During his career, Jung furnished several different definitions of it. Jung defined synchronicity as an "acausal connecting (togetherness) principle," "meaningful coincidence," and "acausal parallelism."

So, a Synchronicity is a coincidence yes, but it actually rises to a higher level than just a coincidence. A Synchronicity is a coincidence with some accompanying evidence, justification, or contains multiple layers of coincidence. For example, it would be a coincidence if you and I showed up at the same place at the same time. But if we showed up at the same place at the same time to buy the same thing, *that* would

73

be a Synchronicity because that has multiple layers of coincidence.

In this chapter I ask for your leniency, as I am including several different topics that may not simply be Synchronicities, but I wanted to include them in this chapter because I feel they are either related to coincidence or Synchronicities, or they should be, or they are mislabeled as a coincidence or Synchronicity.

Also, let's have some leniency in using the words Synchronicity and Coincidence interchangeably, but we all know now that a Synchronicity rises to a higher level than a single Coincidence.

So, how do coincidences and synchronicities happen in the Universe and in our lives? Who makes them happen? Does God and the Universe make them happen? Do you make them happen? Are they part of some pre-ordained design? Or are they manifestations we directly cause? Oh, what a mess of questions. What a tangled knot we have here. We will now go about untying this knot by picking at one section of it at a time.

The first step in doing this, is invoking The Hunter Equation. We do this because Synchronicities are basically a question of Destiny or Free Will because we are asking who creates them. Does God and the Universe create them (Destiny?) Or do we ourselves create them (Free Will)? Answering the question of who creates them might lead us to figuring out how they are created and why.

In the previous chapter, we already determined there are no valid laws of Destiny or Free Will. Both of them only exist partially in some circumstances. So rather than such matters being either Destiny or Free Will, the Hunter Equation states that these matters of Synchronicities are a product of (Intent + Actions + External Forces + Random Luck).

Using the above equation, how does a coincidence or Synchronicity form? Well, indeed they partly occur from our Intents, our desires, dreams, goals, wants, needs. But they are also a result of certain Actions, such as what jobs we take, places we go, where we live, who we choose to communicate with, and so on. External Forces also play a role, in that we may be forced into a Synchronicity by the fact of where we are working or living or things we are obligated to do. Finally, coincidences and Synchronicities can also be partly a result of just being in the right place at the right time as dumb luck would have it.

Thus, Synchronicities exist from a varying combination of the above four elements of the Hunter Equation. So, anyone who says Synchronicities are only from God, or only you are manifesting them, can agree or disagree, but you will know for sure I completely disagree with those statements. If only life was that simple, right? Life is never simple. Life is difficult and complex. I will never agree with anyone who gives such simple explanations and solutions, and then when they don't work out, there is always an excuse.

In a Universe that is always growing, expanding, and changing, you must expect that all elements of the Universe, such as Synchronicities, will also be moving and bending. The Universe is a tricky thing. So are Synchronicities.

Let's now examine some individual topics that are related to Synchronicities. Let me preface by saying my definitions or terms may be different from definitions you have seen in other books or from other Spiritual leaders. I march to my own drumbeat and believe in the information I am given from the higher powers of the Universe. I am not afraid to disagree with other spiritual professionals.

SOUL MATES

I define a Soul Mate as another person who you feel deeply connected with on a soul level. What does "on a soul level" mean? It means you do not just find them sexy, or interesting, or kind, or intellectually stimulating. It is more. You feel as if you already know them or have known them in a past life. You feel an unusual comfort and familiarity with them. There may be a deep trust that is immediate without them having earned it. It feels as if maybe you could be related to them, but you are not.

The test is really about how you feel vs. what you know. Meaning, if you do not know them or do not know much about them, yet you feel totally safe, comfortable, familiar, trusting, and perhaps have strong favorable feelings for them, then they could be a Soul Mate.

The other test is asking if you feel as if you knew them in a different lifetime or dimension. I say this because I believe Soul Mates are often people with Soul Energy that you have encountered before in the Universe. I have two theories on this. The first is that your Soul Energy has indeed had significant substantial contact with their Soul Energy somewhere in the Universe before. Therefore, naturally, you would feel as if you already know them, because you do. The two humans may not have ever met, but your Souls may have already met.

My other theory is that a Soul Mate is another person who has at least one particle of your Soul Energy in them. Remember, due to Soul Splitting, it is possible you have a piece or two of your Universe Soul Energy in other places or other people at the same time. So perhaps when we meet another person who happens to have a piece of our own Soul Energy within them, we totally freak, our ears perk up, and we are totally drawn to this other person because they are indeed part of us. This would explain why we sometimes feel as if we are joined to, or a part of, another person we consider to be a Soul Mate. We feel as one with a Soul Mate. Maybe it is because we share the same Soul Energy with them.

However, another possibility is that different Soul Energies are more highly compatible with certain Soul Energies. Think of it as blood types, except if there were millions of blood types. When our Soul Energy bumps into another person with the same "type," there is an immediate strong connection, as if the Souls of a feather want to flock together.

It is important to mention that a Soul Mate can be anyone. It is not automatically a lover. In fact, it is often not a lover. A Soul Mate can be a friend, teacher, mentor, family member, or yes, a lover or spouse. My point is that a Soul Mate is not about romance. A Soul Mate is purely about the deep soul connection.

76

A person can have more than one Soul Mate. As I described my theories above, finding a Soul Mate involves the Synchronicity of bumping into another person with your same Soul Energy, or Soul Energy you have met before, or Soul Energy of your exact ideal match type. Therefore, a person may meet many Soul Mates in their life, or not meet any. There is some random luck involved in Synchronicities as I have explained.

So many spiritualists would say this next topic belongs in the chapter about Karma. But I will explain why it is very closely related to Soul Mates.

SOUL CONTRACTS

Soul Contracts are thought to be agreements you enter into before you are born into this lifetime. They are agreements to interact, help, or have some significant impact on other person in this lifetime. Or, vice versa, agreements or obligations others have to you.

Soul Contracts are usually one-way agreements. Here is how to recognize them. First, you may have an overwhelming compulsion or sense of responsibility to help a specific person, even if you have no logical obligation to them. You may not even know them that well. Conversely, you may have another person who seems to be going out of their way to help you, even though you never asked, can never repay them, or don't even particularly want their help.

Soul Contracts often feel involuntary, yet at the same time, there is such a strong compulsion to fulfil them. Soul Contracts could also be described as "Soul Ties." It is a strong compulsion or obligation you feel deep inside on a Soul Level, even though logically there is no obligation.

What Soul Contracts have in common with Soul Mates, is that there is an unexplainable tie between two souls to interact. How Soul Contracts differ from Soul Mates, is that a Soul Mate is permanent, not feel the same way.

Can someone be my Soul Mate, but I am not their Soul Mate? Yes. The definition of a Soul Mate is more one sided than the definition of a Twin Flame. Therefore, as long as your Soul Energy recognizes their Soul Energy as a match, then it is a Soul Mate match for you. It could be the other person's Soul Energy does not recognize your Soul Energy as a match because of a difference in perception. For example, let us say your Souls met in a different lifetime. Your Soul became very attached to them and liked them. But perhaps their Soul Energy never really noticed your Soul Energy and did not develop the same feelings. Well then, in the next current life you are in now, their Soul Energy might not really recognize yours, or may not have the same reaction because the prior connection was not as strong for them as it was for you.

What if I find a Soul Mate or Twin Flame, but lose them? Meaning, we never come together in a solid way, or we break up, or we are separated and lose our connection? Well, the problem with Synchronicities is that sometimes things do not fall into sync, and a synchronicity is not formed or completed. Part of the pesky Hunter Equation is that External Forces or Random Luck can screw it all up for us. The Universe is a tricky place. But you can fight back. Use the Hunter Equation to fight back and find them or regain them. Use the four elements to your full advantage to find them, win them over, and get them. Some things are worth searching for, waiting for, and fighting for. Your Intent needs to make those decisions so that your Actions know what to do next.

Some of you might say, "What if I am starting to not like this Hunter Equation stuff, and other Spiritualists have told me that Law of Attraction can get me anything I want, and it's easier." Well, okay, let us talk about that.

LAW OF ATTRACTION

What is The Law of Attraction? Don't quote me. Different people define it slightly different ways. Related to "The Secret," it is a philosophy that says we bring into our life what we think. So, if we have negative thoughts or specific fears, we will end up creating a self-fulfilling prophecy, and those negative things will then come into our lives. Conversely, if we only think positive thoughts with a clear intention of something we want in our lives, then that thing we want will somehow come into our lives.

The Law of Attraction is basically saying we can manifest anything we want based on a clear intention and positive thinking focused on our desired goal. Yeah, there is more to it, but if we are all honest with ourselves, I have summed it up well.

Here is why it does not work. Well first, let me apologize for completely rejecting it out of hand without any fanfare, since millions of people live by it. But firstly, the entire principle is flawed because it violates the Hunter Equation.

Law of Attraction assumes that the Destiny and Free Will are totally valid and are completely determined by Intention and Actions. It thinks the other two elements of External Forces and Random Luck, either do not exist, or are not a factor. It is an inconvenient truth that External Forces and Random Luck *do* exist and *are* a factor.

Sometimes it does not matter how strong of an intention we have, how many actions we take, or how hard we work, sometimes things do not work out the way we desire. Fact of life.

We all know this. Yet, Law of Attraction somehow gives us false hope that we missed something and maybe there is a magic trick that can make the realities of life just go away. The inconvenient reality of life is that External Forces and Random Luck exist. Those two elements alone, are enough to destroy any dreams you have simply based on having a positive attitude, intentions, and focus on what you want to attract.

My gosh, I'm such a bummer and bubble buster, aren't I?

While Law of Attraction is totally false to me, and just a great way to dangle carrots in front of people and make money on their hopes for an easy magic trick, I do think Law of Attraction has some benefit. The benefit is that Law of Attraction has taught people the importance of Intention. Intention, or Intent, is one of my four elements in my equation, and thus very important. If a person has learned how to very effectively create a strong Intent through studying Law of Attraction, then they have helped themselves a great deal. Despair not, all you Law of Attraction people, as you have learned very important lessons and skills when it comes to the element of Intent.

Honestly, I think I have provided enough support to debunk Law of Attraction. But let me add another angle. This is the angle I use often as it makes me very angry about Law of Attraction.

I get very angry when Law of Attraction gurus blame people for their unfortunate outcomes. If you end up in a very poor situation, a Law of Attraction expert would tell you that *you* created your bad situation yourself by your own thoughts and intent. This is narcissistic at its basic level. This assumes that all bad things that happen to us are our fault due to our thoughts and intentions.

I raise the question of what about little kids that get cancer? Did the little child have a negative thought and bring cancer into their lives? Is it their fault they have cancer? I think not. What about the soldier who gets his leg blown off by an IED? Did that soldier make that happen to himself by his intentions and negative thoughts? Seriously? Personally, I get offended by such assertions.

However, usually what will happen is that a Law of Attraction person will ignore all the negative things and just focus on the positive outcomes. They will claim victory on the job landed using Law of Attraction, but they will not claim ownership over the kid who got cancer. I'm sorry, but you cannot have it both ways. A Universal principle is either Universal or it is not. It is either a law or it is not. You cannot ignore one side of an equation. We all must be honest with ourselves and look at Truth, even if it is an inconvenient Truth. With all that above said, I could still put a positive spin on the Law of Attraction to give some of you some comfort and solace. Let us just say that the Hunter Equation *builds upon* the Law of Attraction, by simply adding the elements of External Forces, and Random Luck to the equation. So, you can still use the Law of Attraction, so long as you add those last two elements of the Hunter Equation.

How is that? Now let us dry those crocodile tears. It will be okay.

This chapter was kind of brutal because the truth can be brutal. Sometimes Synchronicities can be a wonderful gift. Other times, we miss them, and they do not happen even though we so desperately want them and need them. The bottom line is that Synchronicities do exist, but we do not control them, nor do they appear upon our demand.

Synchronicities, like everything else, are driven by the Hunter Equation and its four elements.

CHAPTER 12

Karma

In Wikipedia, Karma is defined as: it refers to the spiritual principle of cause and effect where intent and actions of an individual (cause) influence the future of that individual (effect). Good intent and good deeds contribute to good karma and future happiness, while bad intent and bad deeds contribute to bad karma and future suffering. Most people would say Karma is reward for good behavior, and punishment for bad behavior. Meaning, if I do bad things, Karma will punish me, but if I do good things, Karma will reward me.

So, what does that mean? Is there some kind of fairy, monster, ghost, God, or troll, that watches us, and if they see us do something bad, they will sneak up on us and punish us? Or is the Karma Master God? Or is Karma some kind of Energy that judges us?

People seem afraid of Karma, in the sense they really believe it exists. Some people will actually say that they do nice things for others, so they can have good Karma. Other people will literally threaten their enemies with bad Karma. So, people do seem convinced Karma is real and exists.

I think we must narrow things down a bit so that we can truly figure out what Karma is, and if it is real. Firstly, can we all agree there is no Karma fairy, monster, ghost, or troll? If we can agree to that, then that means Karma must be from God (the Universe) or some kind of Energy (the Universe). Based on what I just said, we seem to have a winner. Karma is from the Universe (God). So how is it that the Universe is judging our actions and deciding if we deserve good Karma or bad Karma? Or perhaps, what we really need to do is look in the mirror. *We* are part of the Universe, and *We* are doing the good and bad actions. Plus, we seem to be judging the actions as good or bad, so *we* are also the judges. Now it is starting to sound like, *we* the humans, are the Karma fairies handing out good or bad Karma. Could it be that we have been afraid of our own shadows all this time, and that we humans are the ones responsible for Karma? I think we are getting somewhere now, are we not?

But let us take another closer look at the definition of Karma. Karma is a "spiritual principle of cause and effect where **intent** and **actions** of an individual (cause) influence the **future** of that individual (effect). Good intent and good deeds contribute to good karma and future happiness, while bad intent and bad deeds contribute to bad karma and future suffering."

If I am not mistaken, I spot two elements from the Hunter Equation there, plus the other half of the equation, being "future." Again,

Hunter Equation:
Future Outcome = (Intent + Actions + External Forces + Random Luck).

have seen what he did and perhaps look for a new job out of fear they will be unfairly fired as well. That would result in hitting the mean boss with some units of negative energy, but certainly not the full 100 units.

As stated above, it is hard to say if the boss will receive bad Karma or not. It depends on all the elements of the Hunter Equation. But let's make this more interesting for a moment. Pretend the boss wakes up in the middle of the night and realizes he was wrong and now he feels bad. Perhaps he fears bad Karma coming his way. How can the boss right this wrong and relieve his selfish fear of bad Karma coming his way?

I have seen humans approach this a few different ways. One way, is they go to the person they have wronged and apologize, hoping it all goes away. Would an apology to the employee fix the situation? No. The problem is that 100 units of negative energy was released, and it was absorbed by many different people. The boss would have to apologize to the spouse, children, parents, car finance company, landlord, and so on. Even then, simple words might not be enough to offset 100 units of negative energy.

I have seen other humans simply go to their place of worship and ask God for forgiveness. If they can leave their place of worship feeling they were forgiven, or their religious leader says they are forgiven, does that mean all is okay again? Well, were the 100 units of negative energy absorbed by all those people offset by this visit to the place of worship and talking to God? Umm, no.

Really, the only way to fix a situation like this is if the boss finds a way to offset the 100 units of negative energy. To do this, he might need to release 100 units or more of positive energy. In other words, some "Action" will be required to release positive energy to offset the negative energy. OR, the boss could go to those people damaged and offset the negative energy by taking it back upon himself. He could do this by paying the late rent due, paying the late car payment, making the children happy instead of scared, and so on and so forth. It is a lot of work to fix the 100 units of damage the boss did. But it could be done.

So, the above scenario is an example of how people see Karma, and how it can float around and boomerang back, or not. More importantly, it is an example of how bad deeds, or bad karma, cannot be fixed by simple thoughts or gestures. There must be real Actions, to match unit for unit, in order to fix it.

In summary, Karma on its surface has some validity. But Karma as a literal definition, principle, and law, is flawed, and cannot function as it is expected. Therefore, Karma is only real if you do not take it too literally.

Additionally, any Karmic rewards or punishments are clearly being dealt by other humans, including yourself.

It is an important footnote to point out that some religious beliefs, such as Buddhism, consider Karma an important part of their belief system. Why is this? I believe, like most religious beliefs, certain principles are used in order to create a moral boundary of behavior. If a belief system says you need to treat others well in order to have good Karma, well who am I to protest? I am in favor of good Intents and good Actions.

If a religious belief wants to promote Karma as important, so that people feel they must treat others well, then I think it is wonderful. I have nothing against it. My goal in this book is not to throw shade on everyone's religious beliefs, or otherwise. My goal is to illuminate Truth as it has been shown to me. Usually the Truth is in the middle. Karma is an excellent example of a principle that is kind of true, but not to the full extent some say.

I would urge everyone, and all religious beliefs, to continue considering Karma as a valuable moral compass, because it is.

CHAPTER 13

How Are Psychics Psychic?

There is much legend and misperception surrounding psychic abilities. Some psychics might say they are super powers given to the worthy and the lucky. Some people think psychic abilities are some kind of clever magic trickery. Some religions view psychics as evil scary people using powers that only God is allowed to use.

People always fear what they do not understand, and anything not fully understood is usually surrounded by conspiracy and suspicion. Since some things are not yet scientifically proven, it allows people to make up anything and say anything they want about it. People once thought the world was flat.

I could probably write an entire book on psychic abilities and being psychic. So, what I am going to do here, just like most topics in this book, is that I am going to give you the cliff notes version, so you can better understand what psychic abilities are, and how some people are psychic.

Psychic abilities are not magic. They are also not super powers. Psychic abilities are more similar to a dog whistle. They are something that intrinsically exist already, but only some people can "hear them." Just like how a dog whistle is there, but only dogs can hear it. Similar to a dog whistle, psychic abilities are there for everyone, but not everyone can engage them.

Again, since I am not writing an entire book on this, and just doing one chapter, I am going to simplify things. Therefore, I ask my psychic friends to please refrain from sending me hate mail on how I over simplified things and did not cover all the various complexities.

Being a psychic is the same as being a radio. A psychic has the ability to tune into many various frequencies. The Universe is the radio stations. The Universe sends out energy in the form of pulse waves. These energy waves carry specific frequencies. A psychic is able to detect these incoming energy waves and tune into the specific frequencies, to "hear" the information.

First, let us talk more about these energy waves from the Universe. They are not necessarily powerful fast-moving waves sent from far away galaxies. Many of these waves are emitted very short distances, or even somewhat static.

Let me give you an example of a more static energy wave. If someone was brutally murdered in a room, there would have been a huge discharge of energy from the event. That energy discharge would have gone into the room, the walls, the furniture, and so on. If a psychic walks into that room, a psychic can sense that energy. The energy is stored in the walls of the room, the objects, and the air. So, the energy waves are not traveling distances. The energy is mostly static in the room. The energy is emanating only a few feet or inches from the walls and objects. Sometimes a psychic needs to actually touch the walls or objects to feel the energy, thus the energy waves are not traveling any distance, except from the object to the psychic's hand. This is an example of energy waves that are effectively static, but the psychic has tuned into the frequency and can hear it.

But in many cases, the energy waves travel significant distances and the psychic must tune into the correct frequency carefully to hear the information. For example, if a psychic is sitting at their desk and their client asks them a question about a future outcome, the psychic must determine the correct frequency to tune into, and then effectively tune into that frequency and listen for the information. The frequency from those energy waves are likely coming from some Universal source, such as the Akashic records, or another person the client is engaging with. The psychic must decide the most effective way to get the answer the client is looking for. The psychic may decide to tune into another living person associated with the client. In this case, the psychic will tune into that frequency of that other person, even if the other person is thousands of miles away.

Everything in the Universe gives off these energy waves with frequencies. The entire Universe consists of energy as we have previously discussed. Energy is everywhere. Any psychic can tell you how "noisy" the world is. That is why some psychics become overwhelmed by the "noise" and need to find a way to "switch off." Basically, the energy of the information is not the problem. The challenge is more in effectively tuning into the energy the best most efficient ways.

A client may also ask a psychic to tune into the energy of a deceased loved one. This is called Mediumship. Psychic Mediums specialize in communicating with the dead. In this case, the psychic specifically tunes into the frequency of energy coming from the deceased person's soul energy. Since a person's soul consists of Universal Energy, that energy gives off energy waves. A psychic can effectively tune into that specific frequency, and that specific energy, in order to hear the information. A very skilled psychic can lock onto that energy and have a back and forth communication with that energy. Thus, a psychic can communicate with the dead.

Communicating with the dead sounds so magical and scary. But really, it is just a matter of tuning into the correct frequency for that soul energy of that specific person and being able to listen and hear what the energy is saying. I feel like I am taking away the magic for some of you, or telling you the Easter Bunny is not real, but the point of this book is to unveil the mysteries of the Universe, right? By the way, the Easter Bunny IS real, for any young people reading this. But I will not cover it further in this book.

Let's look at another angle. A client will often ask the psychic what is in their future. How can a psychic see the future? Well, in my personal opinion, a psychic does not specifically see the future. The reason being that the future is not written in stone. But, before you all yell at me, a psychic sees something very similar to the future. A psychic is able to tune into all the frequencies surrounding a person, hear, read, and interpret those energy waves, and then calculate the most likely future.

In other words, a psychic can tune into the energy, read all the energy, and then calculate the trajectory of all that energy. The psychic can view the trajectory of the energy and where all the actions are heading, and with high accuracy predict what will happen in the future. The complicated part of this is the psychic is often tuning into a huge multitude of sources to gain their information.

For example, if a person asks me if they will get a job they are applying for, I would have to tune into many different energy sources. I would tune into the client, the prospective employer, the employer's industry, the employer's customers, the location of employment, Universal sources such as the Akashic records, and so on and so forth. I would draw from many different energy sources before I would come up with my "read" on what I think will happen or what I "see" happening in the future.

Not to burst any bubbles, but I do not believe in looking into a crystal ball and seeing a movie of what will happen. I believe in tuning into a multitude of real actual Universal energies and reading that energy the best I can. By the way, I *have* looked into crystal balls before, and I've seen things and it is fun. But like reading palms, it is kind of for entertainment only. So, have fun. Do it. But when it's time to get serious, you need a psychic who tunes into the frequencies of all the Universal energies to accurately compute the most likely future outcome.

With all that said above, I should point out that many psychics, me included, *do* see images or short movies of the future. But it is still based upon our calculations of the most likely outcomes. The final outcome cannot be seen, because there are too many variables that can change the Future Outcome, such as uncalculated random events.

Another major source of psychic ability is by tuning into a psychic's "Guides," or "Spirit Guides." "Guides" are actual entities, most of which could have been living humans at some point. As we already discussed, a psychic can tune into the soul energy of a deceased person. A "Spirit Guide," or "Guide," is an entity, or deceased person, which the psychic has *locked* onto their energy. So, the energy of this entity is always with the psychic and easily tuned into. Since the psychic does not have to spend much time or effort finding the right frequency or tuning into that energy, the psychic can very easily and quickly tap into that energy of the Guide. The psychic can then ask that energy questions and listen for an answer. It is very similar to doing psychic medium work with the dead. However, with guides, the energy follows the psychic wherever they go and is always present.

Very often, I am asked to tune into a client's Guides and describe to the client who their Guides are. Since everything is energy, and their Guides emit energy, I can tune into that energy and often describe what I am hearing, seeing, and picking up on. The Guide often turns out to be some deceased loved one, ancestor, or someone the client has always resonated with.

Much of what I have discussed above is about the Universal energy going outward, and how it is transmitted to the psychic. I would be remiss if I did not briefly go into more detail about the psychic or "radio" end of things. Like a good radio or TV, a good psychic is able to clearly tune into the correct signal using all possible methods.

A psychic can often see, hear, and feel the energy. A psychic, tunes into the correct frequency, then listens to the energy on all levels in order to gain the most accurate "read" of the energy. So, when I am doing a reading and tuning into the energies, I am opening myself up to seeing anything that comes into my mind, hearing anything that comes into my mind, and feeling or sensing anything that comes into my mind, heart, and soul. I am opening up all my senses to the frequency, and hoping some information is received.

I also want to cover a more advanced psychic skill. Have you ever wondered how a psychic can do "energy work?" Energy work is when a psychic is able to influence, manipulate, or control energy in the client's favor. A couple examples might be when a psychic healer is able to somehow perform healing work from a distance. Or when a psychic is seemingly able to influence an outcome for you, such as you meeting a new person? Is this all for real? How does it work?

Like any profession, anyone can claim to be able to do anything even if they cannot. So, there are some psychics who try to dupe clients into paying for such energy work when they cannot deliver results.

However, a talented skilled psychic *can* influence and manipulate energy for the purposes of healing or providing a desired outcome. I could write an entire book explaining the complexities and details of how this is done. But let me give you a brief explanation.

Basically, a psychic can manipulate energy by using a few tools all at the same time. First, remember the Hunter Equation is always in play and one of the elements is External Forces. A skilled psychic is able to influence the External Forces. How do they do this?

Psychics can push upon the External forces by asking Spirit Guides to provide an External Force, or by pushing upon the Energy waves themselves. Some psychics can impact and move Energy by thought. Energy consists of various waves and particles, and these can be moved like anything else. Healing is often performed by speeding up certain energy around the injury, such as spinning energy at a high speed around a wound, which then speeds up recovery. I was actually taught how to do this in a tiny old empty church in England once, by

be very powerful Angels that humans can call upon for help. Well I believe that to be true. As God is the Universe, I believe the Archangels are symbols of the benevolent Soul Energy that exists to serve the Universe, and thus humanity. An Archangel is the "face" we put to this soul energy, just as God is the "face" we put to the Universe. Having archangels with specific names help us humanize this soul energy of the Universe which actually exists and helps us.

I am even willing to go so far as to say there are different energy signatures for different soul energies, and thus this makes the soul energy seem like "individuals", which can be separated into different archangels.

So as God exists, so do Archangels. The Universe is what it is, and truth is truth. But we all have the freedom to view the Universe through whatever prism we choose. I think Archangels is a totally valid and good way to view the benevolent soul energy within the Universe Energy Collective.

SPIRIT GUIDES

Spirit Guides are souls, or soul energy, which are specific to you and each human. They often consist of loved ones or relatives who have passed, or those with some kind of soul connection to you. Spirit Guides often serve very specific purposes. For example, you might have one Spirit Guide who helps you make decisions, and another Spirit Guide who provides you comfort during rough emotional times. I personally have numerous Spirit Guides who provide me with expertise in certain areas when needed. Often there is a primary Spirit Guide who looks over us and acts as our primary support.

A person can be taught to communicate with their Spirit Guide, just as psychics can often sense and describe your Spirit Guide for you. Spirit Guides are wonderful blessings of soul energy that always remain close to us that we can draw upon as needed.

GHOSTS

Ghosts are essentially energy that is "Earth bound," or still here with us on the ground, as opposed to back in the Universe Energy Collective. However, Ghosts come in different forms.

An active Ghost, or what I might call a "Living Ghost," is actual soul energy of a person that has not left the ground. This is the type of ghost that most people are afraid of, because it still is capable of moving about with free will. The soul energy for one reason or another did not go up to the Universe Energy Collective. It did not go up to the light, or back to God, so to speak.

The reasons may vary. Perhaps the soul energy got confused, trapped, or is held on Earth by some unresolved issue. Perhaps it is only still on Earth temporarily. But for whatever reason, the soul energy is still here.

Since the energy is so strong with this type of Ghost, the Ghost can often be seen with the human eye, as vapor of some sort. This type of ghost can also be communicated with if it wishes to cooperate.

Another type of Ghost is what I call "Static Remnant Energy." It is really not a ghost at all, but since it feels like a ghost, I call it a ghost. This is energy that has been left behind by an event. Let's say a person died in a room. Some of the energy that was released during the death process, may be imbedded into the air, walls, floor, or ceiling of the room. This energy may be strong enough to emit a ghostly feel to it. People will think it is a ghost. But really, it is leftover energy that is just sitting there. So, it is not an active living ghost per se. But it is still ghostly and creepy.

Ghosts can also come and go, flash in and flash out. I consider these ghosts to be the troublemakers. These ghosts are fully capable of going to the light up to the Universe Energy Collective, but for some reason choose to still "haunt" the ground. They have unresolved issues, or just like causing mayhem. They usually cannot be seen with the human eye. But can be felt and detected.

POLTERGEIST

A Poltergeist is a concentration of ghost energy, soul energy, or Universe Energy, which is strong enough to have direct contact with this dimension of the living. Meaning, this energy is able to move objects, touch things, and make noises. This is obviously terrifying to most people. Poltergeists can be from active ghosts, flash in and out ghosts, or Demons, which we will talk about next. A lot more research needs to be done on Poltergeists, as they seem capable of things that are logically impossible. But to me, it is completely logical in the sense that enough energy highly concentrated, could certainly be expected to move objects.

DEMONS

Demons are considered to be those paranormal entities which are malevolent or evil in intent. So, a Demon may be a Ghost, Poltergeist, or a collection of energy from the Universe, but is meant to cause harm.

Demons are possibly the most feared entity by humans. They are not understood, usually given very scary appearances, very difficult to get rid of, and capable of stirring the darkest scariest hysteria.

Where there is light, there is dark. Where there is good, there is bad. There is much light in the Universe. I have spent this entire book talking about the light pretty much. But there is also darkness. A Demon would consist of dark energy. This is energy that has negative intent. Energy may contain negative intent for various reasons. I think of it as hundreds of water faucets giving the life of water to everyone, but then what wastewater goes down the drain, empties into the sewer system, and comes out in one awful sewer pipe, full of the dirtiest most awful substance; that would be your dark energy. The dark dirty energy exists somewhere. Where did you think it went? It exists in the form of Demons.

To be honest, I have rarely come into contact with genuine Demons. I have dealt with many living humans who I felt were just as bad as Demons, but no actual paranormal Demons, except a couple times. So, for me at least, Demons are rare. But they exist.

Demons feed on fear and live in the form of hate. Feeling fear only feeds the Demon and makes it more capable of harm. Its energy output is in the form of hate. So, it is fear going in, and hate coming out. It is important to remember this, so the next time you are dealing with a Demon you know how to disarm it.

Actually, do not mess with Demons. Call someone. Ghost Busters maybe. Or me!

CHAPTER 15

Divine Intervention

Wikipedia defines Divine Intervention as a purported miracle caused by a deity's active involvement in the human world. Let us examine that. So, it is a miracle caused by a deity's active involvement in the human world. What I would rephrase that to, is: Divine Intervention is a miracle (desired outcome) caused by God's (The Universe's) active involvement in the human world. Or we can say, Divine Intervention is a desired Future Outcome caused by the Action of the Universe Energy, as an External Force toward humans.

Divine Intervention is sounding like a very Hunter Equation kind of event. The definition itself essentially contains multiple elements of the Hunter Equation.

Yes, some people are probably doing an eye roll and saying I have just complicated it. Most think of Divine Intervention as God stepping in to help us. But that is exactly what I am saying. God (The Universe), does step in (take Actions) to help us (External Force), to create miracles (desired Future Outcomes).

So, the good news is that I am totally on board with this Divine Intervention stuff. It passes the smell test from a Theologian point of view, as well as a Hunter Equation point of view. It is as if it is scientific and logical, in addition to being, a major pillar of religious and spiritual faith. Don't you just love it when all kinds of contrarian lines cross and overlap, and it just confirms that something *has* to be true!

Therefore, I am a total believer in Divine Intervention. Just like humans have the ability to have Intent and take Action, so does the intelligent Energy of the Universe. It is quite similar to how non-human Angelic beings have the ability to create Action and Intent that results in an External Force that affects humans in a benevolent way.

Why does Divine Intervention happen? I believe there are two possible answers for this. First, some energy in the Universe decides to make it happen. Secondly, humans decide to make it happen. Let me explain further.

Energy in the Universe is intelligent, especially entities such as Angels and Spirit Guides. Angels and Spirit Guides specifically, exist to provide support for souls existing in human form. Our Spirit Guides and Angels are there to help us and protect us. It is only logical that in the normal course of them doing so, they would proactively initiate Actions to provide External Forces which will result in giving us some positive result or outcome that we so desperately need. We humans would interpret such an act as a miracle coming from the heavens, which is exactly what it is. For some reason, these entities from the Universe intelligently determined or intended that we humans needed the assistance. So, they assisted in their own way.

The other way Divine Intervention can occur is through the initiation of a human. A person asks for help or asks for this miracle. This is most commonly referred to as "prayer." A human prays for a certain Future Outcome.

Who or what do they pray to? They pray to God (the Universe), or even specifically to the Angels or their Spirit Guides. What is prayer? Prayer is a very strong intense specific request for a Future Outcome. The prayer is almost always given with a very strong Intent.

I hate to do this to you again, but basically, when someone prays, they are using the Hunter Equation because they are requesting a Future Outcome using very strong Intent, and hoping the Universe takes an Action that creates an External Force, that gives them what they are requesting. Since none of this can be proven and it is all invisible, it can also feel to the human like Random Luck is involved. Thus, all elements of the Hunter Equation are engaged.

Therefore, I am also a total believer in the power of prayer. Here is the only caveat. Usually when I talk about taking Actions within the Hunter Equation, I am referring to Actions that you personally need to take yourself. People are responsible for themselves and their own Actions and need to take control and responsibility over their own life equation. But sometimes when things are desperate, we are tired, and we need help, it's okay to ask for help. Prayer is that way of asking for help.

So how can I make my prayer as effective as possible? Simply apply the Hunter Equation to your prayers. Meaning, be mindful to make your Future Outcome specific and righteous. Do not ask for something meaningless or out of greed. Then pray with deep Intent. Furthermore, to help your prayer along, think of any Actions you personally can take which may assist in the success of the Future Outcome you are praying for. Finally, clear the way of any External Force obstructions you can clearly see coming, but also be open to the fact that your prayer may be answered through an unexpected External Force.

For example, if you pray for a pony, do not expect a pony to show up on your doorstep. What might happen is you find out that a friend of a friend had a friend who was taking care of a pony, but had to move, and they need someone to take over the pony. This would be a weird External Factor coming at you, which is actually the result of

106

your prayer. You need to be awake and savvy enough to recognize it when you see it and take advantage of it.

When we pray, we are giving up control over the equation, so that means the Future Outcome might be provided in a weird way we would have never expected or chosen. So be ready to see it, and be ready to accept it, even if you do not think the circumstances are ideal. You gave up your control over the circumstances the moment you gave it over to prayer, instead of your direct Hunter Equation control of Actions.

Know that there is intelligent Universe Soul Energy up there, and here, in the Universe, that is willing and capable to help us by causing External Forces that might be in our favor. All you have to do is ask through prayer. All you prayer warriors, can now make your prayers even more powerful by applying the Hunter Equation to your prayer process.

CHAPTER 16

The Human Experience

S o far we have spent a lot of time looking at the Universe and its contents. Now it is time to focus more closely on humans.

Let me preface this chapter by saying I will be taking many liberties in defining things how I personally see them, taken from how they have been described to me by higher powers in the Universe. I will also be looking at things from the perspective of the Universe, rather than a fellow human on the ground. I am looking at things as if I was an alien or a being from the outer Universe. But obviously all of that will be mixed with the fact that I have inside knowledge and experience as a human on Earth.

So, with that said, a Human is a Homo Sapiens. A person. An Earthling. An organic living being, such as animals that roam the Earth, but far more advanced in its cognitive thinking. I think we all know what a human is.

What I really aim to discuss is what a human is, in comparison to other beings. In other words, what makes humans special and unique? What is it like to be human? What does it mean to be human? What is the human experience?

In my opinion, what makes humans special from other creatures and beings in the Universe, is the capacity to experience intense sensations and emotions. I am willing to bet that humans are among the most emotional creatures out there. Emotions and Sensations are very intense for humans.

Thus, experiencing sensations and emotions is the definition of The Human Experience.

Therefore, the more sensations and emotions you experience, the more human you are. We talked before about how your Soul is hoping to have amazing experiences and adventures in its various lives. These human lives add to the Soul's overall depth of existence, growth, and evolution. When a Soul lives a human life, it is no doubt in search of sensations and emotions. It is like when you go into a pizza shop, and most people will order a pizza instead of a salad. You can order a salad if you insist, but the full experience of being in a great pizza shop is ordering a great pizza. So, it would be the same for Souls who inhabit a human for its latest life experience. To gain the fullest experience as a human, the Soul would want to experience as many sensations and emotions as possible. It is the essence of life. To experience sensations and emotions, is to live. Let us look at that.

We will talk about Sensations and Senses first. Some popular human sensations are Touch, Taste, Sight, Smell, and Hearing. You all know those. But I want to add a few more to the conversation. Let us add Pleasure, Pain, and Sex. Those three are also emotion based, but they are key human sensations as well.

Touching something as a human is amazing. Our fingers are so sensitive and can pick up tons of information by touching something. Touching things like Jello, cool water, chalkboards, and other humans, can give us amazing experiences just in themselves. Everyone can think of their favorite things to touch.

Taste is one of my favorites. Humans must eat to survive, just like animals and probably many creatures of the Universe. Humans need fuel for life. But for a human, taking in food, fuel, and sustenance, is not just a necessary chore. It is actually one of the most pleasurable things a human does on a daily basis. The sense of Taste gives us various sensations that can barely be described by words. You know a sensation is special when it cannot be described by words. Therefore, Taste ranks right up there. It certainly has to be one of the greatest most unique sensations and experiences in the Universe; and humans are among the lucky ones to have this.

Sight is pretty obvious. It is also fairly necessary. However, plenty of blind people get through life just fine without sight, by using their other senses. Sight is special because through sight a person can take in more bits of data in a shorter time than any other sense. A picture is worth a thousand words. If you want to convey the most amount of information to someone in the shortest amount of time, you would want to use Sight as your vehicle for that. Our ability to see things is amazing. Our sight is not very good as far as optimal functionality though. Most animals have far better sight than humans do, and thus I am sure plenty of Universal beings do as well. However, sight for humans is not just about functionality. It's about a human's ability to see beauty in sight, and thus experience pleasure, just by using Sight. Pretty extraordinary really.

Smell is an interesting sense because it gives us one of the most diverse human reactions when we experience Smell. Smell can put us in heaven or put us in hell. Smell is a very love or hate sensation. Everyone has their favorite smells, but also smells which can evoke the most repulsive reactions. A human can literally become sick just by the smell of something. That is amazingly powerful.

Hearing is similar to Sight in that it is very necessary to functionality. However, plenty of deaf people do fine in life without hearing. Aside from its obvious functionality of communication, safety, and efficiency, it can also provide us with pleasure. Only behind communication, music would be the next most important experience with the sense of Hearing. Listening to music and enjoying music is probably one of the most epic and popular of all human experiences.

Now for the sensations I added, starting with Pleasure. The Sensation of Pleasure is related to all the senses and Sensations mentioned above. But Pleasure is so important and so key to the human experience that I wanted to mention it separately. Pleasure may very well be one of the reasons we live and endure. Without Pleasure, why bother? Pleasure is *that* important. Pleasure is our incentive for living. We endure all experiences in hopes of experiencing Pleasure, even if fleeting. Once a human dies, I suspect the sensation they miss the most is Pleasure. So that is pretty significant, don't you think?

The equal opposite to Pleasure is Pain. No human wants to experience Pain. However, Pain is very necessary because without Pain, we would not fully appreciate Pleasure. In addition to that, Pain is our most effective safety warning system. When we feel Pain, we immediately know something is wrong, and we take immediate corrective action. This applies to physical pain and mental pain. I would argue that Pain is actually necessary for life, more so than the others. Without Pain, we would surely do stupid things and die early.

Then of course, there is Sex. I may be touching the third rail by saying this, but how can you possibly have a human experience without experiencing Sex. I hope I am not making any virgins out there feel uncomfortable or inadequate, but I have to keep it real.

Sex as a human can be amazing. It can also be horrible if a person has had a horrible experience with sex, such as rape or abuse. But Sex is likely the most intense Sensation of them all. Sex is a sensation that absolutely cannot be described in words. People do not even try to describe it in words. So, without a doubt that makes it epic and amazing. The sensation of Sex, the desire, the yearning, the connection, and the orgasm, are all so intense, that humans are literally shaking and barely keeping themselves together, during and after the experience. I venture to say this sensation is more powerful and intense for humans than most other creatures of the Universe.

After looking at all those senses and sensations, we can see how the human experience is packed with amazing things. All of those make life worth living, and make Souls want to live a life as a human. If that is not enough, we also have all our human Emotions. Emotions in humans are even stronger, more intense, and deeper, than our senses and sensations. Our human Emotions make our senses and sensations seem shallow and simple in comparison.

Emotions are hard to list because there are many, including some not fully defined yet. Also, emotions come in many different shades and moods. But we will cover a few of them. Some common Emotions include Happiness, Sadness, Excitement, Pride, Love, Hate, Anger, Fear, and Greed.

Happiness, or Joy, is a wonderful Emotion. It really cannot be explained in words. It is something that must be experienced to be understood. Imagine life with no Happiness ever experienced. Notice I said, "ever experienced." I totally understand there are some humans who experience very little happiness. But at some point, in every Soul's human experience, some level of Happiness is felt and experienced.

The flip side is of course Sadness. Happiness would have little meaning without also experiencing Sadness. Sadness is a cruel emotion. There really is not anything good about it, except for the fact it is necessary to experience so that we more fully appreciate Happiness.

Excitement, or Anticipation, are very fun human emotions to experience. Most of us have fond memories of experiencing these emotions as a child.

Excitement is certainly more powerful as a child. As we grow older, we intentionally make the emotion of Excitement duller, in order to avoid the emotion of Disappointment. Certainly, Excitement is a very fleeting emotion that we push to the side as we get older, and even when we experience it, the emotion often only lasts for some minutes before fading off. But it was well worth mentioning.

Pride is not often mentioned, except sometimes as a negative or bad thing. But I feel Pride is worth mentioning as a positive emotion worth

112

experiencing. Humans are feeble creatures who often struggle and suffer much. Pride is our reward to enduring the struggles and troubles. The feeling of Pride is a great reward and is something we all strive for, even if some of us will not admit to it for religious, cultural, or other reasons.

Perhaps Love should have been mentioned first or last. Love is the most important human emotion. Love is the most important Universal emotion. Love is the language of the Universe and the language of God. Love is everything. It is the sun that makes us live. Without Love, there is no life really. If there is life, it is empty without Love. We know what Love is. My point here is just to remind everyone of its central importance to humans and the Universe. Love is indescribable. But Love is the deepest of all emotions. True love is eternal.

The opposite of Love is Hate. However, Hate is weak and fleeting. Hate is run by impulse. Hate is also far from eternal. Hate is often very fleeting, although it can last a long time in limited circumstances. Hate is the same as Hurt. Hate is Pain. Hate is the symbol of Pain. Hate is not a worthy human emotion to experience, but Hate, similar to Pain, is a great reminder and warning that something is wrong. Hate is an affliction and an illness.

Anger is a very common emotion that causes us the most problems. Anger is usually fleeting. However, Anger is most likely to cause us to do stupid things we later regret. Anger is one of the most intense emotions a human can experience. Anger is unusual because even though it is so intense, it is very shallow at the same time. Some humans can have a deep anger for a long time, but those humans really are classified as mentally ill or damaged on some level. Nobody should experience Anger for more than short moments. If you feel Anger for long periods of time, you should seek help or something bad is most certainly going to happen.

While Love is the most important, the emotion of Fear is one of the most powerful. Fear is our Achilles heel. Fear can grip us and lock us into paralysis, both physically and mentally. Fear is our destruct button that can stop us in our tracks and shut us down. For this reason, Fear is the most dangerous of all the human emotions. Fear always causes bad decisions. Fear degrades all the other emotions. Fear strips us of our humanity. Where Love is the life of us, Fear is the death of us. Anyone locked in Fear is not living. Fear will be discussed at length later on as well.

I have decided to include Greed as an emotion worth mentioning, because like Fear, Greed has the capacity to destroy humanity. Greed will also be discussed more at length later on. But Greed is the disease or virus implanted into the human. It is the "bug" that needs to be removed if they come out with Humans 2.0, because Greed has proven to be something all humans feel, and if acted upon, always hurts humanity.

That is quite a collection of Emotions. I could write an entire book on just Emotions. However, my goal is just to make my point in the power, intensity, and importance of Emotions to the human experience.

Between Sensations and Emotions, we can clearly see why being human is an amazing experience that any Soul would want to have, and perhaps even needs to have. Being human provides a wide expanse of experiences that totally symbolize the essence of life.

Even so, I would be remiss if I did not include the capacity of Memory, or memories, in this chapter. Memories play an important role in the Human Experience. Humans spend lots of time thinking of their memories. These memories can then initiate all of the emotions we listed. Memories is that bank of buttons at our finger tips for experiencing any array of emotions we wish to experience, without leaving the comfort of our home, chair, or bed. Just by the thought of memories, we can fully live out an experience and emotions, without even moving. How cool is that?

What is the best part of being human? Well, each person is encouraged to have their own answer, and likely does have their own answer. But for me, I think the best part of being human is the wide diverse set of Sensations and Emotions that are experienced. The

Human Experience guarantees a wild ride that will not be forgotten.

Conversely, what is the worst part of being human? Same answer. The worst part of being human is the wide array of intense emotions that can at times be very painful, uncomfortable, and draining. Being human is exhausting, difficult, and even scary at times.

But the bottom line is that being human offers a powerful experience for our Soul Energy, which allows for growth and evolution.

CHAPTER 17

Human Vulnerabilities

I will start this chapter by first commenting on the basic strength and vulnerabilities of the Universe and God. The main vulnerability of the Universe/God is that the concept and its details cannot be proven. The strength of the Universe/God is that the concept and details cannot be disproven. Science has its limitations where the Universe is concerned. Therefore, there is still lots of wiggle room for personal opinion and perception. It's much more fun that way.

Humans are not so lucky. Science has done a great job at defining and explaining humans in most every detail. This includes human psychology of course. Therefore, without as much wiggle room to wiggle, humans have to acknowledge and accept a laundry list of weaknesses and vulnerabilities. I spoke in the last chapter of the wonderful reasons to be human. Now it is time to look at the darker side. By looking closely in the mirror without pretty filters, we can more quickly learn, grow, and evolve into a better species, hopefully.

The first and most obvious vulnerability is the fact humans are organic creatures and very open to disease. Humans have open mouths and noses and congregate very closely with other humans. Humans also have hands and fingers which they use to touch everything around them, and then have a natural habit of touching their mouths and noses afterward. This set of circumstances is like a lemming marching off a cliff. It is a guarantee of illness and disease.

However, the irony is that the most serious and deadly diseases humans fall victim to, are often caused by humans themselves. Bad sanitation, self-destructive behaviors such as drinking and drug use, along with poisoning their own food with chemicals that increase the profit of sales, all contribute to humans basically poisoning themselves on purpose.

More damaging than "accidentally" poisoning and harming themselves, humans poison and harm themselves on purpose in the form of vices, or bad habits, and addictions.

Humans will literally and purposely smoke cigarettes, knowing almost for a fact that they will end up with a debilitating lung disease, or deadly cancer. Yet, humans march onward toward the cliff anyway.

Of course, we cannot delay in mentioning Drinking. Alcohol drinking obviously, which gradually kills a human over time by directly ingesting a poison.

Then there is drug use. This includes both legal and illegal drug use. Illicit drugs such as Crack and Heroine will kill anyone quicker than anything else. But Cocaine and huffing fumes are not far behind. Pills and medications used irresponsibly is the equivalent of directly poisoning yourself as well.

Humans are very vulnerable to these vices. Why is this? Well, it comes down to something that make being human a most wonderful experience. Emotions. In the earlier chapter I made the case that the range and intensity of human emotions are what makes being human worth the experience and effort.

However, these same emotions make humans very vulnerable. Humans are unable to control their emotions. The emotions are very strong, intense, and they often come and go, ebb and flow, without warning or control. Emotions are usually out of control, and sometimes in an exaggerated way.

Emotions such as anger and sadness can cause Depression and self-destructive behaviors that can be very harmful. This self-sabotaging behavior can manifest in the form of increased intensity of vices, or outright self-harm such as cutting, self-injury, or suicide.

Human emotions can become so intense and overwhelming that they literally cause a human to kill themselves. I do not know about you, but I would call that a design flaw! It is the equivalent of an electric overload that causes an automatic self-destruct sequence. Not good.

Human emotions also leave humans more vulnerable to manipulation by others. Dubious actors use a person's emotions to manipulate them into giving or doing things that a clear-thinking person would not do. Being open to manipulation is one of the biggest vulnerabilities of all and is worthy of a book of its own.

As if disease and out of control emotions are not bad enough, humans have some very insidious psychological behaviors that make them particularly vulnerable. There are many we could come up with, I am sure; but I am just going to mention a few that I think are absolutely key.

The first is Greed. Humans are never satisfied. They always want more. And more. And more. This insatiable appetite that is never satisfied is a terrible psychological behavior that results in many problems. Obviously, there is a logical reason for limits on most activities and things. Too much candy makes us sick. Cutting down too many trees destroys the Earth. Killing too many animals destroys not only the eco system, but future food sources as well. Raising prices too much can result in nobody buying your product. Cutting expenses too much result in poor quality. This concept of Greed causes humans to intentionally exceed logical smart limits. Thus, humans will intentionally engage in destructive behaviors and acts that directly hurt themselves. It is very illogical. But to be illogical is to be human.

Another one is "Group Think." Group Think is a well-researched behavior where humans tend not to think independently. I hate to use the analogy, but humans can be a little like sheep. When one sheep goes, the rest follow. Plenty of studies have been done on this. Humans are very open to the power of suggestion. If one person states an opinion that seems plausible, and a second person validates it by supporting it, the chances are good that everyone else in the group will agree and go along with it, even if they do not understand it, or fully agree on a full intellectual level.

The path of least resistance for a human is to always agree with the group. Humans seem to have a switch in their brain that shuts off all independent intellectual thought once a certain threshold of group consensus has been reached. Humans avoid confronting a group opinion. It is much easier to simply go along with the group opinion, even if the individual has not fully processed and validated it individually.

Similar to Group Think is "Tribalism." Tribalism is when a human not only goes along with the Group Think, but also aggressively agrees and supports the group's position, even if it is factually or morally wrong. What a human wants more than being right, is to be included. If you give a human a choice between being correct and alone, or wrong and liked, they will almost always go with being wrong as long as they feel included and accepted by a group.

Tribalism is why and how humans are able to justify doing horrific acts within a group, even though intellectually they may know it's wrong. Tribalism is dangerous to not only individual humans, but also humanity as a whole. Human history is littered with examples of how Group Think and Tribalism allowed great atrocities and destruction to occur without any hesitation, even though intellectually and spiritually, these same humans knew it was wrong on some deeper level. Being accepted and included in a group was more important to them than being morally or factually correct.

But I would argue there is another human vulnerability that is even more dangerous and proven to be deadlier over time. This is the psychological trait of humans needing an idol to worship. On an innocent level, humans have a need to believe in something or someone greater than themselves. This in itself seems harmless and fine. Most of us humans have some kind of religious or spiritual belief, or faith, that we hold dearly because it helps us get through hard times.

This only proves my point. The point being, that humans must have something greater, often an idol, to look up to and lead them, or guide them. This "idol" is most often a religious figure. But it can also be a business leader, gang leader, family member, or the almighty currency of money. There is always something a human chooses as being worthy of following and pursuing, even if it goes beyond logic, fact, and common sense. It can also go beyond what is moral and right.

A human without that idol seems lost and lonely without purpose. Why is this? Why must humans have some person or thing to worship or follow?

I think if you look at the psychology of it all, the answer is that humans, in concept, are unable to lead themselves. Humans seem unable to function well without an outside leader or influence. Humans also require an external force of inspiration. Humans need something or someone to look up to, or they feel lost and even despondent. Humans need to know there is someone greater than them, that know better than them, how to live. Humans need to be told what to do, and even how to think, or again, they feel lost and confused. I suppose it would be like separating a flock of sheep until each sheep is alone. How would each sheep know when to move, feed, or leave? They are used to just going with the flock without any individual thought. So alone, they might become confused and apathetic. I would say it is definitely a vulnerability when humans have not yet surpassed the psychology of a sheep.

But let us be fair. Why is this a problem? What is the harm in humans needing a higher influence or idol to worship or follow? The answer is that a group of humans blindly following an idol or leader without individual intellectual thought can be very dangerous. An idol, leader, or general group belief can be very harmful to humanity as a whole. What if the belief, idol, or leader, instructs the group to harm other humans? That is a rhetorical question obviously, since our history is full of this behavior. Religious bigotry against others, and wars, are all started based upon this behavior of following the leader, idol, or belief.

Most individual people have no desire to harm another person. But if the idol or leader instructs them to do so, the human will often do so without hesitation or independent thought. This need for an idol or leader opens humans up to brainwashing, manipulation, and being used to harm humanity.

I believe this need to mindlessly follow an idol or leader, without any individual intellectual thought or fact basis, is the great cancer of humanity. It is basically humanity killing itself from within. That brings us full circle back to the beginning where I spoke of humans purposely poisoning and harming themselves.

In short, humanity, or a human's greatest vulnerability, is their propensity to harm and kill themselves. Very ironic for one's greatest threat to be themselves.

CHAPTER 18

What Is Your Idol?

In the previous chapter, I alluded to the fact that a major human vulnerability is the need to have some sort of Idol to look up to and follow. We need to take a closer look at that and examine the upsides as well as the downsides. At this point in human evolution, people need some sort of idol. They need something greater than themselves to look up to, guide them, and steer toward. As I have said before, humans are much like sheep in that they have a natural tendency to follow something. Most humans are afraid of being alone, so following something they view as greater than themselves, gives them comfort, and doing this with a group of other people gives them even greater comfort.

In my view, there are basically five different idols used or followed by the huge majority of humans. They are Religion, God, Specific Mentors, Nature, and Themselves. Obviously, the fifth I mentioned, "Themselves", is not following anything else so it's a violation of the entire "idol" concept, but I include it because it is what evolution is driving us to eventually. I will explain each of the four idols in detail.

RELIGION

Religion is the most common idol. This book is not about religion, nor does it aim to be pro-religion or anti-religion. Therefore, I will not be going into too much detail regarding the different religions, or my opinions of them.

With that said, a majority of humans on Earth believe in some sort of religion. There are plenty of people who do not believe in any religion, or follow any religion, but they are in the minority.

Religions are based upon a rulebook. Different religions have different rulebooks. But the general principle is that a "culture of rules" are contained in the book and they must be followed. The rulebooks illustrate the rules in the form of stories of what happens when you do not follow the rules.

Religions are based on fear and reward. Based upon the rulebook, the religion will scare its followers into following the rules by explaining or showing the awful things that will happen to them if they do not follow the rules. Whether it be not going to heaven, or going to hell, or violent punishment, the fear is ever present for those who do not follow the rules of the book.

At the same time, the rulebook promises wonderful rewards for those who follow the rules. Whether it is entry into a wonderful bountiful heaven, a guaranteed afterlife, forgiveness of all sins, validation as a person, or a multitude of virgins waiting for each man upon death, the rulebook promises wonderful things if you follow all the rules.

But of course, humans are far from perfect. Nobody can follow all the rules. So, religions have in place ways you can repent and not be punished for breaking the rules. Certain acts, deeds, punishments, or even payments to the religious organizations, can "fix" your sin or mistake, and all is well again.

I apologize if any of that sounds cynical or disrespectful. My aim is to look at this from a purely objective point of view.

However, on the cynical darker side, some religions may use their influence for dubious gain. Some religions use their influence to cause their followers to commit horrible atrocities in the name of their religion. Additionally, religions tend to use their influence to encourage or force monetary payments from their followers for the purpose of profit.

Using a "carrot and stick" approach, allows religions to have huge emotional influence over their followers. Dangling fear over their heads, while also offering amazing rewards can get most humans to do most anything.

But I will stop being cynical for a moment and look at the brighter more positive side of religion. Religions also create a very strong sense of community amongst its followers. A person can have a true sense of belonging within a religion. Many people who have no family and are quite lonely, feel a real sense of family and community by being active within their religion.

Additionally, many religions participate in charitable activities. Religions naturally raise money constantly from followers, so they have the funds to donate to good causes.

I view the advantages of having Religion as your idol to be, the fact it creates a very strong sense of community that can even replace a family. There can also be a strong sense of charity helping those less fortunate.

I view the disadvantages of having Religion as your idol to be, the fact it is based on Fear, and the fact the rulebook can contain scripture that is bigoted, discriminatory, harmful, or even violent to certain people. The fact it is based on fear also opens up the potential for manipulation and profiting from its followers.

Religion has been around forever. It is based on a faith that you believe in something that cannot be proven. It is based on rulebooks written by anonymous authors for the most part. The rulebooks are often changed over the centuries.

Most followers of religion these days tend to follow their religion to a certain degree, but not literally. Many people will tell you that they only participate in religion for the sense of community and family it offers. But there are always some that follow it because they truly believe in the rulebook and attempt to follow the rulebook to the letter of the law as much as possible.

Regardless of which religion you may follow, or your purpose for following it, it would be considered your idol if you participate in religion. Let us move onto the next idol.

GOD & THE UNIVERSE

As you will remember, we are using the terms "God" and "Universe" interchangeably, because to me they are the same thing. For the purposes of this section I will use the term "God" only but bear in mind I am also referring to the Universe as well.

Living with God as your idol is very different from living with Religion as your idol. While Religion is based upon fear and a "carrot/stick" approach, living with God as your idol is based entirely and solely on Love. Love is the language of God and the Universe. So, anything based on God, will also be based on Love.

Therefore the "rules" of living by God are very different, and yet quite simple. Using God as your idol means you live by Love. You aim to love all people and all creatures. There are no rules and no exceptions to this. There is no discrimination, and you operate under the concept of inclusion rather than exclusion.

When you do not know what to do, you simply ask, "What would God do?" You will also hear some people following this type of spirituality saying, "What would Jesus do?" It is a sticky wicket bringing Jesus into this because that references religion. But some who believe in following God, also believe Jesus was a real historical figure.

Jesus has obviously been adopted by the Christian religion as their idol. But outside of that, Jesus is seen as a real historical figure who we can look at independently from any religion. Additionally, since God has never been viewed as an actual earthly person, looking to Jesus as God's face allows us to better relate to God. So, whether you want to only consider God, or whether you want to consider Jesus as the face of God, both are relevant to the type of spirituality I am discussing. Also, as I discuss all this, keep in mind that Muhammad would be inserted as the direct prophet of God, rather than Jesus, if you follow Islam. But for simplicity sake, I am going to continue with the Christian - Jesus example.

Either way, God and Jesus by most all accounts can be viewed as Loving entities that aimed to teach, love, and support those who follow them. God as the Universe is exactly that. It is a collection of soul energy that yearns to learn, grow, and evolve, while engaging in the language of love, for which is the language of the Universe.

Living with God as our idol forces us to set aside any bigotry, discrimination, or hate toward others. It forces us to do what God and Jesus would have done, which is to listen, comprehend, guide, support, accept, forgive, and love, without exception.

If we make mistakes and fall short of this nearly impossible goal, we simply learn, grow, and try harder in the future. There is no penance, payment, or punishment necessary. No fear scare tactics are involved, but also no amazing rewards offered. It is simply a Universal law and handshake.

People who are deeply into a religion often cannot understand how a person outside of religion can still feel so close to God. Hopefully this is explaining that concept, because indeed people with this spirituality are very close to God, always asking and thinking what God would do, and trying to stay in alignment with those values.

I view the advantages of living with God as your idol to be, the fact it is based solely on love rather than fear, as well as inclusion rather than exclusion, and does not include any bigotry or discrimination. The other advantage is that you are not tethered to a rulebook that you are constantly in danger of violating.

I view the disadvantage of living with God as your idol to be, the fact it is a solitary experience. It is up to the individual to create the bond with God and follow it without the prompting of a "leader." The biggest disadvantage in my view is that it does not offer the sense of community and family that Religion offers.

Now onto our next idol.

MENTORS

Some people do not see Religion or God/Universe as viable idols. They might not believe in religion or God and are not engaged with the concept of the Universe. But that does not leave them immune from the common human need for an idol.

Thus, they often choose and adopt a person important to them to be their idol. In a very cute way, we often see examples of this in young children who look up to their older sibling. They may be too young to fully understand and engage with religion and God, but they totally understand the concept of the Mentor, which in their case could be an older sibling.

A Mentor can be a variety of people. It might be a sibling, parent, teacher, friend, sports hero, music or entertainment hero, human legend, or an actual mentor in the business or educational sense. But the point is that this person ends up being the one person they look up to most.

The follower tends to mimic the behavior of the idol. This can be a double-edged sword depending on the actual behavior of the idol.

The advantage of having a Mentor as your idol is that your idol is an actual person that you may be able to have personal contact with. This creates a very close bond with your idol and access which is impossible with the previously mentioned idols.

The obvious disadvantage of a Mentor as an idol, is that nobody is perfect, and the follower will start to mimic any bad behavior which the idol exhibits. We see this with gang leaders being an idol for young kids, and then the young kids want to be in a gang. We see this with sports heroes who end up disappointing us with their behavior.

When having a Mentor as an idol, one must be careful to choose carefully and have the ability to change their idol should something go wrong with their current idol. It is a slippery slope for sure, but a common idol for many people, especially those who do not believe in Religion, God, or understand the Universe.

Our next idol is what I call, the Ancient Idol.

NATURE

Having Nature, or the Earth, as your idol is from the ancient ways. Honestly, I think it is also the most genuine balanced idol of them all so far. Having Nature or the Earth as your idol means you are putting yourself in total alignment with Nature. You are in tune with all that is around you, including the animals, the Earth, and the weather.

Being in tune with Nature and following the cues of Nature is a very peaceful and Zen experience. As an American, I point to the Native Americans as being the masters at using Nature as an idol. The Native Americans took clues and cues from all the animals, birds, sky, and everything around them. They respected Nature, hoping it would respect them back in the form of providing what they needed to survive. They lived one with Nature.

Living with Nature as your idol is about a mutual respect for Nature, being in tune with Nature, and seeking all your signs from Nature. In my opinion, it is probably most closely in alignment with how humans were intended to behave and exist.

I call Nature the ancient idol, because it no longer exists on a grand scale. In fact, the opposite exists. Humans now exploit Nature for profit, even if it means absolute destruction of Nature. Humans have abandoned being in alignment with Nature, and instead invest in technologies to destroy Nature for the most convenient short-term gains. It is an interesting turn evolution has taken indeed.

But still the same, I keep Nature in this book as a major idol because it once was a major idol, it should still be a major idol, and there are still some very spiritual people who use Nature as their idol.

Now for our final idol, and most difficult.

SELF

Living with "Self" as your idol is perhaps a paradox. How can your idol be yourself? This concept is difficult for many humans. However, it is important I discuss it because it is likely the future for humans as we continue to evolve.

Living with your own sense of self as your moral compass means you must self-define all your precepts. You must create your own guiding principles. You must create your own moral values, your own rules. You must have totally developed your own sense of self and fully understand yourself, your goals, your values, your weaknesses, and your own inspirations. Basically, you must be the master of your own self. You must be able to think independently and have the self-discipline to enforce your own values upon yourself.

Living with Self as your idol means having no external force to look up to, and nobody to tell you what to do, or how to behave. It means self-correcting when you go wrong. Imagine having the discipline to do this effectively. Living with Self-means being a self-contained unit who knows what they believe in, why they believe in it, where they are going, and why they are going there. It means knowing the guidelines, rules, and values you have decided to follow, and to provide your own self-discipline to abide by them.

Perhaps this is beginning to sound like utopia or impossible. I agree it sounds difficult, but it is certainly not impossible. Some among us already engage in this to some degree. It is always a work in progress. I could probably write an entire book on just this perhaps.

The advantages of living with Self as yourself idol are tremendous. You are free from all external manipulation, control, and interference. You maintain strong independent thought at all times. You get to define your own set of values that you want to live by. You have amazing freedom in living how you want to live. You are truly the master of your own self.

The disadvantages are also obvious. It is extremely difficult to do this. It requires a person to have great independence of thought, creativity, confidence, self-awareness, and amazing discipline. You pretty much need to be a Jedi.

But a Jedi is very cool, yes? Imagine if everyone had the strength of character to live this way. There would be no more "sheep mentality" or groups ganging up on other groups. Each individual would be guided by independent thought rather than dangerous "group think."

In other words, we would have more highly evolved humans living in a more highly evolved society. But much work and evolution would need to happen first for the majority of the populace to choose this type of idol.

So, there are your five idol concepts. Perhaps you will consider which is your idol, and maybe you even have a mixture of more than one. That is entirely possible as well. But if you have none of the above, you are likely not human.

CHAPTER 19

Good Vs. Evil

Wikipedia defines "Good" as: In its most general context, the concept of good denotes that conduct which is to be or should be preferred when posed with a choice between a set of possible actions. Good is generally considered to be the opposite of evil.

Wikipedia defines "Evil" as: Evil, in a general sense, is the opposite or absence of good. It can be an extremely broad concept, though in everyday usage is often used more narrowly to denote profound wickedness.

In my opinion, those definitions are kind of wordy. I wanted to make it easier for people to understand the different between Good and Evil. Right and Wrong. So here it is.

Good is Love. Evil is Fear.

When something is coming out of a place of love, or done out of love, or love is intended, then it is Good. When something is coming out of a place of fear, or done to make people fear, or creating fear, then it is Evil. Is that simple enough? Love vs. Fear.

Feel free to take my definition for a test drive to see how it feels. Run down different scenarios in your mind, determine if you are feeling love, or feeling fear, then label it Good or Evil. See if it works.

This world is a tricky place. It is full of dubious people who are always trying to accomplish something by labeling things as Good, when they are not necessarily good. Conversely, there are many people who are often persecuted and slandered as bad, but they are actually good.

Good people come in many colors, shapes, and sizes. Dirty, full of tattoos, scary clothes and hair, nicely dressed in suits, dressed in clergy uniforms, politicians, and the list goes on.

Evil people also come in many colors, shapes, and sizes. Dirty, full of tattoos, scary clothes and hair, nicely dressed in suits, dressed in clergy uniforms, politicians, and the list goes on.

Oh wait. Those lists above for good people and bad people are the same. Yes, they are. So how can I tell who is good and who is bad? Which clergy is good and which clergy is bad? Which tattoo covered scary looking dude is good and which is bad? Well, how do they act toward you? Do they come from a place of love, extend love, and make you feel love? Or do they come from a place of fear, extend fear, and make you feel fear? That is how to tell.

We will take clergy for an example because I feel it is the best example. If someone of the clergy talked to me about how I should fear God and I will go to hell if I do not shape up and do what he says, I would say that is coming from a place of fear. However, if a clergy told me to feel the love of God, and know God loves me no matter what, then I would feel that is coming from a place of love. I would then know which clergy is good and which is not. This example applies to everyone.

Let us now look at some symbols of good and evil. Satan is viewed as a symbol of evil. What does Satan look like? Is Satan a red monster with horns? Or is Satan a figurative symbol of evil things and evil people? Or is Satan a person on earth who does evil things? I always find it interesting how people refer to Satan and the Anti-Christ as the same thing. Yet, Satan is a red monster with horns, and the Anti-Christ is a yet to be known clever businessman in a suit who will make us think he is our savior before he destroys us. The monster with horns sounds more mythological, while the clever evil man in the suit sounds like some people I've seen here on Earth in my everyday life. But we know both are evil because they come from a place of fear with fearful evil intentions.

Now for some symbols of good. Many view Jesus Christ as a symbol of good, regardless of your religious nature. By many accounts, Jesus was a modest man of modest means, wearing a simple gown, and getting by as a carpenter. But Jesus was preaching love and came from a place of love. Therefore, Jesus is a symbol of good. Mother Teresa is another symbol of good. She was a living angel who only gave from love. A simple older woman living a simple life. Yet, she was drenched in so much love, making her deserving of Sainthood.

When people point to things and tell me they are good and bad, I do not just accept that judgment. If you point to a homeless person and say they are bad, I would ask, "What does the homeless person do and how do they treat other people?" If a homeless person gives his only coat to another homeless person because they needed it more, then I would say the homeless person is a symbol of good because they acted out of love. If someone points to a place of worship and says it is good, but I come to find out it preaches hate against other people, then I would say it is a symbol of evil. When I see a nice-looking person in a suit, I will not know if they are good or evil until I witness their actions and intentions.

Nobody should be judged without given a chance to show their intentions and actions of either love or fear. Then once they show which card they are playing, you can know what you are dealing with. This applies to the lowest most disadvantaged of our society, as well as the wealthiest most powerful of our society. They each have an equal chance at being good or evil, depending on whether they act out of a place of love or a place of fear. The Universe is a light and dark place. It is full of good and evil. Good and evil is everywhere, including within ourselves. Examine your inner thoughts and memories. There are times you have used fear against someone to get what you wanted. There are times you have used love unconditionally because you knew it was the right thing. In this example, you have acted with evil intent, and acted with good intent. We are human, and we are all over the place with our emotions and behavior.

The purpose of this chapter is not to cure and banish evil from the Universe. That is not likely to happen. My purpose here is to make it easier and more obvious for you to recognize good and evil when you see it.

Instead of the "smell test," we have the "feel test." Ask yourself how something makes you feel. Do you feel love, or do you feel fear? That is the easiest way to tell if something is good or evil.

When you detect evil, you can step back and block it so that you do not fall victim to it. When you detect good, you can trust that it's okay to step closer and check things out further. This can be used in business, relationships, choosing a spiritual outlet, buying a car, almost anything.

You want to get to the point where you are in alignment with only good things. When you get good at detecting good vs. evil, you will naturally by reflex, either move away quickly, or step closer. There are no guarantees, and we are all fooled from time to time, but this is a better guide than trying to look at how someone appears and taking a wild hopeful guess of their intentions.

Most importantly of all, we all must police ourselves and constantly monitor as to whether we are acting from a place of love or a place of fear. Look at how you treat others and how you treat yourself. Always strive to be coming from a place of love so that you can be a symbol of good for the Universe and humanity.

CHAPTER 20

Your Place In The Universe

Have you wondered what your place in the Universe might be? Why are you here? What is your purpose? What are you doing here?

Humans often feel lost and wander aimlessly. Sometimes it is helpful to take a step back and see if we can make some sense of it all. We will try to do that now. Why are you here? Humans are host bodies for your soul. Your soul's goal is to have as many varied experiences as possible so that it may learn, grow, and evolve. So really, the point of your existence is driven by your Soul, not your body, or your opinionated brain. A soul does not necessarily care what specific experiences it has, as long as it has them. So, this is where you and your opinionated brain get to have some influence.

But really, it is not about our opinionated brain. It is more about what our emotions are dictating. Humans are led by their emotions. While your soul is gaining experience, your human life is allowing you to experience all the emotions and amazing things that humans get to feel and experience. Why not enjoy the ride?

So here is my take. I believe we are here to enjoy the human adventure while our souls are gaining as much experience as possible so that our souls can learn, grow, and evolve. So, it is a dual purpose. Our soul is all business and needs to experience things to evolve. But we also get to feel and experience the journey of being human in such a diverse species, environment, and world. Business and pleasure. Like a mullet, business in front and party in the back. So, make the most out of both.

So that is why you are here in principle. But as I said, your soul does not care as much what experiences it is having, so long as it is having them. That means you, your mind, emotions, and preferences, get to decide which experiences you have.

Ideally, a person would go through a deep, well considered process to determine which adventures they want to have. At this point, we set aside our soul. Our soul is fine and just wants adventure. We need to now fully consider our human existence to figure out the rest. So, let us do that.

The first step is to know thyself. What excites you? What inspires you? What interests you? Answer those three questions. Then you need to take inventory of yourself. You need to determine your strengths, weakness, available resources, and such things. But wait, this is starting to feel like a Hunter Equation moment. So here we go.

After answering the three questions I asked above, you should start coming up with some ideas for your desired Future Outcomes. Again, base your Future Outcomes on what excites you, what inspires you, and what interests you. Think hard. There are no wrong answers. No limitations yet.

Now look at your Intent. What would like to do? What fills you with love? Remember, Intent is about love and positivity. So, what in life fills you with love and positivity? List some of those things under Intent. Then, look at Actions. What Actions would be most fun for you to do? What Actions would you enjoy taking? What Actions are realistic and possible for you to do? What Actions are impossible for you to do? You are looking for the Actions you would enjoy taking, while having them realistic and possible to do, based upon the inventory of yourself that you took.

Next, you are looking at the External Forces involved. These are both good and bad. Good External Forces might be family connections or opportunities you have. What advantages do you have, simply due to your circumstances in life? Conversely, what things out there would be blocking you and making certain things difficult or impossible? Look at all that stuff and cross-reference them with each other. Hopefully, you can find some positive External Forces that might help your possible Actions, and spot some very negative External Forces that might rule out some of your possible Actions.

Finally, we have the Random Luck factor that reminds us that life often leads us to places we never expected. Keep this in mind and be open to the fact you do not have total control over your life. Things will happen you do not expect. So, expect that.

Your scratch paper should be full of notes and cross outs and questions marks. Hopefully, you have some key words and ideas that have not been crossed out. Clean up your equation and see what you are left with. That should give you an idea of some directions and passions you might want to consider in life. This process might very well give you your purpose in life; or tell you what you should be doing here while you are here.

So let us see, so far we have your soul which is here for business gaining any experiences it can, your human life is here to enjoy the ride of being human, and you have taken inventory and given thought about your "Self" to figure out what you should be doing here while you are alive.

Now you can look at how you want to live. Consider laying out some guidelines and rules for yourself. Who or what will be your idol, if anyone or anything? We took an entire chapter to discuss this.

What type of values and morals do you want to live by? This is not a rhetorical question. This is a real genuine question. For example, a person who wants to be the greatest richest businessman in the world, will likely have values that state, "I can do anything necessary for success as long as nobody dies in the process." Some would not even worry about if someone dies in the process. Conversely, someone who feels a passion for serving people might say, "I won't do anything that hurts another person." These are two very different value structures. Both are valid, and both are commonly used. There is plenty of room in between those as well. So, what is your value and moral structure? Give it lots of thought and decide what kind of person you want to be, and make sure it is in alignment with your life purpose you worked out with the Hunter Equation.

Next, you want to consider that your soul is not the only thing that wants to learn and grow. Most humans on an emotional level also want to learn and grow. Give some thought on your feelings about education, spiritual growth, ascension, evolution, and things like that. Decide which of those, if any, you have a passion in pursuing. Obviously, it is easier to start on a path of intense education when we are younger, but that is not always the case, and life does not always work out that way. But my point is that the sooner you figure out what you want to engage in, the better.

Finally, think about what lasting changes you would like to make in this world. How would you like to leave your mark on this world in this human life? Will you be able to affect change in a direction you wish to see it go? What contribution can you make to humanity while you are here? Consider ways you can leave a lasting mark on this world so that your stamp is here long after you are gone.

Do not be afraid to be unique, take risks, and express yourself. When I asked, what your place in the universe is, I mean for you to answer that yourself. But part of the answer is that you must make your own place in the Universe. So, make it.

What is the meaning of life? The ideal meaning of life is to make a positive difference while enjoying the journey.

CHAPTER 21

Using The Hunter Equation In Your Life

People approach life in different ways. Some people just live life as it comes and learn things the hard way from mistakes. Other people carefully calculate everything before each move and hope their calculations are correct. Others figure that as long as they think positive thoughts, they can do anything they want, and positive things will come into their life.

All of the above approaches use a piece of the Hunter Equation. Just to remind, the Hunter Equation is:

Future Outcome = (Intent + Actions + External Forces + Random Luck)

People who just kind of glide through life, and suffer the consequences as they go, tend to react to External Forces, while they are at the mercy of Random Luck. People who carefully calculate their every move, tend to focus mostly on what Actions they will be taking, not realizing that their logical outcome will never happen because the External Forces and Random Luck of the Universe will make sure they do not happen. Those who think the positive thinking of Law of Attraction is all you need, are mostly just focusing on Intent, while they have disappointments waiting for them as Random Luck ravages their happy day.

There are many possible life strategies and approaches, but most all of them only give heavy weight to one or two of the Hunter Equation components. This is why most people in life struggle and experience disappointment, despite their best well intended efforts. Life does not work on one or two elements. It is just not that simple, and it is just not that easy.

Life operates on all four elements of the Hunter Equation. For this reason, it is only logical that we carefully take into account all four elements with our approach to life. Yes, it makes life more complicated. But it makes life better and gives us a better possible outcome.

Using the Hunter Equation requires a shift in thinking. Most people are used to thinking in one or two dimensions. What I mean by this is they are used to thinking about keeping their intent (attitude) positive, or just thinking about what actions they are taking; or just reacting to all the external forces being thrown at them. With the Hunter Equation, you have to shift your thinking to multi-dimensional. You need to be able to imagine all four balls in the air at the same time. You need to be able to consider all four elements at the same time and view how they may react to each other. This is not easy and may take practice.

My suggestion on proceeding is to first be sure you have all four elements memorized so they are automatic. Then, whenever you encounter a life decision or life problem, you train yourself to first take a breath, take a pause, and this shall be your cue to recall the four elements of the Hunter Equation. Then consider each of the elements in how to proceed with a life challenge, or how to solve a life problem.

I will now talk about different ways the Hunter Equation can be used for different life situations. This will hopefully give you a better idea of how to apply the Hunter Equation, and some practical scenarios of how it would be done.

MANIFESTING & ACHIEVING A GOAL OR DESIRED RESULT

Historically, we have all been taught that if you want to manifest, achieve goals, or set a goal, what you need to do is write them down, think positive thoughts, and take regular action toward those goals. It's not such a horrible approach really.

However, under the Hunter Equation, let us look at it this way. Firstly, clearly define what you want your Future Outcome to be. What are you manifesting? What do you want to achieve? What is your desired end result? Remember, the equation actually starts with "Future Outcome =" So clearly define what you want your Future Outcome to be.

Secondly, set your Intent. In setting your Intent, look at what your intent is for this goal. Why do you want this Future Outcome? What do you think this goal or outcome will give you, or do for you? What is your expectation? All of these questions are part of your analytical portion of your Intent. Then set your attitude intent. This requires applying Love to the Intent, the goal, the Future Outcome. Love this Future Outcome and embrace it. Feel the positivity around it. Feel the positive feelings you will have after you achieve your goal.

Next, you want to examine the Actions required. First, examine the analytical side of the Actions required. This means do your research. Know what is required in achieving the goal you set. Research, read, ask questions, and learn. Know the actual Actions. Then, you want to look at the Actions and apply Love to them. This is done in order to inspire you to take these Actions. Become inspired and excited about taking all the required Actions.

Notice above how we looked at Intent and Actions separately, but then we looked at them in a combined way as well.

Now we have our Intent set and we are feeling the love; and we have our Actions mapped out, and we are feeling inspired to do them.

Now we look at External Forces. Looking at External Forces means playing Devil's Advocate. Consider, and even write down, all possible External Forces that could possibly affect your plan. Basically, what are all the things that could go wrong? This of course would be a violation of the Law of Attraction to do this. It is why I love this part of the process so much, and why you have now stepped beyond the Law of Attraction into a much more effective process. Now you are taking into account all the possible downsides, limitations, and things that could upset the apple cart. You are anticipating the potential problems and limitations.

After you have taken into account all the possible External Forces you can think of, you want to work backwards. Meaning, you now want to look at what potential Actions could be taken in response to such External Forces. This would be called Contingency Planning by most. So, get your Contingency Plans (Actions) in place. Then walk back another step and revisit Intent by showing all your Contingency Plans some Love and positive thought, by knowing you have done the work to anticipate problems, and that you should feel good about yourself for doing this.

Finally, consider Random Luck. This is a reminder that even the best-laid plans may not work. There are no guarantees in life. When thinking of Random Luck, you want to first consider that External Forces can change the equation at any time Randomly, by luck or bad luck. Most importantly, you want to assess if there are any Actions you can take to increase your odds of success. In other words, can you take any Actions that might put luck a little more in your favor? Luck is about probability. So, any Actions you can take to move luck more into your favor is a good thing. Then step back again into Intent and show that Random Luck some Love. Always love that dice before you throw it.

At this point, you have a complete Goal Setting task done by using the Hunter Equation. Good job. You can see how you would have taken into account many different things. You remembered to look at all four elements sitting in the air, all at the same time. You also interacted all the elements with each other, going forwards and backwards, and forwards again.

Now remember this. The Hunter Equation is a Universal equation from the Universe. This means it is alive and always moving. Certainly, Random Luck and External Forces are always changing, because those are two things you do not control. So always keep an eye on your equation, as it changes and shifts. When you see changes in your equation, revisit all the elements to make any necessary changes. When one element changes, it affects the other elements, along with your Future Outcome. So always keep an eye on that equation and be ready to make changes as needed. That is real life. I again apologize for life being so complicated and difficult. I'm truly sorry. I too, wish that I could just think positive thoughts, go to work every day, and have my life turn out like roses. It would be wonderful. Too bad, too sad, it does not work that way. But hopefully now you have a more advanced accurate template to work with for better Future Outcomes.

CAREER/JOB

Let us look at applying the Hunter Equation to maximizing career, job growth, and benefits.

If you want to do well in your career, you can use the Hunter Equation to improve your Future Outcome. Obviously, your Future Outcome will be to thrive in your career or job, meaning promotion and pay most likely. But please be as specific as possible in defining the Future Outcome you are seeking.

Then look at your Intent. First the analytical side. Revisit why you want this Future Outcome relating to your job. Are you sure you really want it? Are you sure you even want this job? If you hate your career or job, then this exercise is pointless, and you need to go backwards and find a new career. So first confirm that you are solid in your chosen career and that you indeed want the defined Future Outcome. Now that you have confirmed that you truly believe in this career and this Future Outcome, you can show it an outpouring of Love and positive thoughts.

Next, what Actions are required to reach this Future Outcome? Any specific training? Certifications? Approval from a specific person? You know the drill. Write it all down. Consider all the possible Actions you must take to get this done. Then show those Actions some Love. Get inspired to do them. Be inspired to do them.

Now consider all the External Forces that may push back against your plan. This might mean considering certain people, bosses, co-workers that might try to block you or sabotage you. Do not just think positive thoughts, bury your head in the sand, and hope for the best. Instead, face your demons and consider all the possible blocks, problems, and difficulties.

Then take one step back and consider your Actions or your contingency plans to deal with such External Forces. For example, if you can anticipate being blocked or sabotaged by a certain person, then be one step ahead of the process, and put an Action into place now, which deals with that person, meaning that External Force. Maybe you can even prevent this person from being a problem if you have an Action in place now which deals with them before it's even a problem. Look at how smart you are being and show it all some Love. Good attitude still matters, especially to the boss. So, keep that positive Intent.

Then remind yourself of that ugly Random Luck. Realize anything can go wrong at any time. Consider the ways your luck could go against you. Then consider any Actions you can take to increase the probability of good luck in this matter. Show those dice some love before you throw them. With any luck, you just improved your chances at a better Future Outcome for your Career and job.

I went slightly faster through that process. Hopefully you are getting the hang of this.

SOLVING PROBLEMS

When solving a problem using the Hunter Equation, first clearly understand and define the problem. Your Future Outcome is going to be how you want the situation to look *after* the problem is solved. In many cases, the Future Outcome will be stated as the exact opposite of the problem. So, for example, if your problem was "I don't have a car," your Future Outcome would be stated as "I have a car." Of course, a problem is not always an object, but very often a situation. But you get the idea.

Look at your Intent. Analytically, is this truly a problem? Or is it just an unfortunate circumstance you can live with? Be sure you truly understand your problem, and that it is truly a problem. Many times, we have a bad situation and we see it as a major problem, but then days later realize it is not really a problem and it is just something bad we did not like, and we are over it and moved on from it. In your Intent, be sure you truly have a confirmed genuine problem in front of you.

Then consider the Intent with which you want to solve it. With problem solving, there are almost always multiple ways to approach the problem. Determine if your Intent is to solve the problem by replacing something, fixing something, ignoring something, or pretending it does not bother you at all. Once you decide how you want to think about it, show it some Love and own your choice.

Next, look at your Actions you think you will take to solve this problem. By this time, your problem should be well defined, you have confirmed you actually need to solve it, and you have decided what mental approach to take in solving it. So, the Actions you need to take should be narrowed down and easier to come up with than you might first suspect.

So, determine all your possible Actions, then show them some Love and realize taking these Actions might be for the best anyways, and thus be inspired and excited to take them.

But now consider all your External Forces. Who or what is going to stand in your way in solving this? Determine those obstacles. Then review your Actions or contingency plans to deal with those External Forces. Show it all some Love.

Realize life is difficult and that things do not go as planned and be aware that Random Luck might mess with you. Take the Actions that increase the probability of success. Take any Actions you can think of which anticipate problems from External Forces. Keep the Love flowing and stay positive in the knowledge that you are doing everything you can to solve your problem.

Watch your equation as it changes and shifts. When problem solving, it can shift very quickly, and often. Be sure to change with it.

RELATIONSHIPS

The Hunter Equation can be applied to your relationships. Probably the trickiest part of applying it to relationships is defining the Future Outcome you actually want. So, you will need to come up with whatever it is that you are truly after. Whether it is "I want more love in my relationship," or "I want to stop fighting," or "I want more sex," etc, you need to clearly determine it. So carefully consider your Future Outcome. Having something like "I want a happy relationship" is not totally invalid, but it is also not very specific. The more vaguely stated the Future Outcome is, the more ephemeral, and out of control your equation will be. So, keep that in mind. Tight definitions equal tighter equations. Tighter equations equal easier management, and better chances of success.

Look at your Intent. Are you sure this is what you *need*? Are you sure this is what you *want*? Are you sure this is the most important aspect of the relationship to focus on first? Are you sure this is truly important to you? Then commit to your choice. Own it. Love it. Smile. Be positive.

Now determine those Actions you need to take. This is so important in relationships. So often in relationships we bitch and moan about things, wish for them to get better, but then do nothing to actually change things ourselves. We hope the other person changes, or we even demand the other person changes. So, with the Hunter Equation, *you* need to determine the Actions *you* are going to take to achieve your stated Future Outcome. Commit to those Actions and carry them out with Love. Carrying out those Actions with resentment will not work.

Anticipate any External Forces that may affect your plans. Take them into account. Do not expect the other person to be all over you with appreciation for what you are doing. External Forces are about what may go wrong most of the time. So, consider the things you may have missed or not taken into account. Try to go back and take Actions to prevent these External Forces. Do it with Love in your heart, matching your Intent.

Life does not always serve us what we are expecting, so realize Random Luck might change the situation on you. Be prepared for this to possibly happen. Consider the External Forces that might be involved and be ready to take new Actions. Stay positive and keep the faith.

When human relationships are involved, feelings, and emotions, the equation can change instantly and often. Care is needed in monitoring this, and patience is often needed even more. But applying the Hunter Equation to your relationship is surely better than not applying it at all.

CHILDREN

For those who have children, nothing is more important than the kids (at least I hope this is the case). Therefore, applying your best thinking to your children only makes sense. So why not apply the Hunter

Equation to them? You can do this in two ways. You can use the equation to improve their lives, or you can actually teach them the Hunter Equation. For right now, let's take a brief look at how we would apply the equation to your children, if you have any.

You should know the drill by now. Choose and define your Future Outcome. Whether it is to correct a behavior, a bad habit, improve grades, or what have you.

Check your Intent on this. Is this Future Outcome in alignment with what the child wants? If you are doing a Future Outcome that conflicts with the child's own desires or best interests, it probably won't work. So, check your Intent is in alignment with the child, and something truly wanted and needed by the child. Then increase your level of Love, including to the child.

Figure out all your Actions that are needed. Remember, these are Actions YOU take. This is not about dumping all kinds of unsolicited Actions upon the child. Obviously, the child may need to participate in some of the Actions, but that is all the more reason why the Future Outcome must be in alignment with the child's wishes, so that they will cooperate with you.

Look at any External Forces you face. They might be distractions, behavioral problems, or other people. Anticipate all this. Walk it backwards to try and mitigate the problems before they happen through Actions. Do all this with Love. Let the child see the Love.

Random Luck may change the situation and your plans. Be prepared for that and be patient if it happens. Be ready to adjust your equation at any time. I am hoping at this point you have the general idea of how to use the equation. You can use the equation in most any situation, problem, and circumstance.

The important thing to remember is to always keep all four elements up in front of you, and to go forwards and backwards cross referencing with each of the elements like we have done. All the elements relate to each other and support each other. When one changes, the entire equation changes. Remember the equation is a living thing, so it will bend and change. Be ready and willing to adjust.

Using the Hunter Equation in your life puts you in better alignment with how the Universe works. Thus, using the equation should give you better results in your life.

over the External Force? Is the External Force trying to protect you from a flawed Future Outcome?

Review the Random Luck factor. Is bad luck the reason you are stuck? Or is it more the other elements? If it is all bad luck, then try it all again. If bad luck is not the primary culprit, then go back to the other elements above.

Basically, you need to try and fix your equation.

What if you cannot fix your equation, or life is still not working? Here is something else to try. Do what we do when your car is stuck in the mud. You rock it back, and, forth right? Give it just a little gas forward, but then let it rock backwards, then gas again forwards. You get that rocking motion going to try and get unstuck. I use what is called "Push - Pull." The Push Pull theory is something I made up myself as a joke. But it is not a joke. It seems to work. In a way, it is based on Newton's Law of "For every action, there is an equal and opposite reaction." It became an inside joke for those who know me best, because it was me going directly against the Law of Attraction. It does this because by using Push Pull, I end up thinking negative thoughts or pushing for the opposite of what I want. What this does is it rocks my car back and forth. Think about it. I first wanted a certain outcome, but it did not happen (gas pedal to go forward). But then I think of not wanting the outcome at all, and even push back against it with negative thoughts (letting the car rock backwards). Then I quietly watch for any reaction from others or the Universe that might allow me an opportunity to quickly press on the gas forward again to go forward toward the outcome I wanted.

What I have found is that very often I can manifest or attain a desired result by pushing back against it, then it sometimes will bounce back again the other way and I can use that momentum to then push it forward again. It is like a Jedi mind trick, but really it is also physics. It will also annoy your Law of Attraction friends as they watch you push against what you want, only to see you grab it again and push it forward to success as it rocks back your way. Like a pendulum in a way. This Push Pull trick takes practice. Like getting your car out of the mud, it does not always work. Sometimes you need a tow truck. But very often it does work, and you have been clever.

An example of how this works in real life is when you are dating, and it is not going well, so you play hard to get. By actually pushing *against* what you want, you can sometimes more easily bring it in. Playing hard to get can sometimes work when in a difficult dating situation under certain circumstances. Or it can get you stuck even more. You have seen it and you get the picture. But this would be Push Pull in motion as well.

The other thing to try is Time. As they often say, if you don't like the weather, just wait a bit and it will change. Same with life. Nothing stays the same. This is a double-edged sword of course. But when things are not going well, use Time to your advantage. Wait. Be like a snail hiding in its shell. Then when it is safe, you can try to crawl away. What a horrible example. Oh well. But you get what I mean hopefully.

Patience is required of course, but sometimes all we have left is just waiting it out. Give time a chance to fix things for you. Time will always change things. That is a guarantee. Very often time changes it for the worse. But when you are stuck, and things are not good, Time becomes your friend and any change is usually beneficial.

What else can you do when you are stuck? Well, ask a friend. Seek advice. Ask for help. Friends can see things from a different perspective and in their own way spot the problem which is obvious to them but was invisible to you.

Or ask an expert like me for advice. That is what we are here for. If I cannot figure out what is broken with my car, I do not just jiggle everything myself and hope time will fix it. I go see an expert who knows about cars. So, go see an expert in whatever field you are having problems with. Perhaps this should be step 1. But as a man, we will never ask for directions until we are completely lost right? So, I put this suggestion near the end.

While you are working all this out, remember to keep love in your heart. That is the language of God and the Universe after all. So maybe the Universe will speak to you and give you an answer to your problem. But you must be speaking the language of the Universe to understand what it says. The only way to do this is to be in tune with love. Be kind to yourself. Keep love in your heart. Keep the faith. Things work out or change at some point. Always.

CHAPTER 23

Humans Who Struggle Vs. Those Who Don't

Why is it that some people just seem to have one bad thing after another happen to them, while others seem to glide through life with nothing but blessings?

Great question. Wish I knew the answer! Ah, just joking. I will answer it now. I will give you my theory on it anyways. Like most answers to complex questions, there are various factors involved. Let's go through them, starting at the beginning.

You will recall a Soul's purpose in reincarnating is to gain experiences so that it can learn, grow, and evolve. Some souls have gained more experience than others have. Think of a soul as a student in school. A student just starting in school has easier classes that are less challenging. The less challenging classes still give the student new knowledge that allows them to learn and grow. Conversely, an experienced student who has already been through many classes and experiences, takes more advanced courses so that they may be adequately challenged. Some students take very advanced difficult classes that seem impossibly difficult for many of us.

The same applies with souls. Different soul energy collections have different levels and amounts of experiences. Some souls do not require as many complex experiences in order to learn and grow. Other soul energies have already been through many varied complex experiences and require a very advanced set of experiences in order to gain new growth.

What makes one human life more challenging or advanced for a soul than another human life? Simple. Problems. Give me a human life with many difficult endless problems, and "bingo" you have a very advanced life opportunity for an advanced soul to be challenged. The more successive difficult problems a human life has, the more challenging and interesting it is for the soul. That is a key point I just made, in that more problems, and difficulty means a higher level of interest for the soul. A soul wants interesting experiences. Numerous complex and difficult problems offer the soul a large amount of challenge that make the life experience so much more interesting. The more interesting a life experience is for a soul, the more valuable it is to the soul because it means learning, growth, and evolution is happening at a faster rate. So, from a soul's point of view, a difficult life is a good thing. Chew on that for a bit.

But I do not think that is the only factor. Another major factor is, wait for it: The Hunter Equation! Your life equation probably dictates most of your difficulty level. Let us look at that in detail.

If I am a human embarking on a life, I start to fill in my Hunter Equation. I choose my Future Outcome. What I choose will affect the difficulty level of my life. If I choose a Future Outcome that is unrealistic or impossible, I may be in for a very rough life. If I choose a Future Outcome that is possible, but fraught with problems, then I am also in for a rough life. Here is an example. If I choose my Future Outcome as becoming head of a gang, that choice is likely to bring me some pretty horrible problems and bad consequences. So that would be an example of picking a bad Future Outcome goal.

156

But really, the equation can go wrong at any point. I may choose a Future Outcome but have a very bad Intent for my choice. Perhaps my Intent is full of hate and revenge. That bad Intent is likely to bring me problems.

If I choose Actions which are very bad choices, those Actions can create very severe consequences and problems. Also, keep in mind that there is often a "snowball effect" or "domino effect," in that one bad choice in the beginning, can affect you and your equation for years to come, and maybe your entire life. So, choosing wrong Actions can certainly result in a human having a very rough life full of nothing but problems.

A person can also be the victim of harsh External Forces that can cause endless problems in their life. Perhaps the person is working for a Future Outcome and taking Actions that are in alignment with very difficult and harsh External Forces. For example, if my Future Outcome is to have my own department store next to Walmart, and I buy a building next to Walmart to start my store, I am likely to have very harsh External Forces hit me as Walmart rolls over me like I'm an ant, and I lose everything. That would be an example of me making choices that put me squarely and predictably in alignment for harsh External Forces to hit me. Try to avoid that.

Conversely, some people may live easy blessed lives from their intentional or accidental equation choices. For example, perhaps someone decides to become a computer programmer, and in doing so takes the Action of going to a particular University. At that University, they meet and fall in love with someone who turns out to be a very wealthy person. The wannabe computer programmer no longer needs to work for a living and lives out their life in luxury. You can see in this example, the person made some logical good choices in their equation that did not hurt things, but really, they hit the lottery in that the Random Luck factor played in their favor and showered them with nothing but wonderful External Forces, which resulted in an even better Future Outcome than they could have hoped for.

The flip side of course, is that one of the major reasons people face problems is because of bad luck. That pesky Random Luck element is in everyone's equation and does not always smile upon us. Some people just experience bad luck and there is not much that can be done to avoid it. That is why those other motivational spiritual concepts such as Law of Attraction, do not have the Random Luck factor within them, because it's too depressing. However, this book is about practical reality and how things really work, so we must be brave and face reality together, okay?

So, if you are a person who has constant problems in their life, consider what I have said above. First, look carefully at your equation to see if you have chosen difficult roads through your own choices. Check to see if you have made bad choices that you can change. Realize that luck plays a part. But if you see nothing wrong with your equation, then it could be that you have a very advanced experienced soul that requires a very advanced human life in order to evolve.

If you determine your soul may be exactly this type, then your only choice is to embrace it and own it. Realize that you are being challenged because it is the only way for you to learn, grow, and evolve quickly. Appreciate the fact that although your life is not easy, your life is full of depth and growth. You can feel it. All of us who have had difficult lives know the secret deep inside, that we have more depth. It is a badge of honor. It is also proof that everything I have said above is true. It is proof that difficult experiences do indeed result in a deeper learning experience that results in a deeper more complex understanding of life. Your soul thanks you.

CHAPTER 24

Ascension

What is Ascension? Wikipedia defines Ascension as: The belief in some religions that there are certain rare individuals that have ascended into Heaven directly without dying first.

In a purely religious sense, Ascension refers to someone who is so pure and worthy, that they gain entry into Heaven without having to die. Obviously, an honor which no human is worthy of, since all humans are sinners according to Christian beliefs. Other religions may look upon the subject differently and have their own specific view as well.

I want to discuss Ascension from a spiritual viewpoint. However, we will still use the official definition, and even the religious views, in our discussions.

So, let's look at this again. Ascension allows you access to Heaven without dying. What does that mean? Well, "Heaven" is the Universe Energy Collective, right? Heaven is where all the Soul Energy goes after it leaves a body. So that is back up into the Universe Energy Collective. That is back home to God, to be with all the other Soul Energy. To be surrounded by love.

So how can a person gain access to the Universe Energy Collective without being dead? I personally do it all the time. But then again, I'm psychic. As a supposedly living person, I "Ascend my mind" into the Universe Energy. I tune into that energy. I can sense, feel, and communicate with Souls that have left bodies after death, and returned to the Universe Energy. In that way, I am visiting Heaven. But I am visiting as only a temporary guest with limited access.

That is more of a spiritual spin on religious ascension. Now let us talk about spiritual ascension. Spiritual ascension is actually quite different. Confused yet? Basically, I am giving you two very different definitions of ascension in the same chapter so that you can understand what ascension means when someone says it, but also recognize you need to know who is saying it in order to know which meaning to apply. Still confused? That is okay.

Let's try to clear up some of the confusion by talking about Spiritual Ascension. Spiritual Ascension is the process of shedding your "old self" and ascending to a higher vibration of existence. So, with spiritual ascension, we are not talking about going to heaven without dying. We are talking about the spiritual process of working on one's "self" so that our thinking is on a higher vibrational level than what it was previously. Some spiritual people refer to it as "awakening."

But what does vibrational level, or a higher vibration mean? Your vibration refers to your level of living and thinking, based upon how much you apply love to your equation. I say this because love is the ultimate ingredient. So, the higher amount of love you incorporate in all your thinking, the higher your vibration frequency will be.

So those people who shed their psyche of anger, resentment, and fear, and replace their thinking with love, are engaging in spiritual ascension.

Thus, a spiritual awakening, or spiritual ascension, is shedding your psyche of those old human vulnerabilities, and replacing them with an evolved view that is based more on love. Doing this raises your vibration, or vibration frequency. Raising your vibration results in a more peaceful, happier, spiritual existence, and promotes the overall evolution of humanity.

As you can see, I have found a way to make both definitions of ascension work. The religious definition of ascension still applies because psychics are able to visit the ascended world in a virtual way even though they are alive. But the definition of ascension you should be concerned about going forward is the spiritual ascension definition.

If you want to evolve, you can engage in ascension to shift your thinking more into patterns of love. What I mean by this is approaching your conflicts with people, your decisions, and your actions, more out of a place of love.

If you disagree with someone, instead of becoming angry and resentful about it, step back and accept the person is in a certain place spiritually and physically, where they feel a certain way about something. Love that person enough to accept their point of view, and then step back from them if you wish.

Approaching conflicts from love does not mean agreeing with someone. It only means accepting that is how they feel, and respecting and loving them enough to allow for that acceptance. Agree to disagree, while wishing them well and hoping they eventually experience growth, education, and evolve from their current position.

Making this shift into approaching everything from love is very difficult, takes lots of self-work, and practice. But a person who has ascended has truly evolved.

CHAPTER 25

Evolution

When most people think of Evolution, they think of the gradual process of human development. For example, they think of Apes becoming Humans, as we know them today. This is not a scientific book on human biology or development. Instead, we are going to discuss Evolution from a psychological and spiritual point of view.

With that said, the human species is about 200,000 years old. However, humankind is thought to have reached its "maturity" 50,000 years ago. So, humanity as we know it is about 50,000 years old. But not really. We can all see that humanity has changed noticeably even in the last 200 years.

My belief is that humanity is evolving on an exponential scale. Perhaps not much evolution occurred thousands of years ago. But as time has gone on, evolution has gradually increased in speed and development.

I believe a primary reason for this, is out of necessity. The Universe and Mother Nature tends to put things in motion when they are necessary, as if it knows when something is needed. This is not surprising, since the Universe is actually intelligent with all that Universal Energy within it.

Perhaps the Universe and the Earth are conspiring to increase the speed of human evolution in an effort to save humanity and the Earth. I think it is safe to say that the answer to human survival is evolution. Humans either evolve out of their self-destructive ways, or they will become extinct.

A humanity with a "Lord Of The Flies" mentality, mixed with powerful destructive technology, is pretty much a recipe for extinction. So, the only answer is for humanity to evolve out of the 'Lord Of The Flies' tribalism mentality.

I judge human evolution by how people treat each other, such as people's level of empathy for each other. Are humans ready to stick a knife in each other's back for the smallest profit, or are people willing to cooperate with each other for the good of the whole?

However, if you did not catch it, what I said in all the paragraphs above is a bit of a paradox, or conflicting. Why would humans evolve out of their current self-destructive behavior, when humans actually evolved INTO their current self-destructive behavior? In other words, humans were creatures living amongst the flora and fauna, and then evolved into very technologically advanced beings that then began exhibiting very destructive psychological behavior. The destructive psychological behavior would be humans destroying the Earth (that sustains them) and destroying each other out of cruelty and tribalism.

So, has evolution been kind to humans? I would say not. It seems to me an existence of living with the Earth, and then transitioning to an existence of killing the Earth, is not a positive evolutionary direction. Furthermore, we have only seen an increase in violent tribalism between different human groups. Humans seem to hate each other more now than 5,000 years ago I would hypothesize. The reason for this is likely competition for declining resources, within an increasing over-population.

Humans have done the worst possible job managing their species and environment. Logic would say you need to increase the output of your resources, while decreasing your population. Humans have done the exact opposite. Humans are on a death march to see how quickly they can over-populate, while destroying the Earth and its resources at the same time.

I would say the evolution of humans over time has been a failure. Yes, we walk upright, communicate with sophisticated languages, and have I-Phones, but we have not evolved at all when it comes to human empathy, compassion, and cooperation. In fact, there would be some people reading this, and laughing at me, as if these traits I just mentioned above are stupid bleeding heart BS. Thus, the positive psychological and behavioral traits humans need for peace, prosperity, and survival, are not valued as much as they should be.

Humans have done a fair job at evolving technologically (for human standards maybe) but have ceased to evolve psychologically. This has resulted in a catastrophic apocalyptic situation that is playing out in super slow motion before our eyes, as we purposely destroy ourselves.

So, my focus is not on how far humans have evolved physically or technologically, but rather how humans are evolving psychologically and intellectually. This evolution, however slow, is critical for human survival long term.

I personally have seen what I feel could be some recent evolution in this area. While I have seen older generations act with complete lack of empathy and with a multitude of greed, I have seen evidence of children and young people seeming less interested in the game of greed. I think somehow in our psyches and DNA there is a shift to a kinder lighter existence. Only time will tell as Millennials become older.

Many people criticize that Millennials are more dependent on outside help and feel a sense of entitlement to receive such help. I would agree. But this thinking also supports the idea that Millennials lean more toward people supporting each other, than it leads to a greedy "winner take all" attitude of older generations. Millennials are also accused of not working as hard as older generations. However, Millennials tend to be more creative, and kind, in place of that. Some would say this is an indication of evolution.

Humanity could be evolving away from an individuality "take what you can for yourself" mindset, and more into a "what works for everyone" mindset. Most Millennials would not think of hoarding food and letting everyone else starve. Yet, some of our older generations were guilty of doing just that not so long ago. I think we have moved beyond that by a slight degree, just in my lifetime. I call that evolution.

In the spirit of adding variety to the conversation, I would also suggest a possible sign of evolution is the seeming increase of psychic and empathic humans. Although hard to prove scientifically, most would agree there seems to be an increase of children who exhibit psychic and empathic abilities. Is this because there is some alien DNA influence? Of is this because there is some influential evolutionary push? Or is it simply because we never noticed psychic children before? I prefer to believe that the Universe is finally encouraging evolution by introducing this sizeable increase in sensitive, empathic, psychic children, many of which are young people and adults now. This sign of evolution is especially important and notable because it is boosting a human's capacity for empathy, which has been sorely lacking.

Conversely, I would introduce a cynical viewpoint for discussion. As I have put forth in the beginning of the book, I believe everything is a sphere, round, and goes in circles and cycles. I would suggest the possibility that Evolution itself does the same thing.

Perhaps evolution really does go in circles. For example, we start as a very primitive species living in caves and playing with rocks. We evolve into a technologically advanced society. But then, due to our immature psychological development, we essentially destroy ourselves. At this point, perhaps if any of our species survives, we are

165

then brought back to living in caves and playing with rocks again. I certainly hope evolution is not a circle, but I feel we should consider that possibility.

But for now, let us go with the assumption that evolution does seem to be proceeding forward in some way. Evolution has been slow, yet I think it has dramatically picked up speed. Now the question to be asked is, how should humans evolve? In what direction? And what is the most efficient way of evolving at the quickest rate?

I think the simple answer is that humans should evolve in order to survive. I do not see humanity surviving without humanity evolving, as I said earlier. So, survival should be the primary reason we can all agree on for evolving.

In which direction we evolve, is up for debate. Some would say stronger and more powerful, while others would say kinder and more intelligent. Humans will argue about this over the foreseeable future. But it seems to me the most logical direction to evolve in would be the direction that secures the longest most solid future for humanity. The second factor might be the direction that gives humans the highest quality of life. But again, humans will argue over that.

One thing we know is that the quickest way to evolve is through education, experience, and thought. Humanity must value education above everything else, engage in as many experiences as possible, and give individual thought and contemplation to all of life's questions.

If humanity violates any part of that equation above or is lacking or slow with any parts of that, then evolution will be slowed. Making education a lower priority will surely slow down evolution. Keeping humans in tribes, rather than providing cultural experiences, will surely slow evolution. Not teaching humans how to think individually will surely slow evolution.

Humanity itself has control over how fast evolution occurs. Everyone reading this can make their own judgments on how we are doing with all that.

One question I would leave you with is, how will you choose to evolve? As an individual, you can choose if you evolve, in what direction, and how you will achieve it. Are you happy with how you are now? Or would you prefer to evolve further? In what direction shall you evolve? Are you willing to take the actions, and put the work into evolving? All questions for contemplation.

One thing for certain, is that evolution is a key factor in human development and survival.

CHAPTER 26

The Ideal Human

There is no ideal human. Meaning, there is no one exact human that is ideal. The reason is that what is ideal would be in the eye of the beholder. We all have our opinions and preferences of what would be ideal. Certainly, this is true in dating, and it is just as true in looking at ideal human creatures.

In addition to the above, we do not want one exact type of ideal human. If we had that, then there would be no variety. Humans love variety (or should). We want different kinds of people. We need variety for a healthy interesting society.

So why am I even writing a chapter titled this way? Because despite what I just said above, there are some basic traits that the ideal human would have. Therefore, I am going to talk about some of those ideal traits that an ideal human would have. I just wanted to make it clear that I am not saying there is only one particular "ideal human race" or such. I am not going there, and neither should you. This chapter is about taking an evolutionary direction toward human traits that maximize success and happiness of humanity. All of these traits can come in all colors, sizes, shapes, national origins, religions, genders, sexualities, and the like. I am suggesting positive evolution to develop ideal traits within everyone, while keeping everyone in all their multiple different styles, personalities, and everything I mentioned above.

The idcal human would have a lot of empathy. High on the empathy scale. If 1 is no empathy and 10 is crying for every squirrel who loses a nut, let us say a 7 on the empathy scale might be nice. Empathy will be the key to human survival. Without all humans having an adequate amount of empathy, we will hate each other, fight, make each other suffer, and eventually snuff each other and ourselves out.

The ideal human would have no need or desire for tribalism. An ideal human would have strong independent values, opinions, thoughts, and positions. They would not need to be led by a group or told who to like and who to hate. Tribalism would be seen as "3rd grade" to an ideal human.

Along the same lines, an ideal human would have high levels of compassion. When someone needs uplifting, the ideal human would be willing to assist and uplift the person in need. Respecting and caring for those less fortunate would be an important and respected part of our society. It creates a sense of security, respect, and caring within a society.

An ideal human is educated and capable of clear reasoning without the interference or help of others. By educated I mean the ideal human understands facts based on reality and science. They understand factual events in reality, not those told to them in fantasy, or with some political or religious agenda. An educated person sees things through clear glasses without filters. An ideal human is capable of learning and using reason to find answers to questions.

An ideal human is capable of thinking in a clear logical way, free from red herrings, subjective opinions, and biased news. An ideal human understands the process of gathering facts, sorting them, determining a correct answer, and then presenting the correct answer.

Additionally, the ideal human is also capable of creativity. Thinking outside the box. Being innovative. The ideal human can use an existing base of knowledge to then come up with a new way of solving a problem or handling a situation. Creativity also in the form of arts for variety and interest would also be valued.

This leads us to the obvious skill of being able to solve problems. The ideal human can be given a problem or obstacle and is able to calmly and efficiently produce a workable solution. This requires education, logic, reasoning, creativity, and a good temperament. Problem solving is critical for human survival.

The ideal human is very proficient at effective communication. The ideal human can fully express their feelings, opinions, ideas, and detailed procedures. It is surprising how many humans today cannot do this well.

The ideal human would have their full range of human emotions, even intense human emotions, but still have them under adequate control. Having emotions under adequate control is necessary for good social interactions, communication, and good decision-making skills. We all know that when our emotions run out of control, we do stupid things we regret, and say stupid hurtful things we regret.

I referenced this earlier, but it bears repeating, the ideal human is able to think independently. The ideal human is able to maintain their own value system and opinions without being told how to think or what to think. This prevents brainwashing and manipulation. If every human were able to think independently, many of our world problems would be solved. This is a critical future skill but requires a good education so that a person knows how to think and reason on their own.

I could probably continue on, but those are a lot of traits I have mentioned above. What do you think? It seems to be regardless of a person's political or religious affiliation, most would agree all of the above traits would be beneficial for humans to have.

So now the fun question. How do you personally measure up to all of the traits mentioned above? Are you strong in many of those traits? Are there some that could use more attention and improvement?

This chapter is not meant to suggest every human be identical and perfect. It is meant to provide a rough template for an evolutionary direction. Are you evolving in the correct direction? Are there things you can work on to evolve more effectively and faster? We could all use this template as a guide to check ourselves.

But while we are working on being the ideal human, do not forget to love and appreciate the unique individuality of who you are now.

CHAPTER 27

The Future Of Humans

The fate of humanity relies on three major factors in my opinion. The first is how well humans evolve in the diminishment of their vulnerabilities. The second is how well humans are able to live in harmony with Earth, rather than destroying it. The third is how well humanity is able to establish adequate levels of empathy within all humans.

Let's start by reminding ourselves of the human vulnerabilities mentioned earlier in the book. They include disease, mental illness, vices, lack of emotional control, need for an Idol, groupthink, greed, and tribalism. Disease and mental illness are somewhat a factor of technological medical advancement. When I say that, I mean both ways, because medical advancements can extend our life, but technological advancements are also contributing to our "self-poisoning" when it comes to our food and over prescribing of medications. In my opinion, medical and technological advancements are not that much of a factor in the survival of humanity. They may be a factor in the life span of each human, but not in the existence of humanity as a whole. Regardless of how and when people die, there are always more humans being born to replace them. The caveat to this is if there is ever a human wide dysfunction in reproduction or DNA. If there is an interruption in human reproduction, it will likely be caused by humans themselves, somehow poisoning themselves to the point of destroying their ability to reproduce with healthy DNA. Vices such as smoking, drinking alcohol, illicit drugs, addictive use of prescription drugs, and such, are all factors in limiting individual life spans. The risk to humanity as a whole would be if there is some substance that comes into being, resulting in a pandemic of addiction that wipes out humans on a large scale.

Lack of emotional control is a tricky one because having many varied emotions is part of the human experience. Yet, not being able to control those emotions can result in very bad decisions, actions, and outcomes. I truly believe that humans will have to strike a better balance between having human emotions to enjoy life as a human vs. controlling those emotions better as to not lead humanity down dangerous paths. Emotions of Love rarely go wrong unless combined with insanity, but emotions of anger, hate, and jealousy, can lead humans to do horrible things. All it will take is one angry hate filled human to develop a new super weapon in his garage, and they could possibly be a real threat to humanity. Controlling one's extreme emotions is critical.

A human's need for an idol is a double-edged sword. On one hand, an idol can be very inspirational to a human and provide direction in life. On the other hand, an idol diminishes a human's individuality and ability for independent thought and contemplation. A human tends to rely completely on their idol for all moral leadership. This can be dangerous if for some reason the idol goes rogue in a destructive direction. It will become critical for humans to begin weaning themselves off depending on idols, and more reliant on critical inward moral analysis and thinking. A group of humans all being led to the same ill-advised direction can be catastrophic, whereas all humans having individual thoughts, creates a check and balance so that if one human goes rogue, the rest are there to stop him.

This leads to the whole issue of groupthink. As stated above, groupthink is very dangerous because it eliminates all checks and balances. It creates a circumstance where one person, or idol, is able to control the thoughts and actions of the masses. The best example of this would be Hitler and the Nazi movement. Germans became so fixated on their leader that they were literally blind to the human atrocities being committed. It is absolutely necessary that humans eliminate groupthink in order to avoid such mass hysteria and catastrophe in the future.

I would say one of the most devastating vulnerabilities in existence is greed. Greed is a vulnerability that all humans possess to some degree. Yet greed is a quality that is never good. Greed, by its nature and by default results in inequality and unfairness. The concept of balance is important in all parts of the Universe, especially in the human psyche and in Mother Nature. Greed specifically seeks out to destroy any sense of balance by causing humans to artificially attain more for themselves than is needed. Greed at its core causes humans to hoard resources, even if other humans die without those resources. Greed justifies injustice, suffering, and death inside a human's mind by making them think it is good to "have more." Greed is so ingrained into the human psyche that it seems almost impossible to think it will ever be eliminated. Yet greed is among the most dangerous of all human vulnerabilities and its elimination or control is critical to the long-term survival of humanity.

Along with greed, tribalism is among the most dangerous of all human vulnerabilities. Tribalism is this mode of thinking where humans must band together into groups, so they can oppose other groups. A human's urge to do this supersedes all logic and common sense. Tribalism is what creates wars. Humans end up no longer thinking with reason or logic. Humans only think in terms of what their tribe needs or thinks. With tribalism, humans often do not even know why they are fighting, or what they are fighting for. That in itself is somewhat a definition of insanity. The insanity of taking positions and actions without even knowing why. Tribalism can literally make people seem insane and act in insane ways. That makes tribalism likely the most dangerous of all human vulnerabilities, and the most likely vulnerability to destroy humanity. Evolving beyond tribalism will be necessary or humanity will not survive. This is especially true with the technological existence of super weapons.

As you can see, human vulnerabilities are a factor for the future of humanity on a sliding scale, with some not as much a critical factor, while others absolutely critical to the eventual survival of humanity. It is up to humanity to either evolve and curb the most critical vulnerabilities or face the consequences.

Logically, some of these human vulnerabilities, such as greed, are causing our second major factor in the survival of humanity, which is our relationship with Earth. Humans are destroying the Earth. Humans are using Earth's resources faster than they can be replaced and polluting the air and water to the point of actually changing the climate. Greed is so strong with humans, there are people who are literally blind to science and facts, just so they can continue polluting the Earth for monetary gain. I am not making any political statement here. I am just stating an objective fact.

What makes our relationship with Earth so interesting is that not very long ago, humans were living in harmony with the Earth. Humans lived close to the Earth and appreciated the cycle and balance between plants, animals, environment, weather, and humans, all living together to provide life. But once the industrial age hit, and humans could exploit the Earth's resources for monetary profit, the balance was destroyed. Profit is much more important to humans than most anything else.

Now we live in a wasteland. Many animals are extinct or scarce. Some fish are too poisonous with mercury and radioactivity to eat, and there is literally garbage floating in the ocean on a grand scale. Then of course, there is the fact that we are cutting trees down and clearing land on a grand scale. Add to that the fact we are dumping poisonous chemicals into our streams and rivers. Water in some communities is now literally poison. Due to all the air pollution, temperatures are rising, ice caps are melting, and the weather is changing in a violent destructive direction. We are literally killing the Earth, and the consequences are biting back. It will only get worse.

Thus, if humans do not kill themselves first, they could become extinct once the Earth is no longer able to support the population. Once our resources are gone, all food sources poisoned, water poisoned, and the environment no longer suitable for human life, the game is over.

It will be critical for humans to reel in their behavior of destroying the Earth. It's really that simple. I am not saying that everyone needs to plant a tree today. I am just saying humans need to *stop* further polluting and destruction. If we simply *stop* the current damage, the Earth will likely regenerate, and all will be fine. Humans absolutely must live in harmony with Earth. There is no negotiation on this one.

But human vulnerabilities and living in harmony with the Earth are not the only factors in the future of humanity. Equally important to our immediate safety, survival, and harmony, is the factor of Empathy within humans. Empathy is a human's ability to understand another human on the deepest level, such that a person can step into that person's shoes and truly feel what they are feeling. Empathy is true understanding.

Humans possess empathy on a sliding scale. Some humans have almost no empathy. These people are sociopathic and think nothing of doing horrible cruel things to other people. They do not think of other humans as people, but rather think of others as objects. They would think of a homeless person as a dirty piece of garbage, or think nothing about torturing animals, or torturing other people for that matter. Those with no empathy have no ability to understand other humans. For this reason, they are capable of the most horrific acts. Hopefully you are getting the picture of how terrifying this is. There

176

truly is nothing more frightening than a person with no empathy, as they will kill and destroy without hesitation, thought, or regret. They have no regret or feelings because they have no empathy.

Contrasting that, are those with an over excessive amount of empathy. Those with an excess of empathy tend to be overly sensitive toward everything. They feel sorry for a tree being cut down. They might have a meltdown if they accidentally run over a squirrel. These people have an overwhelming desire to help any person in need, even at their own expense. They would give the shirt off their back or their last dollar to someone who needed it more than them. People with an excessive amount of empathy forsake themselves and put themselves at risk to help others.

Those with an excessive amount of empathy make horrible landlords because they would let everyone stay for free. They also would make horrible bosses because they would never terminate or discipline anyone that needed it for the sake of the business. I believe the term "bleeding heart liberal" would have come from the existence of such a person with an over-abundance of empathy.

Obviously and hopefully, most people are somewhere in the middle. A balance of empathy is required for a healthy prosperous life. It is not good to be a monster with no empathy, but it is also not good to cry every time a blade of grass is cut, and to forsake all your own necessary needs for the benefit of a random stranger.

The true danger in humanity is the existence of those with no empathy. They are the true destroyers of the world. However, just as important to point out is the existence of those with a tiny bit of empathy, who tend to be the enablers of those with no empathy.

A monster with no empathy will appear strong as steal to his followers. His followers respect this strength. The monster will ruthlessly show his strength by executing, terminating, or punishing people for reason or no reason. The followers will deep down inside be terrified of this and might even know it is wrong. But they will allow the monster to do it because the monster may have convinced them it's for the greater good. Or, the followers might be too scared of the monster, or the followers respect the monster for being so strong and wish they were equally as strong.

People with very little empathy can easily brush aside any empathy they may have had. For example, only a monster with no empathy would send innocent humans to the gas chamber for no reason. But a person with little empathy would follow the orders they are given by simply not thinking about what they are doing. They might have a small amount of empathy, but it is small enough where they can set it aside and not think about it.

A person with adequate amounts of empathy is unable to set their empathy aside. They would be unable to carry out the orders against the innocent people because they would identify with those persecuted personally. A person with adequate amounts of empathy thinks of themselves as being in the other person's shoes. A person with empathy treats others the way they would like to be treated. A person with adequate empathy rescues others if they themselves would want to be rescued under the same circumstances.

A person very high on the empathy scale will risk their own life to save a stranger. They would go out of their way to give blood or donate organs. People high on the empathy scale find it necessary to go above and beyond the call of duty for others because they truly feel the pain of other people. People with high empathy can easily spot someone in pain having a bad day, while those lower on the empathy scale walk right by the person in pain without even noticing.

So how is humanity as a whole balancing empathy at the moment? We see lots of monsters out there with no empathy. We see lots of apathetic people out there with very little empathy, enabling the monsters. We also see people with healthy amounts of empathy, and some light workers with excessive amounts of empathy. Right now, humanity has a very extreme diverse mix. However, humanity also seems to have more people in positions of power who have no or little empathy. This means there might be too many apathetic people with small amounts of empathy who are letting the "monsters" rule.

To me, the future of humanity will depend on how the balance of empathy in our societies shifts over time. If more humans lose their empathy, I believe humanity is certainly doomed. If more humans shift into higher levels of empathy, I believe humanity can survive.

A humanity that loses empathy will see an increase in cruelty. It will see leaders who make choices based on the benefit of a few instead of the majority. Without empathy, all decisions will be based on greed for the few and themselves. Destruction of millions for the benefit of the few will be the mode of thinking without hesitation. This type of mentality will most certainly result in the eventual destruction of humanity, as the most powerful monsters fight each other to the death, while all the innocents are killed as collateral damage. The remaining monster, as victor, will actually self-destruct as his thirst for conquering can no longer continue, and his emptiness inside consumes him until he wilts away and dies without the support of the masses.

Humanity with adequate amounts of empathy will consider the needs of the majority to be the rule, while also leaving nobody behind. An empathic society would not be able to leave the weakest behind, since they would want to be helped if they were in the position of being the weakest. Greed will not be the order of the day because too many people will be thinking of the needs of other people. An empathic society will value peace and prosperity for as many members of their society as possible. Humanity with empathy does a much better job of resolving conflict with others because they are able to put themselves in the shoes of the opposing person. By doing this, communication is enhanced, and both sides are able to work out a peaceful resolution that benefits the most people.

Humanity with empathy is a humanity that operates with love. Anyone who operates with love, is operating under the Universal language of God and the Universe, and thus is in alignment with the Universe as a whole. Anyone who is in proper alignment with themselves, each other, the Earth, the Universe, and God, is likely to live long and prosper.

CHAPTER 28

Your Life, Your Future

Whenyou picked up this book, you may have thought it was going to be just about the Universe, or some equation I made up. But this book is really about you. This book is meant to give you a basic tour around the Universe, life, death, the paranormal, and some new life skills. This book is meant to make your life better.

Hopefully you have a better understanding of how the Universe might work and how we are all connected. But mostly, I hope you take the Hunter Equation and apply it to your life. Apply it to the good, the bad, and the ugly. Life is not easy. Sometimes life is downright scary and unbearable. If you apply your best life skills, along with lots of faith, persistence, and time, you can prevail.

I also talked a lot about evolving, ascending, and great positive traits to have as a person. Perhaps you can be inspired to invest more in yourself, learn, grow, improve, and evolve yourself as you see fit.

Here is my final suggestion to you. First thing to do is take inventory of yourself. What I mean by this is write down all your human vulnerabilities that you feel are a detriment to you now. Then write down where you feel you sit on the empathy scale, from 1 to 10. That gives you a pretty good picture of who you are today.

Then write down who you wish to be. Write down where you think you should be or want to be on the empathy scale from 1 to 10. Then write down which human vulnerabilities you want to get under control, so they are no longer a negative factor in your life. Write down any major life goals you want to accomplish. This gives you a pretty good picture of who you want to be in the future.

So now you have point A and point B. How do you get from point A to point B? Three methods. Through Ascension, Self-Evolution, and by applying The Hunter Equation.

Take the life goals you wrote down and start applying the Hunter Equation to manifest those goals. Each goal would be the Future Outcome, and you know the rest of the process to go through.

Then consider any change you want to make to your level of empathy. Consider any other spiritual or vibrational changes you want to make in your life. Then start to go through Ascension to achieve that new state of mind. Shed the old you and come into the new you. You must admit to who you are, see who you want to be, face your fears, and learn and grow into the new you. Use meditation, reading, exercise, thinking, or any process that works for you.

Then examine all the human vulnerabilities you feel are a problem for you. Decide to evolve out of those. You can even apply the Hunter Equation to change and evolve out of those. But you must do the self-work necessary. It takes time, work, and practice. Each day you can make progress and become a better person. To a large degree, you control your own evolution. So, take control of it. Be the master of your destiny.

If you go through this process I have outlined, you can change yourself, and change your life. You can be whoever you want to be.

You can be a better person. You can be a happier person. You are a critical part of the Universe, and thus you deserve the best the Universe has to offer. You just have to choose to walk toward it and claim it. Much love to you on your journey.

ACKNOWLEDGEMENTS

Thank you Sarah Delamere Hurding
for your editorial assistance,
and your endless support.

Made in the USA
Middletown, DE
27 May 2021